Theology of Hope

Theology of Hope

For the 21st Century

Jürgen Moltmann

With a new Introduction
by James Hawkey

scm press

Translated by James W. Leitch from the German
Theologie der Hoffnung
5th edn, Chr. Kaiser Verlag, Munich, 1965
Translation © SCM Press 1967, 2002
Preface © Richard Bauckham 2002
Introduction © James Hawkey 2021

This edition published in 2021 by SCM Press
Editorial office
3rd Floor, Invicta House,
108–114 Golden Lane,
London EC1Y OTG, UK
www.scmpress.co.uk

SCM Press is an imprint of Hymns Ancient & Modern Ltd
(a registered charity)

Hymns Ancient & Modern® is a registered trademark of
Hymns Ancient & Modern Ltd
13A Hellesdon Park Road, Norwich,
Norfolk NR6 5DR, UK

British Library Cataloguing in Publication data

A catalogue record for this book is available
from the British Library

978 0 334 06011 6

Typeset by Regent Typesetting
Printed and bound by
CPI Group (UK) Ltd

TO MY WIFE

Contents

II PROMISE AND HISTORY

III THE RESURRECTION AND THE FUTURE OF JESUS CHRIST

IV ESCHATOLOGY AND HISTORY

V EXODUS CHURCH

Preface

Richard Bauckham

It was with this book (in its German original of 1964 and its English translation of 1967) that the theology of Jürgen Moltmann burst onto the international theological scene and began its history of profound influence in the Christian churches world-wide. It was a timely book. Other German theologians, notably Wolfhart Pannenberg, Johann-Baptist Metz and Gerhard Sauter, were also turning to the themes of hope and the future, with a similar emphasis on Christian hope as hope for the future of the world. Some of the liberation theologians of Latin America were shortly, in their own ways, to follow suit. Moreover, in the world outside the churches, the decade of the 1960s was characterized, as Moltmann himself later put it, by an 'outburst of hope'. This may have been the last flowering of that optimism about human progress that has characterized the modern age from its inception. In the 1960s an open future seemed to offer unlimited possibilities in every area of life, and there was an enthusiastic confidence that freedom and fulfilment, once desired, could easily be seized. Moltmann's *Theology of Hope* undoubtedly spoke to this mood, but it was certainly no mere reflection of it. It has proved not only timely but also enduring. In decisive ways it set the direction for the whole of Moltmann's subsequent theological work. Its insistent claim that 'from first to last, and not merely in the epilogue, Christianity is eschatology, is hope' (Introduction, §1), has exercised incalculable influence in theology and the churches. However, whether the real theological substance of this book has been taken fully seriously by many who have been in some way inspired or influenced by it is another question, to which I shall return at the end of this preface. But in my view there is still much that the Church needs to learn from *Theology of Hope* about the foundation and goal of genuinely Christian hope.

This is not the place to discuss the intellectual influences on theology of hope.[1] But readers may find it helpful to know two dimensions of its relationship to its background and context. One is Moltmann's relationship to the tradition of (mainly German Protestant) theology to which he is indebted and from which he significantly departs in his understanding of eschatology. The function of Chapter 1 of *Theology of Hope*, which is difficult for readers not already familiar with the German theologians it discusses, is to position Moltmann's theology of hope in relationship to interpretations of biblical eschatology from Albert Schweitzer to Wolfhart Pannenberg. Since Johannes Weiss and Albert Schweitzer demonstrated that future eschatology is of determinative significance for biblical faith, systematic theology had attempted to appropriate this eschatological dimension while at the same time depriving it of its reference to the real temporal future of the world. Schweitzer, Bultmann and others thought that genuinely future eschatology could only appear to the modern world as an incredible mythology. Eschatology had to be transmuted into some kind of experience of transcendence in the present. It was the remarkable achievement of Moltmann, along with Pannenberg and some others, to rehabilitate future eschatology as a proper and necessary dimension of contemporary Christian faith and theology. They appropriated biblical eschatology in such ways that future eschatology became no longer an embarrassing obstacle to contemporary faith but, quite the opposite, precisely the way to make Christian faith credible and relevant to the modern world. In Moltmann's treatment, the promise of the coming of God's kingdom at the end of history enables Christian faith to engage with the modern experience of history as a process of constant and radical change in a hopeful search for a new future.

Secondly, we must refer to Moltmann's rather complex relationship with modernity. In his early work he often observed how, in the modern period, hope emigrated from the Church and inspired instead the secular movements for change and progress in history. The Church's God without hope confronted the world's hope without God. More precisely, he meant that hope *for the world* left the Church, which focused in a reductive way on the individual's expectation of other-worldly life after death and thus merited the criticism by Marx and others that Christianity deprived people of motivation for improving life in this world. It was Moltmann's purpose in *Theology of Hope* to restore to the Church *its hope for the future of the world.* Opening the Church to future eschatology simultaneously opens it to the world. In all this Moltmann displays a fundamental sympathy for the modern age as the great age of hope and especially for those modern movements of hope that aim at radical change for the sake of the oppressed and the victims of history. However, the Christian solidarity with secular hopefulness that this suggests is not just a matter of adopting the forms hope takes in modernity. The solidarity is a critical solidarity, since Christianity has its own hope for the world, a theological foundation for hope that is not available without Christian faith and a theological expectation of the coming of God's kingdom in all creation that only God can achieve and that goes beyond the possibilities of secular hope. This authentically Christian hope is what enables the Church to seek, with others, the possibilities for change in the contemporary world, to promote them against all tendencies to stagnation, and to give them eschatological direction towards the future kingdom of God. Moltmann in no way reduces the Church's ultimate hope for God's new creation of all things to the possibilities of social and political change here and now, as some readers have feared; rather, he repositions the latter within the former. The Church's ultimate hope does not exclude the more proximate hopes that enable change in the historical future; on the contrary, it positively inspires and sustains them.

Moltmann's relationship to modernity in his early work is predominantly affirmative, for the reasons just explained.[2] But it was never Moltmann's intention simply to endorse the modern ideology of progress. It is a serious mistake to read *Theology of Hope* as envisaging an incremental process of improvement that results in the kingdom of God. Moltmann has come increasingly to recognize the dark underside of modernity, the 'progress' that benefits the powerful at the expense of the oppressed. But the disjunctive and dialectical character of his eschatology has always been a safeguard against its assimilation to the superficial optimism of the successful. It is the victims of history who hope for the world to be different, and the tradition of Christian eschatology has been authentic when it has expressed their hope or hoped in solidarity with them.

The key theological concepts of *Theology of Hope*, which define its eschatology, are three: the notion of divine promise; the understanding of the resurrection of Jesus as promise; and the understanding of history as mission. Moltmann's understanding of promise is established in Chapter 2: he reads the Old Testament story as the history of God's never exhausted promises for the future. Eschatology is not based on prediction but on promise. In other words, it is not some kind of fatalistic knowledge of what will happen, but God's promise to his people and to his world. It involves the freedom and the faithfulness of God, and it calls for obedient human response: those who believe God's promises live in the present in ways that are oriented to God's future fulfilment of these promises.

This understanding of promise then informs Moltmann's interpretation in Chapter 3 of the resurrection of Jesus as God's ultimate promise for the new creation of all things. By raising the crucified Jesus to new life, God guaranteed and, so to speak, enacted his promise. The promise of the universal kingdom remains outstanding, because only Jesus was raised, but he has been raised from the dead for the sake of the future eschatological resurrection of all the dead and the renewal of all creation. Jesus' resurrection *entails* this universal future. In this way, the christological centre and eschatological horizon of Moltmann's theology are established as the necessary implications of each other. Without the coming kingdom of God Jesus' resurrection has no meaning. But without the resurrection of Jesus the Christian hope would not be properly Christian. As Moltmann says in the Introduction to *Theology of Hope* (§1), 'Christian eschatology does not speak of the future as such' but 'of Jesus Christ and *his* future'. All its statements about the future must be based on the person and history of Jesus.

In this understanding of the resurrection of Jesus as eschatological promise, it is essential that the one whom God raised was the crucified Jesus. Because Jesus in his death was identified with the whole of this world's reality and because it was this Jesus who was raised, his resurrection is not a promise of another world but the promise of the transformation of this world into its glorified eschatological future in the presence of God. Again, because Jesus in his death was identified with this world in its most negative aspects – godlessness, godforsakenness and death – his resurrection is God's promise of a new future for the godless, the godforsaken and even the dead. Finally, because it was the dead Jesus whom God raised, because, in other words, the continuity between the dead and the risen Jesus was not the result of some immanent capacity of the human Jesus to rise to new life but could only be given by God, Christian hope is not solely in the possibilities inherent by its nature in this world, but in the transcendent possibilities of the God who can give life to the dead and who will give eternal life to the creation which of itself would lapse into nothing. It is essential to grasp the nature of this radical hope, grounded in the resurrection of the crucified Christ, if we are also to understand the way in which, precisely because it transcends the possibilities of hope available to a purely secular view of the world, it can also ground and sustain within itself all more proximate hopes that accord with the nature of God's coming rule. Anyone who hopes for everything from God, as it were, may also hope for the anticipations and fragments of the kingdom which God gives along the way to his ultimate coming to his creation.

The promise creates history: 'The promise which announces the *eschaton*, and in which the *eschaton* announces itself, is the motive power, the mainspring, the driving force and the torture of history' (Chapter 3, §4). The promise shows that present reality is not yet what it can and will be. It shows that the world is transformable in the direction of its promised future. It inspires hope for the promised future and action in accordance with this promised future. Believers in the promise are liberated from accommodation to the present state of things and, insofar as the promise contradicts it, are set critically against it. They suffer the contradiction between what is and what is promised. But this critical distance also enables them to seek and to activate those present possibilities that lead in the direction of the kingdom of God. This produces no more than anticipations of the kingdom, but they are real anticipations, and it is precisely the kingdom's transcendence beyond all its anticipations within history that is the source of its power to affect history. Hope for the universal transformation of all reality thrusts believers into the worldly reality for whose future they hope, but it keeps them always unreconciled to its present condition, 'a constant disturbance in human society' and 'the source of continual new impulses towards the realization of righteousness, freedom and humanity here in the light of the promised future that is to come' (Introduction, §2). In this way the promise creates history in the form of the universal mission of the Church.

Theology of Hope does not go far towards specifying the praxis of hope involved in the Church's mission, though it makes it abundantly clear that Christian hope does entail self-involving and world-transforming praxis. Moltmann echoes Marx's well-known statement about the philosophers (they 'have only interpreted the world in various ways; the point, however, is to change it'[3]) when he says that 'The theologian is not concerned merely to supply a different *interpretation* of the world, of history and of human nature, but to *transform* them in expectation of a divine trans-formation' (Chapter 1, §7). Chapter 5 puts the critical and creative role of Christian hope in society only in rather general terms. It was in the years immediately after writing *Theology of Hope*, and partly following the lead of his Tübingen colleague J.-B. Metz, that Moltmann developed his theology of hope into a more explicitly 'political theology'.[4] But the theological impetus and conceptual structures for this were already established in *Theology of Hope*.[5]

I have often advised first-time readers of *Theology of Hope* to omit Chapters 1 and 4. They should, of course, read the dazzling Introduction, which immerses them in both the spirit and the conceptuality of Moltmann's understanding of Christian hope, and they should then go on to Chapters 2 and 3, which contain the theology of hope itself, and Chapter 5, which adumbrates its implications for the Church's mission in society. A few comments on Chapters 1 and 4 may help those readers who persevere into these more demanding but nevertheless important chapters – more demanding for most readers because they engage expertly with major German theologians and philosophers of the nineteenth and twentieth centuries. As we have already noted, Chapter 1 serves to situate Moltmann's theology of hope in relation to the German theological tradition, and this focuses on the concept of revelation, which in many ways dominated twentieth-century German theology up to the 1960s, and relates it to the problem of eschatology. This chapter therefore contains Moltmann's critique of notions of divine revelation as an already completed process or the presence of eternity in the non-historical moment, or even as interpretation of salvation history or universal history (Pannen-berg). Rather, revelation occurs in God's promises for the future. Revelation in this sense is neither unrelated to history nor simply read off the events of history, but opens up the future and itself cre-ates history. God reveals himself in making promises and remaining faithful to his promises. This chapter is, of course, by no means Moltmann's last word on his great theological predecessors. He returns to them again and again in later work, approaching them from many angles and nuancing his judgements on their work. In this chapter they are discussed only from a particular, though very significant, perspective.

Moltmann has always held that Christian theology, because of its claim to speak about all reality, must engage in critical dialogue with other interpretations of the world and human experience. Its eschatological orientation opens it to the world and at the same time gives it the task of opening the world to its future. In *Theology of Hope* this is particularly the function of Chapter 4, in which Moltmann engages with the modern experience of history as reflected in historiography and philosophy of history. It highlights the eschatological tendencies of these approaches, which in one way or another seek an end of history within history, and claims that they can be transcended in a Christian missionary understanding of history that keeps history on the move towards the still future eschatological horizon. Secular historicism and Christian traditionalism alike try to suppress the movement of revolutionary change which is the modern experience of history and to close off the open future it implies. But a hermeneutic of Christian mission, which recalls the revelatory events of the past not in order to remain in the past but for the sake of their promise of the future, can meet the modern experience of history by giving it eschatological direction. Contemporary readers of this chapter may well be reminded of Francis Fukuyama's more recent claim that we have reached 'the end of history',[6] and Moltmann himself has engaged with Fukuyama among others in his own more recent return to this theme, in a thoroughgoing critique of premature attempts to realize the eschatological within history.[7]

Theology of Hope is less about the content of Christian hope than about the eschatological orientation which the whole of Christian theology should have. It set the eschatological direction of all Moltmann's own later work. But not until 1995 did he finally publish a systematic eschatology: *The Coming of God*.[8] This is his mature eschatological vision, the fitting culmination of the whole theological project that began in earnest with *Theology of Hope*. *The Coming of God* does not replace *Theology of Hope*. The two books are not competitive; they have different roles in Moltmann's opus. *Theology of Hope*, with its innovative excitement and argumentative power, retains its own distinctive ability to orient both theology and life towards the coming of God in his eschatological kingdom.

In my opening paragraph I raised the question of whether the real theological substance of this book has been taken fully seriously by many who have been in some way inspired or influenced by it. Some seem to have read it as more or less a theological gloss on the optimistic progressivism of the modern age. This, as we have already noticed, is a disastrous misreading. Moltmann's theology of hope, much as it encourages Christians to engage on their own terms with others who seek the hopeful possibilities for change in every actual situation, is grounded not in the inherent potential of this world for human progress, but in the promises of the God who transcends this world, who raised Jesus Christ from death in his thoroughly material solidarity with this created world, and who will make all things new when he comes to his creation in the end. This is why the hope of which Moltmann writes can survive the demise of modern optimism and challenge the post-modern tendency to escape from hopelessness into a reduction of time to the present.

Richard Bauckham
Professor of New Testament Studies
and Bishop Wardlaw Professor
University of St Andrews
December 2001

Notes

1 See Moltmann's own account in J. Moltmann, *Experiences in Theology* (tr. M. Kohl; London: SCM Press, 2000), pp. 87–93; also M. D. Meeks, *Origins of the Theology of Hope* (Philadelphia: Fortress, 1974); R. Bauckham, *Moltmann: Messianic Theology in the Making* (Basingstoke: Marshall Pickering, 1987), Chapter 1.

2 For Moltmann's most recent reflections on modernity, see the essays collected in J. Moltmann, *God for a Secular Society* (tr. M. Kohl; London: SCM Press, 1999).

3 K. Marx, 'Eleventh Thesis on Feuerbach', quoted in J. Moltmann, *Theology Today* (tr. J. Bowden; London: SCM Press, 1988), p. 93.

4 See Moltmann's own account in *Experiences in Theology*, pp. 113–17.

5 For Moltmann's early political theology; see R. Bauckham, *The Theology of Jürgen Moltmann* (Edinburgh: T&T Clark, 1995), Chapter 5.

6 F. Fukuyama, *The End of History and the Last Man* (London: Penguin, 1992).

7 J. Moltmann, *The Coming of God* (tr. M. Kohl; London: SCM Press, 1996), chapter III, §§3–5, 8–9.

8 On this see R. Bauckham (ed.), *God Will Be All in All: The Eschatology of Jürgen Moltmann* (Edinburgh: T&T Clark, 1999; Minneapolis: Fortress, 2002).

Preface by the Author

The following efforts bear the title *Theology of Hope*, not because they set out once again to present eschatology as a separate doctrine and to compete with the well known text-books. Rather, their aim is to show how theology can set out from hope and begin to consider its theme in an eschatological light. For this reason they enquire into the ground of the hope of Christian faith and into the responsible exercise of this hope in thought and action in the world today. The various critical discussions should not be understood as rejections and condemnations. They are necessary conversations on a common subject which is so rich that it demands continual new approaches. Hence I hope they may make it clear that even critical questions can be a sign of theological partnership. I have thus to thank all who have stimulated, and all who have opposed me.

For the reading of the proofs and for many of the references I am grateful to my assistant, Mr Karl-Adolf Bauer.

Jürgen Moltmann
10 September 1964

Introduction

Theology of Hope –
Looking Forward and Back

James Hawkey

I.

The 1974 Accra meeting of the Faith and Order Commission of the World Council of Churches produced a remarkable report entitled 'Uniting in Hope'. After their previous plenary meeting in Louvain (1971), further study had been commissioned to articulate the meaning of the Gospel for the contemporary world under the inspiration of a verse from 1 Peter, 'Giving an account of the hope that is in us'. Alongside more traditional theological discussions on topics relating to the unity of the Church, this project invited the churches to give testimony to their own experience of Christian discipleship, and to share that experience with other churches from highly diverse Christian traditions.[1] The Accra meeting drew together many strands of study from different parts of the Christian world. In his introduction to *Uniting in Hope*, Lukas Vischer, the Swiss Reformed chairman of the commission wrote,

> As long as [the churches] continue to deal with the differences inherited from the past, they are not yet ready to enter the One committed fellowship which they are called to constitute in the world. Only as they recognize each other as living in and proclaiming the same faith, will they have the freedom to move forward together; and only then will they become the One body of Christ within the tensions and conflicts of the present world.[2]

The 1974 meeting, and the preparatory sessions that led up to it, signified a turning point in theological method for Faith and Order. It was an exercise in what some have come to call theology 'from below'. While not dismissing creedal or confessional formulae, the Commission posed the question about where an ecumenical journey of intensified Christian fellowship might most helpfully begin. Statements forged in the heat of theological disagreement were considered perhaps not the most fruitful seed-bed for contemporary explorations in Christian unity. Confident in the movement of the Holy Spirit, this project encouraged the churches to begin with their own life of faith, and to articulate the reason for their hope in the reality of their contexts. Could the same hope be articulated, uncovered, in diverse situations and environments? This sharing of hope was an attempt to articulate the basics of the Christian faith as something received and lived, a response to the call of the Gospel, which unites Christians in a broad fellowship.

Professor Jürgen Moltmann was a member of the Faith and Order Commission at Accra, alongside other theological luminaries including Desmond Tutu and Mary Tanner.[3] Although none of the Accra text is attributed to particular authors, his influence on the report is profoundly recognizable. A decade earlier, Moltmann had written a theology that sets out from hope:

> To believe, means to cross in hope and anticipation the bounds that have been penetrated by the raising of the crucified. If we bear that in mind, then this faith can have nothing to do with fleeing the world, with resignation and with escapism. In this hope the soul does not soar above our vale of tears to some imagined heavenly bliss, nor does it sever itself from the earth.[4]

From its earliest pages, Moltmann's *Theology of Hope* implicitly articulated an ecclesiology *in via*, as the Church is constantly called to give an account of the hope within her by engaging with the world around in a way that celebrates new insights in the light of Christ's eternally promised future.[5]

Moltmann was a key drafter of the sections of the Faith and Order report *Uniting in Hope*, which articulated the hope that Christians can hold together. The final version is full of resonance with *Theology of Hope*. The report states that as humanity is 'liberated from presumption and desperation, we are in life and death captives of hope'.[6] That hope, which stirs us to action, does not allow the Christian to be conformed to an 'enslaved and divided world', but rather compels the Christian to strive, joyfully, for liberation and peace. All this is rooted in the events of Christ's self-sacrifice and resurrection, which have filled us 'with an indestructible hope in eternal life, in spite of sin, death and demonic powers'.[7]

Moltmann presented the first draft of part B, 'Affirmation of Hope in Christ' to the Accra plenary session.[8] Other German theologians at the meeting criticized Moltmann's presentation of this section of the report on the grounds that it was limited to a biblical worldview, 'too pietist, too conservative'. Anyone who has ever attempted to draft a document for ecumenical consensus will recognize the challenge of finding both a style and an approach that is acceptable to everyone! But however the material was presented on that occasion, there is no doubt that Moltmann's voice is recognizable in the final text, and that solidarity and the need for societal change are themes that emerge from the biblical exegesis. The centrality of eschatology as a starting point for the Christian life and all theological reflection – so fundamental for Moltmann – comes out clearly towards the middle of section B of *Uniting in Hope*. The voice is unmistakable, 'This hope in the coming of Christ gives meaning to all our experience and our historical activity. This is what makes suffering bearable, keeps love alive, and gives boldness to faith.'[9] Or as he put it in his introduction to *Theology of Hope*, 'Christianity is eschatology, is hope, forward looking and forward moving, and therefore also revolutionizing and transforming the present ... The eschatological is not one element of Christianity, but it is the medium of Christian faith as such, the key in which everything in it is set, the glow that suffuses everything here in the dawn of an expected new day.'[10]

Despite the criticism of some of Moltmann's fellow countrymen, section B of *Uniting in Hope* testifies to the animating power of eschatology behind all moves in the direction of human flourishing:

[a] yearning for God ... directs us to an earnest struggle for God's rights over his creation ... In, along with, and behind the struggle for freedom, for the dignity of human life, for the awakening of a living hope, we hope for God's coming and we look forward to the perfect joy of his Kingdom.[11]

Indeed, it is the very hope of this coming Kingdom which inspires us with an 'incentive to participate in efforts to build a more human social order in the perspective of the Kingdom of God'. There are other strong echoes of Moltmann's voice – a brief discussion of social order and institutions, the role of individual Christians and of the Church in society, and a plea for a more 'human'[12] society. All these themes are explored in *Theology of Hope*, warning against any tendency to luxuriate in the abstract, alongside an encouragement to engage confidently with the world as it is. Towards the middle of his final chapter, 'Exodus Church', Moltmann articulates it like this:

> [salvation] does not mean merely salvation of the soul, individual rescue from the evil world, comfort for the troubled conscience, but also the realization of the eschatological hope of justice, the humanizing of man, the socializing of humanity, peace for all creation. This other side of reconciliation with God has always been given too little consideration ... it is only in the light of this other side of reconciliation that Christians ... can gain new impulses for the shaping of man's public, social and political life.[13]

It is these very themes that so much of his subsequent work has gone on to unpack. Since its initial publication, the reception of *Theology of Hope* has been more significant and more diverse than the writings of many of Moltmann's peers, including among those who ultimately disagree with him on wider theological questions.

2.

A Culture of Life in Defiance of the Deadly Threats of This Age is Professor Moltmann's response to a request to articulate a theology of hope for the twenty-first century. The Charles Gore Lecture was inaugurated in 1935 as a permanent memorial to Bishop Charles Gore, a Canon of Westminster between 1894–1902. Many distinguished theologians have delivered this lecture since its inception, and since 2016 the Gore Lecture has formed a centrepiece of Westminster Abbey Institute's public spring programme. The 2019 series of Institute spring lectures focused on the broad theme of hope, with contributions from journalist and author Jenny McCarthy, and former director of Oxfam Dame Barbara Stocking, alongside my own lecture, re-written during the COVID-19 pandemic, which explored hope as a virtue, and argued for tangible, public signs of hope and recovery to be allied to developments in public policy.

Moltmann's text emerges from a lifetime of Christian thought and prayer, and reveals his deep emotional and intellectual engagement with the profound challenges facing humanity and the survival of the earth itself. This piece of writing represents the distilled commitment and energy of a Christian thinker with the hinterland of a vast frame of reference. Moltmann wears his learning lightly, and the reader may be surprised by the disarming simplicity of his arguments. His debts to Hegel and the German romantic tradition are merely acknowledged with a single quote from the *Phenomenology of Spirit*. This is the Moltmann of personal responsibility, solidarity, social justice, and peace, raging at the deadly dangers human culture has embraced. Some of the themes in *A Culture of Life* were initially explored with greater demonstrable reliance on scripture in his 1989 book *Creating a Just Future*, where Moltmann asks whether Christianity has become so fused with modern society (which he sees arising out of the Industrial Revolution) that Christians simply share that society's many ambiguities and moral contradictions? If so, the loss of a particularly Christian hope is devastating not only for communities of faith, but for broader society, and the earth itself.

Moltmann's audience on this occasion represented a further broadening in the reception of his thinking. Westminster Abbey Institute was founded in 2013 to revitalize moral and spiritual values in public life and service. Through public lectures and symposia, as well as private, invitation-only events for government departments, the Institute seeks to nurture the gift of public service and offer support for those who work in government, civil service and those institutions that in some way contribute towards the health of public life in the UK. It was to this broad community of public service that Moltmann's lecture was primarily directed. Many of those who attended the lecture were Christians, some were theologians; but among the audience who appreciated Moltmann's analysis and challenge were those of other faiths, and many for whom any form of religious adherence is certainly not explicit.

Thus the theological language that characterizes much of his other writing is not frequently deployed here, there is no exegesis of scripture (only an allusion to 2 Corinthians 1:20 at the very end), and the vision of God, while clearly and distinctively Christian, has the potential for wide application. This is a manifesto, rooted in Moltmann's own deep and rich faith, intended for an audience far beyond those who would ordinarily read the works of one of our most influential living theologians.

3.

The night before the Gore Lecture, Professor Moltmann spoke informally to a group of theologians in Westminster Abbey's Jerusalem Chamber. Many of his themes included areas he would subsequently address in his Gore Lecture. He also outlined an increasing nervousness around the doctrine of the *imago Dei*, in particular how it has been misused to remove human beings from their organic context within broader creation. On both nights, privately and publically, he spoke much about his own history, and of how his theology was rooted in his own life and hope. 'Without the experience of captivity, I would never have been a theologian,' he told me. Moltmann's first Prisoner of War Camp was in Kilmarnock, Ayrshire, where he encountered Scottish families who greeted him with a hospitality he found both shameful and embarrassing. The solidarity and common expression of humanity he encountered from his captors and local people alike moved him greatly and left an indelible mark on his memories of Britain.

In the summer of 1946, it became clear that captivity was going to last longer than Moltmann had initially thought. He was moved to Norton Camp, near Mansfield, to continue his education under the auspices of the YMCA. The Camp existed to train teachers and protestant pastors for post-War Germany. Here, he immersed himself in Rilke and the novels of Thomas Mann, as well as learning Hebrew and Greek. In his own words, 'Norton Camp was Britain's generous gift to German POWs ... I have never lived so intense an intellectual life as I did in Norton.'

Moltmann describes the first international SCM Conference at Swanwick in the summer of 1947 as an event of profound importance. 'It turned my life upside down,' he said, to arrive as one of a small group of uniformed German prisoners fearfully anticipating questioning about Nazi war crimes and the mass murder of Jews in Auschwitz. In fact, he discovered a fraternal welcome as a brother in Christ, and the transformative ability to sing and pray with other young Christians from all over the world. It was here at Swanwick that he decided to focus his life on theology, rather than the physics and mathematics he had previously explored. In the notes he left me of our conversations, he has simply written: 'Reconciliation, not atom bombs' at the bottom of this reflection. The acceptance of his group of POWs among the wider variety of Christian young people, speaking openly and praying with them, made it possible for Moltmann to confess what he described as the 'collective guilt' of Germany.

In 1995, the survivors of the German group returned to England to visit the site of Norton Camp. Moltmann recalls that although the Nissan Huts had now vanished, the strong old oak trees – 'resilient nature' – had remained. The group remembered those who had shown them such a transformative Christian welcome, praying together and singing hymns. The former prisoners invited the camp's old commander, Major Boughton, to join them. The Major dryly remarked that he'd never before heard of prisoners returning to their prison of their own free will, and praising God for what they had experienced there. 'But that was exactly what we did, with great joy and thankfulness,' reflected Moltmann.

4.

In a highly personal short book, *Resurrected to Eternal Life*, published in 2021, Moltmann reminisces about how he and his late wife were both deeply influenced by Dietrich Bonhoeffer's insistence that there is a profound 'this-worldliness' inherent in Christianity. Bonhoeffer wrote from prison to Eberhard Bethge:

> During the last year or so I've come to know and understand more and more the profound this-worldliness of Christianity ... By this-worldliness I mean living unreservedly in life's duties, problems, successes and failures, experiences and perplexities. In doing so, we throw ourselves completely into the arms of God ...[14]

Theology of Hope and *A Culture of Life* both represent this strand of Moltmann's faith and theology, open to the world for which Christ died and rose, while, as he puts it, taking the world's 'horizons up into the eschatological horizon of the resurrection, and thereby disclos[ing] to modern history its true historical character'.[15] *Resurrected to Eternal Life* explores something of the balance of the 'other-worldliness' which is also an essential part of the Christian proclamation[16] and inseparable from what we might have to say about death.

Even when writing in the mode of an activist, Moltmann's insight never begins with experience or ideology, but rather with theology – with the eschatological hope that characterizes Christian engagement with the world. It is precisely this that allows his profound and passionate insights to be harvested by a wide variety of interlocutors. In an age of renewed debate about nuclear weapons, of passionate and urgent concern for the environment, of the dangers of ideological populism, his voice remains one of insistent wisdom and great freshness. Our churches have moved on from the heady days of Accra, and the so-called ecumenical spring of earlier decades. We wrestle with issues of theological anthropology, tradition, providence, and knotty questions around revelation and culture. If Christians could once again engage with the surrounding world from the firm basis of a genuinely shared hope – which is nothing less than 'the future of the crucified one'[17] who has promised to gather all people to himself – our mission may become more credible and more transformative. Returning to this fundamental wellspring, which engages with the reality of human frailty and sin, is itself a sign of the triumph of resurrection life. Can this really be the shared territory from which all Christian engagement emerges? We would find ready partners beyond the Church's environs, as well as a refreshed sense of our own Christian mission and vocation. A greater familiarity with Moltmann's thinking will challenge us to embrace such an essential project, both for the Church's unity, and for the flourishing of the world Christ came to save.

James Hawkey
Canon Theologian of Westminster Abbey

Notes

1 *Uniting in Hope: Accra 1974: Reports and Documents from the Meeting of the Faith and Order Commission*, Faith and Order Paper No. 72 (Geneva: World Council of Churches, 1975).

2 *Uniting in Hope*, Preface V.

3 Dame Mary became a member of the Commission the following year, but attended the Accra meeting as a substitute for her supervisor Geoffrey Lampe. I am grateful to her for sharing memories of this meeting.

4 Jürgen Moltmann, *Theology of Hope: For the 21st Century* (London: SCM Press, 2021), p. 6.

5 These themes are developed more fully and explicitly in his final section 'Exodus Church'.

6 *Uniting in Hope*, p. 29.

7 *Uniting in Hope*.

8 *Uniting in Hope*, pp. 28–32.

9 *Uniting in Hope*, p. 30.

10 *Theology of Hope*, p. 2.

11 *Uniting in Hope*, p. 31.

12 *Uniting in Hope*, p. 32.

13 *Theology of Hope*, p. 312–13.

14 Dietrich Bonhoeffer, *Letters and Papers from Prison*, ed. Eberhard Bethge, 2nd ed. (London, SCM Press, 1971), p. 369.

15 *Theology of Hope*, p. 287.

16 Jürgen Moltmann, *Resurrected to Eternal Life: On Dying and Rising* (Minneapolis: Fortress Press, 2021).

17 Moltmann, *Resurrected to Eternal Life*.

Abbreviations

AGFNRW	Veröffentlichungen der Arbeitsgemeinschaft für Forschung des Landes Nordrhein-Westfalen
ET	English translation
EvTh	*Evangelische Theologie*
ExpT	*Expository Times*
NF	Neue Folge
NTS	*New Testament Studies*
RGG	*Religion in Geschichte und Gegenwart*
TLZ	*Theologische Literaturzeitung*
TWNT	*Theologisches Wörterbuch zum Neuen Testament*
VT Suppl.	Supplements to *Vetus Testamentum*
WA	Complete Works of Luther, *Weimarer Ausgabe*
ZTK	*Zeitschrift für Theologie und Kirche*

Lecture

'But where there is danger, salvation also grows'

A Culture of Life in Defiance of the Deadly Threats of This Age

*Originally delivered at Westminster Abbey,
as the Charles Gore Lecture on 3 March 2020*

Jürgen Moltmann

I would like to speak about an issue that has been stirring people for quite some time: a culture of life stronger than the barbarianism of killing. A love for life that defies the imminent destruction of the world we live in. I would like to begin with a verse by the German poet Friedrich Hölderlin and follow his gaze into the universal future of the world:

> But where
> there is
> danger,
> salvation
> also grows.
> (*Wo aber gefahr ist, wächst das rettende auch.*)

We will have to see whether this statement offers comfort or a threat to us as we inquire into the possibilities for a culture of life in the face of the tangible destruction menacing us and our world.

I will set out to examine some of the dangers, and offer in response dimensions of a world capable of supporting life, and which is, in a quite literal sense, worthy of our love. At the end, I would like to return to the first verse of Friedrich Hölderlin's celebrated poem 'Patmos':

Near and
Hard to grasp is
God.
(*Nah ist Und schwer zu fassen der Gott.*)

1. The Terror of Death

The Misery of Hate

Human life itself is in danger today. The life of humanity is threatened. Human life is not in danger because it is menaced by death, that has always been the case. It is in danger because it is no longer respected and affirmed – it is no longer loved. After the Second World War, Albert Camus stated: 'The secret of Europe is that it no longer loves life.' Anyone who took part in the Second World War knows what he meant.

After 70 years of peace in Europe, we are facing a new ideology of enmity today. In the twentieth century we experienced state-operated 'terror from above' in the forms of fascism and Stalinism; today we are experiencing private 'terror from below'.

'Your young people love life,' Mullah Omar of the Taliban told Western journalists, 'our young people love death.' Suicide assassins love the death of their enemies and their own death. That is the Islamist ideology of terror of the so-called IS (Islamic State) in Iraq and of Boko Haram in Africa towards the supposedly godless Western world that they feel threatened by. The mentality of victimhood always leads to anger and to hate.

These days, this form of terror has been joined by 'white terror'. Norway, New Zealand, Texas and Germany have witnessed the terror of white supremacy, essentially white racism. In many western nations, a climate of hate has been fostered, promoting such hatred against those perceived as outsiders. In the 1970s, Germany experienced 'terror from the Left', and now we are experiencing 'terror from the Right' against migrants, Jews and unpopular politicians.

Our public atmosphere has been poisoned ever since we have had the ability to post anonymously on Twitter and elsewhere on the internet. Hate via the world-wide-web – death threats made to politicians you don't like, hate speech against foreigners, insults, vicious slander and fake news are kindling a new kind of underground civil war. Nazi language is emerging again in Germany. It had never been overcome, just repressed. It is the language of arrogance and enmity, the language of fear and aggression, the language of falsehood: the language of death. And all too often, words that aim to injure are followed by actions that kill.

How can human civilization prevail against such odds?

Neo-Nationalism

Neo-nationalism is to blame for much of this. Due to nationalist power politics [of Putin in Russia, Trump in the USA, and Xi in China] the nations of the world are at war in the midst of peace. This is a hybrid war of economic sanctions and cyber wars with fake news. In the struggle for power, the new nationalists seem to believe in the 'survival of the fittest' because they believe their own nation to be the strongest.

Neo-Nationalism can offer no genuine future for humankind, but rather will lead it into ruin – and not just for humankind alone, but also for the whole interrelated community of our earth. This new nationalism began at the end of the East-West Conflict in 1990. Since the end of the Second World War, the world had been divided into two blocs: the socialist world in the East and the 'free world' in the West. Then the Soviet Union dissolved itself, Gorbachev lost, and Yeltsin won in 1993. The Soviet Union disintegrated into larger and smaller nations, Russia felt overburdened to be the 'protecting power of socialism'. The socialist dream of the equality of all people died.

The so-called free world dissolved rather more slowly. The alliance of democratic states did not disintegrate until President Trump asserted the USA's neo-nationalism under the slogan of 'America first'. The USA felt overburdened to be the 'protecting power of the free world'. The USA rescinded multilateral treaties of the United Nations, and reneged upon the Paris Climate Protection Agreement of 2015, the INF Treaty of 1987 banning nuclear short-range missiles in Europe, and the Iran Nuclear Deal. In 2018, the USA stepped back from the United Nations Human Rights council. Right wing neo-nationalism is also stirring in the nations of the European Union.

In nations that see themselves as somehow 'ethnically pure', members of one's own clan or tribe are considered 'fellow human beings' while everyone else is a foreigner. A line is drawn between 'us' and 'the others'. The friend-foe category is the existential category of neo-nationalism, as Hitler's professor for constitutional law, Carl Schmitt taught.

Does this mean that the democratic dream for humanity has died as well?

The Nuclear Suicide Programme

Such a new focused concentration on one's own nation poses a particular threat to the survival of humankind, considering that atomic bombs are still in the hands of individual nations. When the atomic bomb was invented and dropped on Hiroshima and Nagasaki in August 1945, not only did the Second World War conclude, but the entire human race also entered its end times. I do not mean this in an apocalyptic sense: this 'end times' is the age when the end of the human race is possible at any moment. The possibility of a large nuclear war unveiled the mass, simultaneous mortality of the whole human race. No one could survive a nuclear winter after a large-scale nuclear war. It is true that since the end of the Cold War in 1990, a great atomic war has not been very likely, but in the USA, Russia, China, the UK, France, India, Pakistan, Israel and North Korea, there are still vast arsenals of atomic and hydrogen bombs ready for the self-destruction of humankind, following the rationale, 'Whoever fires first, dies second.'

This is the mutually assured destruction that paradoxically has been ensuring world peace since 1945. It is a latent but ever-present 'suicide programme' for the nations, as the Russian nuclear scientist Sakharov put it, which many have forgotten because it has been repressed from public awareness. Years ago in Prague, President Obama reminded us of the ideal of a world without nuclear weapons, but President Putin applauded Russia's new weapons in 2018, and President Trump rescinded the INF Treaty banning nuclear short-range missiles in Europe, which Reagan and Gorbachev had agreed in 1987. A new phase of nuclear armament has begun, a sinister feature of which is the missile boosters that reduce warning times to a bare minimum. The great atomic war looms over humankind like a sinister fate, and we feel its effects on public awareness through what American psychologists call 'nuclear numbing'. We repress our anxiety, try to forget the threat, and live as if this danger did not exist. And yet it gnaws at our subconscious and impairs our love for life.

Will the nations reach an agreement on a world without nuclear weapons, or will the nations continue to menace each other with threats of the nuclear murder of humankind?

The Ecological Catastrophe of Our World

In contrast to the nuclear threat to humanity, the ecological catastrophe discussed under the seemingly harmless moniker 'climate change' is no longer merely a threat, but already an incipient catastrophe in some parts of the earth. This is not only a latent problem, but one that has a prominent place in much public consciousness. Greta Thunberg's wake-up call 'Fridays for Future' has been heard worldwide. At the United Nations Climate Change Conference in Paris in 2015, the nations paid attention to the 'cry of the suffering earth' for the first time. People can see climate change, feel its heat and smell its polluted air.

The biosphere of the earth is the only living-space available to humanity. But globalization has led human civilization to its limits, and is in the process of overstepping these limits so that the earth's biosphere is substantially and permanently altered. The extinction of species which goes hand in hand with climate change is a clear warning to us. Air pollution with carbon dioxide is destroying the ozone layer and warming the climate, the polar ice caps and mountain glaciers are melting, and as a result, sea levels are rising. The deserts are expanding, and soon we will have a tropical climate in Europe.

The ecological catastrophe has come to pass exactly as the Club of Rome predicted in its report 'The Limits to Growth' in 1972. We know all of this and yet we are paralyzed, because we continue to believe in 'growth' on its own terms – producing more, consuming more, in a type of superstitious worship as if growth would bring more joy to our life!

Protecting the environment is fine in the minds of much of the general population and our opinion leaders as long as it does not cost us anything. While we remain paralyzed, the costs of so-called environmental protection over the next 20 years are growing out of all control. With a hint of sarcasm, one might say that while some don't know what they are doing, others aren't doing what they know.

It has been said that it is too late for pessimism. Climate change and the extinction of species are signals for a major adjustment which challenges our scientific-technological civilization, should we wish to survive. This concerns both our common world view and our personal way of life.

Will we find time and energy enough to change ourselves and our world so that our children can live?

We do not know whether humankind will survive its self-induced fate and be able to liberate itself from these suicide traps. And that is surely a good thing. If we knew that we had no chance of surviving, we would do nothing about our predicament, it would be futile, 'after us, the deluge', as the saying goes. Equally, if we knew that we were definitely going to survive, we wouldn't do anything either. Only if the future is open to both possibilities will we be compelled to do what is necessary to avert the pending calamity. Because we do not know whether humankind will survive, we must act today as if the future of humankind depended on us, and yet trust that we and our children will be able to survive and thrive.

But need the human race survive at all? One might ask cynically: didn't the dinosaurs also come and go? The existential question we face is – is humankind to be, or not to be? It is the Hamlet-question of humankind.

There are more than seven billion human beings living on earth today. The earth could just as well be uninhabited: It existed without humans for the longest period of time and in all likelihood would continue to exist for millions of years, if the human race succumbed to its demise. Are we here merely by chance, or is it inherent to the blueprint of evolution that we humans were to appear? If nature had a 'strong anthropic principle', then we could feel 'at home in the universe', as the book title by Stuart Kauffman promises. Such a 'strong anthropic principle' is, however, perhaps not verifiable. If we search the cosmos for an answer to our existential question, we will arrive at Steve Weinberg's observation: 'The more the universe seems comprehensible, the more it also seems pointless.' The silence of space and the coldness of the universe already terrified Blaise Pascal. Neither the stars in the sky nor the genes in our bodies tell us whether humankind should exist on earth or not.

But how can we love life and affirm our existence if, in the end, it is an accident of nature, basically superfluous, and without relevance for the course of the world? Is there a 'duty to exist', or a 'duty to ensure a future', as Hans Jonas inquired, taking the existential question of humankind seriously? If we do not answer this question, every culture of life will remain uncertain and subject to barbarianism.

2. A Culture of Life is a Culture of Common Life of Humankind and the Earth

Are the threats greater than the powers of salvation?

Human Rights and Humanity

Past nationalisms led us into the madness of the two world wars of the twentieth century. They led us to Verdun and Stalingrad. As a survivor of the Second World War, I know what I am talking about. Neo-nationalism is spreading underground in our societies with death threats and individual murders. It is not difficult to predict that this will only lead the people into a mass grave. In Germany today, its past, neo-nationalism, and the National Socialist underground have come together, and once more we have Aryan nationalism.

Yet at the beginning of the American and European modern era, humanism was born: human riqhts and an ethos of humanity. Exclusively Christian, brotherhood expanded into a general human brotherhood, *fraternité*, *philadelphia*. Everyone knows the 'Ode to Joy' by Friedrich Schiller, set to music at the end of Beethoven's 9th Symphony:

Joy, thou beauteous godly lightning,
Daughter of Elysium,
Fire-drunken we are entering,
Heavenly, thy holy home!

Thy enchantments bind together,
What did custom stern divide,
Every man becomes a brother,
Where thy gentle wings abide.

This piece is also the anthem of the European Union. The first article of the Universal Declaration of Human Rights also praises the 'spirit of brotherhood'. The American Declaration of Independence codified human rights in 1776, affirming the belief that all men are created equal and free. The French Revolution spread these rights in Europe in 1789: 'liberty – equality – fraternity'. Immanuel Kant considered the 'commonwealth of humankind', based on human rights, to be not only the ultimate objective of human history, but also the 'final end of creation', thus spanning the human and the natural world. Kant anticipated such a commonwealth of humankind would bring about 'eternal peace'.

After the grueling Second World War with its 55 million dead people, the United Nations was founded in 1945 and the Universal Declaration of Human Rights proclaimed in 1948. The International Covenant on Economic, Social and Cultural Rights followed in 1966, and the Convention on the Rights of the Child in 1989. Modern democracies are based on human rights and are anticipations of a politically organized world community, the Commonwealth of Humankind.

Democracy is based on the sovereignty of the people. All power emanates from the people, and therefore from all the citizens, not from people of one race, or one class, or one gender.

Democracy is based on human rights. Human dignity is inviolable. So-called 'people's democracies' were not human rights democracies. Today, protecting human rights is a crucial aspect of international democratic politics – 'Make the world safe for democracy', as President Wilson proclaimed in 1917. Domestically, democracies are concerned with human rights, not with ethnic or class rights. Humanity trumps nationality.

Gottfried Ephraim Lessing described the meaning of humanity in his famous drama 'Nathan the Wise' of 1779:

Were Jews and Christians such, e'er they were men?
And have I found in thee one more, to whom
It is enough to be a man?

One might feel tempted to apply this to today's nationalist conflicts:

Were Americans and Hispanics…
Were Croats and Serbs…
Were Europeans and Africans…

Ah, and have I found in thee one more, to whom
It is enough to be a human being?

Those who have drowned in the Mediterranean fleeing from conflict and disaster teach us what humanity really means. Humanity means brotherhood, and brotherhood and sisterhood mean solidarity: taking part in one another's lives and sharing one's own life.

Living with the Bomb

The dream of a world without nuclear weapons is only a dream. Nobody expects humans to someday cease being able to do what they can do today. Whoever has learned the formula of nuclear world destruction can never forget it. Since Hiroshima, humankind has lost its nuclear innocence.

Hiroshima changed the quality of human history. Our time has become limited time, as the end can come at any moment. Our own generation and those that will follow us eke out our lives under the threat of the bomb. Life is no longer a matter of course; life and survival have become the main tasks of political culture – a life against death.

And yet the nuclear age is also the first common age of all nations. Since Hiroshima, the separate histories of the nations have become intertwined in a common world history of humankind, because they all may fall victim to the nuclear age. In this situation, survival is only conceivable if nations unite as a collective agent for peace. Only the international community of nations can organize partnership for security and thus pave the way for a transnational federation of humanity.

Such a life-saving union of humankind in the age of nuclear threat would require that the individual interests of nations be focused on the common interest of humankind's survival.

We must finally get started with nuclear disarmament. Nuclear bombs are not military, but purely political weapons. And the political security of nations can just as well be guaranteed by means of peace-treaties. The United Nations can 'ostracize' nuclear weapons, just as chemical warfare and land mines were ostracized as military weapons. Chemical weapons were not used in the Second World War.

Deterrence can no longer be said to secure peace, because suicide bombers cannot be deterred. Only just can we secure lasting peace. It has been said that peace is not the absence of violence, but the presence of justice. Consequently there is no peace where injustice and acts of violence rule, even if law and order are enforced. The financial expense of security goes through the roof where there is no political and social justice to secure peace. Systems of injustice can only be upheld by means of violence. There is no peace where such violence, fear and distrust reign. Systems of violence are built on sand – their days are numbered.

Planetary Solidarity

On 5 November 2019, President Donald Trump withdrew the USA from the 2008 Paris Climate agreement which had been ratified under President Obama. That same day, thousands of scientists published a memorandum warning of the countless human fatalities that would accompany the forthcoming catastrophes for the earth's ecosystem. This illustrates the dilemma very well. If nature's dying leads to a crisis within a life-system that connects human society with surrounding nature, this logically implies a crisis of the entire system. The current ecological crisis is such a total crisis. It can therefore not be solved by technology alone, but rather demands a change of our entire outlook on life as well, of our way of life (right down to what we choose to eat), a change of our society's fundamental values.

Which basic values rule our modern, scientific-technological civilization? It is predominately the will to have power over the nature of the earth: 'Knowledge is power'. Modern industrial societies are no longer oriented towards harmony with the cycles and rhythms of the earth as agrarian societies once were, but are rather geared towards growth, progress and globalization according to humanity's own projects. The modern anthropocentrism supplanted the old cosmos-orientation.

There is a well-known ecological joke: 'Two planets meet in space. One asks: "How are you doing?" The other answers: "I'm not well at all. I'm quite ill, I've got homo sapiens." The first one replies: "I'm so sorry for you. That's rough. I had that too, once. But don't worry, you will get over it quickly."'

That is the new planetary perspective on humankind. Will the human planetary disease pass as the human race does away with itself, or will it pass because the human race grows wise and heals the wounds it has inflicted on planet earth up to and including this very day? Humankind will learn in the end, either by means of discernment or by means of catastrophes. I am in favor of discernment and foresight.

The ecological catastrophe requires a change in our basic values to a focus on 'reverence for life' (Albert Schweitzer) – that means reverence for every single form of life and for the great community of all living things. Modern anthropocentrism will be replaced by a new ecological biocentrism.

We cannot return to a premodern cosmos-orientation, but we can begin the ecological transformation of industrial society. It is a question of sustainably integrating human society into the living conditions of the earth. The linear concept of progress in production – consumption – and more and more garbage needs to be replaced by cycles. Only cyclical approaches do not result in decay: the cycles of 'renewable energies' and recycling economy. (What became of your last cell phone?)

The Earth Charter of 2000 points to this future for life:

Humanity is part of a vast evolving universe. Earth, our home, is alive with a unique community of life ... The protection of Earth's vitality, diversity, and beauty is a sacred trust.

Human life implies not only the gift of life, but also the responsibility of being humane. Embracing and accomplishing this in times of terror requires a great courage to truly live. Terrorized consciousness paralyses the will to live, and promotes a retreat into private life. But this only paves the way for public terror and future catastrophes. Life must be lived, private, public, and political life! Life must be lived today in defiance of terror and dangers! Life, one's own and common, universal life, must be lived in defiance of universal death!

The German philosopher Friedrich Hegel, a friend of Hölderlin's since their time studying together in Tübingen, expressed it in the following words:

Not a life that shrinks from death
and remains untouched by devastation,
but a life that endures death and maintains itself in it
is the life of the Spirit.

'Near and hard to grasp is God ...'

In conclusion, let me speak as a theologian:

* Should humankind exist, or are we superfluous?
* Do we have a duty to exist?

These existential questions are not answered by means of rational arguments, but foremost by pre-rational orientations, by people's basic trust or their mistrust, they have learned by experience.

It is not the distant God that is 'hard to grasp', but rather God's being near to us. God is closer to us than we are to ourselves. That is why we cannot grasp God.

We however are grasped by God, we know the answer to the existential question of humanity:

* In God's eternal YES to creation, we affirm our existence in spite of death.
* In God's eternal love, we love this life and resist its destruction.
* With God near, we trust in salvation, even if dangers grow.

'Near and Hard to grasp is God. But where there is danger, Salvation also grows.'

Introduction: Meditation on Hope

1. What is the 'Logos' of Christian Eschatology?

Eschatology was long called the 'doctrine of the last things' or the 'doctrine of the end'. By these last things were meant events which will one day break upon man, history and the world at the end of time. They included the return of Christ in universal glory, the judgment of the world and the consummation of the kingdom, the general resurrection of the dead and the new creation of all things. These end events were to break into this world from somewhere beyond history, and to put an end to the history in which all things here live and move. But the relegating of these events to the 'last day' robbed them of their directive, uplifting and critical significance for all the days which are spent here, this side of the end, in history. Thus these teachings about the end led a peculiarly barren existence at the end of Christian dogmatics. They were like a loosely attached appendix that wandered off into obscure irrelevancies. They bore no relation to the doctrines of the cross and resurrection, the exaltation and sovereignty of Christ, and did not derive from these by any logical necessity. They were as far removed from them as All Souls' Day sermons are from Easter. The more Christianity became an organization for discipleship under the auspices of the Roman state religion and persistently upheld the claims of that religion, the more eschatology and its mobilizing, revolutionizing, and critical effects upon history as it has now to be lived were left to fanatical sects and revolutionary groups. Owing to the fact that Christian faith banished from its life the future hope by which it is upheld, and relegated the future to a beyond, or to eternity, whereas the biblical testimonies which it handed on are yet full to the brim with future hope of a messianic kind for the world, – owing to this, hope emigrated as it were from the Church and turned in one distorted form or another against the Church.

In actual fact, however, eschatology means the doctrine of the Christian hope, which embraces both the object hoped for and also the hope inspired by it. From first to last, and not merely in the epilogue, Christianity is eschatology, is hope, forward looking and forward moving, and therefore also revolutionizing and transforming the present. The eschatological is not one element *of* Christianity, but it is the medium of Christian faith as such, the key in which everything in it is set, the glow that suffuses everything here in the dawn of an expected new day. For Christian faith lives from the raising of the crucified Christ, and strains after the promises of the universal future of Christ. Eschatology is the passionate suffering and passionate longing kindled by the Messiah. Hence eschatology cannot really be only a part of Christian doctrine. Rather, the eschatological outlook is characteristic of all Christian proclamation, of every Christian existence and of the whole Church. There is therefore only one real problem in Christian theology, which its own object forces upon it and which it in turn forces on mankind and on human thought: the problem of the future. For the element of otherness that encounters us in the hope of the Old and New Testaments – the thing we cannot already think out and picture for ourselves on the basis of the given world and of the experiences we already have of that world – is one that confronts us with a promise of something new and with the hope of a future given by God. The God spoken of here is no intra-worldly or extra-worldly God, but the 'God of hope' (Rom. 15.13), a God with 'future as his essential nature' (as E. Bloch puts it), as made known in Exodus and in Israelite prophecy, the God whom we therefore cannot really have in us or over us but always only before us, who encounters us in his promises for the future, and whom we therefore cannot 'have' either, but can only await in active hope. A proper theology would therefore have to be constructed in the light of its future goal. Eschatology should not be its end, but its beginning.

But how can anyone speak of the future, which is not yet here, and of coining events in which he has not as yet had any part? Are these not dreams, speculations, longings and fears, which must all remain vague and indefinite because no one can verify them? The term 'eschato-*logy*' is wrong. There can be no 'doctrine' of the last things, if by 'doctrine' we mean a collection of theses which can be understood on the basis of experiences that constantly recur and are open to anyone. The Greek term *logos* refers to a reality which is there, now and always, and is given true expression in the word appropriate to it. In this sense there can be no *logos* of the future, unless the future is the continuation or regular recurrence of the present. If, however, the future were to bring something startlingly new, we have nothing to say of that, and nothing meaningful can be said of it either, for it is not in what is new and accidental, but only in things of an abiding and regularly recurring character that there can be logical truth. Aristotle, it is true, can call hope a 'waking dream', but for the Greeks it is nevertheless an evil out of Pandora's box.

But how, then, can Christian eschatology give expression to the future? Christian eschatology does not speak of the future as such. It sets out from a definite reality in history and announces the future of that reality, its future possibilities and its power over the future. Christian eschatology speaks of Jesus Christ and *his* future. It recognizes the reality of the raising of Jesus and proclaims the future of the risen Lord. Hence the question whether all statements about the future are grounded in the person and history of Jesus Christ provides it with the touchstone by which to distinguish the spirit of eschatology from that of utopia.

If, however, the crucified Christ has a future because of his resurrection, then that means on the other hand that all statements and judgments about him must at once imply something about the future which is to be expected from him. Hence the form in which Christian theology speaks of Christ cannot be the form of the Greek *logos* or of doctrinal statements based on experience, but only the form of statements of hope and of promises for the future. All predicates of Christ not only say who he was and is, but imply statements as to who he will be and what is to be expected from him. They all say: 'He is our hope' (Col. 1.27). In thus announcing his future in the world in terms of promise, they point believers in him towards the hope of his still outstanding future. Hope's statements of promise anticipate the future. In the promises, the hidden future already announces itself and exerts its influence on the present through the hope it awakens.

The truth of doctrinal statements is found in the fact that they can be shown to agree with the existing reality which we can all experience. Hope's statements of promise, however, must stand in contradiction to the reality which can at present be experienced.

3

They do not result from experiences, but are the condition for the possibility of new experiences. They do not seek to illuminate the reality which exists, but the reality which is coming. They do not seek to make a mental picture of existing reality, but to lead existing reality towards the promised and hoped-for transformation. They do not seek to bear the train of reality, but to carry the torch before it. In so doing they give reality a historic character. But if reality is perceived in terms of history, then we have to ask with J. G. Hamann: 'Who would form proper concepts of the present without knowing the future?'

Present and future, experience and hope, stand in contradiction to each other in Christian eschatology, with the result that man is not brought into harmony and agreement with the given situation, but is drawn into the conflict between hope and experience. 'We are saved by hope. But hope that is seen is not hope; for what a man seeth, why doth he yet hope for? But if we hope for that we see not, then do we with patience wait for it' (Rom. 8.24, 25). Everywhere in the New Testament the Christian hope is directed towards what is not yet visible; it is consequently a 'hoping against hope' and thereby brands the visible realm of present experience as a god-forsaken, transient reality that is to be left behind. The contradiction to the existing reality of himself and his world in which man is placed by hope is the very contradiction out of which this hope itself is born – it is the contradiction between the resurrection and the cross. Christian hope is resurrection hope, and it proves its truth in the contradiction of the future prospects thereby offered and guaranteed for righteousness as opposed to sin, life as opposed to death, glory as opposed to suffering, peace as opposed to dissension. Calvin perceived very plainly the discrepancy involved in the resurrection hope: 'To us is given the promise of eternal life – but to us, the dead. A blessed resurrection is proclaimed to us – meantime we are surrounded by decay. We are called righteous – and yet sin lives in us. We hear of ineffable blessedness – but meantime we are here oppressed by infinite misery. We are promised abundance of all good things – yet we are rich only in hunger and thirst. What would become of us if we did not take our stand on hope, and if our heart did not hasten beyond this world through the midst of the darkness upon the path illumined by the word and Spirit of God!' (on Heb. 11.1).

It is in this contradiction that hope must prove its power. Hence eschatology, too, is forbidden to ramble, and must formulate its statements of hope in contradiction to our present experience of suffering, evil and death. For that reason it will hardly ever be possible to develop an eschatology on its own. It is much more important to present hope as the foundation and the mainspring of theological thinking as such, and to introduce the eschatological perspective into our statements on divine revelation, on the resurrection of Christ, on the mission of faith and on history.

2. The Believing Hope

In the contradiction between the word of promise and the experiential reality of suffering and death, faith takes its stand on hope and 'hastens beyond this world', said Calvin. He did not mean by this that Christian faith flees the world, but he did mean that it strains after the future. To believe does in fact mean to cross and transcend bounds, to be engaged in an exodus. Yet this happens in a way that does not suppress or skip the unpleasant realities. Death is real death, and decay is putrefying decay. Guilt remains guilt and suffering remains, even for the believer, a cry to which there is no ready-made answer. Faith does not overstep these realities into a heavenly utopia, does not dream itself into a reality of a different kind. It can overstep the bounds of life, with their closed wall of suffering, guilt and death, only at the point where they have in actual fact been broken through. It is only in following the Christ who was raised from suffering, from a god-forsaken death and from the grave that it gains an open prospect in which there is nothing more to oppress us, a view of the realm of freedom and of joy. Where the bounds that mark the end of all human hopes are broken through in the raising of the crucified one, there faith can and must expand into hope. There it becomes παρρησία and μακροθυμία. There its hope becomes a 'passion for what is possible' (Kierkegaard), because it can be a passion for what has been made possible. There the *extensio animi ad magna*, as it was called in the Middle Ages, takes place in hope. Faith recognizes the dawning of this future of openness and freedom in the Christ event. The hope thereby kindled spans the horizons which then open over a closed existence. Faith binds man to Christ. Hope sets this faith open to the comprehensive future of Christ. Hope is therefore the 'inseparable companion' of faith. 'When this hope is taken away, however eloquently or elegantly we discourse concerning faith, we are convicted of having none. ... Hope is nothing else than the expectation of those things which faith has believed to have been truly promised by God. Thus, faith believes God to be true, hope awaits the time when this truth shall be manifested; faith believes that he is our Father, hope anticipates that he will ever show himself to be a Father toward us; faith believes that eternal life has been given to us, hope anticipates that it will some time be revealed; faith is the foundation upon which hope rests, hope nourishes and sustains faith. For as no one except him who already believes His promises can look for anything from God, so again the weakness of our faith must be sustained and nourished by patient hope and expectation, lest it fail and grow faint. ... By unremitting renewing and restoring, it [hope] invigorates faith again and again with perseverance.'[1] Thus in the Christian life faith has the priority, but hope the primacy. Without faith's knowledge of Christ, hope becomes a utopia and remains hanging in the air. But without hope, faith falls to pieces, becomes a fainthearted and ultimately a dead faith. It is through faith that man finds the path of true life, but it is only hope that keeps him on that path. Thus it is that faith in Christ gives hope its assurance. Thus it is that hope gives faith in Christ its breadth and leads it into life.

To believe means to cross in hope and anticipation the bounds that have been penetrated by the raising of the crucified. If we bear that in mind, then this faith can have nothing to do with fleeing the world, with resignation and with escapism. In this hope the soul does not soar above our vale of tears to some imagined heavenly bliss, nor does it sever itself from the earth. For, in the words of Ludwig Feuerbach, it puts 'in place of the beyond that lies above our grave in heaven the beyond that lies above our grave on earth, the historic *future*, the future of mankind'.[2] It sees in the resurrection of Christ not the eternity of heaven, but the future of the very earth on which his cross stands. It sees in him the future of

---

1 Calvin, *Institutio* III.2.42 ET: *Institutes of the Christian Religion* (Library of Christian Classics vols. XX and XXI), ed. John T. McNeill, trans. Ford Lewis Battles, 1961, p. 590.

2 *Das Wesen der Religion*, 1848.

the very humanity for which he died. That is why it finds the cross the hope of the earth. This hope struggles for the obedience of the body, because it awaits the quickening of the body. It espouses in all meekness the cause of the devastated earth and of harassed humanity, because it is promised possession of the earth. *Ave crux – unica spes!*

But on the other hand, all this must inevitably mean that the man who thus hopes will never be able to reconcile himself with the laws and constraints of this earth, neither with the inevitability of death nor with the evil that constantly bears further evil. The raising of Christ is not merely a consolation to him in a life that is full of distress and doomed to die, but it is also God's contradiction of suffering and death, of humiliation and offence, and of the wickedness of evil. Hope finds in Christ not only a consolation *in* suffering, but also the protest of the divine promise *against* suffering. If Paul calls death the 'last enemy' (I Cor. 15.26), then the opposite is also true: that the risen Christ, and with him the resurrection hope, must be declared to be the enemy of death and of a world that puts up with death. Faith takes up this contradiction and thus becomes itself a contradiction to the world of death. That is why faith, wherever it develops into hope, causes not rest but unrest, not patience but impatience. It does not calm the unquiet heart, but is itself this unquiet heart in man. Those who hope in Christ can no longer put up with reality as it is, but begin to suffer under it, to contradict it. Peace with God means conflict with the world, for the goad of the promised future stabs inexorably into the flesh of every unfulfilled present. If we had before our eyes only what we see, then we should cheerfully or reluctantly reconcile ourselves with things as they happen to be. That we do not reconcile ourselves, that there is no pleasant harmony between us and reality, is due to our unquenchable hope. This hope keeps man unreconciled, until the great day of the fulfilment of all the promises of God. It keeps him *in statu viatoris*, in that unresolved openness to world questions which has its origin in the promise of God in the resurrection of Christ and can therefore be resolved only when the same God fulfils his promise. This hope makes the Christian Church a constant disturbance in human society, seeking as the latter does to stabilize itself into a 'continuing city'. It makes the Church the source of continual new impulses towards the realization of righteousness, freedom and humanity here in the light of the promised future that is to come. This Church is committed to 'answer for the hope' that is in it (I Peter 3.15). It is called in question 'on account of the hope and resurrection of the dead' (Acts 23.6). Wherever that happens, Christianity embraces its true nature and becomes a witness of the future of Christ.

3. The Sin of Despair

If faith thus depends on hope for its life, then the sin of unbelief is manifestly grounded in hopelessness. To be sure, it is usually said that sin in its original form is man's wanting to be as God. But that is only the one side of sin. The other side of such pride is hopelessness, resignation, inertia and melancholy. From this arise the *tristesse* and frustration which fill all living things with the seeds of a sweet decay. Among the sinners whose future is eternal death in Rev. 21.8, the 'fearful' are mentioned before unbelievers, idolaters, murderers and the rest. For the Epistle to the Hebrews, falling away from the living hope, in the sense of being disobedient to the promise in time of oppression, or of being carried away from God's pilgrim people as by a flood, is the great sin which threatens the hopeful on their way. Temptation then consists not so much in the titanic desire to be as God, but in weakness, timidity, weariness, not wanting to be what God requires of us.

God has exalted man and given him the prospect of a life that is wide and free, but man hangs back and lets himself down. God promises a new creation of all things in righteousness and peace, but man acts as if everything were as before and remained as before. God honours him with his promises, but man does not believe himself capable of what is required of him. That is the sin which most profoundly threatens the believer. It is not the evil he does, but the good he does not do, not his misdeeds but his omissions, that accuse him. They accuse him of lack of hope. For these so-called sins of omission all have their ground in hopelessness and weakness of faith. 'It is not so much sin that plunges us into disaster, as rather despair', said Chrysostom. That is why the Middle Ages reckoned *acedia* or *tristitia* among the sins against the Holy Spirit which lead to death.

Joseph Pieper in his treatise *Über die Hoffnung* (1949) has very neatly shown how this hopelessness can assume two forms: it can be presumption, *praesumptio*, and it can be despair, *desperatio*. Both are forms of the sin against hope. Presumption is a premature, selfwilled anticipation of the fulfilment of what we hope for from God. Despair is the premature, arbitrary anticipation of the non-fulfilment of what we hope for from God. Both forms of hope-lessness, by anticipating the fulfilment or by giving up hope, cancel the wayfaring character of hope. They rebel against the patience in which hope trusts in the God of the promise. They demand impatiently either fulfilment 'now already' or 'absolutely no' hope. 'In despair and presumption alike we have the rigidifying and freezing of the truly human element, which hope alone can keep flowing and free' (p. 51).

Thus despair, too, presupposes hope. 'What we do not long for, can be the object neither of our hope nor of our despair' (Augustine). The pain of despair surely lies in the fact that a hope is there, but no way opens up towards its fulfilment. Thus the kindled hope turns against the one who hopes and consumes him. 'Living means bury-ing hopes', says Fontane in one of his novels, and it is these 'dead hopes' that he portrays in it. Our hopes are bereft of faith and confidence. Hence despair would seek to preserve the soul from disappointments. 'Hope as a rule makes many a fool.' Hence we try to remain on the solid ground of reality, 'to think clearly and not hope any more' (Camus), and yet in adopting this so-called realism dictated by the facts we fall victim to the worst of all utopias – the utopia of the *status quo*, as R. Musil has called this kind of realism.

The despairing surrender of hope does not even need to have a desperate appearance. It can also be the mere tacit absence of meaning, prospects, future and purpose. It can wear the face of smiling resignation: *bonjour tristesse!* All that remains is a certain smile on the part of those who have tried out the full range of their possibilities and found nothing in them that could give cause for hope. All that remains is a *taedium vitae*, a life that has little further interest in itself. Of all the attitudes produced by the decay of a non-eschatological, bourgeois Christianity, and then consequently found in a no longer Christian world, there is hardly any which is so general as *acedia*, *tristesse*, the cultivation and dandling manipulation of faded hopes. But where hope does not find its way to the source of new, unknown possibilities, there the trifling, ironical play with the existing possibilities ends in boredom, or in outbreaks of absurdity.

At the beginning of the nineteenth century the figure of pre-sumption is found at many points in German idealism. For Goethe, Schiller, Ranke, Karl Marx and many others, Prometheus became the great saint of the modern age. Prometheus, who stole fire from the gods, stood in contrast to the figure of the obedient servant of God. It was possible to transform even Christ into a Promethean figure. Along with that there frequently went a philosophical, revo-lutionary millenarianism which set itself to build at last that realm of freedom and human dignity which had been hoped for in vain from the God of the divine servant.

In the middle of the twentieth century we find in the literary writings of the existentialists the other form of apostasy from hope. Thus the patron saint that was Prometheus now assumes the form of Sisyphus, who certainly knows the pilgrim way, and is fully acquainted with struggle and decision and with patient toil, yet without any prospect of fulfilment. Here the obedient servant of God can be transformed into the figure of the honest failure. There is no hope and no God any more. There is only Camus' 'thinking clearly and hoping no more', and the honest love and fellow-feeling exemplified in Jesus. As if thinking could gain clarity without hope! As if there could be love without hope for the beloved!

Neither in presumption nor in despair does there lie the power to renew life, but only in the hope that is enduring and sure. Pre-sumption and despair live off this hope and regale themselves at its expense. 'He who does not hope for the unexpected, will not find it', runs a saying of Heraclitus. 'The uniform of the day is patience and its only decoration the pale star of hope over its heart' (I. Bachmann).

Hope alone is to be called 'realistic', because it alone takes seriously the possibilities with which all reality is fraught. It does not take things as they happen to stand or to lie, but as progressing, moving things with possibilities of change. Only as long as the world and the people in it are in a fragmented and experimental state which is not yet resolved, is there any sense in earthly hopes. The latter anticipate what is possible to reality, historic and moving as it is, and use their influence to decide the processes of history. Thus hopes and anticipations of the future are not a transfiguring glow superimposed upon a darkened existence, but are realistic ways of perceiving the scope of our real possibilities, and as such they set everything in motion and keep it in a state of change. Hope and the kind of thinking that goes with it consequently cannot submit to the reproach of being utopian, for they do not strive after things that have 'no place', but after things that have 'no place *as yet*' but can acquire one. On the other hand, the celebrated realism of the stark facts, of established objects and laws, the attitude that despairs of its possibilities and clings to reality as it is, is inevitably much more open to the charge of being utopian, for in its eyes there is 'no place' for possibilities, for future novelty, and consequently for the historic character of reality. Thus the despair which imagines it has reached the end of its tether proves to be illusory, as long as nothing has yet come to an end but everything is still full of possibilities. Thus positivistic realism also proves to be illusory, so long as the world is not a fixed body of facts but a network of paths and processes, so long as the world does not only run according to laws but these laws themselves are also flexible, so long as it is a realm in which necessity means the possible, but not the unalterable.

Statements of hope in Christian eschatology must also assert themselves against the rigidified utopia of realism, if they would keep faith alive and would guide obedience in love on to the path towards earthly, corporeal, social reality. In its eyes the world is full of all kinds of possibilities, namely all the possibilities of the God of hope. It sees reality and mankind in the hand of him whose voice calls into history from its end, saying, 'Behold, I make all things new', and from hearing this word of promise it acquires the freedom to renew life here and to change the face of the world.

4. Does Hope Cheat Man of the Happiness of the Present?

The most serious objection to a theology of hope springs not from presumption or despair, for these two basic attitudes of human existence presuppose hope, but the objection to hope arises from the religion of humble acquiescence in the present. Is it not always in the present alone that man is truly existent, real, contemporary with himself, acquiescent and certain? Memory binds him to the past that no longer is. Hope casts him upon the future that is not yet. He remembers having lived, but he does not live. He remembers having loved, but he does not love. He remembers the thoughts of others, but he does not think. It seems to be much the same with him in hope. He hopes to live, but he does not live. He expects to be happy one day, and this expectation causes him to pass over the happiness of the present. He is never, in memory and hope, wholly himself and wholly in his present. Always he either limps behind it or hastens ahead of it. Memories and hopes appear to cheat him of the happiness of being undividedly present. They rob him of his present and drag him into times that no longer exist or do not yet exist. They surrender him to the non-existent and abandon him to vanity. For these times subject him to the stream of transience – the stream that sweeps him to annihilation.

Pascal lamented this deceitful aspect of hope: 'We do not rest satisfied with the present. We anticipate the future as too slow in coming, as if in order to hasten its course; or we recall the past, to stop its too rapid flight. So imprudent are we that we wander in times which are not ours, and do not think of the only one which belongs to us; and so idle are we that we dream of those times which are no more, and thoughtlessly overlook that which alone exists. ... We scarcely ever think of the present; and if we think of it, it is only to take light from it to arrange the future. The present is never our end. The past and the present are our means; the future alone is our end. So we never live, but we hope to live; and, as we are always preparing to be happy, it is inevitable we should never be so.'[3] Always the protest against the Christian hope and against the transcendent consciousness resulting from it has stubbornly insisted on the rights of the present, on the good that surely lies always to hand, and on the eternal truth in every moment. Is the 'present' not the only time in which man wholly exists, which belongs wholly to him and to which he wholly belongs? Is the 'present' not time and yet at once also more than time in the sense of coming and going – namely, a *nunc stans* and to that extent also a *nunc aeternum*? Only of the present can it be said that it 'is', and only present being is constantly with us. If we are wholly present – *tota simul* – then in the midst of time we are snatched from the transient and annihilating workings of time.

Thus Goethe, too, could say: 'All these passing things we put up with; if only the eternal remains present to us every moment, then we do not suffer from the transience of time.' He had found this

---

3 Blaise Pascal, *Pensées*, No. 172. ET by W. F. Trotter (Everyman ed.), 1943, pp. 49f.

eternally resting present in 'nature' itself, because he understood 'nature' as the *physis* that exists out of itself: 'All is always present in it. Past and future it does not know. The present is its eternity.' Should not man, too, therefore become present like nature?

> Why go chasing distant fancies?
> Lo, the good is ever near!
> Only learn to grasp your chances!
> Happiness is always here.

Thus the true present is nothing else but the eternity that is immanent in time, and what matters is to perceive in the outward form of temporality and transience the substance that is immanent and the eternal that is present – so said the early Hegel. Likewise Nietzsche endeavoured to get rid of the burden and deceit of the Christian hope by seeking 'the eternal Yea of existence' in the present and finding the love of eternity in 'loyalty to the earth'. It is always only in the present, the moment, the *kairos*, the 'now', that being itself is present in time. It is like noon, when the sun stands high and nothing casts a shadow any more, nor does anything stand in the shadow.

But now, it is not merely the *happiness of the present*, but it is more, it is the *God of the present*, the eternally present God, and it is not merely the present being of man, but still more the eternal presence of being, that the Christian hope appears to cheat us of. Not merely man is cheated, but still more God himself is cheated, where hope does not allow man to discover an eternal present. It is only here that the objection to our future hopes on the ground of the 'present' attains to its full magnitude. Not merely does life protest against the torture of the hope that is imposed upon it, but we are also accused of godlessness in the name of the God whose essential attribute is the *numen praesentiae*. Yet what God is this in whose name the 'present' is insisted upon as against the hope of what is not yet?

It is at bottom ever and again the god of Parmenides, of whom it is said in Fragment 8 (Diels): 'The unity that is being never was, never will be, for now it Is all at once as a whole' (νῦν ἔστιν ὁμοῦ πᾶν). This 'being' does not exist 'always', as it was still said to do in Homer and Hesiod, but it 'is', and is 'now'. It has no extension in time, its truth stands on the 'now', its eternity is present, it 'is'

13

all at once and in one (*tota simul*). In face of the epiphany of the eternal presence of being, the times in which life rises and passes fade away to mere phenomena in which we have a mixture of being and non-being, day and night, abiding and passing away. In the contemplation of the eternal present, however, 'origin is obliterated and decay is vanished'. In the present of being, in the eternal Today, man is immortal, invulnerable and inviolable (G. Picht). If, as Plutarch reports, the divine name over the portal of the Delphic temple of Apollo was given as *EI*, then this, too, could mean 'Thou art' in the sense of the eternal present. It is in the eternal nearness and presence of the god that we come to knowledge of man's nature and to joy in it.

The god of Parmenides is 'thinkable', because he is the eternal, single fulness of being. The non-existent, the past and the future, however, are not 'thinkable'. In the contemplation of the present eternity of this god, non-existence, movement and change, history and future become unthinkable, because they 'are' not. The contemplation of this god does not make a meaningful experience of history possible, but only the meaningful negation of history. The *logos* of this being liberates and raises us out of the power of history into the eternal present.

In the struggle against the seeming deceit of the Christian hope, Parmenides' concept of God has thrust its way deeply indeed into Christian theology. When in the celebrated third chapter of Kierkegaard's treatise on *The Concept of Dread* the promised 'fulness of time' is taken out of the realm of expectation that attaches to promise and history, and the 'fulness of time' is called the 'moment' in the sense of the eternal, then we find ourselves in the field of Greek thinking rather than of the Christian knowledge of God. It is true that Kierkegaard modified the Greek understanding of temporality in the light of the Christian insight into our radical sinfulness, and that he intensifies the Greek difference between *logos* and *doxa* into a paradox, but does that really imply any more than a modification of the 'epiphany of the eternal present'? 'The present is not a concept of time. The eternal conceived as the present is arrested temporal succession. The moment characterizes the present as a thing that has no past and no future. The moment is an atom of eternity. It is the first reflection of eternity in time, its first attempt as it were to halt time.' It is understandable that then the believer, too, must be described in parallel terms to the Parmenidean and

Platonic contemplator. The believer is the man who is entirely present. He is in the supreme sense contemporaneous with himself and one with himself. 'And to be with the eternal's help utterly and completely contemporaneous with oneself today, is to gain eternity. The believer turns his back on the eternal so to speak, precisely in order to have it by him in the one day that is today. The Christian believes, and thus he is quit of tomorrow.'

Much the same is to be found in Ferdinand Ebner, whose personalist thinking and pneumatology of language has had such an influence on modern theology: 'Eternal life is so to speak life in the absolute present and is in actual fact the life of man in his consciousness of the presence of God.' For it is of the essence of God to be absolute spiritual presence. Hence man's 'present' is nothing else but the presence of God. He steps out of time and lives in the present. Thus it is that he lives 'in God'. Faith and love are timeless acts which remove us out of time, because they make us wholly 'present'.

Christian faith then means tuning in to the nearness of God in which Jesus lived and worked, for living amid the simple, everyday things of today is of course living in the fulness of time and living in the nearness of God. To grasp the never-returning moment, to be wholly one with oneself, wholly self-possessed and on the mark, is what is meant by 'God'. The concepts of God which are constructed in remoteness from God and in his absence fall to pieces in his nearness, so that to be wholly present means that 'God' happens, for the 'happening' of the uncurtailed present is the happening of God.

This mysticism of being, with its emphasis on the living of the present moment, presupposes an immediacy to God which the faith that believes in God on the ground of Christ cannot adopt without putting an end to the historic mediation and reconciliation of God and man in the Christ event, and so also, as a result of this, putting an end to the observation of history under the category of hope. This is not the 'God of hope', for the latter is present in promising the future – his own and man's and the world's future – and in sending men into the history that is not yet. The God of the exodus and of the resurrection 'is' not eternal presence, but he promises his presence and nearness to him who follows the path on which he is sent into the future. YHWH, as the name of the God who first of all promises his presence and his kingdom and makes them prospects for the future, is a God 'with future as his essential nature', a God of promise and of leaving the present to face the future, a God whose freedom is the source of new things that are to come. His name is not a cipher for the 'eternal present', nor can it be rendered by the word *EI*, 'thou art'. His name is a wayfaring name, a name of promise that discloses a new future, a name whose truth is experienced in history inasmuch as his promise discloses its future possibilities. He is therefore, as Paul says, the God who raises the dead and calls into being the things that are not (Rom. 4.17). This God is present where we wait upon his promises in hope and transformation. When we have a God who calls into being the things that are not, then the things that are not yet, that are future, also become 'thinkable' because they can be hoped for.

The 'now' and 'today' of the New Testament is a different thing from the 'now' of the eternal presence of being in Parmenides, for it is a 'now' and an 'all of a sudden' in which the newness of the promised future is lit up and seen in a flash. Only in this sense is it to be called an 'eschatological' today. 'Parousia' for the Greeks was the epitome of the presence of God, the epitome of the presence of being. The parousia of Christ, however, is conceived in the New Testament only in categories of expectation, so that it means not *praesentia Christi* but *adventus Christi*, and is not his eternal presence bringing time to a standstill, but his 'coming', as our Advent hymns say, opening the road to life in time, for the life of time is hope. The believer is not set at the high noon of life, but at the dawn of a new day at the point where night and day, things passing and things to come, grapple with each other. Hence the believer does not simply take the day as it comes, but looks beyond the day to the things which according to the promise of him who is the *creator ex nihilo* and raiser of the dead are still to come. The present of the coming parousia of God and of Christ in the promises of the gospel of the crucified does not translate us out of time, nor does it bring time to a standstill, but it opens the way for time and sets history in motion, for it does not tone down the pain caused us by the non-existent, but means the adoption and acceptance of the non-existent in memory and hope. Can there be any such thing as an 'eternal Yea of being' without a Yea to what no longer is and to what is not yet? Can there be such a thing as harmony and contemporaneity on man's part in the moment of today, unless hope reconciles him with what is non-contemporaneous and disharmonious? Love does not snatch us from the pain of time, but takes the pain of the temporal upon itself. Hope makes us ready to bear the 'cross of the present'. It can hold to what is dead, and hope for the unexpected. It can approve of movement and be glad of history. For its God is not he who 'never was nor will be, because he now Is all at once as a whole', but God is he 'who maketh the dead alive and calleth into being the things that are not'. The spell of the dogma of hopelessness – *ex nihilo nihil fit* – is broken where he who raises the dead is recognized to be God. Where in faith and hope we begin to live in the light of the possibilities and promises of this God, the whole fulness of life discloses itself as a life of history and therefore a life to be loved. Only in the perspective of this God can there possibly be a love that is more than *philia*, love to the existent and the like – namely, *agape*, love to the non-existent, love to the unlike, the unworthy, the worthless, to the lost, the transient and the dead; a love that can take upon it the annihilating effects of pain and renunciation because it receives its power from hope of a *creatio ex nihilo*. Love does not shut its eyes to the non-existent and say it is nothing, but becomes itself the magic power that brings it into being. In its hope, love surveys the open possibilities of history. In love, hope brings all things into the light of the promises of God.

Does this hope cheat man of the happiness of the present? How could it do so! For it is itself the happiness of the present. It pronounces the poor blessed, receives the weary and heavy laden, the humbled and wronged, the hungry and the dying, because it perceives the parousia of the kingdom for them. Expectation makes life good, for in expectation man can accept his whole present and find joy not only in its joy but also in its sorrow, happiness not only in its happiness but also in its pain. Thus hope goes on its way through the midst of happiness and pain, because in the promises of God it can see a future also for the transient, the dying and the dead. That is why it can be said that living without hope is like no longer living. Hell is hopelessness, and it is not for nothing that at the entrance to Dante's hell there stand the words: 'Abandon hope, all ye who enter here.'

An acceptance of the present which cannot and will not see the dying of the present is an illusion and a frivolity – and one which cannot be grounded on eternity either. The hope that is staked on the *creator ex nihilo* becomes the happiness of the present when it loyally embraces all things in love, abandoning nothing to annihilation but bringing to light how open all things are to the possibilities in which they can live and shall live. Presumption and despair have a paralysing effect on this, while the dream of the eternal present ignores it.

5. Hoping and Thinking

But now, all that we have so far said of hope might be no more than a hymn in praise of a noble quality of the heart. And Christian eschatology could regain its leading role in theology as a whole, yet still remain a piece of sterile theologizing if we fail to attain to the new thought and action that are consequently necessary in our dealings with the things and conditions of this world. As long as hope does not embrace and transform the thought and action of men, it remains topsy-turvy and ineffective. Hence Christian eschatology must make the attempt to introduce hope into worldly thinking, and thought into the believing hope.

In the Middle Ages, Anselm of Canterbury set up what has since been the standard basic principle of theology: *fides quaerens intellectum – credo, ut intelligam*. This principle holds also for eschatology, and it could well be that it is of decisive importance for Christian theology today to follow the basic principle: *spes quaerens intellectum – spero, ut intelligam*. If it is hope that maintains and upholds faith and keeps it moving on, if it is hope that draws the believer into the life of love, then it will also be hope that is the mobilizing and driving force of faith's thinking, of its knowledge of, and reflections on, human nature, history and society. Faith hopes in order to know what it believes. Hence all its knowledge will be an anticipatory, fragmentary knowledge forming a prelude to the promised future, and as such is committed to hope. Hence also *vice versa* the hope which arises from faith in God's promise will become the ferment in our thinking, its mainspring, the source of its restlessness and torment. The hope that is continually led on further by the promise of God reveals all thinking in history to be eschatologically oriented and eschatologically stamped as provisional. If hope draws faith into the realm of thought and of life, then it can no longer consider itself to be an eschatological hope as distinct from the minor hopes that are directed towards attainable goals and visible changes in human life, neither can it as a result dissociate itself from such hopes by relegating them to a different sphere while considering its own future to be supra-worldly and purely spiritual in character. The Christian hope is directed towards a *novum ultimum*, towards a new creation of all things by the God of the resurrection of Jesus Christ. It thereby opens a future outlook that embraces all things, including also death, and into this it can and must also take the limited hopes of a renewal of life, stimulating them, relativizing them, giving them direction. It will destroy the *presumption* in these hopes of better human freedom, of successful life, of justice and dignity for our fellow men, of control of the possibilities of nature, because it does not find in these movements the salvation it awaits, because it refuses to let the entertaining and realizing of utopian ideas of this kind reconcile it with existence. It will thus outstrip these future visions of a better, more humane, more peaceable world – because of its own 'better promises' (Heb. 8.6), because it knows that nothing can be 'very good' until 'all things are become new'. But it will not be in the name of 'calm despair' that it seeks to destroy the presumption in these movements of hope, for such kinds of presumption still contain more of true hope than does sceptical realism, and more truth as well. There is no help against presumption to be found in the despair that says, 'It will always be the same in the end', but only in a persevering, rectifying hope that finds articulated expression in thought and action. Realism, still less cynicism, was never a good ally of Christian faith. But if the Christian hope destroys the presumption in futuristic movements, then it does so not for its own sake, but in order to destroy in these hopes the *seeds of resignation*, which emerge at the latest with the ideological reign of terror in the utopias in which the hoped-for reconciliation with becomes an enforced reconciliation. This, however, brings the movements of historic change within the range of the *novum ultimum* of hope. They are taken up into the Christian hope and carried further. They become precursory, and therewith provisional, movements. Their goals lose the utopian fixity and become provisional, penultimate, and hence flexible goals. Over against impulses of this kind that seek to give direction to the history of mankind, Christian hope cannot cling rigidly to the past and the given and ally itself with the utopia of the *status quo*. Rather, it is itself summoned and empowered to creative transformation of reality, for it has hope for the whole of reality. Finally, the believing hope will itself provide *inexhaustible resources* for the creative, inventive imagination of love. It constantly provokes and produces thinking of an anticipatory kind in love to man and the world, in order to give shape to the newly dawning possibilities in the light of the promised future, in order as far as possible to create here the best that is possible, because what is promised is within the bounds of possibility. Thus it will constantly arouse the 'passion for the possible', inventiveness and elasticity in self-transformation, in breaking with the old and coming to terms with the new. Always the Christian hope has had a revolutionary effect in this sense on the intellectual history of the society affected by it. Only it was often not in church Christianity that its impulses were at work, but in the Christianity of the fanatics. This has had a detrimental result for both.

But how can knowledge of reality and reflection upon it be pursued from the standpoint of eschatological hope? Luther once had a flash of inspiration on this point, although it was not realized either by himself or by Protestant philosophy. In 1516 he writes of the 'earnest expectation of the creature' of which Paul speaks in Rom. 8.19: 'The apostle philosophizes and thinks about things in a different way from the philosophers and metaphysicians. For the philosophers fix their eyes on the presence of things and reflect only on their qualities and quiddities. But the apostle drags our gaze away from contemplating the present state of things, away from their essence and attributes, and directs it towards their future. He does not speak of the essence or the workings of the creature, of *actio, passio* or movement, but employs a new, strange, theological term and speaks of the expectation of the creature (*exspectatio creaturae*).' The important thing in our present context is, that on the basis of a theological view of the 'expectation of the creature' and its anticipation he demands a new kind of thinking about the world, an expectation-thinking that corresponds to the Christian hope. Hence in the light of the prospects for the whole creation that are promised in the raising of Christ, theology will have to attain to its own, new way of reflecting on the history of men and things. In the field of the world, of history and of reality as a whole, Christian eschatology cannot renounce the *intellectus fidei et spei*. Creative action springing from faith is impossible without new thinking and planning that springs from hope.

For our knowledge and comprehension of reality, and our reflections on it, that means at least this: that in the medium of hope our theological concepts become not judgments which nail reality down to what it is, but anticipations which show reality its prospects and its future possibilities. Theological concepts do not give a fixed form to reality, but they are expanded by hope and anticipate future being. They do not limp after reality and gaze on it with the night eyes of Minerva's owl, but they illuminate reality by displaying its future. Their knowledge is grounded not in the will to dominate, but in love to the future of things. *Tantum cognoscitur, quantum diligitur* (Augustine). They are thus concepts which are engaged in a process of movement, and which call forth practical movement and change.

'*Spes quaerens intellectum*' is the first step towards eschatology, and where it is successful it becomes *docta spes.*

I

Eschatology and Revelation

1. The Discovery of Eschatology and its Ineffectiveness

The discovery of the central significance of eschatology for the message and existence of Jesus and for early Christianity, which had its beginnings at the end of the nineteenth century in Johannes Weiss and Albert Schweitzer, is undoubtedly one of the most important events in recent Protestant theology. It had a shattering effect, and was like an earthquake shaking the foundations not only of scientific theology, but also of the Church, of piety and of faith as existing within the framework of nineteenth-century Protestant culture. Long before world wars and revolutions had awakened the Western consciousness of crisis, theologians like Ernst Troeltsch had the as yet hardly comprehended impression that 'everything is tottering'. The recognition of the eschatological character of early Christianity made it clear that the automatically accepted idea of a harmonious synthesis between Christianity and culture was a lie (Franz Overbeck). In this world with its assured and axiomatic religious positions in the realm of thought and will, Jesus appeared as a stranger with an apocalyptic message that was foreign to it. At the same time there arose a feeling of estrangement and a sense of the lost and critical state of this world. 'The floods are rising – the dams are bursting', said Martin Kähler. It is all the more astonishing that the 'new' element in the discovery of the eschatological dimension of the whole Christian message was considered to represent for traditional Christianity in its present and existing form only a 'crisis' which had to be assimilated, mastered and overcome. None of the discoverers took his discovery really seriously. The so-called 'consistent eschatology' was never really consistent, and has therefore led a peculiar shadow-existence to this day. The very concepts in which attempts were made to comprehend the

23

peculiarity of the eschatological message of Jesus manifest a typical and almost helpless inadequacy. Johannes Weiss in his pioneer work, *Die Predigt Jesu vom Reiche Gottes*, in 1892 formulated his insight as follows: 'The kingdom of God is in Jesus' view an absolutely supra-worldly factor which stands in exclusive contrast to this world. ... The ethico-religious use of this concept in recent theology, which wholly strips it of its original eschatological and apocalyptic sense, is unjustified. It is only seemingly biblical, for it uses the expression in a different sense from Jesus.'[1] As compared with the picture of Jesus advanced by his father-in-law Albrecht Ritschl, this statement provides a sharp antithesis. But is the 'supra-worldly' already the 'eschatological'? Jesus here no longer appears as the moral teacher of the Sermon on the Mount, but with his eschatological message he becomes an apocalyptic fanatic. 'He has nothing more in common with this world, he has one foot already in the next.'[2] Thus after his sally into the no-man's-land of eschatology Johannes Weiss returned again at once to the liberal picture of Jesus.

It was no different with Albert Schweitzer. The greatness of his work lay in the fact that he took seriously the foreignness of Jesus and his message as compared with all the liberal nineteenth-century pictures of Jesus. 'Eschatology makes it impossible to attribute modern ideas to Jesus and then by way of "New Testament Theology" take them back from Him as a loan, as even Ritschl not so long ago did with such *naïveté*.'[3] But the startling thing about Schweitzer's work on the other hand is that he had no eschat-

---

1 J. Weiss, *Die Predigt Jesu vom Reiche Gottes*, 1892, pp. 49f.

2 *Ibid.*, 2nd ed., p. 145. On the limitations of the recognition of the eschatological message of Jesus in Johannes Weiss, cf. F. Holmström, *Das eschatologische Denken der Gegenwart*, 1936, pp. 61ff.: 'Weiss, it is true, seeks to root out the Ritschlian idea of the kingdom of God from New Testament theology, yet it remains still unbroken in systematic and practical theology' (p. 62); 'For Christianity today, normative significance thus attaches not to the eschatological figure of Jesus, but to the traditional liberal ideal picture of the moral teacher of wisdom' (p. 71). 'The "time-conditioned" character of Johannes Weiss' own view of the significance of the eschatological motif can thus be seen from the fact that he regards it merely as a time-conditioned element in Jesus' own preaching.'

3 A. Schweitzer, *Von Reimarus zu Wrede. Eine Geschichte der Leben-Jesu-Forschung*, 1st ed. 1906, p. 322. ET by W. Montgomery: *The Quest of the Historical Jesus: a critical study of its progress from Reimarus to Wrede*, 2nd English ed., 1911 (trans. of 1st German ed. of 1906), p. 250. (The 3rd English ed. of 1954 has a new Introduction by the author, but is otherwise the same as in 1911.)

ological sense at all – neither for theological nor for philosophical eschatology. The consequences which he drew from his discovery of the apocalyptic of Jesus were aimed at the final conquest and annihilation of what he considered an illusionary eschatologism. His philosophy of life and of culture is governed by the over-coming of that painful impression which he described as follows in the first edition of his *Quest of the Historical Jesus*: 'There is silence all around. The Baptist appears and cries: "Repent, for the Kingdom of Heaven is at hand." Soon after that comes Jesus, and in the knowledge that He is the coming Son of Man lays hold of the wheel of the world to set it moving on that last revolution which is to bring all ordinary history to a close. It refuses to turn, and He throws Himself upon it. Then it does turn; and crushes Him. Instead of bringing in the eschatological conditions, He has destroyed them. The wheel rolls onward, and the mangled body of the one immeasurably great Man, who was strong enough to think of Himself as the spiritual ruler of mankind and to bend history to His purpose, is hanging upon it still. That is His victory and His reign.'[4] The 'wheel of history', symbol of the eternal recurrence of the same cycle, takes the place of the eschatological arrow-flight of history. The experience of two thousand years of delayed parousia makes eschatology impossible today.

After the first World War the founders of 'dialectical theology' took the eschatology that had thus been suppressed by idealism and condemned to ineffectiveness, and set it in the centre not only of exegetical but now also of dogmatic study. In the second edition of his *Römerbrief*, Karl Barth in 1921 makes the programmatic announcement: 'If Christianity be not altogether and unreservedly eschatology, there remains in it no relationship whatever to Christ.'[5] Yet what is the meaning of 'eschatology' here? It is not history, moving silently and interminably onwards, that brings a crisis upon men's eschatological hopes of the future, as Albert Schweitzer said, but on the contrary it is now the *eschaton*, breaking tran-scendentally into history, that brings all human history to its final crisis. This, however, makes the *eschaton* into a transcendental eternity, the transcendental meaning of all ages, equally near to

---

4 *Ibid.* 1906, p. 367, ET pp. 368f. This passage was deleted in the later (German) editions.

5 *Der Römerbrief*, 2nd ed. 1922, p. 298 (ET by E. C. Hoskyns: *The Epistle to the Romans*, 1933, p. 314).

all the ages of history and equally far from all of them. Whether eternity was understood in transcendental terms, as in Barth, who spoke of the unhistorical, supra-historical or 'proto-historical', or whether the *eschaton* was understood in existentialist terms, as in Bultmann, who spoke of the 'eschatological moment', or whether it was axiologically understood, as in Paul Althaus, who saw 'every wave of the sea of time break as it were on the strand of eternity', – everywhere in these years, even as they strove to get the better of the historic eschatology which was construed by religion in terms of saving history and by secularism in terms of belief in progress, men became the victims of a transcendental eschatology which once again obscured rather than developed the discovery of early Christian eschatology. It was precisely the transcendentalist view of eschatology that prevented the break-through of eschatological dimensions in dogmatics. Thus all that remains as the outcome of the 'eschatological struggle of today' is in the first instance the unsatisfactory result that there certainly exists a Christian eschatology which sees history in terms of saving history and regards eschatology as concerned merely with the final, closing events of history, that there certainly exists a transcendental eschatology, for which the *eschaton* as good as means the transcendental 'present of eternity', and that there exists an eschatology interpreted in existentialist terms, for which the *eschaton* is the crisis of kerygmatic involvement, but that Christian eschatology is not yet by any means in a position to break through the categories which provide the framework of these forms of thinking. This, however, is the inescapable task of theological thought, if the 'discovery' sixty years ago of the eschatological message of early Christianity is to be properly understood and is to involve consequences for theology and for the existence of the Church.

Now these forms of thinking, in which the real language of eschatology is still obscured today, are entirely the thought forms of the Greek mind, which sees in the *logos* the epiphany of the eternal present of being and finds the truth in that. Even where the modern age thinks in Kantian terms, this conception of truth is at bottom intended. The real language of Christian eschatology, however, is not the Greek *logos*, but the *promise* which has stamped the language, the hope and the experience of Israel. It was not in the *logos* of the epiphany of the eternal present, but in the hope-giving word of promise that Israel found God's truth. That is why history was here experienced in an entirely different and entirely open form. Eschatology as a science is therefore not possible in the Greek sense, nor yet in the sense of modern experimental science, but only as a knowledge in terms of hope, and to that extent as a knowledge of history and of the historic character of truth. These differences between Greek thought and that of Israel and Christianity, between *logos* and promise, between epiphany and *apokalypsis* of the truth have today been made clear in many fields and by various methods. And yet Georg Picht is right when he says, 'The epiphany of the eternal present of being distorts to this day the eschatological revelation of God.'[6] In order to attain to a real understanding of the eschatological message, it is accordingly necessary to acquire an openness and understanding *vis-à-vis* what 'promise' means in the Old and New Testaments, and how in the wider sense a form of speech and thought and hope that is determined by promise experiences God, truth, history and human nature. It is further necessary to pay attention to the continual controversies in which the promise-centred faith of Israel found itself, in every field of life, engaged with the epiphany-based religions of the world about it, and in which its own truth came to light. The controversies continue also through the New Testament, especially where Christianity encountered the Greek mind. They are part of Christianity's task also today – and that, too, not only in what modern theology has to say for itself, but also in reflecting on the world and in the experience of history. Christian eschatology in the language of promise will then be an essential key to the unlocking of Christian truth. For the loss of eschatology – not merely as an appendix to dogmatics, but as the medium of theological thinking as such – has always been the condition that makes possible the adaptation of Christianity to its environment and, as a result of this, the self-surrender of faith. Just as in theological thought the blending of Christianity with the Greek mind made it no longer clear which God was really being spoken of, so Christianity in its social form took over the heritage of the ancient state religion. It installed itself as the 'crown of society' and its 'saving centre', and lost the disquieting, critical power of its eschatological hope. In place of what the Epistle to the Hebrews describes as an exodus from the fixed camp and the continuing city, there came the solemn

---

6 G. Picht, *Die Erfahrung der Geschichte*, 1958, p. 42.

27

entry into society of a religious transfiguration of the world. These consequences, too, have to be borne in mind if we are to attain to a liberation of eschatological hope from the forms of thought and modes of conduct belonging to the traditional syntheses of the West.

2. Promise and Revelation of God

In addressing ourselves to the combined topic of 'promise' and 'revelation' the purpose is not only to enquire into the relation between the two, but also to develop a view of the 'revelation of God' which is 'eschatological' in so far as it seeks to discover the language of promise. The concepts of revelation in systematic theology have been fashioned throughout in adoption of, and controversy with, the Greek metaphysic of the proofs of God. 'Revelation theology' today consequently stands in emphatic antithesis to so-called 'natural theology'. That means, however, that these concepts of revelation are constantly preoccupied with the question of whether or not God can be proved. On this front, a theology of revelation can ally itself with a negative natural theology and be derived from the dogma of the non-provability of God. But a concept of revelation arrived at in this way is threatened with the loss of all its content. Its reduction of everything to the problem of the knowledge of God brings about the much lamented formalism of revelation theology.

But now the more recent theology of the Old Testament has indeed shown that the words and statements about the 'revealing of God' in the Old Testament are combined throughout with statements about the 'promise of God'. God reveals himself in the form of promise and in the history that is marked by promise. This confronts systematic theology with the question whether the understanding of divine revelation by which it is governed must not be dominated by the nature and trend of the promise. The examination in the field of comparative religion of the special peculiarity of Israelite faith is today bringing out ever more strongly the difference between its 'religion of promise' and the epiphany religions of the revealed gods of the world around Israel. These epiphany religions are all 'religions of revelation' in their own way. Any place in the world can become the epiphany of the divine and the pictorial transparency of the deity. The essential difference here is accordingly not between the so-called nature gods and a God of revelation, but between the God of the promise and the gods of the epiphanies. Thus the difference does not lie already in the assertion of divine 'revelation' as such, but in the different ways of conceiving and speaking of the revelation and self-manifestation of the deity. The decisively important question is obviously that of the context in which the talk of revelation arises. It is one thing to ask: where and when does an epiphany of the divine, eternal, immutable and primordial take place in the realm of the human, temporal and transient? And it is another thing to ask: when and where does the God of the promise reveal his faithfulness and in it himself and his presence? The one question asks about the presence of the eternal, the other about the future of what is promised. But if promise is determinative of what is said of the revealing of God, then every theological view of biblical revelation contains implicitly a governing view of eschatology. Then, however, the Christian doctrine of the revelation of God must explicitly belong neither to the doctrine of God – as an answer to the proofs of God or to the proof of his non-provability – nor to anthropology – as an answer to the question of God as asked by man and given along with the questionableness of human existence. It must be eschatologically understood, namely, in the field of the promise and expectation of the future of the truth.[7] The question of the understanding of the world in the light of God and of man in the light of God – this was the concern of the proofs of God – can be answered only when it is plain which God is being spoken of, and in what way or with what purpose and intention he reveals himself. We shall therefore have to take some of the concepts of revelation in more recent systematic theology and examine them first in regard to the view of eschatology by which they are governed and secondly in regard to their immanent links with traditional proofs of God.

The other reason for understanding revelation in the light of promise arises from the theology of the Reformers. The correlate of faith is for the Reformers not an idea of revelation, but is expressly described by them as the *promissio dei: fides et promissio sunt correlativa.* Faith is called to life by promise and is therefore essentially hope, confidence, trust in the God who will not lie but will remain faithful to his promise. For the Reformers, indeed,

---

7 So also G. Gloege, *RGG*[3] IV, col. 1611: 'The concept of revelation belongs to eschatology.'

the gospel is identical with *promissio*. It was only in Protestant orthodoxy that under the constraint of the question of reason and revelation, nature and grace, the problem of revelation became the central theme of dogmatic prolegomena. It was only when theology began to employ a concept of reason and a concept of nature which were not derived from a view of the promise but were now taken over from Aristotle, that the problem of revelation appeared in its familiar form. There arose that dualism of reason and revelation which made theological talk of revelation increasingly irrelevant for man's knowledge of reality and his dealings with it. The result of this unhappy story is, that our task is to set the subject of divine revelation no longer in antithesis to man's momentary understanding of the world and of himself, but to take this very understanding of self and the world up into, and open its eyes for, the eschatological outlook in which revelation is seen as promise of the truth.

The formalism which is everywhere so striking in the modern concept of revelation has its ground in the approach which adopts the seemingly perfectly natural method of deriving the theological content of 'revelation' from the word 'revelation'. 'In general, we understand by revelation *the disclosure of what is veiled, the opening up of what is hidden*' (R. Bultmann).[8] 'In the New Testament, ἀποκαλύπτειν refers to the removing of a veil, φανεροῦν to the emerging of the hidden, δηλοῦν to the making known of what is otherwise unknown, and γνωρίζειν to the imparting of what is otherwise not available' (O. Weber).[9] 'A closed door is opened, a covering is taken away. In the darkness light dawns, a question finds its answer, a riddle its solution' (K. Barth).[10] This general explanation of the word then results for Bultmann in what for him is the decisive question whether revelation is an importation of knowledge or an event which transposes me into a new state of my self.[11] As long as every man knows of his death, and his existence is placed by it in a state of radical questionableness, he can also know

---

8 *Glauben und Verstehen*, III, 1960, p. 1 (ET by Schubert M. Ogden, Existence and Faith, 1960, p. 59).

9 *Grundlagen der Dogmatik*, I, 1955, p. 188.

10 *Das christliche Verständnis der Offenbarung* (Theologische Existenz heute, NF vol. 12), 1948, p. 3 (cf. ET by R. Gregor Smith in *Against the Stream: Shorter Post-war Writings 1946–52*, 1954, p. 205, slightly altered). Cf. also p. 5 (ET p. 207): 'Revelation in the Christian sense of the term means revelation, disclosure of something which is *hidden* from man not only in fact but *in principle*.'

11 *Glauben und Verstehen*, III, 1960, p. 2 (ET p. 59).

in advance what revelation and life is. God's revelation proves to be an event affecting the peculiar existence of the particular individual, and therewith an answer to the question raised by the questionableness of his being. Barth on the other hand defined the general use of the word revelation in the Christian sense by saying that here revelation is the self-revelation of the Creator of all that is, of the Lord of all being, and hence transcendent self-revelation of God. While Bultmann endeavours to bring out as against the supra-naturalistic orthodox concept of revelation the fact that revelation has the character of an event in history, Barth was concerned for the absolute independence, unprovability, underivability and incomparability of the self-revelation of God. Just as Bultmann developed his understanding of revelation within the framework of a new proof of God from existence, so the concept of the self-revelation of God developed by Barth corresponds with Anselm's ontological proof of God as interpreted in his book *Fides quaerens intellectum* (1930). This book on Anselm contains highly significant prolegomena to the *Church Dogmatics*. This means, however, that both writers are wrestling with specific theological traditions and find in the *concept* of revelation the starting point for a new way of speaking of the revelation of God, without first asking what is the reference and bearing of the words for the revelation of God in the Old and New Testaments. To set out from a general explanation of terms means to let these expressions remain in the first instance where they originally belong, i.e. where they stand in the epiphany religions. It then becomes all the more difficult later on to discover specifically in the 'revelation of God' the new content of the biblical proclamation. Too little attention is paid to the fact that the expressions for 'revelation' in the biblical scriptures have completely broken out of their original religious context and are employed with a meaning of a different kind. This different kind of meaning is mainly determined by the events of promise.

3. Transcendental Eschatology

What is the underlying view of eschatology which governs and dominates the concept of the 'self-revelation of God' as found in Barth, and the understanding of revelation as the 'disclosure of authentic selfhood' as found in Bultmann?

We shall find that the idea of self-revelation both in its theological and in its anthropological form has been formulated under the spell of a 'transcendental eschatology'. I choose the expression 'transcendental eschatology', which Jakob Taubes and Hans Urs von Balthasar have used to designate Immanuel Kant's doctrine of the end, because it accords better than the usual designation 'presentative eschatology' with the categories of thought in which the corresponding view of revelation is here formulated.

Within the framework of a transcendental eschatology, the question of the future and the goal of revelation is answered by means of a reflection: the wherefore and the whence are the same, the goal of revelation is identical with its origin. If God reveals nothing other than 'himself', then the goal and the future of his revelation lies in himself. If revelation happens to man's self, then its goal is that man should attain to his authenticity and primordiality, that is, to himself. This means, however, that revelation and the *eschaton* coincide in either case in the point which is designated God's or man's 'self'. Revelation' does not then open up a future in terms of promise, nor does it have any future that would be greater than itself, but revelation of God is then the coming of the eternal to man or the coming of man to himself. It is precisely this reflection on the transcendent 'self' that makes eschatology a transcendental eschatology. 'Revelation' consequently becomes the apocalypse of the transcendent subjectivity of God or of man.

The classical philosophical form of transcendental eschatology is found in Immanuel Kant. Its basic features recur wherever Kantian thinking is found in the revelational theology of modern times. In his short, almost forgotten treaties on *Das Ende aller Dinge* (1794), Kant addressed himself to the eschatology of the eighteenth century as expressed in terms of cosmology and saving history, and subjected it to a critique corresponding to his great critiques of theological metaphysics.[12] There can be no such thing as an intellectual knowledge of the 'last things', since these 'objects ... lie wholly beyond our field of vision'.[13] It is therefore idle to 'brood over what they are in themselves and in essence'.[14] Taken as particular objects accessible to the intellect, they are 'wholly void'.[15]

---

12 Quoted according to the edition: I. Kant, *Zur Geschichtsphilosophie (1784–1798)*, ed. A. Buchenau, Berlin 1947, pp. 31ff. For an analysis and assessment, cf. Hans Urs von Balthasar, *Prometheus*, Studien zur Geschichte des deutschen Idealismus, 1947, pp. 91ff.; J. Taubes, *Abendländische Eschatologie*, 1947, pp. 139ff.; H. A. Salmony, *Kants Schrift: Das Ende aller Dinge*, 1962.

13 *Op. cit.*, p. 40.

14 *Ibid.*

15 *Ibid.*

No provable and convincing knowledge of them can be attained. Yet they are not for that reason to be considered 'void' in every respect. For what the intellect finds itself certainly bound to dismiss as null and void, acquires through the practical reason a significance of its own that is highly existential, namely moral. The ideas of the last things have therefore to be ethically examined, and considered in the sphere of the moral reason, of the practical ability to be a self. The method will be to start as if we had 'here to do merely with ideas ... which reason creates for itself', as if we were 'playing' with ideas which 'are given us by the legislative reason itself with a practical purpose', in order to reflect on them according to 'moral principles concerned with the ultimate goal of all things'.[16]

Now with this critical appropriation of traditional eschatological ideas Kant has not only brought about an ethical reduction of eschatology. Rather, its immediate effect is, that through excluding the eschatological categories of hope, the reality appearing to, and perceptible by, the theoretic reason can now be rationalized on the basis of eternal conditions of possible experience.[17] If the *eschata* are supra-sensible and as such beyond all possibility of knowledge, then eschatological perspectives are in turn also completely

---

16 *Op. cit.*, p. 44. The whole passage runs: 'Since we have here to do merely with ideas (or are *playing* with ideas) which *reason creates for itself*, the objects of which (if they have any) lie wholly beyond our field of vision, yet which, although for speculative knowledge they are extravagant, are nevertheless *not for that reason to be considered void in all respects*, but are given us by the legislative reason itself with a practical purpose, not in order that we should brood over what their objects are in themselves and in essence, but in order that we should ask what we have to make of them with a view to the moral principles concerned with the ultimate goal of all things (with the result that these things which *would otherwise be wholly void* acquire *objective, practical reality*) – since all this is so, we have a clear field before us to take *this product of our own reason*, the general concept of an end of all things, and to classify it and order its subordinate concepts according to the relation it bears to our perceptive faculty' (my italics).

17 Kant: 'The abiding and unchanging "I" (of pure apperception) forms the correlate of all our representations' (*Critique of Pure Reason*, A 123, ET by N. Kemp Smith, 1929, p. 146). 'Thus the time in which all change of appearances has to be thought, remains and does not change' (*ibid.*, B 225, ET p. 213). 'Time is nothing but the form of inner sense, that is, of the intuition of ourselves and of our inner state' (*ibid.*, B 49, ET p. 77). On this, cf. Picht, *op. cit.*, p. 40: 'The abiding present of eternity – that is the ground of the concept of time in Kant. ... It is the religious experience of traditional metaphysical theology, which conceived God as the Absolute, i.e. as the immutable substance of Being in its eternal presence.'

irrelevant for the knowledge of the world of experience. 'And since our intuition is always sensible, no object can ever be given to us in experience which does not conform to the condition of time.'[18] Whereas for Herder eschatology still meant the inner impetus and the orientation towards the future of a dynamically open cosmos of all living things, Kant has the sensual impression of a 'world machine' and a 'mechanism of nature'.[19] The *res gestae* of history are consequently for the intellect the same in principle as the *res extensae* of nature. Thus along with cosmological eschatology his criticism applies also to every conceivable eschatology expressed in terms of history and saving history. It is not simply that its place is taken by an ethical eschatology of moral ends. That is only one consequence. Rather, the *eschata* form themselves into eternal, transcendental conditions for the possibility of experiencing oneself in a practical way. Man, who 'as belonging to the sensuous world recognizes himself to be necessarily subject to the laws of causality', nevertheless becomes 'in practical matters, in his other aspect as a being in himself, conscious of his existence as determinable in an intelligible order of things'.[20] In moral action man gets 'beyond the mechanism of blindly working causes'[21] 'into an order of things totally other than that of a mere mechanism of nature'.[22] He attains to the non-objective, non-objectifiable realm of freedom and of ability to be a self. Thus, as Hans Urs von Balthasar aptly remarks, 'transcendental philosophy becomes the method towards inward apocalypse'.[23] In place of cosmological and historic eschatologies comes the practical realization of eschatological existence.

G. W. F. Hegel in his early treatise *Glauben und Wissen* with the sub-title *oder die Reflexionsphilosophie der Subjektivität* (1802) has impressively described his dissatisfaction with the results of this reflective philosophy:

The great form of the world spirit, however, which has discovered itself in these philosophies, is the principle of the North and, from the religious point of view, of Protestantism, the subjectivity in which

---

18 *Critique of Pure Reason*, B 52, ET p. 78.
19 *Critique of the Practical Reason*, A 174 (ET by L. W. Beck, Chicago 1948 and London 1949, p. 202).
20 *Ibid.*, A 72 (ET p. 152).
21 *Ibid.*, A 191.
22 *Ibid.*, A 74.
23 Hans Urs von Balthasar, *op. cit.*, p. 92.

beauty and truth presents itself in feelings and dispositions, in love and understanding. Religion builds its temples and altars in the heart of the individual, and sighs and prayers seek the God whose contemplation is forbidden because there is always the danger of the intellect, which would see the contemplated object as a thing, the forest as firewood. It is true that the inward must also become outward, the intention attain to reality in action, the immediate religious feeling express itself in outward movement, and the faith that flees the objectivity of knowledge take objective form in thoughts, concepts and words; but the objective is very carefully distinguished by the intellect from the subjective, and it is the element which has no value and is nothing, just as the struggle of subjective beauty must be precisely to take all due precautions against the necessity of the subjective's becoming objective ... It is precisely as a result of its fleeing the finite and holding fast to subjectivity that it finds the beautiful turned altogether into things, the forest into firewood, pictures into things that have eyes and do not see, ears and do not hear, while the ideals that cannot be taken in wholly intelligible reality like sticks and stones become fabrications of the imagination and every relation to them is seen as empty play, or as dependence on objects and as superstition.[24]

This critique of the reflective philosophy of Kant's transcendental subjectivity Hegel later developed further in his critique of romanticism.[25] In doing so he had in view what has been called the 'dual track in the history of modern thought' (J. Ritter) in which Descartes' methodizing approach to world experience is inevitably joined dialectically by Pascal's *logique du cœur*, the rational system of the Enlightenment by aesthetic subjectivity, historical scepticism by the non-historical mysticism of the solitary soul, the positivism of a science that is independent of values (Max Weber) by the appealing tones of the philosophy of existence (Karl Jaspers). For theology, this resulted in the dilemma that according as the story of Christ became for the intellect an 'accidental truth of history', so faith was transformed into an immediate contemplation of

---

24 Quoted according to the edition in the Philosophische Bibliothek 62b, ed. F. Meiner, 1962, p. 3. Note the almost verbal polemical allusion to the Kant passage quoted above, p. 33 n 1.

25 Cf. G. Rohrmoser, *Subjektivität und Verdinglichung: Theologie und Gesellschaft im Denken des jungen Hegel*, 1961, pp. 75ff.; O. Pöggeler, *Hegels Kritik der Romantik*, Phil. Diss., Bonn 1956; J. Ritter, *Hegel und die französische Revolution* (AGFNRW 63), 1957.

'eternal truths of reason' – that according as the proclamation in history degenerated into the 'mere historical faith of the Church', so faith exalted itself into the 'pure, immediately God-given faith of reason'. Hegel here perceived that both elements in this process, objectification and subjectivity, are abstract products of reflective philosophy and therefore dialectically condition each other. Both involve a negation and a break-away from history: 'The world has congealed, as it were, it is not a sea of being, but a being that has turned into mechanical clockwork.'[26] A new concept of the cosmos in terms of natural science obscures the experience of reality as history; while on the other hand human existence pales to an ineffable, solitary subjectivity, which must flee all contact with reality and all concessions towards it in order to abide by itself. This cleavage into objectification and subjectivity is not to be escaped – nor can theology escape it in bringing the gospel to the modern world – by declaring one side of this kind of thinking to be vain, deficient, corrupt and decadent. Rather, theology will have to take the hardened antitheses and make them fluid once more, to mediate in the contradiction between them and reconcile them. That, however, is only possible when the category of history, which drops out in this dualism, is rediscovered in such a way that it does not deny the antithesis in question, but spans it and understands it as an element in an advancing process. The revelation of God can neither be presented within the framework of the reflective philosophy of transcendental subjectivity, for which history is reduced to the 'mechanism' of a closed system of causes and effects, nor can it be presented in the anachronism of a theology of saving history, for which the 'forest' has not yet become 'firewood' and 'sacred history' has not yet been subjected to critical historical thinning. Rather, the essential thing will be to make these abstract products of the modern denial of history fluid once more, and to understand them as forms assumed in history by the spirit in the course of an eschatological process which is kept in hope and in motion by the promise grounded in the cross and resurrection of Christ. The conditions of possible experience which were understood by Kant in a transcendental sense must be understood instead as historically flowing conditions. It is not that time at a standstill is the category

---

26 K. Jaspers, *Descartes und die Philosophie*, 2nd ed. 1948, p. 85.

of history, but the history which is experienced from the eschato-logical future of the truth is the category of time.

4. The Theology of the Transcendental Subjectivity of God

Karl Barth gave as one of the reasons for the complete recasting of his commentary on Romans in the second edition of 1921 the fact that he was indebted to his brother Heinrich Barth for 'better acquaintance with the real orientation of the ideas of Plato and Kant'.[27] It will be owing to this influence that the eschatology which in the first edition of 1919 was not unfriendly towards dynamic and cosmic perspectives retreated from now on into the background of Barth's thinking, and that early dialectical theology set to work in terms of the dialectic of time and eternity and came under the bane of the transcendental eschatology of Kant. Here 'end' came to be the equivalent of 'origin', and the *eschaton* became the transcendental boundary of time and eternity. 'Being the transcendent meaning of all moments, the eternal "Moment" can be compared with no moment in time', says Barth in comment on Rom. 13.12: 'The night is far spent, the day is at hand.'[28] 'Of the *real* end of history it may be said at any time: The end is near!'[29] His exposition of I Cor. 15 shows a corresponding lack of interest in an eschatology that deals with the history of the end: 'The history of the end must be for him [the radical biblical thinker] synonymous with the pre-history, the limits of time of which he speaks must be the limits of all and every time and thus necessarily the origin of time.'[30]

From the point of view of the history of philosophy this transcendental eschatology was working with a combination of Ranke's saying that 'every epoch has an immediate relation to God' and Kierkegaard's dictum that 'where the eternal is concerned there is only one time: the present'. 'Every moment in time bears within it the unborn secret of revelation, and every moment can thus be *qualified*', said Barth in 1922, and Bultmann in 1958 in the last

---

27 *Der Römerbrief*, 2nd ed. 1922, Preface VI (cf. ET p. 4).
28 *Ibid.*, p. 484 (ET p. 498).
29 *Die Auferstehung der Tolem*, 2nd ed. 1926, p. 60 (ET by H. J. Stenning: *The Resurrection of the Dead*, 1933, p. 112)
30 *Ibid.*, p. 59 (ET p. 110).

paragraph of *History and Eschatology* says the same in almost the same words – though to be sure with the addition, 'You must awaken it.'[31]

What do these eschatological statements – if we would call them 'eschatological' – imply for the understanding of the revelation of God?

Karl Barth's doctrine of the 'self-revelation' of God was first developed in detail in 1925 in his essay on 'The Principles of Dogmatics according to Wilhelm Herrmann', in taking up and surmounting the celebrated 'self' of Herrmann.[32] The idea of 'self-revelation' has a previous history in the nineteenth century in the school of the Hegelian theologians. For the twentieth century, however, and especially for Barth and Bultmann, the emphasizing of 'self' in connection with revelation comes from Herrmann, whose pupils both of them were in Marburg. Without entering further into Herrmann's theology,[33] we can preface our enquiry here by a quotation from his book *Gottes Offenbarung an uns* (1908), in order to indicate the problem involved in the idea of 'self-revelation': 'We have no other means of knowing God except that he reveals himself to us ourselves by acting upon us.'[34]

With the actualism which in this statement links together revelation, action, and knowledge of God, Barth and Bultmann are in agreement. The question – not for the understanding of the statement as Herrmann meant it, but for the point at which Barth and Bultmann start with, and depart from, Herrmann – is how the content is to be understood. Does the statement mean that God himself must reveal himself to us, or that God must reveal himself to us ourselves? Does the 'self' of the self-revelation refer essentially to God or to man?

What Herrmann meant by this statement is plain. Revelation is not instruction, and not an emotional impulse. Revelation of God

---

31 Cf. *Römerbrief*, 2nd ed. 1922, p. 483 (ET p. 497) and R. Bultmann, *History und Eschatology*, 1957, p. 155.

32 In *Die Theologie und die Kirche* (Ges. Vortrage II), 1928, pp. 240ff. (ET by L. P. Smith: *Theology and Church*, 1962, pp. 238ff.).

33 On this cf. the latest study by T. Mahlmann, 'Das Axiom des Erlebnisses bei Wilhelm Herrmann', *Neue Zeitschrift für systematische Theologie*, 4, 1962, pp. 11ff.

34 *Gottes Offenbarung an uns*, 1908, p. 76. (The German – *dass er sich uns selbst offenbart* – can also mean, 'that he himself reveals himself to us' – Translator.)

cannot be objectively explained, but it can certainly be experienced in man's own self, namely, in the non-objectifiable subjectivity of the dark, defenceless depths in which we live the moment of involvement. The revealing of God in his working upon ourselves is therefore as unfathomable, as non-derivable, as much grounded in itself as the living of life, which no one can explain, but everyone can experience.[35] That is why no catchword is more characteristic of the theology of Herrmann than the word 'self' in an anthropological sense. Barth, however, argues in his essay that the word 'self' in this sense cannot after all be the last word in the theology of revelation. 'Herrmann knows that one does *not* "experience" God the Father, Son and Holy Spirit, the mystery of God. "Even where he reveals himself, God continues to dwell in darkness."'[36] Precisely when it comes to the doctrine of the Trinity, he says, there appears a reservation even in Herrmann, despite all the emphasis on our own personal experience. Whether this is true of Herrmann need not concern us here. For the development of Barth's theology it is important that he starts at this point, and goes on by putting the subjectivity of God in place of the subjectivity of man which Herrmann means by 'self'. He asks whether in speaking of 'the majesty of the Triune God', we have not to think of 'the unabrogable subjectivity of God, who exclusively determines *himself*, and is knowable exclusively through *himself* in the "purest act" (*actus purissimus*) of his Triune Personality'.[37] 'The lion breaks his cage; a wholly different "Self" has stepped on to the scene with *his* own validity.' 'Man asks about his "self" only because and if God is pleased to give him knowledge of *his* "Self", only because and if God's Word is spoken to him. Dogmatics should *begin* with "God said" (*Deus dixit*), repudiating the wholly futile attempt to recover it, if at all, only as a mere "reflection of faith" on the heights of some alleged "experience" (as if there were such a thing as an "experience" of it!).'[38] For Barth, the science of theology is

---

35 These are ideas and parallels arrived at by Herrmann in his encounter with the rising vitalist philosophy of Bergson, Simmel and Driesch. Cf. T. Mahlmann, *op. cit.*, p. 29: 'Life creates its own justification by its action (*ZTK* 12, 1912, p. 75). That life is grounded in itself, has its origin only in itself, accordingly means that life is self-assertion, that it asserts itself continually without demonstrable ground.'

36 K. Barth, *op. cit.*, p. 262 (ET p. 254).

37 *Ibid.*, p. 264 (ET p. 256, slightly altered).

38 *Ibid.*, pp. 266f. (ET p. 258, slightly altered).

accordingly grounded not in religious experience, but in the *auto-pistia* of Christian truth, in the fact that it is grounded in itself, and 'what is already established can well be left without proof'.[39]

Herrmann – this was his Kantian heritage – had taken it to be self-evident that revelation cannot be objectively grounded, proved to the theoretic reason. The non-objectifiability of God and the non-objectifiability of each peculiar existence or each peculiar 'self' constituted one and the same mystery for him. The ungroundable character of God and the ungroundable character and *gratuité* of life that is lived merged for him into one. That is why he held knowledge of God to be the 'defenceless expression of religious experience'. He saw the 'danger' of the intellect and of objectification precisely as Hegel had described it. 'Everything that science can grasp is – dead.'[40] 'To know a thing is to gain control of it, to make it serviceable to us. The living world, inaccessible as it is to science ... is disclosed to us through *self-reflection*, i.e. through honest reflection on what we in actual fact experience.'[41] For that reason we cannot say of God what he himself objectively is, but only what effect he has on ourselves.

For Barth, however, this defenceless non-groundability of religious experience cannot yet claim the required *autopistia* and *autousia*, but can only be a pointer towards the ground that is really grounded in itself, that 'is never in any sense "object", but is always unchangeably subject'.[42] It is the sovereignty of the self-existent God in contrast and in counter to all propositions of man's consciousness. Nor does the negative talk of the non-provability, the non-groundability and the non-objectifiability of God yet achieve that change of thought which Barth demands – the change to the transcendental subjectivity, expressed in trinitarian terms, of the God who reveals himself to man in the act of the *Deus dixit*. It is a change of thought that was foreshadowed in the ontological proof of God in Anselm and then executed by Hegel, and was later carried further by Barth in the idea of the self-revelation of God in his name.

---

39 *Ibid.*, p. 267 (ET p. 258).
40 *Realencyklopädie für prot. Theol. und Kirche* 16, p. 592, quoted by T. Mahlmann, *op. cit.*, p. 21.
41 ZTK 22, 1912, p. 73, quoted by T. Mahlmann, *op. cit.*, p. 35.
42 K. Barth, *op. cit.*, p. 269 (ET p. 260).

In this way Herrmann's 'self' acquires in Barth a *theological* form. Yet it should be noted that it still retains all the attributes, all the relations and distinctions, in which it had been formulated by Herrmann.

God cannot be proved, neither from the cosmos nor from the depths of human existence. He proves himself through himself. His revelation is the proof of God given by God himself.[43] No one reveals God but himself alone. Who this God is, is first learned from his revelation. He reveals not this and that, but himself. By being the one who acts in his revelation, God is the one who describes himself.[44] God cannot be commended and defended in his self-revelation, but he can only be believed – and that, too, as a result of his making himself credible.[45] His word, in which he himself is present, cannot and need not be proved. It vindicates itself. Where the knowledge of God stood in Herrmann as the 'defenceless expression of religious experience', there we now have the self-revelation of God in the proclamation of the *Deus dixit* in the same defencelessness – namely, non-groundable and therefore indestructible, unprovable and therefore irrefutable, grounding and proving itself.

Now all these reflections on the subjectivity of God could also be sublime speculations on God. Barth, however, when he speaks of the self-revelation of God, would speak of nothing else but 'that little bundle of reports' on the existence of Jesus Christ which date from the days of the Roman Empire. But it is just here, where this history is concerned, that there arises a series of questions:

Does 'self-revelation of God' mean God's eternal self-understanding? Does the doctrine of the Trinity mean the eternal trinitarian reflection of God upon himself? Does 'self-revelation' mean the pure present of the eternal, without history or future? The adoption of the term 'self' still retains even in the idea of the self-revelation of God its old reflective note from the thought of Herrmann. It contains the reflection that arises when God can no longer be proved from the world after the manner of the proofs of God, and it is to that extent a polemic term encumbered by the problem complex of the provability of God. It is therefore difficult

43 *Das christliche Verständnis der Offenbarung* (Theologische Existenz heute, NF 12), 1948, p. 7 (ET p. 209).

44 *Ibid.*, p. 8.

45 *Ibid.*, p. 13.

to apply it to that bundle of reports about Jesus of Nazareth, for these statements and communications did not arise in the realm of the Greek metaphysics of the proofs of God, but in a wholly different context.

In itself it would here be a simple matter to transfer to God the structures of personality, personal selfhood, personal self-reflection and self-disclosure. Barth, however, did not take this path towards theological personalism, but developed the idea of self-revelation in the context of the doctrine of the Trinity and linked it with the proclamation of the lordship of God. The doctrine of the Trinity results from the developing of the self-revelation, i.e. from the questions of the subject, predicate and object of the event, *Deus dixit*. God himself is the revealer, the act of revealing, and the revealed.[46] Whereas in the first outline of Barth's dogmatics, in his *Christliche Dogmatik* I (1927), Herrmann's idea of subjectivity is still dominant, in the *Church Dogmatics* I/1 (1932) it recedes in favour of a detailed doctrine of the immanent Trinity. Yet even here the immanent form of the divine Trinity appears to give the revelation of God the character of transcendental exclusiveness as a 'self-contained novum'.[47] What seems in this context to be more important than the trinitarian development of the self-revelation of God is the connecting of it with the 'lordship of God'. That God reveals 'himself' means that he reveals himself '*as* God and Lord'. Self-revelation accordingly does not mean for Barth personalistic self-disclosure of God after the analogy of the I-Thou relationship between men. God reveals himself in actual fact as 'somebody' and 'something' for man, not as pure, absolute Thou. That would in any case, like the individual, be 'ineffable'. He reveals himself 'as' the Lord. The announcing of the *basileia* is the concrete content of the revelation. The meaning of God's lordship, however, is again to be learned from his concrete action in relation to man in his revelation, so that here, too, act and content still fall together in the first instance. What does 'self-revelation' mean in this context? It means that in his revelation God does not disguise himself, does not appear behind a mask, does not identify himself with some-thing other than what he himself is – that what he reveals himself *as*, he is 'beforehand in himself' – that consequently in the reve-lation of God *as* the Lord, man has to do with God *himself*, can

---

46 *Christliche Dogmatik* I, 1927, pp. 127, 140, 154ff.
47 *Kirchliche Dogmatik* I/1, 1932, p. 323 (ET p. 352).

depend on himself. Thus in revealing 'something' (his lordship) and 'somebody' (namely, himself in his Son), God reveals himself.

Once this connection is realized, then G. Gloege's and W. Pannenberg's criticism[48] of Barth's theology of self-revelation, in which they suspect a gnostic use of terms and a modern personalism, proves to be unjust. But then W. Kreck's interpretation of self-revelation also appears questionable: 'We must therefore here abide by Barth's fundamental epistemological proposition: God (and therefore also man as God's creature and image) can be known only through God.'[49] Kreck sets this proposition in antithesis to any knowledge of God by way of the *analogia entis*. This well-known proposition, however, is not one of Christian theology, but has its source in Neoplatonic gnosticism, appears in the reflections of mediaeval mysticism, and is found also in Hegel's philosophy of religion. Taken in itself, it represents the highest stage of the self-reflection of the Absolute that was attained within the sphere of Greek philosophy of religion. On this principle the question of revelation and of knowledge of God would form a dosed circle which is strictly speaking impenetrable. It is not applicable to that bundle of historic reports from which Christian faith lives, but rather to an esoteric gnosis. 'Revelation', however, must at once involve the crossing of the boundary between like and unlike, if it is to be revelation. Where there is knowledge of God on the ground of revelation, we should sooner have to assert the opposite principle: only unlikes know each other. God is known only by non-God, namely by man, as 'God' and 'Lord'. Now of course Kreck in this proposition is thinking of pneumatology: 'No man can say that Jesus is the Lord, but by the Holy Spirit' (I Cor. 12.3). But this Spirit has his place in the event of Christ and in the word, not in a divine circle *supra nos*. The immanent form of the doctrine of the Trinity is always in danger of obscuring the historical and eschatological character of the Holy Spirit, who is the Spirit of the resurrection of the dead.

Barth later himself revised the transcendental eschatology of his dialectical phase. 'It showed that although I was confident to treat the beyondness of the coming kingdom with absolute seriousness, I

---

48 G. Gloege, art. 'Offenbarung, dogmatisch', *RGG*, 3rd ed., col. 1611. W. Pannenberg, *Offenbarung als Geschichte*, 1961, p. 14.

49 In *Antwort. Festschrift für Karl Barth*, 1956, p. 285.

had no such confidence in relation to its coming as such.'[50] On the passage we quoted from the commentary on Rom. 13.12 he now says: 'It is also clear that ... I missed the distinctive feature of the passage, the teleology which it ascribes to time as it moves towards a real end ... The one thing that remained as the only tangible result was precisely that one-sided supra-temporal understanding of God which I had set out to combat.'[51] That, however, surely means that in this 'supra-temporal understanding' the truth of God, in regard both to the concept of the *eschaton* and to the concept of revelation, had been taken as epiphany of the eternal present and not as apocalypse of the promised future. But now if, as we have seen, Barth's concept of the self-revelation of God was shaped precisely by this transcendental eschatology, must there not then come a corresponding revision in the understanding of revelation? Can the impression then be allowed to stand that 'self-revelation of God' means the 'pure presence of God', an 'eternal presence of God in time', a 'present without any future'?[52] Can it then be said that the story of Easter 'does not speak eschatologically'? If that were so, then the event of the resurrection of Christ would in itself already be the eschatological fulfilment, and would not point beyond itself to something still outstanding that is to be hoped for and awaited. To understand the revelation in Christ as self-revelation of God, is to take the question as to the future and the goal indicated by revelation, and answer it with a reflection on the origin of revelation, on God himself. With this reflection, however, it becomes almost impossible to see the revelation of the risen Lord as the ground for still speaking of an outstanding future of Jesus Christ. If the idea of self-revelation is not to change tacitly into an expression for the God of Parmenides, then it must have an open eye for the statements of promise in the third article of the Creed. Yet this must not happen in such a way that the future redemption which is promised in the revelation of Christ would become only a supplement, only a noetic unveiling of the reconciliation effected in Christ, but in such a way that it gives promise of the real goal and true intention of

50 *Kirchliche Dogmatik* II/1, p. 716 (ET p. 635, slightly altered), cf. also I/2, pp. 55ff. (ET pp. 50ff.).
51 *Ibid.*, II/1, p. 716 (ET p. 635, slightly altered).
52 *Kirchliche Dogmatik* I/2, pp. 125f. (ET pp. 114f.). Also in I/1, pp. 486f. (ET pp. 530f.), 'eschatological' can be synonymous with 'related to the eternal reality', and 'future' with 'what accrues to us from the side of God'.

each other. Man by his creation is appointed to be himself. Hence questionableness is the structure of human existence. Man is by nature in quest of himself. In and with the question raised by his existence there arises the question of God. 'We cannot speak about our existence when we cannot speak about God; and we cannot speak about God when we cannot speak about our existence. We could only do the one along with the other ... If it is asked how it can be possible to speak of God, then the answer must be: only in speaking of us.'[60] Hence man attains to himself only in God, and only where he attains to himself does he attain to God. To both – God and the human self, or rather each peculiar existence – belongs the characteristic of non-objectifiability. The closed system of cause and effect in the discernible, explicable, objectively demonstrable world of things and of history is therefore set aside (*a*) when I speak of God's action, and (*b*) when I speak of myself. 'In faith the closed weft presented or produced by objective observation is transcended ... when it (faith) speaks of the activity of God. In the last resort it is already transcended when I speak of myself.'[61] The statements of scripture arise out of existence and are addressed to existence. They have not to justify themselves at the forum of an objectifying science of nature and history, since the latter does not even set eyes on the non-objectifiable existence of man.[62] That determines the programme of existentialist interpretation and of demythologizing. This interpretation is governed by the question of God that is given with the questionableness of existence, and it is accordingly directed towards an understanding that has neither mythical nor scientific objectivity but is in each several instance individual appropriation in the spontaneity of that subjectivity which is non-objectifiable because transcendental.[63]

Whereas Barth broke away from Herrmann by separating, as we have seen, the non-objectifiable subjectivity of God in the act of the *Deus dixit* from the subjectivity of man, that is, God's 'self' from 'man's self', Bultmann remains under the spell of the hidden correlation of God and self. Hence for him the self-revelation of God

---

60 *Glauben und Verstehen*, I, 1933, p. 33.

61 *Kerygma und Mythos*, IT, 1952, p. 198 (ET by R. H. Fuller: *Kerygma and Myth*, 1957, pp. 198f.).

62 *Ibid.*, p. 187.

63 On Bultmann's equating of theological anthropology with the anthropology of transcendental subjectivity, cf. W. Anz, 'Verkündigung und theologische Reflexion', *ZTK* 58, 1961, Beiheft 2, pp. 47ff., esp. 68ff.

finds its measure and development not in a doctrine of the Trinity, but in place of that we find the disclosing of the authenticity or selfhood of man. It is true that God's action, God's revelation, God's future are unprovable, yet that does not by any means imply that our statements are arbitrary, but all the statements in question find non-objectified verification, so to speak, in man's coming to himself. The place of the proofs of God from nature and from history is taken, not by an unprovability of God that opens the door to arbitrariness, but by an *existential proof of God*, by speaking and thinking of God as the factor that is enquired after in the question raised by man's existence. That is an advanced, deepened and reshaped form of the only proof of God left over by Kant – the moral proof of God supplied by the practical reason. God is – objectively – unprovable, and so likewise is his action and revelation. But he proves himself to the believing 'self'. This is no proof of the existence of God, but a proof of God through existing authentically. It is true that in this interpretation the Christian hope leaves the future as God's future 'empty' as far as mythological, prognosticative pictures of the future are concerned, and renounces all wishful thinking. Yet there is a very precise criterion for determining what God's 'future' then is – namely, 'the realization of human life'[64] which is the object of the question raised by the questionableness of human existence. 'Eschatology has wholly lost its sense as goal of history, and is in fact understood as the goal of the individual human being.'[65] It is therefore just as impossible for Bultmann as for Kant that eschatology should provide a doctrine of the 'last things' in the world process, but the *logos* of the *eschaton* becomes the power of liberation from history, the power of the desecularization of existence in the sense of liberating us from understanding ourselves on the basis of the world and of works.

This proof of God from existence, in the framework of which theological questions are here asked and theological statements made, has a long previous history in dogmatic thought. Karl Jaspers points out that 'existence and transcendence' is the rendering in philosophical language of what the language of myth calls 'soul and God', and that in both languages it is defined as 'not world'.[66]

64 'The Christian Hope and the Problem of Demythologizing', *ExpT* 65, 1954, p. 278.
65 'History and Eschatology in the New Testament', *NTS* 1, 1954, p. 13.
66 *Philosophie* II, 1932, p. 1.

of God that arises from the questionability of human existence, involves the same presupposition as the proofs of God from the world or from history. It presupposes an antecedently given relation to God of the soul, the self or existence, even if this relation cannot be objectively proved but only subjectively experienced in the experience of certainty. In the restless heart that is due to his creation, man is engaged in the quest for God, whether he knows it or not.

The peculiar radicality of this proof of God from existence is due to the form now assumed by subjectivity as a product of reflective philosophy. Inasmuch as this subjectivity understands itself as the incomprehensible immediacy of our existing, it is attained by distinguishing itself from the non-self, from the world of observable, calculable and disposable things and of our own objectifications. If he is to be able to be a person in the proper sense, man must distinguish himself radically from his world. All statements on the relation of the person to God become definable only by means of the opposite, relation to the world. Man then continually distinguishes between his being part of the world and his being his own self, and so makes the world a secularized world and his self the pure receiving of his person from God. This process of abstracting our own individual subjectivity from all relationships to the world in endless reflection is a modern phenomenon. The proof of God from existence was not found in this antithesis either in Augustine or in the Reformers. On the contrary, they knew of God's working – albeit a hidden working – in the world, in nature and in history, and expounded it in the doctrine of created orders. The concept of science which Herrmann and Bultmann have taken over from Kantianism, however, no longer allows of this. For them, scientific knowledge is thought to be of an objectifying kind and its categories are designed for a 'closed system of cause and effect' and a world-order regulated by set laws, both in natural and in

---

observing of the 'radical questionableness of reality', has certain things in common with the undertaking of the so-called proofs of God. This analogy, however, is at once restricted by Ebeling: 'The problem of true transcendence seems to us to arise at a totally different point from where the usual so-called proofs of God placed it: not with the question of the *primum movens* or such like, but with the problems relating to personal being, like the question of meaning, the question of guilt, the question of communication, etc.' These questions which arise in the realm of personal being, however, are not 'totally different' from those posed by experience of the world.

historical science. For the experience we have of reality under these categories, God and his action remain hidden in principle. Hence the result is, as for Kierkegaard, the alliance of a theoretic atheism and a believing heart. Theological importance can therefore attach only to these scientific efforts as such – and that, too, for the existing subject of the act of knowing. If this scientific way of thinking about reality and of dealing with it has its ground in man's practical turn of mind and his will to power, in his desire to command, to survey, to calculate, to assert himself and make himself secure, then from the theological point of view that comes near to man's attaining to self-assurance from his works. This means that for the man who is confronted by the message of grace, the dimension 'world' is now relevant only within the framework of the question of justification – in the question whether he seeks to understand himself 'from the world' as the disposable realm of his works, or 'from God' the Indisposable. For the subject in search of himself, 'world' and 'God' thereby become radical alternatives. Man comes to stand 'between God and the world' (Gogarten). There is no need to mention that this view of 'God' and 'world' as alternatives has a previous history in gnosticism and in mysticism. More important is the fact that this kind of theological understanding of 'world' forces both man's scientific and his practical dealings with reality into a legalism which does not accord with this reality. Does the objective knowledge of the world and of history necessarily fall, in the view of theology, under 'the law'? Is any self-understanding of man conceivable at all which is not determined by his relation to the world, to history, to society? Can human life have subsistence and duration without outgoing and objectification, and without this does it not evaporate into nothingness in endless reflection? It is the task of theology to expound the knowledge of God in a correlation between understanding of the world and self-understanding.

The categorical framework of a transcendental subjectivity also dominates Bultmann's understanding of revelation. The revelation of God is accordingly a matter of man's coming to himself, truly understanding himself. 'Revelation means *that opening up of what is hidden which is absolutely necessary and decisive for man if he is to achieve "salvation" or authenticity.*'[73] This presupposes for one thing that man cannot of himself attain to his authenticity, but

---

73 *Glauben und Verstehen* III, 1960, p. 2 (ET p. 59).

must seek for revelation, but secondly that he is necessarily destined to come to his authenticity. If his authenticity is disclosed to him by revelation, then the divinity of God discloses itself to him therein. Christian proclamation and Christian faith answer this anterior question of man about himself – the question which in virtue of his questionable nature he himself is – not by what they say and what they mediate, but by what they are. 'Revelation does not mediate any speculative knowledge, but *it addresses us.* The fact that in it man learns to understand himself, means *that he learns to understand each several "now" of his life, each several moment, as one qualified by the proclamation.* For to be in the moment is his authentic being.'[74] Revelation in this sense is the event of preaching and faith. Revelation is the coming about of the ἀκοὴ τῆς πίστεως. 'The preaching is itself revelation and does not merely speak about it.'[75] 'It is only in faith that the object of faith is disclosed; therefore, faith itself belongs to revelation.'[76] Not in *what* the word of proclamation says or in what it points to, but in the fact that it 'happens', addressing, accosting, appealing, lies the event of revelation. '*What, then, is revealed?* Nothing at all, so far as the quest for revelation is a quest for doctrines. ... But everything, so far as *man has his eyes opened regarding himself and can understand himself again.*'[77] Thus here the event of the proclamation that addresses us, and of the decision of faith that understands and appropriates it, is itself revelation. Since the governing question of revelation is constituted by the questionableness of human existence itself, the revelation discloses a self-understanding in authenticity, certainty and identity with oneself. The active event of revelation is itself the presence of the *eschaton*, for 'to be in the moment' of proclamation and faith is the 'authentic being' of man. Authentic being, however, means the restoring of man's original being in the sense of creatureliness and the attaining of finality in the sense of eschatology. Both are fulfilled in the historicality determined by word and faith. In the 'moment' of revelation, creation and redemption coincide.[78] *What*

---

74 *Glauben und Verstehen* III, 1960, p. 30 (ET p. 86, slightly altered).

75 *Ibid.*, p. 21 (ET p. 78).

76 *Ibid.*, p. 23 (ET p. 79).

77 *Ibid.*, p. 29 (ET p. 85, slightly altered).

78 *Ibid.*, p. 29: 'There did not appear in Jesus a different light from the light that always shone already in the creation. Man does not learn a different understanding of himself in the light of the revelation of redemption from the

is revealed is identical with the event, the fact *that* revelation takes place.

Here two questions arise:

1. When the questionableness of human existence is exclusively made the governing question of revelation and salvation, and this question is narrowed down to the alternative of understanding oneself either from the disposable 'world' or the indisposable 'God', then the self-evidence of the 'self-understanding' is manifestly not called in question, neither hermeneutically in relation to the received texts nor theologically. Yet why should the anterior understanding which causes man to ask for 'revelation' be only an 'unknowing knowledge' 'about himself' and 'not a knowledge of the world'?[79] Why is the word that has all along been the light of men 'naturally ... not a cosmological or theological theory but ... an understanding of oneself through acknowledging the Creator'?[80] Why does revelation not supply a '*Weltanschauung*', but a new 'self-understanding'? What Bultmann presupposes in this context as a 'natural' and self-evident alternative, is not in the least 'natural', but is an exact description of a definite *Weltanschauung*, a definite view of history and a definite analysis of time, according to which man has become questionable to himself in his social, corporeal and historic relations to the world and attains his self-hood by differentiation from the external world and reflection upon his objectifications. Basically, however, '*Weltanschauung*' and 'self-understanding' lie on the same plane. The one presupposes the other and is inseparably bound up with it. Only in his outgoing towards the world does man experience himself. Without objectification no experience of oneself is possible. Always man's self-understanding is socially, materially and historically mediated. An immediate self-consciousness and a non-dialectical identity with himself is not possible to man – that is shown precisely by the dialectical antithesis of world and self in Bultmann.

2. The theological question arises whether it is really true that in the event of revelation in proclamation and faith man already

---

understanding he ought always to have of himself already in view of the revelation in creation and law, namely, as God's creature' (cf. ET p. 86).

79 *Ibid.*, p. 26 (ET p. 83): 'Thus there is a "natural revelation". ... But ... the knowledge of it is not a knowledge of the world, a theistic view of God. Rather it is a knowledge by man of himself.'

80 *Ibid.*, p. 26 (ET p. 82): cf. also *Das Evangelium des Johannes*, 12th ed., 1952, pp. 27ff.

comes 'to himself' in that authenticity which is at once both original and final. In that case faith would itself be the practical end of history and the believer would himself already be perfected. There would be nothing more that still awaits him, and nothing more towards which he is on his way in the world in the body and in history. God's 'futurity' would be 'constant' and man's openness in his 'wayfaring' would likewise be 'constant' and 'never-ending'.[81] This, however, is just what would cause believing existence, understood in an 'eschatological' sense of this sort, to turn into a new form of the 'epiphany of the eternal present'.[82] If Jesus with his word has already reached his 'goal'[83] in faith itself, then it is hardly conceivable that faith is directed towards *promissio* and that faith has itself a goal (I Peter 1.9) to which it is on the way, that 'it doth not yet appear what we shall be' (I John 3.2), and that faith is thus out for something which is promised to it but which is not yet fulfilled. If it is precisely believers who wait for the redemption of the body, on the ground of the eschatologically understood 'earnest of the Spirit' who is the Spirit of the raising of the dead, then in so doing they make it known that they have not yet attained to

---

81 *Glauben und Verstehen* III, p. 121: '... his constant futurity is his beyondness'. P. 165: '... the God of history ... the ever coming God'. *Das Urchristentum im Rahmen der antiken Religionen*, 2nd ed., 1954, p. 228 (ET by R. H. Fuller: *Primitive Christianity in its Contemporary Setting*, 1956, p. 208): 'The openness of Christian existence is never-ending.'

82 J. Schniewind already saw and criticized this, *Kerygma und Mythos* I, pp. 100ff. (ET pp. 75ff.). P. 103 (ET p. 78): 'If the "eschatological attitude" means a life based on invisible, intangible realities, that is much too wide a definition. For it is then identical with religion as such.' P. 105 (ET p. 81): 'Eschatology deals with the *eis ti* and the *telos*, with the meaning and goal of the time process, but not with the eternal present.'

83 G. Ebeling, *Das Wesen des christlichen Glaubens*, 1959, pp. 68, 72 (ET by R. Gregor Smith: *The Nature of Faith*, 1961, pp. 60, 62), *Wort und Glaube*, 1960, p. 311 (ET p. 298) and frequently. This does not prevent Ebeling from understanding faith as 'essentially a faith that relates to the future' (p. 248; ET p. 241) and saying, '... faith ... is the future' (*Wesen des christlichen Glaubens*, p. 231, ET p. 175). This future of faith, however, appears only in reflection on the dimension of faith itself, and is understood as 'pure (that surely means unmediated) future' or 'futurity'. But that is to regard faith as being eternally hope. Future in the sense of futurity, and hope in the sense of hoping, thereby become dimensions or ecstatic extensions of the 'now of eternity'. Cf. *Theologie und Verkündigung*, 1962, pp. 89f. (ET by John Riches, *Theology and Proclamation*, 1966, pp. 89f.), and the criticism of H. Schmidt, 'Das Verhältnis von neuzeitlichem Wirklichkeitsverständnis und christlichem Glauben in der Theologie G. Ebelings', *Kerygma und Dogma* 9, 1963, pp. 71ff.

identity with themselves, but that in hope and confidence they are living to that end and here defy the reality of death. It is precisely in the context of the eschatological distinction of 'not yet', in which faith stretches out towards the future, that it becomes possible to perceive a world that is not identical with 'world' in the antithetical sense in which the doctrine of justification uses the term to denote the epitome of corruption, law and death. If faith awaits the 'redemption of the body', and a bodily resurrection from the dead, and the annihilation of death, then it begins to see itself in a profound bodily solidarity with the 'earnest expectation of the creature' (Rom. 8.19ff.), both in its subjection to vanity and in the universal hope. Then it does not regard the world from the standpoint of the 'law'. It sees it not merely as 'world' in the sense of being unable to understand itself from the world, but perceives it in the eschatological perspective of promise. The world itself is subjected along with it to vanity, in hope. The future which the promise of the God of the resurrection opens to faith is given to the creature along with it and to it along with the creature. The creature itself is a 'wayfarer', and the *homo viator* is engaged along with reality in a history that is open towards the future. Thus he does not find himself 'in the air', 'between God and the world', but he finds himself along with the world in that process to which the way is opened by the eschatological promise of Christ. It is not possible to speak of believing existence in hope and in radical openness, and at the same time consider the 'world' to be a mechanism or self-contained system of cause and effect in objective antithesis to man. Hope then fades away to the hope of the solitary soul in the prison of a petrified world, and becomes the expression of a gnostic longing for redemption. Talk of the openness of man is bereft of its ground, if the world itself is not open at all but is a closed shell. Without a cosmic eschatology there can be no assertion of an eschatological existence of man. Christian eschatology therefore cannot reconcile itself with the Kantian concepts of science and of reality. The very mode of our experience of the world is not adiaphorous. On the contrary, world-picture and faith are inseparable – precisely because faith cannot suffer the world to become a picture of God, nor a picture of man.

6. 'Progressive Revelation' and the Eschatology of Salvation History

The intention behind the old idea of understanding God's revelation as 'progressive revelation' was to construe revelation in historic terms and see the history of the world as revelation. Ideas of this kind go back to late federal theology (J. Cocceius) and the early pietistic theology of history, the so-called 'prophetic' and 'economic' theology of the seventeenth and eighteenth centuries.[84] In contrast to Orthodoxy's supranaturalistic and doctrinaire view of revelation, the Bible was here read as a history book, as the divine commentary upon the divine acts in world history. This new historic understanding of revelation had its ground in the rebirth of eschatological millenarianism in the post-reformation age. It was the start of a new, eschatological way of thinking, which called to life the feeling for history. The revelation in Christ was accordingly seen in the light of history as a transitional stage in a more far-reaching 'kingdom of God' process, and taken as an ultimate datum for the future, yet also one that points beyond itself. The revelation of God is consequently not an 'eternal moment', and the *eschaton* that comes to light in it is not a *'futurum aeternum'*, but the revelation in Christ is then the last, decisive element in the history of a kingdom whose pre-history begins in the Fall and indeed already in the Creation – whether with the proto-gospel of Gen. 3.15 or with the promise of the divine image in Gen. 1.28 – and whose final history extends historically and noetically beyond the revelation in Christ. The revelation in Christ is thus placed under the head

---

84 G. Schrenk, *Gottesreich und Bund im älteren Protestantismus, vornehmlich bei J. Cocceius*, 1923; G. Möller, 'Föderalismus und Geschichtsbetrachtung im 17. und 18. Jahrhundert', *Zeitschrift für Kirchengeschichte*, 3rd Series, I, vol. 50, 1931, pp. 397ff.; J. Moltmann, 'J. Brocard als Vorläufer der Reich-Gottes-Theologie', *Zeitschrift für Kirchengeschichte*, 4th Series, IX, vol. 71, 1960, pp. 110ff.; G. Weth, *Die Heilsgeschichte*, 1931; F. W. Kantzenbach, 'Vom Lebensgedanken zum Entwicklungsdenken in der Theologie der Neuzeit', *Zeitschrift für Religions- und Geistesgeschichte* 15, 1963, pp. 55ff.; E. Fülling, *Geschichte als Offenbarung*, 1956. For a critical assessment cf. K. G. Steck, *Die Idee der Heilsgeschichte. Hofmann – Schlatter – Cullman* (Theologische Studien 56), 1959. Steck's concluding recommendation that new consideration should today be given to Fichte's statement, 'It is only the metaphysical that brings blessedness, and not by any means the historical; the latter brings only prudence', certainly does not seem to me to offer any solution, in view of the context in which this statement stands in Fichte himself.

of a history of revelation, whose progressiveness is expressed in the idea of the developing of salvation stage by stage according to a previously fixed plan of salvation, This theology of the 'plan' of saving history has many striking parallels with the scientific deism of the seventeenth and eighteenth centuries and is in every sense a religious product of the Enlightenment. For that reason it can find expression in terms both of pietism and of rationalism, both of history of salvation and of history of progress.[85] Yet its real appeal lies not so much in the enlightened explanation of the divine saving plan of history, but rather in taking the testimonies of scripture, which point historically towards each other and also beyond themselves, and using them to turn history into a 'system of hope' (J. A. Bengel) by which to answer the question of the future and goal which the Christian revelation contains for the nations, for our bodily existence, for nature and for Israel. This theology of a progressive revelation of God in the history of salvation – conceived as esoteric knowledge on the part of those in initiated circles – is 'economic' to the extent that it brings to light the 'economies', or saving dispensations, of God in the past and thus turns past history into comprehended history, while on the other hand it draws conclusions for God's future action from his ways in the past. It is 'prophetic' in the ultimate sense, since it seeks to take prophecies and events in the past which point beyond the present, and use them as a means of discovering and portraying the future.

Its truth surely lies in the mere fact of its taking the trouble to enquire at all into the inward tendency and eschatological outlook which the divine revelation in history has towards the future. Its mistake, however, is to be seen in the fact that it sought to discover the eschatological progressiveness of salvation history not from the cross and the resurrection, but from other 'signs of the times' – from an apocalyptic view of the corruption of the Church and the decay of the world, or from an optimistic view of the progress of culture and knowledge – so that revelation became a predicate of history, and 'history' was turned deistically into a substitute for God.

---

85 One need think only of the astonishing parallel between pietistic and enlightened millenarianism, of Bengel and Lessing, C. A. Crusius and Ötinger, Herder and Menken, Hegel and von Hofmann, Rothe and Blumhardt. On this point cf. F. Gerlich, *Der Kommunismus als Lehre vom tausendjährigen Reich*, 1921.

What made this theology of salvation history possible was that resurgence of apocalyptic thought and hope which both in the theological and in the secular realm accompanied the birth of the 'modern age'. Yet it is an apocalyptic which is evolved from the standpoint of cosmology and world history and based on a historico-theological proof of God from history. It did not pass through the fires of Kantian criticism, nor did it – even in its nineteenth-century representatives – ever submit itself to that criticism, while for its own part it was hardly ever critical of that criticism either. Where it appears in the theology of salvation history in nineteenth-century romanticism, it retains this uncritical character throughout. That means, however, that it never really entered into the spirit of the modern age but assumed the remoteness of esoteric church teaching. Yet that is not to dismiss the truth contained in this kind of theological thinking. Its underlying polemic against an abstract materialism and an unhistoric historicism must be noted, even if that polemic failed on the whole to succeed.

In the pietism of Württemberg, history was understood by J. A. Bengel and F. Ötinger as a living 'organism'. Ötinger's *Theologia ex idea vitae deducta* (1765) introduced the concept of life into theology and attempted by this means to make room for thinking of a comprehensive kind.[86] This concept of life and of organism was not so much naturalistic, but rather had an eschatological orientation towards the awaited break-through of the glorious heavenly life in the resurrection. Its polemic was directed against the mechanistic world picture of the natural science of the Enlightenment, and against the idealistic subjectivism which went along with it. History, it maintained, should not be regarded as a collection of facts existing outside of man, but should be understood as a 'stream of life' which 'organically' surrounds man. Although the terms employed are derived from the life of nature and appear little suited for the comprehending of history, yet the criticism they express of Lamettrie's *L'homme machine* and of the unhistoric scientific materialism of the Enlightenment of Western Europe is noteworthy. The idea of the 'world machine' and of the 'forest' that has turned to 'firewood' is assailed by the salvation history school's theology of life. The new central concepts 'history' and 'life' thereby acquire significance for the overcoming of the modern

---

86 W. A. Hauck, *Das Geheimnis des Lebens: Naturanschauung und Gottesauffassung Fr. Chr. Ötingers*, 1947.

antithesis of 'subjectivity and objectification'. They were also taken over by Hegel in this sense, presumably from the Württemberg tradition. At all events it is in harmony with the intentions of Ötinger when Karl Marx in his critique of abstract scientific materialism and of Ludwig Feuerbach says: 'As soon as we have this active life process before us, history ceases to be a collection of dead facts, as in the still abstract thought even of the empiricists, or a series of imagined actions on the part of imagined subjects, as with the idealists.'[87] Both abstractions, subjectivity and objectification, acquire reality and lose their abstract, non-historic character in the dialectical process. The only question is, what constitutes this process, what is the subject of it, and what is its goal.

The idea of salvation history has furthermore an emphatically anti-historical tenor. Auberlen declared: 'The task of theology today consists in overcoming rationalistic unhistorical historicism ... through the knowledge of sacred history.'[88] The only noteworthy thing about this statement is the assertion that historicism is 'unhistorical'. The overcoming of it by means of a manifestly non-rational knowledge of 'sacred history' remains an illusion unless and until a new understanding of *ratio* can be acquired. The theology of salvation history was never itself able to bring about a critical change in the epistemological principles of historical science, and consequently always appears in the age of critical historical research to be an anachronistic means of glossing over the crisis in which the theology of revelation finds itself in the modern age. The 'disenchanting' of history by historical science certainly

87 *Frühschriften*, ed. Landshut, 1953, p. 350. Cf. also p. 330: 'Of the inborn attributes of matter, movement is the first and foremost, not merely in the sense of mechanical and mathematical movement, but still more as the impetus, the vital spirit, the tension, the pain (to use Jacob Böhme's word) of matter. ... In the course of its further development materialism becomes one-sided. ... Sensuality loses its blossom and becomes the abstract sensuality of the geometrist. Physical is sacrificed to mechanical or mathematical movement. Materialism becomes misanthropic', because, as it is said elsewhere (pp. 338, 346, 354), it 'shuts itself off from history'. This romanticist struggle on Marx's part against the sensual materialism of Feuerbach and against abstract, scientific materialism repeated itself in the Russian revolution in practical terms in the conflict between Trotsky and Stalin. Trotsky understood the revolutionary not as the 'mechanic of force', but as 'doctor' to the life process of the social organism. This conflict repeated itself in theoretical terms in the discussion between G. Lukács, K. Korsch and Lenin.
88 Quoted by G. Weth, *op. cit.*, p. 97.

cannot be undone by weaving a romantic, metahistorical, believing spell into history again. Only when critical historical science discovers its own historicality and learns to take it as a presupposition and a methodological principle, is there any chance of its realizing the possibility of attaining a 'historic' understanding of history and getting beyond an 'unhistorical historicism'. The traditional theology of salvation history bears much the same relationship to historical criticism as does Goethe's theory of colour to Newton's analysis of light. It has aesthetic and poetic categories of its own, but none by which the reality of history today could be grasped and altered.

The real concern of the theology of salvation history, however, lay not so much in the metahistorical grasp of 'sacred history', but was rather to show that revelation has a face towards world history and eschatology. This purpose underlies the concept of 'progressive revelation'.

Within the confines of a transcendental eschatology, revelation, as we have seen, becomes indifferent towards the ages of history. All ages are given an equally immediate relation to eternity, and history becomes the epitome of transience. R. Rothe rightly observes in his celebrated essay on revelation: 'It (scripture) shows us a revelation of a totally different kind. It describes it above all as a series – and that, too, a constantly self-coherent series – of wondrous *facts of history* and *dispensations in history* which then form the starting point for instances of supernatural prophetic illumination that have a definite pragmatical connection with them and assume manifold forms, as visions and as inward experiences of being addressed by the Spirit of God, not so much in order to communicate new knowledge of religious truth as to give advance intimation of future events in history.'[89] Both forms of revelation, that of 'outward manifestation' and that of 'inward inspiration' – a distinction which is made again and again between 'revelation in act' and 'revelation in word' – are historically conditioned, from which it follows that the divine revelation takes place gradually through the dialectic of word and event in a succession of happenings which are foretold and come to pass, and that it presses towards an end in which it is itself fulfilled. 'The advancing development of the kingdom of the Redeemer is at the same time also a

---

89 R. Rothe, *Zur Dogmatik*, 1863, p. 59.

continually advancing revelation of the absolute truth and perfection of the same.'[90] Thus in R. Rothe, and then with modifications also in Biedermann and E. Troeltsch, God's revelation is certainly understood as self-revelation, yet is linked with the idea which the concept of salvation history provides of an eschatological and progressive, dialectically advancing self-realization of the Revealer. That means, however, that present history, the history of the modern age in its cultural, scientific and technical progress, must be represented as an element in the process of the self-realizing revelation of God and his kingdom. When, therefore, an outmoded and antiquated Christianity raised the apologetic question of its own present relevance, the theology of progressive revelation characteristic of cultural Protestantism had to answer by showing that the modern age which was superseding traditional Christianity was secretly Christian or had a secret part in the history of the kingdom. 'Why is the Church opposed to cultural development?' asked R. Rothe, and answered: 'Oh, I blush to set it down: because it fears for belief in Christ. That is for me not faith, but faint-heartedness. But that is precisely what comes of disbelief in the real, effective world-dominion of the Saviour.'[91] In E. Troeltsch this question takes the form: 'Are we still to be seen in continuity with Christianity, or are we growing towards a religious future which is no longer Christian?'[92] His answer was the idea of a progressive revelation which in every age anew brings the spirit of the age into synthesis with the traditional Christian message. Similar questions and answers played an active part in the circles around the Blumhardts and among the 'religious socialists'.

Although the theology of progressive revelation never succeeded, in Rosenstock-Huessy's phrase, in 'overcoming modernity', yet it does contain elements that are not to be dismissed simply by the fact that a transcendental eschatology makes all ages of history indifferent. Although the idea of salvation history is philosophically anachronistic and theologically deistic, yet it does preserve the question of the eschatological future outlook which the Christian revelation holds for a world involved in history. That is to say, all the themes of the eschatology of salvation history – such as

---

90 *Ethik*, 1867, §570. Cf. also A. E. Biedermann, *Christliche Dogmatik*, 1884, §987.
91 R. Rothe, *Vorträge*, 1886, p. 21
92 *Glaubenslehre*, 1925, p. 49.

the mission to the nations, the discussion of the future of Israel, the future of world history, of creation and of the body – are the proper themes of Christian eschatology as such, only they cannot be conceived in the traditional terms of salvation history. The decisive question is, whether 'revelation' is the illuminating interpretation of an existing, obscure life process in history, or whether revelation itself originates drives and directs the process of history; whether consequently, as Barth has asked, revelation is a predicate of history, or whether history has to be understood as a predicate of the eschatological revelation and to be experienced, expected and obediently willed as such.

7. 'History' as Indirect Self-revelation of God

Another attempt to free theological consideration of the 'self-revelation' of God from the fetters of the reflective philosophy of transcendental subjectivity – an attempt, moreover, which in many respects leaves the discussion still open – is found in the programmatic volume *Offenbarung als Geschichte* (1961) by W. Pannenberg, R. Rendtorff, U. Wilckens and T. Rendtorff.[93]

Since Kant's critique and the concept of science that was based on it, the impression had arisen that there can be no proof of God and of his action in history, and no objective demonstration of revelation, and this had compelled theology to speak of revelation only in the context and framework of transcendental subjectivity. That, however, is not by any means to say that theology had at last settled down to its own business, but rather that it had entered into a negative alliance with a particular, modern mode of experiencing the world. If this spell is to be broken and an alternative to this kind of theology of revelation is to be found, then that must of necessity be bound up with an alternative to the modern, post-Kantian concept of science, to the critical concept of reason, and to the historicism of a critical historical treatment of reality. An

---

93 Cf. further, W. Pannenberg, 'Heilsgeschehen und Geschichte', *Kerygma und Dogma* 5, 1959, pp. 218–237, 259–288; R. Rendtorff, '"Offenbarung" im Alten Testament', *TLZ* 85, 1960, cols. 833–838; K. Koch, 'Spätisraelitisches Geschichtsdenken', *Historische Zeitschrift*, Aug. 1961; W. Pannenberg, 'Hermeneutik und Universalgeschichte', *ZTK* 60, 1963, pp. 90ff.; R. Rendtorff, 'Geschichte und Wort im Alten Testament', *EvTh* 22, 1962, pp. 621ff.

alternative to faith's theology of revelation must then also bring criticism to bear on that critique of knowledge which Kant set up 'in order to find a place for faith'. It must raise the question of God no longer in an exclusive sense on the ground of the questionableness of man's subjectivity, but in an inclusive sense on the ground of the questionableness of reality as a whole, and it is in this comprehensive context that it must speak of God's revelation and action.

Offenbarung als Geschichte therefore sets out not from the proof of God from existence, or from showing that the question of God arises from the questionableness of existence. Rather, it starts from the proof of God from the cosmos, or by showing that the question of God arises from consideration of the question of reality as a whole. The place of the 'kerygma theology', and of the idea of an immediate self-revelation of God in the appeal of the word, is therefore taken by the recognition of an 'indirect self-revelation of God in the mirror of his action in history'.[94] 'The facts as acts of God shed a reflected light on God himself, tell us indirectly something about God himself.'[95] Since, however, each individual event, taken as an act of God, only partially illumines the nature of God, revelation in the sense of the full self-revelation of God in his glory can be possible only where the whole of history is understood as revelation. 'History as a whole is thus revelation of God. Since it is not yet finished, it is only in the light of its end that it is recognizable as revelation.'[96] Hence the full self-revelation of God takes place 'not at the beginning but at the end of the revealing history'.[97] The apocalyptic writers of late Judaism had extraordinary visions in which they foresaw such an end of history in the general resurrection of the dead. In the (risen) 'destiny' of Jesus of Nazareth the end of history has accordingly been forestalled. For in his resurrection there has already happened to him what still awaits all men.[98] If his resurrection is the 'forestalling', the anticipation, the prolepsis of the universal end, then it follows that in his destiny God himself is indirectly revealed as the God of all men.[99]

---

94 *Offenbarung als Geschichte*, p. 15.
95 *Ibid.*, p. 17.
96 R. Rendtorff, *TLZ* 85, 1960, col. 836.
97 *Offenbarung als Geschichte*, p. 95.
98 *Ibid.*, p. 104.
99 *Ibid.*, pp. 98, 104ff.

This theology of universal history obviously intends in the first instance to extend and supersede the Greek cosmic theology. The place of the cosmological proof of God, which argued from 'reality as cosmos' to the one divine *arche* and so provided proof of a cosmological monotheism, is taken by a theology of history which argues back in the same way from the unity of 'reality as history' to the one God of history.[100] The epistemological method remains the same, only in place of the self-contained cosmos whose eternally recurring sameness makes it a theophany in its symmetry and harmony, we have an open-ended cosmos with a teleological trend towards the future. 'History' thus becomes the new summary term for 'reality in its totality'.[101] In place of the metaphysical point in which the unity of the cosmos culminates, we have the eschatological point in which history finds its unity and its goal. Just as in the light of that culminating metaphysical unity the cosmos could be recognized as indirect revelation of God, so now in the light of the end of history, history can be recognized as indirect revelation of God. The retention of the retroflexive argument in the knowledge of God – 'in the mirror of his acts in history' – has the result that knowledge of God becomes possible in principle only *post festum* and *a posteriori*, in looking back upon completed facts in history and on prophecies that have come true in it. That, however, would be knowing God with the eyes of 'Minerva's owl', which according to Hegel begins its flight only 'when a form of life has grown old and reached perfection'.[102] The place of the *kerygma* theology, which perceived God in the event of being addressed by the word, would then be taken by a theology of history, which hears God in the 'language of the facts'. Just as in Greek cosmic theology the eternal being of God is indirectly manifest in that which is, and can be inferred from it, so here God's being would be recognized

---

100 For the application of the retroflexive argument cf. W. Pannenberg, 'Die Aufnahme des philos. Gottesbegriffes als dogmatisches Problem', *Zeitschrift für Kirchengeschichte* 70, 1959, p. 11; 'Heilsgeschehen und Geschichte', *op. cit.*, p. 129; *Offenbarung als Geschichte*, p. 104. This retroflexive argument presupposes an unbroken link between God and history, on the ground of which we can argue back from it to him. Since this is also the basis of the cosmological proof of God, 'history' is here understood as indirect theophany, just as the cosmos then was in Greek cosmology. It is a question, however, whether this is a biblical understanding of history.

101 'Heilsgeschehen und Geschichte', *op. cit.*, p. 222.

102 G. W. F. Hegel, *Grundlinien der Philosophie des Rechtes*, ed. J. Hoffmeister, 4th ed., 1956, Vorrede 17.

in the has-beens of history. Now of course the fact that the 'end of history' is not yet here, but has only been forestalled in the destiny of Jesus, also makes the recognition of God in history into a knowledge that is always only of proleptic, anticipatory character. Yet the basic Old Testament insight that 'history is that which happens between promise and fulfilment' – the insight from which Pannenberg and Rendtorff set out – is ultimately abandoned in favour of an eschatology which is expressed in terms of universal history and which proves itself by reference to 'reality as a whole' in an effort to improve on Greek cosmic theology.[103] This eschatology acquires its eschatological character only from the fact that reality cannot yet be contemplated as a whole because it has not yet come to an end. With this, however, the Old Testament God of promise threatens to become a θεὸς ἐπιφανής, whose epiphany will be represented by the totality of reality in its completed form. The world will one day be theophany, indirect self-revelation of God *in toto*. Because it is not yet so, reality is open-ended towards the future and all knowledge of God and the world has an eschatologically qualified 'provisional' character. This, however, would mean that the thought structures of Greek cosmic theology remain in principle, and are simply given an eschatological application. The retention of the retroflexive method thereby leads to a view of 'historic fact' which, with its implied concept of being, of 'mirror' and 'image', appears to resist any combination with faith and hope and even with 'history'.[104] It remains unclear whether the place of

---

103 This critical observation has already been made also by James M. Robinson, 'The Historicality of Biblical Language', *The Old Testament and Christian Faith*, ed. B. W. Anderson, 1963, pp. 128f.

104 Here H. G. Geyer, 'Geschichte als theologisches Problem', *EvTh* 22, 1962, p. 103, is right when he says: 'A fact is a completed event (*factum*) and as such has had its day, and the form of consciousness appropriate to it is memory and its methodically developed form in the knowledge of historical science; promise, however, always has its day still ahead of it.' To be sure, there is also such a thing as hope in the *modus* of memory and as a historical event that has its future still ahead of it. Only that would have to be formulated in a new concept of memory and historical knowledge. Cf. J. Moltmann, 'Verkündigung als Problem der Exegese', *Monatsschrift für Pastoraltheologie* 52, 1963, pp. 24ff.; K. Barth, *Römerbrief*, 2nd ed., 1922, p. 298 (ET p. 314): 'All that is not *hope*, is wooden, dead, hampering, as ponderous and awkward as the word reality. There there is no freedom, but only imprisonment.' E. Bloch, *Das Prinzip Hoffnung* I, 1959, p. 242: 'A fact (*factum*) is a lump of dead matter *alien to history*.'

the theophany in nature is taken merely by a theophany in history regarded as open-ended nature, or whether what is meant is the fundamentally different condition on which it becomes possible to perceive reality as history, namely, from the standpoint of promise. This theology of history as opposed to the theology of the word remains subject to Kant's critique of theological metaphysics, as long as it itself fails to undertake critical reflection on the conditions of the possibility of perceiving reality as history in the eschatological and theological sense. We are told that this 'theology of history' differs from the traditional theology of salvation history in that it seeks to be 'historically verifiable in principle'.[105] But that is just what cannot be maintained, unless and until the concept of the 'historical' is transformed and the theology of history becomes the very ground of its redefinition.

As long as this theology of history regards 'God' as the object that is in question when we enquire about the unity and wholeness of reality, then its starting point is obviously different from that of the question about God and his faithfulness to his promises in history – a question which first arises only in the context of promise and expectation, as in the Old Testament. This is certainly not to say that Pannenberg's question as to an appropriate understanding of the world on the part of theology, or a proof of its statements about God by reference to the whole of reality, is any less relevant than the question as to an appropriate self-understanding or the proving of our statements about God by reference to human existence in Bultmann. On the contrary, the 'theology of history' is a necessary supplement to the 'theology of existence'.

The conflict between a theology of revelation in terms of word and one in terms of history is irresolvable, unless and until these two end-products of abstraction from reflective philosophy are surmounted by a third view which is either comprehensive or open in character. This attempt is made in a second aspect of the development of 'revelation as history' in the concept of the *'history of tradition'*.[106] When history is regarded as the history of tradition, then we have no longer an alternative to the kerygma theology, as in the expression 'language of the facts' (which was after all

---

105 W. Pannenberg, 'Heilsgeschehen und Geschichte', *op. cit.*, p. 287.

106 This phrase is used with special emphasis in the essays by W. Pannenberg and R. Rendtorff in *Studien zur Theologie der alttestamentlichen Überlieferungen*, 1961.

intended only polemically), but we have here an attempt to bring together again the separated elements, namely, 'word', word-event, interpretation, evaluation, etc., on the one hand, and *'factum'*, facts and coherent groups of facts on the other. The theology of history with its 'language of the facts' does not mean the *bruta facta*, which present themselves to positivistic historicism as the end-products of abstraction from tradition, but means the divine 'language of the facts in that context of tradition and expectation in which the events in question take place'.[107] In this sense 'history is always also the history of tradition'.[108] 'History of tradition is in fact to be regarded as the profounder term for history as such.'[109] The events which reveal God must be taken in and with the context in tradition in which they took place and along with which alone they have their original significance. Thus when history is regarded as the history of tradition, the modern distinction between 'factuality' and 'significance' is set aside in a way analogous to that of G. Ebeling's 'theology of the word-event'. As in the latter case the events are asserted along with the word in which they were originally announced, so here the words and traditions are asserted along with the historic events.[110] The decisive question, however, is *how* the Cartesian and Kantian distinction between reality and the perception of it is overcome. If our intention is to see real events in that original context in experience and tradition in which they found expression at the time, then we can set out either hermeneutically from the word-event or in terms of universal history from the particular event in the totality of historic reality. In both cases, however, we must stand the test of that historical criticism to which the traditions are, and must be, subjected by the modern consciousness. The fact that the past encounters us in the 'language of tradition' and is accessible only therein has never been disputed. The only question has been, whether this 'language of the tradition' is 'correct' as far as the reality accessible to historical criticism is concerned. The historical criticism of the Christian traditions has ever since the Enlightenment presupposed with increasing radical-

107 W. Pannenberg, *Offenbarung als Geschichte*, p. 112.
108 *Offenbarung als Geschichte*, p. 112.
109 W. Pannenberg, *Studien zur Theologie der alttestamentlichen Über-lieferungen*, p. 139.
110 G. Ebeling, *Theologie und Verkündigung*, 1962, p. 55 (ET p. 57).

ness a crisis in the traditions, if not indeed a revolutionary break in them.[111] Since this crisis and this criticism, 'tradition' is no longer 'taken for granted'. The relationship to history as tradition has become one of reflection and has lost its immediacy. If, therefore, we would understand 'history as tradition', then we shall have to find a new concept of 'tradition', which cancels out historical criticism and its sense of the crisis in history, yet without negating or muzzling it. This problem is not solved simply by showing that in many and devious ways modern historic thinking derives by historic tradition from the historic thinking of the Bible, for of course the point is not so much the origin of the modern historical consciousness, but rather its future.

Particularly difficult from the theological standpoint is the thesis that the raising of Jesus from the dead is the historically demonstrable prolepsis, the anticipation and forestalling of the end of universal history, so that in it the totality of reality as history can be contemplated in a provisional way. The thesis that this event of the raising of Jesus must be 'historically' verifiable in principle, would require us first of all so to alter the concept of the historical that it would allow of God's raising the dead and would make it possible to see in this raising of the dead the prophesied end of history. To call the raising of Jesus historically verifiable is to presuppose a concept of history which is dominated by the expectation of a general resurrection of the dead as the end and consummation of history. Resurrection and the concept of history then contain a vicious circle for the understanding.

The important question for theology, however, is whether such an apocalyptic view of history – and, moreover, one reduced to the expectation of a general resurrection of the dead – is adequate to embrace the Easter appearance of the risen Lord in the context of tradition and expectation in which it was perceived by the disciples. If it were solely the risen 'destiny' of Jesus that constituted the forestalling of the end of all history and the anticipation of the 'destiny' still awaiting all men, then the risen Jesus himself would have no further future. Nor would it be for Jesus himself that those who know him would wait, but only for the repetition of his destiny in themselves. The Church would be waiting for that which has

---

111 Cf. J. Ritter's verdict in the discussion on J. Pieper, *Über den Begriff der Tradition* (AGFNRW 72), 1958, pp. 45ff.

already happened to Jesus to be repeated for itself, but not for the future of the risen Lord. Certain as it is that the Easter appearances of Jesus were experienced and proclaimed in the apocalyptic categories of the expectation of the general resurrection of the dead and as a beginning of the end of all history, it is nevertheless equally certain that the raising of Jesus was not merely conceived solely as the first instance of the final resurrection of the dead, but as the source of the risen life of all believers. It is not merely said that Jesus is the first to arise and that believers will attain *like him* to resurrection, but it is proclaimed that he is himself the resurrection and the life and that consequently believers find their future in him and not merely *like* him. Hence they wait for their future by waiting for his future. The horizon of apocalyptic expectation is not by any means wide enough to embrace the post-Easter apocalyptic of the Church. The place of apocalyptic self-preservation to the end is taken by the mission of the Church. That mission can be understood only when the risen Christ himself has still a future, a universal future for the nations. Only then does the Church's approach to the nations in the apostolate have any historic meaning. The apocalyptic outlook which interprets the whole of reality in terms of universal history is secondary compared with this world-transforming outlook in terms of promise and missionary history.

Finally, from the theological standpoint it may be due to the one-track character of the apocalyptic of universal history that the theological significance of the cross of Jesus recedes in favour of his resurrection. Between the expectations of late Jewish apocalyptic and of Christian eschatology stands the cross of Jesus. Hence all Christian resurrection eschatology bears the mark of an *eschatologia crucis*. That is more than merely a break in the coherent historic tradition of apocalyptic expectations. The contradiction of the cross permeates also the whole existence, life and theological thinking of the Church in the world.

If the programme of 'Revelation as History' is concerned to construct on the basis of the resurrection hope theological concepts and approaches to reality which will put an end to the above-mentioned negative alliance with the spirit of the modern age, then it is completely in accord with the demand made by Barth and Bonhoeffer that the 'lordship of Christ' must be consistently testified and presented all the way to the very heart of secular reality. Whether the statement about 'proving the divinity of the biblical God by reference to the totality of the momentary experience of reality'[112] is appropriate to this, remains the question, for that is a task which will end not so much in confirming or superseding as in conflict and divergence. The uncritical use of such terms as 'historical', 'history', 'facts', 'tradition', 'reason', etc., in a theological sense, appears to show that the methodical, practical and speculative atheism of the modern age is here circumvented rather than taken seriously. If this very atheism – as it has been most profoundly understood by Hegel and Nietzsche – derives from the nihilistic discovery made on the 'speculative Good Friday', that 'God is dead'[113] then the only real way of vindicating theology in face of this reality, in face of this reason, and in face of a society thus constituted, will be in terms of a theology of resurrection – in fact, in terms of an eschatology of the resurrection in the sense of the future of the crucified Lord. Such a theology must accept the 'cross of the present' (Hegel), its godlessness and god-forsakenness, and there give theoretical and practical proof of the 'spirit of the resurrection'. Then, however, revelation would not manifest and verify itself as history of our present society, but would disclose to this society and this age for the very first time the eschatological process of history. The theologian is not concerned merely to supply a different *interpretation* of the world, of history and of human nature, but to *transform* them in expectation of a divine transformation.

8. The Eschatology of Revelation

It is ultimately always a result of the influence of Greek methods of thought and enquiry when the revelation of God which is witnessed in the biblical scriptures is understood as 'epiphany of the eternal present'. That describes the God of Parmenides rather than the God of the exodus and the resurrection. The revelation of the risen Christ is not a form of this epiphany of the eternal present, but necessitates a view of revelation as apocalypse of the promised future of the truth. In the light of this future of the truth, manifest in the promise, man experiences reality as history in all its

---

112 *Offenbarung als Geschichte*, p. 104 n. 17, and frequently.
113 G. W. F. Hegel, *Glauben und Wissen*, ed. F. Meiner (Philosophische Bibliothek 62b), 1962, pp. 123f.

possibilities and dangers, and is broken of that fixed view of reality in which it becomes an image of the deity.

Christian theology speaks of 'revelation', when on the ground of the Easter appearances of the risen Lord it perceives and proclaims the identity of the risen one with the crucified one. Jesus is recognized in the Easter appearances as what he really was. That is the ground of faith's 'historical' remembrance of the life and work, claims and sufferings of Jesus of Nazareth. But the messianic titles, in which this identity of Jesus in cross and resurrection is claimed and described, all anticipate at the same time the not yet apparent future of the risen Lord. This means that the Easter appearances and revelations of the risen Lord are manifestly understood as foretaste and promise of his still future glory and lordship. Jesus is recognized in the Easter appearances as what he really *will be*. The 'vital point' for a Christian view of revelation accordingly lies neither in 'that which came to expression in the man Jesus' (Ebeling) nor in the 'destiny of Jesus' (Pannenberg) but – combining both of these – in the fact that in all the qualitative difference of cross and resurrection Jesus is the same. This identity in infinite contradiction is theologically understood as an event of identification, an act of the faithfulness of God. It is this that forms the ground of the promise of the still outstanding future of Jesus Christ. It is this that is the ground of the hope which carries faith through the trials of the god-forsaken world and of death.

'Revelation' in this event has not the character of *logos* determined illumination of the existing reality of man and the world, but has here constitutively and basically the character of promise and is therefore of an eschatological kind. 'Promise' is a fundamentally different thing from a 'word-event' which brings truth and harmony between man and the reality that concerns him. 'Promise' is in the first instance also a different thing from an eschatologically oriented view of reality as universal history. Promise announces the coming of a not yet existing reality from the future of the truth. Its relation to the existing and given reality is that of a specific *inadaequatio rei et intellectus*. On the other hand, it does not merely anticipate and clarify the realm of coming history and the realistic possibilities it contains. Rather, 'the possible', and therewith 'the future', arises entirely from God's word of promise and therefore goes beyond what is possible and impossible in the realistic sense. It does not illuminate a future which is always somehow already inherent in reality. Rather, 'future' is that reality which fulfils and satisfies the promise because it completely corresponds to it and accords with it. It is only in that event which is spoken of as 'new creation out of nothing', as 'resurrection of the dead', as 'kingdom' and 'righteousness' of God, that the promise contained in the resurrection of Christ finds a reality which accords with it and completely corresponds to it. The revealing of the divinity of God therefore depends entirely on the real fulfilment of the promise, as *vice versa* the fulfilment of the promise has the ground of its possibility and of its reality in the faithfulness and the divinity of God. To that extent 'promise' does not in the first instance have the function of illuminating the existing reality of the world or of human nature, interpreting it, bringing out its truth and using a proper understanding of it to secure man's agreement with it. Rather, it contradicts existing reality and discloses its own process concerning the future of Christ for man and the world. Revelation, recognized as promise and embraced in hope, thus sets an open stage for history, and fills it with missionary enterprise and the responsible exercise of hope, accepting the suffering that is involved in the contradiction of reality, and setting out towards the promised future.

This certainly does not mean that the need to attain to an appropriate understanding of existence and to find our bearings in universal history is rendered superfluous. Only both of these, the illumination of the historic character of human existence and the anticipatory illumination of contexts and prospects in terms of universal history, will have to be coordinated with the apostolic process of history which God's revelation calls to life in promise. The God-revealing event of promise can find articulated expression only in the midst of, and by reference to, the questionableness of the world as a whole and of human nature itself, but it is neither exhausted therein nor identical therewith. It takes up both into the peculiar context of its own enquiry, in which context the knowledge of the truth presents itself in the form of a question that is open towards the fulfilment of the promise.

If it is true that the appearances of the risen Lord are to be taken as a foretaste of his own future, then they are to be understood in the context of the Old Testament history of promise, and not in analogy to an epiphany of the truth in the Greek sense. The witnesses of Easter do not recognize the risen Lord in a blaze of heavenly, supra-worldly eternity, but in the foretaste and dawn of his eschatological future for the world. They do not regard him as the one who has been 'immortalized', but as the one who 'is to come'. They saw him not as what he is in timeless eternity, but as what he will be in his coming lordship. We can therefore say: the risen Lord encounters us as the living Lord, inasmuch as he is in motion, on the march towards his goal.[114] 'He is still future to himself.'[115] With the resurrection, his work is 'not yet completed, not yet concluded'.[116] These statements come from Barth's later work and show plainly the direction which the revision of his eschatology of eternity must take. The appearances of the risen Lord were recognized as the promise and anticipation of a really outstanding future. Because in these appearances a process was manifestly perceptible, they provoked testimony and mission. The future of the risen Lord is accordingly here present in promise; it is accepted in a hope that is prepared to suffer, and it is grasped by the critical mind that reflects on men and things in hope.

But what does it mean to say that the risen Lord in his revelation is the promise of his own future? It would have to mean that Jesus reveals and identifies himself as the Christ both in identity with himself and in differentiation from himself. He reveals and identifies himself as the crucified one, and to that extent in identity with himself. He reveals himself as the Lord on the way to his coming lordship, and to that extent in differentiation from what he will be. The revelation of his future in his appearances is therefore a 'hidden' one. He is the hidden Lord and the hidden Saviour. Through hope the life of believers is hidden with him in God – yet in a hiddenness that is made for future unveiling, and aims at it,

---

114 K. Barth, *Kirchliche Dogmatik* IV/3, p. 377 (ET pp. 326f.): 'He Himself encounters us here as the *living One* also in the concrete sense that ... precisely here He obviously finds Himself in *motion* or on His *way* as divine-human Mediator, *striding* from His commencement to the goal already included and indicated in it. ... As the Revealer of His work He has not yet reached His goal. He is still moving towards it. He is marching from its beginning in the revelation of *His* life to the end of His not yet accomplished revelation of the life of *all* men and *all* creation as enclosed in His life, of their life as new creation on a new earth and under a new heaven.' Whereas in Barth's doctrine of revelation the resurrection event stands under the head of the 'pure presence of God', in his doctrine of reconciliation it comes to stand under the head of 'anticipation' of the universal redemption and consummation.

115 *Ibid.*, p. 378 (ET p. 327, slightly altered).

116 *Ibid.*, p. 385 (ET p. 334).

and presses towards it. The future of Jesus Christ is in this context the revelation and manifestation of him who has come. Faith is directed in hope and expectation towards the revelation of what it has already found hidden in Christ. And yet the future of the risen Lord, that which in his resurrection is promised, intended and held in prospect, involves not merely a noetic expectation. His future is not merely the unveiling of something that was hidden, but also the fulfilment of something that was promised. The revelation in the appearances of the risen Christ has therefore to be described not only as 'hidden', but also as 'unfinished', and has to be related to a reality which is not yet here. It is still outstanding, has not yet come about, has not yet appeared, but it is promised and guaranteed in his resurrection, and indeed is given along with his resurrection as a necessary consequence: the end of death, and a new creation in which amid the life and righteousness of all things God is all in all. Thus the future of the risen Lord involves also the expectation of a creative act. The word in which this comes to expression is therefore gospel and promise in one. If 'revelation' in the context of the Easter appearances does not refer to a completed, self-contained process or to the presence of eternity, then it must be understood as an open-ended revelation that points forwards and leads forwards. This, its eschatological openness, will certainly not be filled up, carried on and completed by the subsequent Church and its history. If it is towards *his* own future and promise that the revelation of the risen Lord is open, then its openness to the future surpasses all subsequent Church history and is absolutely superior to it. The remembrance of the promise that has been given – of the promise in its givenness (*Er-gangenheit*), not in its pastness (*Ver-gangenheit*) – bores like a thorn in the flesh of every present and opens it for the future. In this sense the revelation of the risen Lord does not become 'historic' as a result of the fact that history continues willy-nilly, but it stands as a sort of *primum movens* at the head of the process of history. It is in virtue of this revelation that the reality of man and his world becomes 'historic', and it is the hope set upon this revelation that makes all reality inadequate and as such transient and surpassable. It is the *promissio inquieta* that is the true source of Augustine's *cor inquietum*. It is the *promissio inquieta* that will not suffer man's experience of the world to become a self-contained cosmic image of the deity, but keeps our experience of the world open to history.

If revelation is promise in this sense, then it has to be related to the process which is brought about by missionary enterprise. The process of witness to the eschatological hope by those who in each succeeding present have to answer for their hope, the apostolate which involves the world of the nations in this process, and the exodus from the present of a self-contained existence into the promised future – these are the things that constitute the history which 'corresponds' to this kind of revelation, because it is called to life by this revelation. Awareness of history is awareness of mission, and the knowledge of history is a transformatory knowledge.

Now this revelation of God in the event of promise can always be expressed only in relation to, and critical comparison with, man's experience of the world and of existence at any given moment. Here lies the justification for the views of revelation we have discussed, which see it in the context of the proof of God from existence or of the proof of God from the totality of reality. If God is not spoken of in relation to man's experience of himself and his world, then theology withdraws into a ghetto and the reality with which man has to do is abandoned to godlessness. Since the days of the early Christian apologists, the *promissio Dei* of which the biblical scriptures speak has always been considered in the form of the Greek *logos*. Yet it should be noted that between the two extreme possibilities of ghetto and assimilation, the *promissio Dei* has always worked as a ferment of destruction of the Greek *logos* – namely, in such a way that the illuminating truth of the Greek *logos* has been given eschatological, and therewith historic, character.

In this process, theology can give polemical and liberating proof of its truth even today. Yet it is just when we perceive the revelation of God in the promise and are thereby led to ask what light this sheds on the humanity of man and the reality of the world, that we then find ourselves in the neighbourhood of the proofs of God and of 'natural theology'.

Following an ancient definition, 'natural theology' is understood as a '*theologia naturalis, generalis et immediata*', i.e. a knowledge of God which is not mediated but given along with reality, universally accessible and immediate. To this there belonged the knowledge that the world is God's world, or that to ask about the origin or the totality of reality is to ask about God, and secondly, the knowledge of man's peculiar standing in the cosmos, a general idea that to be man is to be subject to the claims of God's law – in other words, the knowledge that the question raised in the questionableness of human existence is the question of God. Whatever the way in which these proofs of God, or indications of the question of God, were presented by Christian theology as universally accessible, they were always so presented as to provide pointers to, and suitable agreements with, the 'supernatural, special and historically mediated' knowledge of God. Whatever Western theology may have taken up and represented in this way as 'natural theology', it was never 'natural' and was neither 'universally human' nor 'immediate'. On closer inspection, 'natural theology' always contained knowledge historically mediated from particular intellectual traditions – from the Stoa, from Plato and Aristotle, etc. The common sense which was appealed to always proves to be a common sense that has developed in history and bears a Western stamp. The 'natural' element in 'natural theology' was thus not at all something that comes 'by nature', but always came from history and was an adoption of what society regarded as natural, i.e. as axiomatic. The Aristotle who was held to be the father of natural theology is no longer by any means identical with the historical Aristotle, but was an Aristotelian heritage worked over by Christian theology. What was called 'nature' and 'universal consciousness of God' in a Christian sense had always already been determined by the content for which it was supposed to provide a general framework. Thus it is true that 'natural theology' is a presupposition of the theology of revelation – in the sense that revelation first posits, creates and fashions it in its specific form. That is not by any means to put an end to the business of natural theology. On the contrary, it is a necessary part of reflection upon nature and human existence in the light of revelation. It therefore continues to be a necessary part of theology as such, if the latter would give expression to the universal sweep of the revelation of God. But as a pre-sup-*position* of theology – a position already pre-determined by theology – it belongs to the presentation of revelation's universal, eschatological outlook of expectation. In this sense H. J. Iwand's thesis is correct: 'Natural theology is not that from which we come, but the light to which we are going. The *lumen naturae* is the reflection of the *lumen gloriae*. ... The reform that is required of theology today consists in assigning revelation to this age, but natural theology to the age to come.'[117] In this sense 'natural theology' – theology of existence and theology of history – is a halo, a reflection of the future light of God upon the inadequate material of present reality,

---

117 H. J. Iwand, *Nachgelassene Werke I, Glauben und Wissen*, 1962, pp. 290f.

a foretaste and advance intimation of the promised universal glory of God, who will prove himself to all and in all to be the Lord. What is called 'natural theology' is in actual truth *theologia viatorum*, an anticipation of the promised future in history as a result of obedient thinking. Hence it always remains historic, provisional, variable and open. If it means perceiving and reflecting upon the reality in which every man stands, but doing so on the basis of faith and hope, then for that reason it does not have the appeal that its statements are 'self-evident', but it is essentially polemical or, as E. Brunner says, 'eristical'. We shall have to turn the proofs of God the other way about and not demonstrate God from the world but the world from God, not God from existence but existence from God – and that, too, in constant critical debate with other ways of asserting truth and showing the meaning of things. In this sense the work of 'natural theology' belongs not to the *praeambula fidei*, but to *fides quaerens intellectum*.

The man who is the recipient of this revelation of God in promise is identified, as what he is – and at the same time differentiated, as what he will be. He comes 'to himself' – but in hope, for he is not yet freed from contradiction and death. He finds the way of life – but hidden in the promised future of Christ that has not yet appeared. Thus the believer becomes essentially one who hopes. He is still future to 'himself' and is promised to himself. His future depends utterly and entirely on the outcome of the risen Lord's course, for he has staked his future on the future of Christ. Thus he comes into harmony with himself *in spe*, but into disharmony with himself *in re*. The man who trusts himself to the promise is of all people one who finds himself a riddle and an open question, one who becomes in his own eyes a *homo absconditus*. In pursuit of the promise, he finds he is in search of himself and comes to regard himself as an open question addressed to the future of God. Hence the man who hopes is of all people the one who does not stand harmoniously and concentrically in himself, but stands excentrically to himself in the *facultas standi extra se coram Deo*, as Luther called it. He is ahead of himself in hope in God's promise. The event of promise does not yet bring him to the haven of identity, but involves him in the tensions and differentiations of hope, of mission and of self-emptying. If revelation encounters him as promise, then it does not identify him by disregarding what is negative, but opens him to pain, patience and the 'dreadful power of the negative', as Hegel has said. It makes him ready to take the pain of love and of self-emptying upon himself in the Spirit of him who raised Jesus from the dead and who quickens the dead. 'Yet it is not the life which abhors death and keeps itself pure of corruption, but the life which endures it and maintains itself in the midst of it, that is the life of the spirit.' 'The power of the spirit is only so great as its outgoing, its depth only so deep as the extent to which in its expending it ventures to spread itself and to lose itself.'[118] Thus the promised identity of man leads into the differentiation of self-emptying. He gains himself by abandoning himself. He finds life by taking death upon him. He attains to freedom by accepting the form of a servant. That is how the truth that points forward to the resurrection of the dead comes to him.

But if the event of promise in the resurrection identifies man by leading him to the emptying of himself, this experience of self is immediately bound up with a corresponding experience of the world. Man does not gain himself by distinguishing himself from 'the world', but by emptying himself into it. But in what way must the 'world' then be experienced? It cannot be taken as a rigid cosmos of established facts and eternal laws. For where there is no longer any possibility of anything new happening, there hope also comes to an end and loses all prospect of the realizing of what it hopes for. Only when the world itself is 'full of all kinds of possibilities' can hope become effective in love. 'To hope there belongs the knowledge that in the outside world life is as unfinished as in the Ego that works in that outside world.'[119] Thus hope has the chance of a meaningful existence only when reality itself is in a state of historic flux and when historic reality has room for open possibilities ahead. Christian hope is meaningful only when the world can be changed by him in whom this hope hopes, and is thus open to that for which this hope hopes; when it is full of all kinds of possibilities (possible for God) and open to the resurrection of the dead. If the world were a self-contained system of cause and effect, then hope could either regard this world as itself the fulfilment, or else in gnostic fashion transcend and reflect itself into the supra-worldly realm. That, however, would be to abandon itself.

---

118 G. W. F. Hegel, *Phänomenologie des Geistes*, ed. J. Hoffmeister (Philosophische Bibliothek 114), 1949, pp. 29 and 15 (cf. ET by J. B. Baillie, *The Phenomenology of Miad*, 2nd ed., 1931, pp. 93 and 74).

119 E. Bloch, *Das Prinzip Hoffnung* I, 1959, p. 285.

On the ground of the promised future of the truth the world can be experienced as history. The eschatological sense of the event of promise in the resurrection of Christ awakes in remembrance and expectation our sense for history. Hence every view which sees the world as a self-contained cosmos, or history as a universal whole that contains and manifests the divine truth, is broken down and transposed into the eschatological key of 'not yet'. Our knowledge, as a knowledge of hope, has a transcendent and provisional character marked by promise and expectation, in virtue of which it recognizes the open horizon of the future of reality and thus preserves the finitude of human experience. To think God and history together on the ground of the event of promise in the resurrection of Christ, does not mean to prove God from the world or from history, but *vice versa* to show the world to be history that is open to God and to the future. Christian theology will thus not be able to come to terms with, but will have to free itself from, the cosmologico-mechanistic way of thinking such as is found in the positivistic sciences – whether in the positivism of the scientific disenchanting of the world, by which the world not only becomes 'godless', as Max Weber has said, but also becomes a world without alternatives, without possibilities and without any future, or in the factualized and institutionalized relationships of the scientific civilization of modern society, which in the same way is threatened with the loss not only of its future but of its own historic character as well. Theology will be able to free itself, however, only by breaking up this kind of thinking and these relationships and striving to set them in the eschatological movement of history. It will not be able to free itself from them by falling back upon a romanticist glorification of reality. The 'firewood' does not again become a 'forest', nor the 'tale of events' again become 'sacred history', and the traditions of the West do not again become unequivocal links in the chain of historic tradition. The experience of the world as history can hardly take the form of again considering the experience of history either in terms of fate, in that passivity in which we suffer birth and death, or in terms of chance. 'The universal endeavour of human reason is directed towards the abolition of chance', as W. Humboldt already aptly remarked. The scientific and technical efforts of the modern age have at least since the French revolution been aimed at bringing about the end of this kind of history, the end of the history of chance, of contingency, of surprise, crisis and catastrophe. To demonstrate to this increasingly rounded scientific and technical cosmos its own historic character does not mean revealing to it the critical nature of its own self, but exhibiting to it and to the men in it that history which is experienced in the light of the promised future of the truth. Both intellectual forms – the objectification of the world and the subjectivity of existence – stand in contrast to *the* history which is experienced in the light of the future of the truth. Hence for Christian theology 'history' cannot mean that it has again to proclaim the truth of God in combination with the old experiences of fate and chance, but that it has to give this world itself a place in the process that begins with the promise and is kept going by hope. The problem of history in the 'modern age' is presented not so much in terms of the difference between Greek glorification of the cosmos and the biblical hope in history, but rather in terms of the difference between a scientific and technical millenarianism, which seeks the end of history in history, on the one hand, and, on the other, an eschatology of history, which arises from the event of promise in the resurrection, and for which the 'end of history' in the 'modern age' can no more be the promised and expected end than the 'modern age' (*Neuzeit*) itself can be the 'new age' (*neue Zeit*) in the apocalyptic sense – as this expression (*Neuzeit*) was surely meant to be. Positivism, which was originally intended by Auguste Comte to have a thoroughly millenarian sense, can therefore be given historic character only by being transcended and superseded by the new expectations of an eschatological outlook. This will reveal its historic form and significance and the finitude of its epistemological horizon.

Christian theology has one way in which it can prove its truth by reference to the reality of man and the reality of the world that concerns man – namely, by accepting the questionableness of human existence and the questionableness of reality as a whole and taking them up into that eschatological questionableness of human nature and the world which is disclosed by the event of promise. 'Threatened by death' and 'subjected to vanity' – that is the expression of our universal experience of existence and the world. 'In hope' – that is manifestly the way in which Christian theology takes up these questions and directs them to the promised future of God.

II

Promise and History

If we would trace out the Old Testament's peculiarly ambiguous, unemphatic and yet widely broadcast observations on 'revelation' and turn them to good account for dogmatics, then it is not advisable to set out from the assumption that every man's existence, threatened as it is by chaos and transience, leads him to ask after 'revelation', nor yet to start with the question how the hidden God, the Origin and the Absolute, becomes manifest to men estranged from him. Rather, it is essential to let the Old Testament itself not only provide the answers, but also pose the problem of revelation, before we draw systematic conclusions. If this is to be attempted in the following pages, it is of course impossible to enter into questions of a detailed exegesis. But it will have to be a case of clarifying and defining the concepts employed in exegesis. In so doing we shall often come upon religious-historical ideas, and shall also have to employ such ideas. That, however, is not intended to imply any general religious-historical presuppositions. Our task is not to take the various religious ideas and forms of belief and subsume them under a general concept of religion. But the contours of what is meant by promise and hope stand out most clearly in face of other religions and forms of belief which are grappled with and contested, and for that reason they can best be illumined in comparison and contrast.

1. Epiphany Religions and Faith in Terms of Promise

If we ask for a summary statement of the conclusions emerging from the study of the history of religion in Israel and the surrounding oriental world, then the Old Testament materials appear from this standpoint to be 'syncretistic documents'. 'Israel achieved a syncretism between the religion of the nomad and of the Canaanite peasant. It is through this syncretism that it became what it was in classical times.[1] The term 'syncretism' here calls for further clarification. It certainly cannot mean an easy blend of disparate elements nor yet, of course, an alliance between hostile brethren against a third, common enemy, as was originally the case with the Cretans. It cannot even mean mere intermixture, but is intended to express the process of struggle between two mutually incompatible forms of faith. It is a struggle which is kindled in various historic situations by various matters about which conflict arises and, precisely from the various tensions, we are enabled to recognize the peculiarity of the contending parties. The exact nature of the two opposing sides cannot at any point be defined in spatial or temporal, and indeed hardly even in clearcut ideological terms. And yet the process of struggle is apparent at every point, both in Israel's conflict with its neighbours and also within the empirical Israel itself. It can be seen specially clearly in specific historic situations. It can also be latent for centuries and obscured to the point of being unrecognizable. While the 'peculiar religious position' of Israel can consequently hardly be stated in terms of a unique 'religion of Israel', it certainly does emerge in the fact that such a process of tense struggle pervades its whole history.

The definition of these tendencies of tension in general terms of the history of culture and of religion has to my mind been most clearly stated by Victor Maag, following Martin Buber and others. He sees the tension in the fact that in the Israel of Palestine the vectoral and kinetic elements of the old nomad religion and the static elements of the peasant religion of Canaan meet each other. 'Nomadic religion is a religion of promise. The nomad does not live within the cycle of seed-time and harvest, but in the world of migration.'[2] 'This inspiring, guiding, protecting God of the nomads differs quite fundamentally in various respects from the gods of the agrarian peoples. The gods of the nations are locally bound. The transmigration God of the nomads, however, is not bound territorially and locally. He journeys along with them, is himself on the move.'[3] The result of this is a different understanding of

---

1 V. Maag, 'Malkût Jhwh', *VT Suppl.* VII (Congress Volume: Oxford 1959), 1960, p. 137.

2 *Ibid.*, p. 140.

3 *Ibid.*, pp. 139f.

existence: 'Here existence is felt as history. This God leads men to a future which is not mere repetition and confirmation of the present, but is the goal of the events that are now taking place. The goal gives meaning to the journey and its distresses; and today's decision to trust in the call of God is a decision pregnant with future. This is the essence of promise in the light of transmigration.'[4]

No doubt Maag's view of the nomad religion of promise in contrast to the mythical and magical religion of peasant culture contains typical ideal elements, but it does make intelligible the tension in which Israel found itself, and – what is still more important – it gives significance to the question how and by what means it came about that when Israel passed from the nomadic and semi-nomadic life to the settled life of Canaan it did not, like all peoples and tribes on crossing this first cultural frontier of human life, abandon the nomad religion and the God of promise in favour of the epiphany gods that sanctify land, life and culture, but was able to take the occupation of the land and the fact of building and dwelling in the land and incorporate them in the original religion of promise as a new experience of history. The peculiar thing about the Israel of history appears to lie neither in its nomadic origin, which it had in common with others, nor in the occupation of the land and the transition to agricultural and municipal life, which it likewise had in common with others, but in the fact which causes this process of conflict and is manifested in various situations – the fact that the Israelite tribes took the wilderness God of promise with them from the wilderness along with the corresponding understanding of existence and the world, retained them in the land amid the totally new experiences of agrarian life, and endeavoured to undergo and to master the new experiences in the land in the light of the God of promise.

The process of conflict which this entailed is seen very clearly in the relationship to God, and here in turn in the ideas of the appearing and revealing of God. The oldest usage, and one presumably common to the whole orient, is found where the deity 'discloses himself'.[5] The Niphal of *ra'ah* is a *terminus technicus* for such hierophanies. These are originally bound to a specific place, which is then honoured in the cultus as a place of the divine epiphany. In

---

4 *Ibid.*, pp. 140.
5 R. Rendtorff, 'Die Offenbarungsvorstellungen im Alten Israel', in *Offenbarung als Geschichte*, 1961, pp. 23f.

Exodus 3.2 we find an expression of this kind: 'And the *mal'ak Jahwe* appeared unto him in a flame of fire out of the midst of the bush.' The land of oriental culture is full to the brim of such appearances through which places are sanctified to become places of the cultus. Stones, waters, trees, groves, mountains, etc., can become the bearers of hierophanies. There arise cult legends which provide the aetiology of such sacred places and rituals which bestow divine hallowing on the land round about and on those who dwell on it and cultivate it. Such places of the cultus are gateways, as it were, through which the gods come to hallow the land, and the men who dwell upon it experience the sanctifying of their cultivation of the land. Men thus 'live as close as possible to the gods' (M. Eliade).[6] In the cultus at the place of the hierophany their culture is secured against chaos by being anchored in the original sacred event of the cosmogony, or by being connected with the sacred centre of the world. Constructive enterprise and residential life is sanctified and protected by means of mythical, magical and ritual relationships of correspondence with the eternal, the original, the holy, and the cosmic order.

In corresponding ways time, whose passage discloses the horrors of chaos, is ordered and sanctified by means of sacred festivals which celebrate the epiphany, the arrival of the gods, and so make men 'contemporaries of the gods'. Time the destroyer is regenerated by means of periodic return to the time of the first beginning. To the sanctification conferred at the places of epiphany upon the area in which man lives and builds, menaced as it is by chaos, there corresponds the sanctification of time in the cyclic recurrence of the epiphany of the gods in times of festival.[7]

Whether men polytheistically worship a number of local deities, or pantheistically find all times and places full of the divine (Thales: πάντα πλήρη θεῶν),[8] whether the invisible, the original

---

6 M. Eliade, *The Sacred and the Profane: the Nature of Religion*, ET by W. R. Trask, 1961, pp. 24ff., 91ff.

7 W. F. Otto, *Die Gestalt und das Sein*, 1955, p. 255: 'The festival always means the return of a world hour at which the most ancient, most venerable and most glorious state is here again; a return of the golden age in which our ancestors had such close intercourse with the gods and the spirits. This is the point of festive exaltation which, wherever there are real festivals, is different from all other gravity and all other joy.'

8 On the fundamental significance of this statement for the religion and philosophy of ancient Greece, cf. W. Jaeger, *Die Theologie der frühen griech-*

divine world, becomes epiphanous through a series of intermediate authorities, whether princes set up as θεὸς ἐπιφανής or teachers and miracle-workers as θεῖος ἀνήρ, or whether this divine, absolute eternal Origin is conceived as becoming epiphanous through itself – all this makes no essential difference here, but is a continuation and sublimation of this epiphany religion which revolves around the θεὸς ἐπιφανής. This epiphany religion forms the presupposition and the abiding foundation of the natural theology of Greek philosophy of religion, and of oriental philosophies of religion. It gives rise to what is here the decisive question of the 'self-disclosing', 'appearing', 'revealing' of the divine. It is here important to see that these epiphanies have their point in themselves, in their coming about. For where they come about, there comes the hallowing of place, of time and of men in that act in which man's ever-threatened culture is granted correspondence with, and participation in, the eternal divine cosmos. The threat to human existence from the forces of chaos and of annihilation is overcome through the epiphany of the eternal present. Man's being comes into congruence with eternal being, understands itself in correspondence and participation as protected by the presence of the eternal.

Now the striking thing is, that Israel was but little concerned to understand the essential meaning of the 'appearances' of Yahweh in terms of such hallowing of places and times, but for Israel the 'appearing' of God is immediately linked up with the uttering of a word of divine promise.[9] Where Yahweh 'appears', it is manifestly not in the first instance a question of cultivating the place and time of his appearance. The point of the appearances to particular men in particular situations lies in the promise. The promise, however, points away from the appearances in which it is uttered, into the as yet unrealized future which it announces. The point

---

ischen Denker, 1953, pp. 31ff.

9 R. Rendtorff, *op. cit.*, p. 24. Likewise also W. Zimmerli, '"Offenbarung" im Alten Testament', *EvTh* 22, 1962, p. 16: 'The sacredness of a place is supposed to be legitimized through the account of the appearing of the deity at this place. Then, however, we find in the Old Testament a development in which it is increasingly only the mainstay of the ἱερὸς λόγος that remains – less and less weight attaches to the sensually perceptible appearing of Yahweh, but instead the divine word of promise is brought out ever more fully as the real content of the scenes of revelation. The emphasis is shifted away from the sensually perceptible appearance, the manifestation of Yahweh, on to the announcement of his action.'

of the appearance then lies not in itself, but in the promise which becomes audible in it, and in the future to which it points. In the various strata of the tradition of such appearances of promise, the concomitant circumstances of epiphany then actually take second place in Israel's faith to the call and the pointer to the future. With that, the concept of revelation found in the epiphany religions is transformed. It is subordinated to the event of promise. Revelation is understood from the standpoint of the promise contained in the revelation. Here Yahweh's revelation manifestly does not serve to bring the ever-threatened present into congruence with his eternity. On the contrary, its effect is that the hearers of the promise become incongruous with the reality around them, as they strike out in hope towards the promised new future. The result is not the religious sanctioning of the present, but a break-away from the present towards the future. If the mythical and magical cults of the epiphany religions have the purpose of annihilating the terrors of history by anchoring life in the original sacred event, and if in tendency they are 'anti-historical' (M. Eliade),[10] then the God who gives his promises in the event of promise is one who makes possible for the very first time the feeling for history in the category of the future, and consequently has a 'historicizing' effect.[11] This tendency to run counter to the mythical world by understanding epiphany and revelation from the standpoint of the event of promise is manifestly the reason why the words for 'revelation' are employed in the Old Testament so ambiguously and unsystematically. Yahweh is not in this sense an 'apparitional God'. The sense and purpose of his 'appearances' lies not in themselves, but in the promise and its future.

The effects of the struggle in the history of Israel between faith in terms of promise and religion in terms of epiphany have been brought out by Old Testament research at many points. Where the bands of Israel enter the land, they receive the land and the new experiences of settled life as 'fulfilment of the promise', as realization of the pledge given in the wilderness by the God of promise who had caused their fathers to journey into it. Life amid the fulness and increase of their own people is likewise understood in the

---

10 M. Eliade, *The Myth of the Eternal Return*, ET by W. R. Trask, 1955, p. 152.

11 G. von Rad, *Theologie des Alten Testamentes* II, 1960, p. 117 (ET by D. M. G. Stalker: *Old Testament Theology*, 1965, p. 104).

light of the promise. Thus the assurance of their own existence is attained through historic remembrance of the previous promise of the God who guided their nomad fathers, and the gift of land and people is seen as the visibly maintained faithfulness of Yahweh. This is an essentially different assurance of existence from what Israel found in the land and fertility cults of Palestine. Land and life are not brought into congruence with the gods by means of an epiphany religion, but are understood as a piece of history in the vast course of the history of promise.[12]

The cyclic annual festivals of nature religion which Israel found waiting for it and duly took over, are subjected to an important 'historicizing'. They are interpreted in terms of the historic data of the history of promise.[13]

The mythical and magical rituals which establish the above-mentioned relationship of correspondence between threatened human existence and the protecting divine being are 'futurized', i.e. they are interpreted in terms of the future of the divine promise. V. Maag has pointed this out in the case of the rituals of the kingdom cult of Jerusalem.[14] What by their origin were magical formulae are integrated into the divine promise for the future. The expression 'eschatology' which is employed at this point for the new sense in which the mythical and magical formulae are re-interpreted, is rightly a disputed term, since it normally means the 'last' things and not merely 'future' things. For that reason it will be better to refer to the basic character of a religion of promise. In this we could find the continuing source and driving force of such reinterpretations in these stages of the history of Israel. As it is impossible to find

---

12 W. Zimmerli, 'Verheissung und Erfüllung', *EvTh* 12, 1952, pp. 39ff.

13 G. von Rad, *op. cit.*, pp. 117ff. (ET pp. 104ff.).

14 V. Maag, *op. cit.*, p. 150: 'When the ritual of Jerusalem spoke of the king who would bring world peace, then the heart of the former nomad still heard this in the categories of expectation and understood it in the same way as the ancestral promises. Thus what was by origin a magical formula became a divine promise for the future.' His observation on p. 114 is also interesting: 'What order is in this world, was settled by the cosmogonic gods once for all at the start. The myth and ritual of the New Year festival provide the most forceful sanction conceivable for what has positive existence and validity in state and society. This static positivism knows no new horizons towards which a people could be led, no God who is on the way to letting men see what they have never yet seen. ... To a positivism of this kind, however, Yahweh never really submitted, even though court and temple circles naturally also tried to impose it on him.'

the source of 'eschatology' in the empty heart that has experienced disappointment with cult and ritual, so it is equally impossible to speak of eschatology of the nomads. But it might well be that the faith which lives in terms of promise could prove to be the *primum movens* which enabled Israel, or at least specific circles in the empirical Israel, to master the situations of the land settlement and later to master the situations of world history. The whole force of promise, and of faith in terms of promise, is essentially to keep men on the move in a tense *inadaequatio rei et intellectus* as long as the *promissio* which governs the *intellectus* has not yet found its answer in reality. It is in promise, which keeps the hoping mind in a 'not yet' which transcends all experience and history, that we find the ground for the breakdown of the mythical and magical relations of correspondence, for the 'historicizing' of the nature festivals in terms of the data of the history of promise, and for the futurizing of their content in terms of the future of the promise. It is from promise that there arises that element of unrest which allows of no coming to terms with a present that is unfulfilled. Under the guiding star of promise this reality is not experienced as a divinely stabilized cosmos, but as history in terms of moving on, leaving things behind and striking out towards new horizons as yet unseen. The real question now is whether and how experiences of a new kind in the occupation of the land and later in the conflicts of world history are mastered by faith in the promise, how they are incorporated into the promise that transcends every present, and how the promise is expounded and unravelled in these experiences.

2. The Word of Promise

If in the word promise we have before us a key-word of Israel's 'religion of expectation', then it must now be explained what we have to understand by 'promise' and more specifically by the 'promise of (the guide-)God'.[15]

(*a*) A promise is a declaration which announces the coming of a reality that does not yet exist. Thus promise sets man's heart on a future history in which the fulfilling of the promise is to be expected. If it is a case of a divine promise, then that indicates that

---

15 For the expression 'guide-God' cf. M. Buber, *Konigtum Gottes*, 2nd ed., 1936, p. xi; *The Prophetic Faith*, ET by C. Witton Davies, 1949, p. 10.

the expected future does not have to develop within the framework of the possibilities inherent in the present, but arises from that which is possible to the God of the promise. This can also be something which by the standard of present experience appears impossible.[16]

(b) The promise binds man to the future and gives him a sense for history. It does not give him a sense for world history in general, nor yet for the historic character of human existence as such, but it binds him to its own peculiar history. Its future is not the vague goal of possible change, nor the hope aroused by the idea of possible change; it is not openness towards coming events as such. The future which it discloses is made possible and determined by the promised fulfilment. It is in the first instance always a question here of Buber's 'hopes of history'. The promise takes man up into its own history in hope and obedience, and in so doing stamps his existence with a historic character of a specific kind.

(c) The history which is initiated and determined by promise does not consist in cyclic recurrence, but has a definite trend towards the promised and outstanding fulfilment. This irreversible direction is not determined by the urge of vague forces or by the emergence of laws of its own, but by the word of direction that points us to the free power and the faithfulness of God. It is not evolution, progress and advance that separate time into yesterday and tomorrow, but the word of promise cuts into events and divides reality into one reality which is passing and can be left behind, and another which must be expected and sought. The meaning of past and the meaning of future comes to light in the word of promise.

(d) If the word is a word of promise, then that means that this word has not yet found a reality congruous with it, but that on the contrary it stands in contradiction to the reality open to experience now and heretofore. It is only for that reason that the word of promise can give rise to the doubt that measures the word by the standard of given reality. And it is only for that reason that this word can give rise to the faith that measures present reality by the standard of the word. 'Future' is here a designation of that reality in which the word of promise finds its counterpart, its answer and its fulfilment, in which it discovers or creates a reality which accords with it and in which it comes to rest.

---

16 For what follows cf. the definitions of promise by W. Zimmerli, 'Verheissung und Erfüllung', *EvTh* 12, 1952, pp. 38ff.

(e) The word of promise therefore always creates an interval of tension between the uttering and the redeeming of the promise. In so doing it provides man with a peculiar area of freedom to obey or disobey, to be hopeful or resigned. The promise institutes this period and obviously stands in correspondence with what happens in it. This, as W. Zimmerli has illuminatingly pointed out, distinguishes the promise from the prophecies of a Cassandra and differentiates the resulting expectation of history from belief in fate.[17]

(f) If the promise is not regarded abstractly apart from the God who promises, but its fulfilment is entrusted directly to God in his freedom and faithfulness, then there can be no burning interest in constructing a hard and fast juridical system of historic necessities according to a schema of promise and fulfilment – neither by demonstrating the functioning of such a schema in the past nor by making calculations for the future. Rather, the fulfilments can very well contain an element of newness and surprise over against the promise as it was received. That is why the promise also does not fall to pieces along with the historical circumstances or the historical thought forms in which it was received, but can transform itself – by interpretation – without losing its character of certainty, of expectation and of movement. If they are God's promises, then God must also be regarded as the subject of their fulfilment.

(g) The peculiar character of the Old Testament promises can be seen in the fact that the promises were not liquidated by the history of Israel – neither by disappointment nor by fulfilment – but that on the contrary Israel's experience of history gave them a constantly new and wider interpretation. This aspect comes to light when we ask how it came about that the tribes of Israel did not proceed to change their gods on the occupation of the promised land, but the wilderness God of promise remained their God in Canaan. Actually, the ancestral promises are fulfilled in the occupation of the land and the multiplication of the people, and the wilderness God of promise makes himself superfluous to the extent that his promises pass into fulfilment. The settled life to which they have attained in the land has little more to do with the God of promise on the journey through the wilderness. For the mastering of the agrarian

---

17 W. Zimmerli, *op. cit.*, p. 44.

culture the local gods are to hand. It could of course be said that the ancestral promises regarding the land have now been fulfilled and liquidated but that, for example, the promises of guidance and protection for the hosts of Israel in the holy wars continue and are still live issues. But it could also be said that the God who is recognized in his promises remains superior to any fulfilment that can be experienced, because in every fulfilment the promise, and what is still contained in it, does not yet become wholly congruent with reality and thus there always remains an overspill. The fulfilments in the occupation of the land do not fulfil the promise in the sense that they liquidate it like a cheque that is cashed and lock it away among the documents of a glorious past. The 'fulfilments' are taken as expositions, confirmations and expansions of the promise. The greater the fulfilments become, the greater the promise obviously also becomes in the memory of the expositor at the various levels of the tradition in which it is handed down. There is no trace here of what could be called the 'melancholy of fulfilment'. This peculiar fact of the promise that goes on beyond experiences of fulfilment could also be illustrated by the traces the promise leaves in the hopes and desires of men. It is ultimately not the delays in the fulfilment and in the parousia that bring men disappointment. 'Disappointing experiences' of this kind are superficial and trite and come of regarding the promise in legalistic abstraction apart from the God who promises. On the contrary, it is every experience of fulfilment which, to the extent that we reflect on it as an experience behind us, ultimately contains a disappointment. Man's hopes and longings and desires, once awakened by specific promises, stretch further than any fulfilment that can be conceived or experienced. However limited the promises may be, once we have caught in them a whiff of the future, we remain restless and urgent, seeking and searching beyond all experiences of fulfilment, and the latter leave us an aftertaste of sadness. The 'not yet' of expectation surpasses every fulfilment that is already taking place now. Hence every reality in which a fulfilment is already taking place now, becomes the confirmation, exposition and liberation of a greater hope. If we would use this as a help towards understanding the 'expanding and broadening history of promise',[18] if we ask the reason for the abiding overplus of promise as compared with history, then we

---

18 G. von Rad, 'Typologische Auslegung des Alten Testamentes', *EvTh* 12, 1952, pp. 25f.

must again abandon every abstract schema of promise and fulfilment. We must then have recourse to the theological interpretation
of this process: the reason for the overplus of promise and for the
fact that it constantly overspills history lies in the inexhaustibility
of the God of promise, who never exhausts himself in any historic
reality but comes 'to rest' only in a reality that wholly corresponds
to him.[19]

3. The Experience of History

Beneath the star of the promise of God it becomes possible to
experience reality as 'history'. The stage for what can be experienced, remembered and expected as 'history' is set and filled,
revealed and fashioned, by promise.

The promises of God disclose the horizons of history – whereby
'horizon', as it is aptly put by H. G. Gadamer, is not to be understood
as 'a rigid boundary', but as 'a thing towards which we are moving,
and which moves along with us'.[20] Israel lived within these moving
horizons of promise and experienced reality within the fields of
tension they involve. Even when the period of nomadic wanderings
ended in Palestine, this mode of experiencing, remembering and
expecting reality as history still remained and characterized this
people's wholly peculiar relation to time. The realm of Palestinian
culture did not turn time for them into a figure of cyclic recurrence, but on the contrary, a historic experience of time repeatedly
asserted itself prevailingly over an unhistoric experience of space
and turned the occupied areas (bewohnte Räume) of the land into
temporal periods (Zeiträume) of an all-embracing history.

What could here be experienced as 'history' in the potential
changes of reality always reached as far as the promises of God
stretched men's memories and expectations. 'Israel's history
existed only in so far as God accompanied her, and it is only this
time-span which can properly be described as her history.'[21] This

---

19 G. von Rad, 'Es ist noch eine Ruhe vorhanden dem Volke Gottes' (1933)
in Ges. Studien zum Alten Testament (Theologische Bücherei 8), pp. 101ff. (ET:
'There Remains Still a Rest for the People of God', The Problem of the Hexa-
tauch and Other Essays, 1966, pp. 94ff.).

20 H. G. Gadamer, Wahrheit und Methode, 1960, pp. 231f., 286ff.

21 G. von Rad, Theologie des Alten Testamentes II, 1960, p. 120 (ET p. 106).

fact of God's accompanying his people, however, was always seen within the area of tension between a manifest promise on the one hand and the expected redeeming of this promise on the other. It was within the span of this tension that history became of interest to Israel. 'Only where Yahweh had revealed himself in his word and acts did history exist for Israel.'[22] This means, however, that the experience of reality as history was made possible for Israel by the fact that God was revealed to Israel in his promises and that Israel saw the revealing of God again and again in the uttering of his promises.

Now, if events are thus experienced within the horizon of remembered and expected promises, then they are experienced as truly 'historic' events. They do not then have only the accidental, individual and relative character which we normally ascribe to historic events, but then they have always at the same time also an unfinished and provisional character that points forwards. Not only words of promise, but also the events themselves, in so far as they are experienced as 'historic' events within the horizon of promise and hope, bear the mask of something that is still out-standing, not yet finalized, not yet realized. 'Here everything is in motion, the accounts never balance, and fulfilment unexpectedly gives rise in turn to another promise of something greater still. Here nothing has its ultimate meaning in itself, but is always an earnest of something still greater.'[23] The overspill of promise means that the facts of history can never be regarded as processes complete in themselves which have had their day and can manifest their own truth by themselves. They must be understood as stages on a road that goes further and elements in a process that continues. Hence the events that are 'historically' remembered in this way do not yet have their ultimate truth in themselves, but receive it only from the goal that has been promised by God and is to be expected from him. Then, however, the events that are thus experienced as 'his-toric' events give a foretaste of the promised future. The overspill of promise means that they have always a provisional character. They contain the note of '*provisio*', i.e. they intimate and point forward

---

22 G. von Rad, 'Offene Fragen im Umkreis einer Theologie des Alten Testa-mentes', *TLZ* 88, 1963, col. 409.
23 G. von Rad, 'Typologische Auslegung', *op. cit.*, p. 29, cf. also p. 30: 'Thus in the presentation of a fact there is very often something that transcends what actually happened.'

to something which does not yet exist in its fulness in themselves. Hence the history that is thus experienced and transmitted forces every new present to analysis and to interpretation. Events that have been experienced in this way 'must' be passed on, because in them something is seen which is determinative also for future generations. They cast their shadow, or shed their light, on the way ahead. On the other hand they may also be freely interpreted and actualized by each new present, since they are never so firmly established that we could restrict ourselves merely to ascertaining what they once were.[24]

The ancient historic traditions give expression to experiences which Israel had of its God and his promises. But if these promises reach out into that future which is still ahead of the present, then the historic narratives concerned cannot merely narrate experiences of the past. Rather, the whole narrative and representation of this past will lead us to open ourselves and our present to that same future. The reality of history (*Wirklichkeit der Geschichte*) is narrated within the horizon of the history of the working (*Wirkungsgeschichte*) of God's promises. The stories of Israelite history – the histories of the patriarchs, of the wilderness, of David – are treated as themes pregnant with future. Even where the historic tradition passes over into legendary tradition, the peculiarly Israelite tradition is still dominated by the hopes and expectations kindled by Yahweh's promises. Since the history that was once experienced contains an element that transcends history in its pastness and is pregnant with future, and to the extent that this is so, two things follow: first, this history must again and again be recalled and brought to mind in the present, and secondly, it must be so expounded to the present that the latter can derive from history an understanding of itself and its future path and can also find its own place in the history of the working of God's promises.

The peculiarity of Israelite accounts of history as 'historiography conditioned by faith in the promise'[25] is particularly outstanding in comparison with the accounts of history in other peoples and other religions. 'In the Greek and Roman mythologies, the past is re-presented as an everlasting foundation. In the Hebrew and

---

24 On this point cf. H. W. Wolff, 'Das Geschichtsverständnis der alttestamentlichen Prophetie', *EvTh* 20, 1960, pp. 218ff., and G. von Rad's comment in 'Offene Fragen', *op. cit.*, pp. 413f.

25 W. Zimmerli, 'Verheissung und Erfüllung', *op. cit.*, p. 50.

Christian view of history the past is a promise to the future; consequently, the interpretation of the past becomes a prophecy in reverse.'[26]

The history of Israel shows again and again that the promises to which Israel owes its existence prove amid all the upheavals of history to be a *continuum* in which Israel was able to recognize the faithfulness of its God.[27] It could perhaps be said that the promises enter into fulfilment in events, yet are not completely resolved in any event, but there remains an overspill that points to the future. That is why reality, as it comes and is awaited and as it passes and is left behind, is experienced as history, and not as a cosmic and ever-recurring constant. It is experienced not in the epiphany of the eternal present, but in expectation of the manifestation and fulfilment of a promised future. That is why the present itself, too, is not the present of the Absolute – a present with which and in which we could abide – but is, so to speak, the advancing front line of time as directed purposefully towards its goal in the moving horizon of promise. If the promise of God is the condition on which it becomes possible to have historic experience of reality, then the language of historic facts is the language of promise – otherwise events can be called neither 'historic' nor 'eloquent'. The promises of God initiate history for Israel and retain the control in all historic experiences.

Where we abstract from the process of promise, historic events are robbed of the outlook that makes them 'historic'. Where the promises lose their power and significance as initiators of history, there the events of history are rounded off, as it were, to become facts of the past, processes complete in themselves. They are then treated and presented in the light of other outlooks. Where God's revelation is no longer seen in promise and mission, we can, for example, reflect upon the eternal, immortal and absolute being of the Deity. Then historic events belong within the sphere of transience. They are then no longer provisional events that point to the future of promise, but transient and relative events that reflect the eternal intransience of the Deity. Then there can in principle be 'nothing new under the sun'. A history of such facts can then be contemplated as a succession of completed processes, a series of images of eternal ideas. In what they have been, we then seek to discover eternal Being. In their coherent working we then seek to

---

26 K. Löwith, *Meaning in History*, 1949, p. 6.
27 H. W. Wolff, 'Das Kerygma des Jahwisten', *EvTh* 24, 1964, p. 97.

discover eternal laws. We have then, however, to look around for other conditions for the possibility of perceiving reality as history. Yet here the question constantly arises, whether this other picture of history and the designations derived from it are really adequate to the understanding of history in a historic sense and can stand theological and philosophical comparison with Israel's experience of history, conditioned as it was by faith in the promise and determined by hope.

The very use of the term 'fact', 'divine fact of history', is incapable of expressing what Israel experienced in history. For this term implies a concept of being, of absoluteness, of immutability and finality, which refuses to be combined with promise, hope and future, and therefore also with 'history'.[28]

Now it has also been observed that very many of the prophets' words about the future, especially their political predictions, did not come to pass in the way they were originally meant, and that history has thus outrun, and thereby antiquated, many words of promise. And this has been made a reason for no longer understanding history from the standpoint of promise but seeing in history a reality which overreaches these words of promise. 'History has outrun the words.'[29] Is it possible where the Old Testament is concerned to speak in principle of 'history's remaining short of the promise',[30] and thus of expectations which again and again transcend the new situations of history and make them 'historic', or does 'history outrun the promises' and does the consciousness of Israel already show some indication of a view of history that no

---

28 The use of the expression 'divine fact of history' in G. von Rad's *Theologie des Alten Testamentes* is at many points unclear and allows manifold interpretations. If according to vol. I, p. 112 (ET p. 106) the 'faith of Israel is fundamentally grounded in a theological view of history', i.e. 'it knows itself founded on facts of history and knows itself fashioned and refashioned by facts in which it saw the hand of Jahweh at work', then it is surely, as von Rad himself goes on to emphasize, the 'faith of Israel' for which these 'facts' are pregnant with future because of the divine promises in which they are interwoven – it is not such an understanding of the facts as results from critical historical examination. If according to vol. II, p. 117 (ET p. 104) the 'historic acts by which Jahweh founded the community are absolute', then this surely means that because they have the character of promise they overreach their temporal transience and move into the future – it does not mean absoluteness in the sense of intransience.

29 T2 W. Pannenberg, *Offenbarung als Geschichte*, postscript to the 2nd ed., p. 132.

30 W. Zimmerli, '"Offenbarung" im Alten Testament', *EvTh* 22, 1962, p. 31.

longer has promise, hope and mission for the future as the condition that makes it possible?

Now it is certain that apart from the promises that fell by the way in the course of history, there are also and above all others to which Israel owed its existence as 'Israel' in a theological and a historic sense, in the constant recalling of which and the ever new embracing and interpretation of which Israel consequently found its identity and continuity. These include not only the 'basic promises' of Exodus and the Sinaitic covenant – 'I am the Lord thy God'[31] – but for example also the promises to Abraham.[32] It cannot be said that mummified formulae of promise were capable of mastering new experiences of history, neither can it be said that some kind of numinous history as it ran mysteriously on rendered the promises obsolete. The process of word and history surely went on in such a way that men were neither concerned to discover from history the formal confirmation of the ancient promises, nor yet to take the promises merely as interpretations of history. Rather, the really new experiences, such as the occupation of Canaan and then later on the collapse of the kingdom, could be taken as explications of the traditional promises by means of new acts of Yahweh, and the new events could be understood in the light of the attested promise of Yahweh's faithfulness. Thus we find promise and history in a process of transformation, in which the traditional accounts of the promises took their place in the mastering of the new experiences of history, while the new experiences of history were understood as transformations and expositions of the promises. The result of these processes of transformation, however, was never the emergence of views of history that were no longer based on promises and no longer bound to them. Never did men reflect on the overwhelming power of history and the powerlessness of the out-dated promises, and abandon the rest of the future to other powers than the God of promise. The tension of promise and fulfilment was not left behind by the simple progress of Israel's history, but was much more strongly creative of Israel's historic progress. As a result of those experiences of history for which the old election traditions were no match, the tension was actually heightened in the prophets. Only, this tension which has its origin in promise and its goal in fulfilment must not be represented in too schematic

---

31 Thus F. Baumgärtel, *Verheissung*, 1952, p. 133.
32 H. W. Wolff, 'Das Kerygma des Jahwisten', *op. cit.*, pp. 95ff.

a form. Between promise and fulfilment there is a whole variety of intermediate links and processes, such as exposition, development, validation, assertion, renewal, etc. Between promise and fulfilment stretches the process of the history of the working of the word – an event of tradition, in which the promise is transmitted to coming generations in interpreted and actualized form, and every new present is exposed to the promised future in hope and obedience. This event of tradition, which creates continuity amid the changes of history, cannot already be taken in itself as a profounder concept of history. The process of tradition, in which we recall history and undergo new historic experiences, is understandable only in the light of the *tradendum* or object to be transmitted – viz., the promise and the future prospect it implies for events.

4. Revelation and Knowledge of God

How does God become knowable, if his revelations are essentially promises which open up new, historic and eschatological horizons for the future? How have we to understand the revelation of God, if election, covenant, promise and mission belong not merely accidentally but essentially to the event of revelation?

For W. Zimmerli,[33] revelation means 'self-presentation', 'self-representation' and 'self-disclosure' of God. This, he finds, is indicated by the recurring formula, 'And they shall know that I am Yahweh.'[34] In the strangely awkward formulation of this statement about the knowledge of God, the place of the object is taken by a noun clause in which Yahweh's 'I' appears as subject. This means that knowledge of God is related not to a predicable object (he – Yahweh), but manifestly to an event of revelation in which Yahweh remains the subject even of the process of knowing. Zimmerli accordingly, calls the stereotype phrase '*ani Yahweh*' a 'formula of self-presentation' and finds in it the standard view of revelation in the Old Testament.

But (1) how does he understand and interpret the exegetical findings in regard to this constantly recurring formula? This self-disclosure of

---

33 Cf. W. Zimmerli, *Gottes Offenbarung. Gesammelte Aufsätze* (Theologische Bücherei 19), 1963, and his essay '"Offenbarung" im Alten Testament' in *EvTh* 22, 1962, pp. 15–31.
34 *Gottes Offenbarung*, p. 16.

Yahweh is a 'word of revelation in which the "I" discloses itself in its "I"-character'.[35] 'Self-presentation' means 'emergence in the unmistakably unique "I"-mystery expressed in the proper name.'[36] 'A hitherto unnamed person emerges from his unknownness by making it possible to know and name him by his own name. The emphasis lies on the naming of Yahweh's proper name, which contains within it the whole fulness and glory of him who here names himself.'[37] In the proper name declared by his own self lies the guarantee that the 'I' is this unmistakably individual person.[38] The declaring of the name is – as also in profane analogies: 'I am Joseph', 'I am David' – not a predicative statement but an act of self-disclosure, 'a thoroughly personal event'.[39] It is 'God proclaiming himself' in his name as subject.[40]

(2) With this personalistic understanding of the self-revelation of God, what is the meaning of 'history'? History is then a 'creaturely tool in the free hand of God',[41] the 'place of the knowledge of God',[42] the 'place where the truth of his word of revelation becomes knowable in its execution'.[43] Events, where Yahweh appoints speakers to proclaim the name of Yahweh over them, can become 'address in bodily form' to man. Then they become events which seek to be heard in our own day as a summons in the name of Yahweh and to be answered in obedience.[44] History is then 'a penultimate thing' and has only a 'subservient function' as compared with the personal self-demonstration of Yahweh.[45]

(3) What is then the goal of the promises of God? If his self-revelation is understood in such personal terms, then the things announced in the promises obviously lose their importance. 'Rather, this formula (viz., the formula of self-presentation) brings out how completely the material content is swallowed up by the sole emergence of the "I".'[46] 'Yahweh himself is the future of which the prophets speak.'[47] 'Everything that Yahweh has to tell his people and to announce to them appears as a

---

35 '"Offenbarung" im AT', op. cit., p. 22.
36 Ibid., p. 21.
37 Gottes Offenbarung, p. 11.
38 '"Offenbarung" im AT', op. cit., p. 21.
39 Gottes Offenbarung, p. 124.
40 Ibid., p. 126.
41 '"Offenbarung" im AT', op. cit., p. 28.
42 Ibid., p. 29.
43 Gottes Offenbarung, p. 22.
44 '"Offenbarung" im AT', op. cit., pp. 28f.
45 Ibid., p. 29.
46 Ibid., p. 21.
47 'Verheissung und Erfüllung', EvTh 12, 1952, p. 44.

development of the basic declaration: I am Yahweh.'[48] The history of the promise then serves towards ever profounder knowledge of God on man's part.

Here several questions arise. With these personalistic descriptions of the revelation of God, which doubtless bring out the indisputable lordship of God even in the process of knowing, is it possible to avoid a transcendental misunderstanding of the self-revelation of God?

If the words of promise are the real content of the Old Testament scenes of revelation, can we then turn things the other way round and make the personal epiphany of Yahweh as Subject the real content of the scenes that constitute the history of the promise? If the revelation of God is understood in such a personal way, why *must* the self-presentation of Yahweh find its explication in the word of promise? But if promise is constitutive for the revealing of Yahweh, does the formula of self-presentation not then contain more than merely a self-disclosing of the mystery of a person – namely, a pledge of faithfulness which points to events to come?[49] Then, however, the history instituted by the promise of Yahweh and by his oath of faithfulness would not be in itself indifferent – the mere place and material for the knowledge of God. Then the name of Yahweh would not merely disclose the secret of his person, but would at the same time also be a name of pilgrimage and a name of promise, which shows what can be relied upon in the darkness of the future. All this Zimmerli says as well,[50] but the personalistic descriptions of the self-revelation of God seem to stand in a certain tension with the recognized theological significance of the promise. Revelation of Yahweh surely stands not only at the beginning of the history of promise, with the result that the promises and commandments are given in his 'name', but there is revelation also in that future to which the promises point and towards which the commandments set us on the way. There, however, it is not only the personal name of Yahweh that will be revealed, but his divinity and glory will be revealed in all lands, so that the ancient promise 'I am Yahweh' will be

---

48 *Gottes Offenbarung*, p. 20.

49 *Gottes Offenbarung*, p. 21, cf. also pp. 100f.

50 '"Offenbarung" im AT', *op. cit.*, p. 19: 'God thereby enters into, and speaks from within, this history whose further future is made visible in the promises that then follow.' *Gottes Offenbarung*, pp. 100f.: 'Rather, the announcing of the name leads on immediately to Yahweh's promise that it is his will to have historic dealings with Israel. Consequently if we would know Yahweh in his name, then it is not a matter of hearing secret things from the dark background of this name, but of paying attention to the historic acts towards Israel (Yahweh, "your God") of the one who thus reveals himself in his name.'

fulfilled in the 'kabod Yahweh', the glory of God, that fulfils all things. But then the things announced in the promises become identical with the fact that the one and only divinity of God is glorified in all things. That 'Yahweh himself' is the future of which the prophets speak, would then have to mean that the whole creation is made good and comes to its own in his all-embracing lordship, his peace and his righteousness as an event that is really to be expected. This, however, can hardly be stated in terms of a personalistic, or indeed transcendental, concept of revelation.

In objection to Zimmerli's view of revelation R. Rendtorff has pointed out that Zimmerli himself says of Exodus 3: 'By pointing back to things already known, or to earlier events, God presents himself as the one who is known.'[51] It is not an unknown God who emerges from his unknownness in naming his name, but 'the same' who was with the fathers. Hence for Rendtorff the real God-revealing factor lies in the reference back to previous and already known history. 'The God who here speaks is he who has hitherto already given repeated proof of his power.[52] 'Thus men's eyes are directed towards coming events; but by being combined with the reference back to the previous action of the God of their fathers, the event which is expected in the future is given its place in the whole history of this God hitherto.'[53] Thus for Rendtorff it is from the complex of the history wrought by him that God becomes manifest, knowable and predicable. Through his historic acts he is known to anyone who looks at events themselves with open eyes. The 'events themselves' can and should produce knowledge of Yahweh in those who see them. Hence the formula 'I am Yahweh' especially when attention is paid to the active verbs which are always combined with it in the subordinate clauses, cannot be taken merely as a formula of personal self-presentation, but is rather a pregnant expression for Yahweh's claim to power as manifested in events. 'Yahweh' would accordingly be not a proper name that reveals the mystery of his 'I', but a divine predicate that is arrived at from the experience of history and is synonymous with 'the mighty one'. It is not the name that is the object of knowledge, but the claim to power contained in it. Yahweh is revealed through his acts in history. 'The aim of this whole history is thus to bring about knowledge of Yahweh, knowledge of the fact that he alone is God and has power.'[54] Our question as to the

---

51 *Offenbarung als Geschichte*, p. 33.
52 *Ibid.*
53 *Ibid.*, pp. 33f.
54 *Ibid.*, p. 36.

full self-revelation of God is answered in the Old Testament by the expression 'kabod Yahweh'. The glory of Yahweh is revealed in historic acts to which Israel looks back. The prophets expect it to be ushered in by a future event. Then all peoples will themselves know the glory of Yahweh.

Here history has not merely the function of serving the personal encounter with God, but history 'itself' is revealing. Yahweh is recognizable as 'the mighty one' in the mirror of his historic acts. The historic connection between God's new action and his action hitherto makes God's divinity recognizable. If, however, history itself is understood in this way as indirect self-revelation of God, then the place of the cosmos as a theophany is obviously taken by history as a theophany.[55] This leads perforce to the idea that the one God can be indirectly known in the unity of universal history as seen from its end. But now, in the Old Testament practice of referring back new revelations of God to things already known, it is not a case of arguing back from effect to cause or from the act to the doer, but it is a question of recognizing again that God is the same God all the way from promise to fulfilment: 'Ye shall know that I, Yahweh, have spoken it, and performed it' (Ezek. 37.14). The promise that was given is remembered where the faithfulness of Yahweh is revealed in the event. So also the future kabod Yahweh, which will reveal the divinity of God to all peoples, is no event without a witness, but Israel is appointed 'for a witness to the peoples' (Isa. 55.4). It is not that consummated history reveals God, but God's universal revelation in the coming of the fulness of his glory brings history to its consummation. Despite these objections, however, we must hold fast to Rendtorff's extension of Zimmerli's concept of revelation: 'God himself' cannot merely mean God in person, God in the mystery of his 'I', but must always also mean God as God and Lord, God in the mystery of his lordship. Where God himself is revealed, there his lordship and his power are revealed, and his lordship and power are revealed where his promises of blessing, peace and righteousness are fulfilled by him himself. To know 'I am Yahweh' and to know his glory which comes to pass, are one and the same thing.

If we are prepared to understand divine revelation and the knowledge of God within the horizon of history as the sphere of promise, then we shall be able to reach the following conclusions:

---

55 Cf. pp. 77f. above.

1. God reveals himself as 'God' where he shows himself as the same and is thus known as the same. He becomes identifiable where he identifies himself with himself in the historic act of his faithfulness. The presupposition for the knowledge of God is the revealing of God by God. To that extent God remains Subject and Lord even of the process of man's knowing. Man's knowing is responsible knowing. But if the revelations of God are promises, then God 'himself' is revealed where he 'keeps covenant and faithfulness for ever' (Ps. 146.6). Where God, in his faithfulness to a promise he has given, stands to that which he has promised to be, he becomes manifest and knowable as the selfsame Self. 'God himself' cannot then be understood as reflection on his transcendent 'I-ness', but must be understood as his selfsame-ness in historic faithfulness to his promises. If God confesses to his covenant and promises in adopting, confirming, renewing, continuing and fulfilling them, then God confesses to God, then he confesses to himself. In proving his faithfulness in history, he reveals himself. For the essence and the identity of the God of promise lies not in his absoluteness over and beyond history, but in the constancy of his freely chosen relation to his creatures, in the constancy of his electing mercy and faithfulness. Hence knowledge of God comes about not in view of a transcendent Super-Ego, nor yet in view of the course of an obscure history, but in view of the historic action of God within the horizon of the promises of God. God reveals himself in his name, which discloses the mystery of his Person to the extent that it discloses the mystery of his faithfulness. The name of God is a name of promise, which promises his presence on the road on which we are set by promise and calling. The name of God and the promises contained in the name of God are therefore not only formulae of self-presentation, but they also tell us something 'about' God, for in them he gives surety for his future. They tell us who he will be. They tell us that he will be found on the road his promises point to the future, and where he will be found on that road. That is why the revelation of God and the corresponding knowledge of God are always bound up with the recounting and recalling of history and with prophetic expectation. These two things are not merely developments of his self-revelation, but are obviously a constitutive part of the revelation of his faithfulness and sameness and uniqueness.

Martin Buber has declared: 'It may be claimed to be a fundamental principle of the history of religion that experience of God begins with the experience of a single phenomenon, but knowledge of God begins with the identification of two, i.e. cognition begins with re-cognition.'[56] This is to my mind a specifically Old Testament thought. To know God means to re-cognize him. But to re-cognize him is to know him in his historic faithfulness to his promises, to know him therein as the selfsame Self and therefore to know himself. The identifying of two experiences is possible only where there is self-identification, or the revelation of historic faithfulness, because this God guarantees his promises by his name.

2. If knowledge of God is a re-cognizing of God, because revelation of God means that God confesses to God in historic faithfulness to his promises, then it can hardly be said that the historic complex of particular historic events 'itself' reveals God. But the history of promise, i.e. the history initiated by promise and covenant and expected as a result of them, does reveal the faithfulness of God to the extent that in it he keeps faith with his promises and thereby remains true to himself. It would again be taking over the Greek concept of knowledge, if we were to say that knowledge of God would always be possible only *a posteriori* on the ground of fulfilled promises if it is in the historic issue that the God of promise proves himself to be the God who gives a successful issue to his prophets. God is not first known at the end of history, but in the midst of history while it is in the making, remains open and depends on the play of the promises. That is why this knowledge must constantly remain mindful of the promises that have been issued and of the past exercise of God's faithfulness, and at the same time be a peculiarly hopeful knowledge. It must be a knowledge that does not merely reflect past history – as a mental picture of completed facts of history – but it must be an interested knowledge, a practical knowledge, a knowledge that is upheld by confidence in the promised faithfulness of God. To know God is to suffer God, says an old adage. But to suffer means to be changed and transformed. Knowledge of God is then an anticipatory knowledge of the future of God, a knowledge of the faithfulness of God which is upheld by the hopes that are called to life by his promises. Knowledge of God is then a knowledge that draws us onwards – not upwards – into situations that are not yet finalized but still outstanding. It is a knowledge not of the looks of past history, but of the outlooks

---

56 M. Buber, *Königtum Gottes*, 2nd ed. 1936, p. xliii.

involved in the past promises and past faithfulness of God. Know-ledge of God will then anticipate the promised future of God in constant remembrance of the past emergence of God's election, his covenant, his promises and his faithfulness. It is a knowledge that oversteps our bounds and moves within the horizon of remem-brance and expectation opened up by the promise, for to know about God is always at the same time to know ourselves called in history by God.

Just as the promises are not descriptive words for existing real-ity, but dynamic words about acts of faithfulness to be awaited from God, so knowledge of God cannot consist in a résumé of the language of completed facts. The truth of the promise lies not in any demonstrable correspondence with the reality which was or which is. It lies not in the *adaequatio rei et intellectus*. The promise here proves its truth, on the contrary, in the specific *inadaequatio intellectus et rei* in which it places the hearer. It stands in a demon-strable contradiction to the historic reality.[57] It has not yet found its answer, and therefore draws the mind to the future, to obedient and creative expectation, and brings it into opposition to the existing reality which has not the truth in it. It thus provokes a peculiar incongruence with being, in the consciousness of hoping and trusting. It does not glorify reality in the spirit, but is out for its transformation. Hence it does not give rise to powers of accommo-dation, but sets loose powers that are critical of being. It transcends reality not by rising to an unreal realm of dreams, but by pressing forwards to the future of a new reality.

3. The guarantee of the promise's congruity with reality lies in the credibility and faithfulness of him who gives it. Yet this argument would remain abstract, and would fail to do justice to the character of the promise as the word in which God promises himself and con-fronts man as 'I Yahweh', if it disregarded the fact that promises effectually strain towards a real, future event of fulfilment. This future to which the promise points can be expressed by a theolog-ical personalism only as the personal future of God 'himself'. Our hope in the promises of God, however, is not hope in God himself or in God as such, but it hopes that his future faithfulness will bring

---

57 Over against Deut. 18.21f. and Jer. 28.9, which see the criterion of true prophecy in the 'coming to pass of the word', do we not find a different criterion in Jer. 23.22 and 29: 'Is not my word like as a fire? saith the Lord; and like a hammer that breaketh the rock in pieces?'?

it also the fulness of what has been promised. To be sure, it can be said that our hope is hope in the coming of the faithfulness of God, that it expects the promised future from the coming of God himself and not apart from him. Yet it would surely be an abstraction which would not do justice to the Old Testament hope, if we were to describe this hope as *spes purissima in Deum purissimum.*[58] Hope, where it holds to the promises, hopes that the coming of God will bring it also 'this and that' – namely, his redeeming and restoring lordship in all things. It does not merely hope personally 'in him', but has also substantial hopes of his lordship, his peace and his righteousness on earth. Otherwise hope itself could unobtrusively change into a kind of fulfilment and there would be nothing more in which our hopes could be fulfilled.

An understanding of the promise must combine both the personalistic and the historic and substantial concepts of truth. Hope's assurance springs from the credibility and faithfulness of the God of promise. Hope's knowledge recalls the faithfulness of this God in history and anticipates the real fulfilment in a multitude of preconceptions, not to say realistic utopias – yet all this without prejudice to the freedom of the God who promises. An assurance of hope without such knowledge would be vague adventuring. A knowledge without such assurance would be historical speculation.

The God who is present in his promises is for the human spirit an ob-ject (*Gegen-stand*) in the sense that he stands opposed to (*entgegen-steht*)[59] the human spirit until a reality is created and becomes knowable which wholly accords with his promises and can be called 'very good'. Hence it is not our experiences which make faith and hope, but it is faith and hope that make experiences and bring the human spirit to an ever new and restless transcending of itself.

---

58 Luther, WA 5, p. 166: *Adeo scil. omnia a nobis aufferenda sunt, ut nec optima dei dona, idest ipsa merita, reliqua sint, in quibus fidamus, ut sit spes purissima in purissimum deum: tunc demum homo vere purus et sanctus est* ('For so completely have we to renounce all things that not even the best gifts of God, i.e. not even his merits, remain to be objects of our faith, that our hope be purely hope purely in God: only then is a man truly pure and holy').

59 The play here on the German words *Gegenstand* and *entgegenstehen* is to some extent contained also in the English word 'object', which by derivation means 'lying before' or 'lying opposite'. – *Translator.*

5. Promise and Law

If the promises of God create an interval of tension between their being issued and their coming to pass, and thereby institute freedom for obedience, then importance attaches to the question of directions for the filling out of this interval and of the existence thus constituted in it. This is understandable, since a promise does not announce an inescapable fate, but sets men on a road that leads to another land and another reality. If we again take our cue from the theme of nomadic life, then we can say that originally promise is combined with obedience, and obedience with a change of place and a change of existence. It is necessary to arise and go to the place to which the promise points, if one would have part in its fulfilment. Promise and command, the pointing of the goal and the pointing of the way, therefore belong immediately together.

In this context the judicial character of promise will also have to be taken into account. Promise is the one side of the covenant in which God's association with the people of his choice is grounded. To this extent promise founds upon election, and election always means being called into the history of promise. Whoever receives the promises, God enters into covenant with him and he with God. In the covenant, God in his freedom binds himself to be faithful to the promise he has given; and if this covenant extends to a future in which fulfilments are to ensue, then it cannot be regarded as a historical fact, but is to be understood as a historic event which points beyond itself to the future that is announced. The covenant will have to be understood as a history-making event which opens up specific possibilities of history. The covenant must be understood as a 'historic process' or, as Jacques Ellul calls it on the basis of parallels in law, a 'contract requiring adherence' which is not exhausted in a single transaction, but whose effects continue until the promised fulfilment.[60] To this extent the promise of the covenant and the injunctions of the covenant have an abiding and guiding significance until the fulfilment.

The obedience which the injunctions demand springs of firm confidence, and is a natural consequence of the promises. To 'keep' the covenant which God has founded means both to 'keep' the

---

60 J. Ellul, *The Theological Foundation of Law*, ET by M. Weiser, 1961, p. 50.

words of the promise and 'to keep his commandments'. We 'keep' the commandments by obedience. We 'keep' the promises when 'with all our heart and all our strength' we trust and hope in them and do not doubt. All the commandments are explications of the one commandment, to love God and to cleave to him (Deut. 6.5), and this one commandment is but the reverse side of the promise. It commands (*gebietet*) what the promise offers (*bietet*). Hence not only disobedience is punished by not experiencing the fulfilment, but so also is resignation, weariness, departure from the living hope. Despondency and despair are sin – indeed they are the origin of all sins.[61] Hence *vice versa* the commandments are 'easy' to fulfil in the power that comes of hoping in God and waiting upon him. The commandments of the covenant, which point our hopes in the promise to the path of physical obedience, are nothing else but the ethical reverse of the promise itself. The promised life here appears as the life that is commanded. Hence the demands for obedience and the demands for hope are alike related to that horizon which opens up before the present in the light of the historic datum of the covenant, and which makes the present the front-line for the onset of the promised new life. In this conjunction with the promises of the covenant, the commandments all have a paracletic and parenetic significance, but they are not legal conditions or what theologians commonly call 'law'.[62] If the commandments are the ethical side of the promise and obedience is the fruit of hope, then the commandments are just as little rigid norms as the promises are, but they go along with the promise, producing history and transforming themselves on the path through the ages towards the fulfilment. They are not abstract norms of ideal orders that always exist and reflect their images in time, but they are a real foreshadowing of the historic prospects extended to specific men by the historic datum of the covenant. The commandments have accordingly just as much a future tenor as the promises. Their goal is the reality of that human dignity which is vouchsafed to men through fellowship with the God of promise.

---

61 Despair and despondency are merely the reverse side of that *superbia* in which Luther saw the origin of all sins. On this point cf. the fine treatise by J. Pieper, *Über die Hoffnung*, 1949, pp. 51ff. and K. Barth, *Church Dogmatics* IV/2, §65: 'The Sloth and Misery of Man'.

62 On this paragraph cf. G. von Rad, *Theologie des Alten Testamentes* II, pp. 402ff.: 'Das Gesetz' (ET pp. 388ff.: 'The Law').

It is therefore plain that theological reflection on the law can begin at the point where the promise itself is rendered questionable by non-realization or by delay in its fulfilment. The theological reflection which separates the law from its future can arise in the vacuum created by the postponement of the promise, and on the basis of historic experiences which contradict the promised future. The non-realization of promises upon which we had depended, the distress that arises when the protection and guidance of the God of promise fail to come, makes the following theological reflections possible:

(a) God lies. They were his promise and his covenant, but he has not kept them. 'Wilt thou indeed be unto me as a deceitful brook, as waters that fail?' (Jer. 15.18, RV).

(b) God is faithful. He does not deny himself. What he says comes to pass. Therefore if it does not come to pass, it was not the promise of God, but the lie of false prophets. History itself proves them to be false prophets. Reflections of this kind were manifestly often brought forward even against the charismatic leaders of Israel.

(c) The reflection turns against the sorely tried, or even already disappointed man himself. The reason for the withholding of the fulfilment, for the distance and absence of God and for his judgment, lies in man, whether because he has departed from the hope in the God of the promise and fallen into idolatry (the golden calf) or the worship of other gods, or because of his disobedience to the injunctions of the commandments. Then the hidden – uncleanness and sin must be searched out and purification and atonement sought, in order to establish the promise once more.

This last reflection, however, turns the promise into an object and regards it in abstraction from the God who promises. It becomes an object whose power can be manipulated by means of repentance and the rites of the cultus. Whereas in essence a divine promise itself contains the power of its fulfilment in the faithfulness and might of the God who promises, in reflection in the vacuum caused by its delay there arises a peculiar conditionalizing of the promise. Its fulfilment is made to depend on obedience, and obedience is understood as a *conditio sine qua non* and as a return achievement on man's part. Perfect obedience to the promise and its injunctions must bring its fulfilment, while every imperfection gives further cause for delay. Here we have a reversal of subjects which is often subtle and from the historical standpoint calls for very careful differentiation: if obedience is a consequence of the promise that incites us to arise and set off towards a definite goal and entrusts the fulfilment to the power of the God who promises, so now *vice versa* the fulfilment can be regarded as the consequence of human obedience. Here the obedience of man need not as yet be understood as the efficient cause of the fulfilment, but can also be taken merely as the occasion for the fulfilment by God himself. But this means that the power of the promise to attain to fulfilment lies no longer in the faithfulness of God himself, but in the obedience of man.

In the Old Testament, too, such reflections are not unknown. It is plain that they already arise very early. They arise at every point where in the absence of the promised salvation, in misfortune and god-forsakenness, the people begin to raise the questions of why and wherefore and how long. These questions become acute in popular complaint, and the attempted answers are given on the basis of the covenant and of divine justice. Is it conceivable that this last reflection dominates the rabbinical teaching of late Judaism? Could it possibly be that the Torah theology of late Judaism has a formative influence in what New Testament scholars often describe as 'delay of the parousia'? In modern Jewish theology the reversing of the subjects is plainly the ground of its remarkable proximity to German idealism, to activistic messianism and to the Russian 'husbandmen of God'. Then 'the redemption of the world is left to the power of our conversion. God has no wish for any other means of perfecting his creation than by our help. He will not reveal his kingdom until we have laid its foundations.'[63]

One could call this 'the promise in the form of the law'. Then it would have to be pointed out in this context that while Paul's controversy with the Judaism of the Torah and with Jewish Christians is certainly on the question of the law, yet its concern is surely the promise (Gal. 3.15ff.). Promise in the form of gospel, or promise in the form of law – that is the question. And it could well be that 'promise in the form of gospel' brings to light once more the

---

63 M. Buber, *Gog und Magog*, 1949, p. 297. H.-J. Kraus, 'Gesprach mit M. Buber', *EvTh* 12, 1952, pp. 76ff. Combined with this is also another thought – that Yahweh mysteriously requires the action of Israel as his son. Cf. L. Baeck, *Das Wesen des Judentums*, 2nd ed. 1959, pp. 132ff.; C. Cohen, *Religion der Vernunft aus den Quellen des Judentums*, 2nd ed. 1929, pp. 140, 172, 233, 431.

original meaning of the law as being the injunctions that are bound up with the promise.

6. Promise in the Eschatology of the Prophets[64]

Since the rediscovery of the eschatological character of the words of the Bible witnesses, the concept 'eschatology' has become hazy. Whereas in orthodox dogmatics it referred to the last, often unrelated and supplementary, article '*de novissimis*', in dogmatics and exegesis today it has acquired various senses and meanings, according to the particular material to which it is applied, simply 'future', or 'extending beyond the present', or 'last age', or 'transcendent', or 'directed towards a final goal', or 'finally valid'. Among Old Testament scholars the terminological dispute narrows down to the question whether hopes within history can already be called eschatological, or whether the term should be reserved for prophecies which speak of the end of history as such, and thus of events which lie outside the realm of history.[65] Can a distinction be made between historic eschatologies and cosmic eschatologies, between eschatologies within history and transcendental eschatologies? Does the *eschaton* mean merely 'future', or is it applied to the absolute future as opposed to history?

It is hardly possible to expound specific complexes of ideas as 'eschatological schemata'. It is also scarcely possible to establish the points at which we can say, 'Here prophetic promise ends, and there eschatology begins.' But it can be said in the first instance that those promises and expectations are eschatological which are directed towards a historic future in the sense of the ultimate horizon. Now, the concept 'horizon', as meaning a boundary of expectation which

64 For what follows cf. M. Buber, *The Prophetic Faith*, ET 1949; T. C. Vriezen, 'Prophecy and Eschatology', *VT Suppl.* I (Congress Volume: Copenhagen 1953), 1953, pp. 199–229; H. W. Wolff, 'Das Geschichtsverständnis der alttestamentlichen Prophetie', *EvTh* 20, 1960, pp. 218–235; G. von Rad, *Theologie des Alten Testamentes* II, pp. 125ff.: 'Die Eschatologisierung des Geschichtsdenkens durch die Propheten' (ET pp. 112ff.: 'History related to Eschatology: Israel's Ideas about Time and History, and the Prophetic Eschatology'); O. Plöger, *Theokratie und Eschatologie*, 1959; D. Rössler, *Gesetz und Geschichte*, 1960; K. Koch, 'Spätisraelitisches Geschichtsdenken am Beispiel des Buches Daniel', *Historische Zeitschrift*, 1961, vol. 193, pp. 1–32.

65 G. von Rad, *op. cit.*, p. 128 (ET p. 114) in the form of a question to G. Hölscher, S. Mowinckel and G. Fohrer.

moves along with us and invites us to press further ahead, already fits in with the general concept of promise. 'Israel's faith in God has a future content.'[66] And it is quite true that picturing the future in terms of the threat of judgment and the promise of salvation is not a specific characteristic of the prophets of classical times, but that it could rather be said, on the contrary, that classical prophecy is a specific characteristic of Israelite belief in the promise.[67] 'This faith that looks to the future took over various themes in order to make plain what the future of God meant in various particular circumstances.'[68] That presupposes faith in the God of promise, who is the God who will be, and cannot be psychologically explained on the basis of disappointment with the cultic θεὸς ἐπιφανής who is subsequently 'eschatologized.'[69]

This would mean, however, that the eschatology of the prophets grew up on the soil of Israel's faith in the promise, and that in prophetic eschatology faith in the promise is wrestling with new experiences of God, of judgment and of history and thereby undergoing new, profound changes. In the prophets, despite all the newness of their message, the God who confronts Israel with his claims is no other than the *Deus spei*, the God of hope.

What part of the promised future is the ultimate future, what part of the historic *novum* is the *novum ultimum*, is determined by the perspective in which the viewer sees the time that is now void but will then be filled. The ideas of time are first determined by the expectations. Here it is quite possible for the eschatological perspectives to expand, and for that which appeared to one generation as 'ultimate' to be seen by a later generation as within history and surpassable. The ideas of 'end' and 'goal' all depend on what a thing is supposed to be the end of and for what it is supposed to be the goal. What is here regarded as 'time' is then concrete time

---

66 Cf. also O. Procksch, *Theologie des Alten Testamentes*, 1950, p. 582. Cf. also M. Buber, *op. cit.*, p. 8.

67 Cf. here the new questions in the study of the prophets: R. Bach, *Die Aufforderung zur Flucht und zum Kampf im alttestamentlichen Prophetenspruch*, 1962; R. Rendtorff, 'Erwägungen zur Frühgeschichte des Prophetentums in Israel', *ZTK* 59, 1962, pp. 145ff.

68 Jepsen, Art. 'Eschatologie' in *RGG³* II, col. 661.

69 Thus e.g. M. Buber, *Königtum Gottes*, 2nd ed. 1936, p. x, and S. Mowinckel, *Psalmenstudien* II, p. 324. On this, G. von Rad, *op. cit.*, p. 130 (ET p. 116): 'If we hold by what the prophets say, it will not do to put the "experience of disillusionment" at the head as the evocative factor proper.'

as seen in the processes of historic and expected changes. To that extent the sense of time and the ideas of time also change along with the expectations. The abstract scientific concept of time, which has categorically determined modern thinking since Kant, must not be applied here until we have tested its eschatological scope – which in Kant's case means its transcendental scope.[70]

But when and how do hopes for history become hopes that are to be called 'eschatological'? When does a promise become an eschatological promise? Is it demonstrable and conceivable that the historic, moving horizon of promise can reach ultimate bounds?

The concept 'eschatology' is here intended to mark the peculiarity of the prophets as distinct from those who had earlier spoken for the religion of Yahweh and also as distinct from later apocalyptic writers.

From the standpoint of the history of religion, the 'mastering' of agrarian culture in Israel's occupation of Canaan has been described as the first decisive frontier crossed by the tribes of Israel. In this 'opening up of the realm of sedentary experience by Yahwism',[71] the latter itself underwent considerable expansion. The 'mastering' of those great experiences in the world history of the seventh and sixth centuries, in which Israel perished as a nation and yet survived itself in the religious sphere,[72] could be called the second major frontier. On this frontier, too, faith in the promise undergoes tremendous expansion: in the message of the classical prophets, which is closely bound up with these experiences of history and of judgment, it develops into the prophetic eschatology.

The message of these prophets arises in the shadow of the increasing menace from Assyria, Babylon and Persia, the gathering storm of destruction that broods over the national, political and Palestinian life of Israel in both kingdoms. The prophets see before them the annihilation of Israel's existence and of the whole history of promise and fulfilment thus far vouchsafed to Israel by its God. They interpret this history of collapse as Yahweh's judgment on his apostate people. This means that the new historic action of Yahweh in the history of the nations, which for Israel becomes the history of its destruction, is seen by them as being on the same level as, and

---

70 Cf. pp. 45ff. above.

71 V. Maag, *op. cit.*, p. 153 n. 1.

72 A. Alt, 'Die Deutung der Weltgeschichte im Alten Testament', *ZTK* 56, 1959, p. 129.

even competing with, the historic acts of Yahweh in their own past as remembered in the cultus and the festivals. This new, and as yet dark and unfathomable action of Yahweh will even go the length of outreaching and replacing his past action upon his people. In the historic judgment on Israel, Yahweh not only annuls the debts of Israel, but he annuls also the institutions of his own covenant in his unfathomable freedom to adopt new ways.

'The message of the prophets has to be termed eschatological wherever it regards the old historic bases of salvation as null and void,' says G. von Rad in his new view of the matter, 'but we ought then to go on and limit the term. It should not be applied to cases where Israel gave a general expression of her faith in her future, or, as does happen, in the future of her sacred institutions. The prophetic teaching is only eschatological when the prophets expelled Israel from the safety of the old saving actions and suddenly shifted the basis of salvation to a future action of God.'[73] This allows no recognition to the psychological explanation of 'eschatology' as given by Mowinckel and Buber following the example of Albert Schweitzer. It was not that the 'disappointments of history' in regard to promises in which they had believed, and which depended on the land, the cultus and the temple, caused men to give eschatological form to their hopes for history. What did cause them to do this was experiences which were understood as judgments of Yahweh, and indeed not merely as judgment upon what by the standard of the ancient covenant ordinances was a disobedient people, but also as judgment on the history of Yahweh's relationship with this people hitherto. How far, amid the breakdown of what has hitherto been and the breaking in of new, hitherto unknown action on God's part, does the message of the prophets become 'eschatological'? This surely cannot lie merely in the break-away from the 'future of the Yahweh who has come', which up to that point had also been known, to the 'future of the Yahweh who is to come', which up to that point had not been known.

The threat that the history of the attacking peoples will bring Yahweh's judgment upon Israel marks a quite decisive universalizing of the divine action. The experience of being crushed between the great world powers is understood as a judgment of Yahweh. Yet even as early as Amos this threat of judgment is universal: God

---

73 G. von Rad, *op. cit.*, pp. 131f. (ET p. 118).

judges all wrong, including that among the peoples who do not know his law. Consequently the God who uses the nations to judge his apostate people is also their Lord and will also be their Judge. For if he appoints the nations to execute judgment on Israel, then he is obviously their God and Lord. If he uses these nations to judge Israel according to his law, then he will also judge these nations according to his law, given though it is in the first instance only to Israel. As a result of their onslaught upon Israel, and because according to the message of the prophets Israel must take this onslaught as a judgment of its God, the nations are involved in the fate of Israel and come within the range of Yahweh's working in judgment and in blessing. On its political deathbed Israel brings the nations, as it were, into the hands of its God and into his future. By this very means Yahweh's threats and promises for the future are set free from their restriction to the one specific people and its particular future in history, and become eschatological. The moving horizon of the assurances for the future given by the God of promise, once it is extended to embrace 'all peoples', then reaches the utmost bounds of human reality as such, and becomes universal and so also eschatological. The horizon of the coming God thereby attains a *non plus ultra*.

However widely it extends to embrace all peoples, and however deeply it goes to the roots of earthly existence, the prophets' message of judgment nevertheless points once more to a different future, to a day of Yahweh, which will arise out of the night of judgment. This judgment certainly means the annihilation of the people and of the history to which this people owes its existence, but it does not mean the annihilation of Yahweh's faithfulness to himself. It can therefore be conceived as a judgment that paves the way for something finally new, and as annihilation for the sake of greater perfection. Thus there arise visions of the end, of the unheard-of new salvation that is on the way, of the new covenant, of the coming glory of Yahweh in his sovereignty over all the earth – and all this, too, not only for Israel, but so to speak for all the peoples that have participated in the judgment upon Israel and have thus been involved in the history of Yahweh's relationship with Israel. It is only through the above-mentioned universalizing of the judgment that the coming salvation of Yahweh first becomes eschatological in its breadth and unrestrictedness.

How is this conceived? To begin with, 'the new thing' whose coming is foretold is conceived in analogy to the previous saving acts of God in the history of the fulfilling of his promises in his people's past – as the occupation of a new land, as the setting up of a new David and a new Zion, as a new exodus, as a new covenant. That is to say, it is conceived as a 'renewal' and return of what is past and lost, so that beginning and end correspond to each other.[74] But these are analogies which seek to interpret the wholly non-analogous. It cannot be a question merely of the restitution of the good old days, for new and unheard-of things have already been done by Yahweh. The judgment has become universal, and therefore the nations – in the first instance those participating in the judgment, then, *pars pro toto*, through them 'all peoples' – are taken up into the new, coming acts of God. Already in the judgment Yahweh glorifies himself upon them. How much more will he glorify himself upon them when his new saving acts in Israel come to light. 'Salvation has become universal, even if it is Israelite and even if it is received via Israel.'[75] To be sure these visions of salvation, which are to be called 'eschatological' in virtue of the fact that in their unrestrictedness they break through all spatial and racial limitations and extend to the utmost bounds of human reality in 'all peoples', are *Israelo-centric eschatologies*. This is already implied in the fact that they are expressed in the form of analogy to the past saving history of Yahweh's relationship with his people and on the ground of the basic experience of judgment in the history that is concentrated upon Israel. Yet the extension to all peoples of the threat of judgment and of the promise of salvation in itself already involves what T. C. Vriezen calls the 'missionary task of Israel' – the task of being a light to the Gentiles and a witness for Yahweh in his controversy with the gods of the nations. But the more the new saving action of God that is to come outstrips all analogies from the history of Israel's dealings with its God in past experience and tradition, and the more the judgment that begins with Israel moves on through the history of the nations, the more clearly there appear the first signs of a *universal eschatology of mankind*. Here, however, we have presumably already the beginning of what must be called apocalyptic.

---

74 G. von Rad, *op. cit.* II, p. 131 (ET p. 117); H. W. Wolff, *op. cit.*, pp. 224f.
75 T. C. Vriezen, *An Outline of Old Testament Theology*, ET, 1958, p. 360.

Thus we can speak of a real 'eschatology' only at the points where, in the limitations and perspectives of history, the horizon of the promised future embraces in the *eschaton* the *proton* of the whole creation, where the horizon of the God who announces himself and is on his way extends to all peoples, for there is nothing that can be conceived as wider in extent than that.

Along with this universalizing, however, there goes also an intensification of the promise up to the limits of existence as such. What the ancient faith in the promise expected from the nearness and then from the presence of the God of promise was guidance, preservation, protection, blessing, fulness of life, etc., and these expectations were given content from the concrete experience of deprivations, of being abandoned to hunger, thirst, wretchedness and the oppression and menace of their enemies. That is, the expectations receive their content in the mind's eye from the contrary experiences that were endured under the absence and hiddenness of the God of promise. The positive content of the ideas is all supplied by negation of the negative. In the same way the visionary ideas of the prophetic promises receive their content from the negative experiences of Yahweh's judgment. This means, however, that the visions of the promised glorifying of Yahweh develop in the light of the new experiences of judgment. Yahweh's coming glory shows itself in overcoming the experienced judgment and turning it to blessing. If this were to be expressed in theological terms, we should have to say: it shows itself in the overcoming of God by God – of the judging, annihilating God by the saving, life-giving God, of the wrath of God by his goodness. If we would illustrate it by the people concerned, then the coming new action of Yahweh must be exemplifiable in the overcoming of the experiences of judgment, in the overcoming of hunger and poverty, of humiliation and offence, of international wars and polytheism, and finally of a god-forsaken death. These conquests of the experienced negative aspects of existence that are understood as judgments of Yahweh are all summed up in the content of the expectation that is bound up with the coming fulness of the glory of Yahweh. The content of the expectation in the 'predictions' is thus supplied on the one hand by recollections and analogies from the history of the fulfilment of Yahweh's promises in the good old days of his people's past whose return is hoped for – while on the other hand it is provided by negation of the negative elements in the new experiences of judgment.

To this end, ideas of international peace, etc., can then also be taken over from other peoples, so far as they can be given eschatological form.

But in the message of the prophets there still remains at first one boundary – *death*. As long as death is felt to be the natural boundary of life, God remains a God of the living. But if death – or at least early death – is experienced as exclusion from the promise of fulness and consummation of life, and thus as an effect of judgment, then the hope of the overcoming of God's judgment by his life-creating glory must be exemplified also in relation to this boundary. Hence on the periphery of the prophetic message death appears as a suffering of divine judgment, and the messianic salvation in which the judgment is annulled is exemplified in a conquest of dying and of death. Yahweh remains a God of the living. The suffering endured at the ultimate boundary of life does not lead to the adoption of Egyptian ideas of a Beyond. But if the death-boundary is understood as a judgment of Yahweh, then his power extends also beyond death. The dead, too, can be recognized as included within the realm of his promise and glory, and even death itself is seen as a transformable possibility in his hand and no longer as a fixed reality that sets a limit to his working. Thus the term 'eschatological' would now have to be used for a promise whose horizon of expectation surmounts and overcomes all experiences of the total judgment of God in life and death. Only when the horizon of expectation extends beyond what is felt to be the final boundary of existence, i.e. beyond the bounds of death, does it reach an *eschaton*, a *non plus ultra*, a *novum ultimum*.

The universalizing of the promise finds its eschaton *in the promise of Yahweh's lordship over all peoples.*

The intensification of the promise finds its approach to the eschatological in the negation of death.

Now of course it must be noted that these limits of the eschatological, as they have here been terminologically defined, are nowhere so plain and clear-cut in the classical prophets. The latter stand in the midst of the history of their people and in the transition from the breakdown of the old to the breaking in of the new. History for them does not stand still as in the apocalyptic visions of the end. They do not, like the apocalyptic sects, stand in unworldly detachment over against the 'world', the nations and the people of Israel, so that they could give themselves over to contemplating the worldliness of the world and its future fate. On the contrary, here everything is still in flux and the history whose future they announce is still mobile. They know that they themselves and their message are a factor in the movement of the history of God. Thus they certainly speak of 'history' as the 'work of Yahweh' or the 'plan of Yahweh' (Isa. 28.29), arid also of the 'whole work of Yahweh' (Isa. 10.12). Yet that is not a history surveyed apocalyptically from the standpoint of the end at which all things stand still, but it is a future announced from the midst of the process of history. When they speak of Yahweh's plan, they are not thinking of insight into the divine determination of the world, but mean the constancy of his historic faithfulness. They see judgment and history in the light of the freedom of Yahweh, not as immutable fate. Hence the plans of Yahweh can be 'repented of' by Yahweh, and the proclamation of them leads the present into decisions which have an influence on the future of the divine action also. As distinct from any fatalistic apocalyptic view of history, the mobility of history as the prophets see it, and as they stand in it with their own witness, can therefore be called 'a purposeful conversation of the Lord of the future with Israel'.[76] It could thus be said that while the prophetic message in its breadth and in its existential depth does reach the utmost bounds of reality and thereby become eschatological, yet these bounds are not predetermined but are themselves flexible.

7. The Historifying of the Cosmos in Apocalyptic Eschatology

It is difficult to explain the phenomenon of late Jewish apocalyptic and its contents.[77] Have we here to do with a legitimate continuation of the prophetic message, or with a falling away from the prophetic faith in the promise? Is it a case of the intrusion of the dualistic world-picture of Iranianism or, if this is so, had an inward openness for it already been prepared by the message of the prophets?

It can be said in the first instance that the futuristic and eschatological outlook is common to both the prophets and the

---

76 H. W. Wolff, *op. cit.*, p. 231.

77 Cf. the completely divergent verdicts of G. von Rad, *op. cit.*, II, pp. 314ff. (ET pp. 301ff.) on the one hand, and on the other hand of K. Koch, *op. cit.*, and W. Pannenberg, *Offenbarung als Geschichte*, 1961, pp. 103ff.

apocalyptists. Then, however, distinctions will at once have to be made.

(*a*) Apocalyptic cherishes a religious, deterministic view of history. The temporal sequence of the aeons is settled from the start and history gradually unfolds a plan of Yahweh's. In the prophets, however, there is no trace of the idea that the *eschata* have been firmly determined since the beginning of time.

(*b*) In apocalyptic the factor standing over against the God who acts in history is the 'world' that lies under the power of evil. In the prophets, however, we have 'Israel and the nations'.

(*c*) The apocalyptic expectation is no longer directed towards a consummation of the creation through the overcoming of evil by good, but towards the separation of good and evil and hence the replacement of the 'world that lies under the power of evil' by the coming 'world of righteousness'. This shows a fatalistic dualism which is not yet so found in the prophets.

(*d*) The judgment is not seen as something which in the freedom of God can be recalled and which can be averted, if it may be, by repentance, but as an immutable fate that is assuredly coming, as a *fatum irreparabile*.

(*e*) The prophets stood in the midst of the people of Israel and thus also in the midst of its history. The apocalyptists stand in the post-exilic congregation of the righteous of Yahweh.[78]

(*f*) The prophets in their predictions quite openly took their stand in their own historic present. From that standpoint they unfold their historic perspectives. The apocalyptist, however, veils his own place in history.

In short, the question arises whether apocalyptic thinking does not ultimately show signs of non-historic thinking. Does the apocalyptic division of world history into periods according to the plan of Yahweh not merely interpret in terms of universal history earlier, foreign schemata of a cosmological kind? Apocalyptic as the 'science of the highest' has such an encyclopaedic character, just like the esoteric apocalyptic of the pietistic theology of saving history in the seventeenth and eighteenth Christian centuries.

On the other hand, it has been pointed out' with good reason how firmly the apocalyptic picture of history is rooted in the historic thinking of Israel and bound up with the prophetic eschatology. In

---

78 O. Plöger, *op. cit.*, pp. 63ff.

this context Daniel becomes the executor of the testament of the prophets with his first 'sketch of world history in terms of universal history'.[79]

This contradictory impression arises from the fact that in the eschatology of the prophets the horizon of the promise, both in its breadth and in its depth, reaches the limits of what can be described as cosmic finitude. When, however, the moving historic horizon of the historic hopes reaches these *eschata*, then there arises the possibility of abandoning the point of perspective in history and reading the course of world history backwards from the end now contemplated, as if universal history were a *universum*, a predetermined cosmos of history. Numerical speculations from ancient cosmology are introduced in order to provide an order for the periods of world history corresponding to the spatial order. The world empires are fixed. The *eschaton* becomes a *fatum*. Then the place of election, which determines the ground of obedience and hope, is taken by providence which determines events. The place of the promise which is trusted in hope contrary to all apparent hope is taken by the end drama. The place of the *eschaton* which is brought about by God in his freedom is taken by a historic finale that comes about in the course of time. The place of the faithfulness of God to which, in his freedom, the fulfilment of the promised future is entrusted is taken by the plan of God which is firmly established from the beginning of time and gradually disclosed by history. In place of a historic theology we have a theology of history and in place of a historic eschatology comes an eschatological contemplation of history. Like the eighteenth-century theology of saving history, apocalyptic contains perceptible traces of the distant God of deism. On the other hand it must not be overlooked that in the speculative apocalypses there is also always a note of exhortation to be found. It is the exhortation to persevere in the faith of the righteous: he who endures to the end will be saved. It follows that faith and unbelief, good and evil, election and reprobation, righteous and unrighteous are firmly established, and what matters is to abide by what we are. This again is wholly in harmony with the place of apocalyptic in the life of those who form a community apart.

What is the result of thus comparing the eschatology of the prophets with the historic hopes of early Israel on the one hand

---

79 K. Koch, *op. cit.*, p. 31.

and with cosmological apocalyptic on the other? In asking this, we are now asking about the systematic consequences for the outline of eschatology as such.

In the first instance we find an extreme contradiction in the theological evaluation of apocalyptic. G. von Rad holds that the characteristic apocalyptic division of world history into periods from the standpoint of the world consummation is 'simply the interpretation and actualization of earlier cosmological schemata found in myth'.[80] K. Koch and W. Pannenberg see it as the first attempt to provide a sketch of world history on the basis of the prophetic eschatology. Both verdicts have their ground in the recognition of the fact that apocalyptic applies cosmological patterns to history, with the result that either 'history' comes to a standstill or else 'history' becomes intelligible as a summary representation of reality in its totality.

But now, when we consider the relation between eschatology and cosmology in apocalyptic, there arises still a third possible interpretation and a third possible theological evaluation. The application of cosmological patterns to history as determined by the *eschaton* naturally does have the effects noted by von Rad and Koch. Yet the peculiarity and the theological significance of apocalyptic could lie contrariwise in the fact that what we have here is not by any means a cosmological interpretation of eschatological history, but an eschatological and historic interpretation of the cosmos. It might well be that the existing cosmic bounds of reality, which the moving historic horizon of the promise reaches in eschatology, are not regarded as fixed and predetermined things, but are themselves found to be in motion. It might well be that once the promise becomes eschatological it breaks the bounds even of that which aetiology had hitherto considered to be creation and cosmos, with the result that the *eschaton* would not be a repetition of the beginning, nor a return from the condition of estrangement and the world of sin to the state of original purity, but is ultimately wider than the beginning ever was. Then it would not be the case that eschatology becomes cosmological in apocalyptic, and is thereby stabilized, but *vice versa* cosmology would become eschatological and the cosmos would be taken up in terms of history into the process of the *eschaton*. This would then be the other side of the

---

80 G. von Rad, *op. cit.* II, p. 321 (ET p. 308).

struggle in apocalyptic between eschatology and cosmology – a side which has hitherto remained unnoticed, because theology was interested only in eschatology but not in cosmology. If, as we might say, in the message of the prophets the Israelite 'hope for history' was struggling with the experiences of world history, and if in this struggle world history was understood as a function of the eschatological future of Yahweh, so it is also in apocalyptic: historic eschatology is here struggling with cosmology and in this struggle makes the cosmos understandable as a historic process of aeons in apocalyptic perspective. Then it would not by any means be the case that in the apocalyptic outlook the history that is motivated by our hopes for history is brought to a standstill, but on the contrary, the now universal hope for history would here be setting the cosmos in motion. In a struggle of this kind eschatology naturally suffers serious losses. Yet we must not look only at these, but must also see what is gained in them. The 'universe' is no longer, as in pagan cosmology, a thing to be interpreted in astro-mythical or pantheistic or mechanistic terms as the sum total of the world and of our satisfaction with it. Instead, it splits into aeons in the apocalyptic process – into a world that is coming and one that is passing away. The *totum* of apocalyptic means a different thing from the universe of cosmology. The whole world is now involved in God's eschatological process of history, not only the world of men and nations. The conversion of man in the prophetic message then finds its correlate in the conversion of the whole cosmos, of which apocalyptic speaks. The prophetic revolution among the nations expands to become the cosmic revolution of all things. Not only the martyrs are included in the eschatological suffering of the Servant of God, but the whole creation is included in the suffering of the last days. The suffering becomes universal and destroys the all-sufficiency of the cosmos, just as the eschatological joy will then resound in a 'new heaven and a new earth'. In other words, while apocalyptic does conceive its eschatology in cosmological terms, yet that is not the end of eschatology, but the beginning of an eschatological cosmology or an eschatological ontology for which being becomes historic and the cosmos opens itself to the apocalyptic process. This historifying of the world in the category of the universal eschatological future is of tremendous importance for theology, for indeed it makes eschatology the universal horizon of all theology as such. Without apocalyptic a theological eschatology remains bogged down in the ethnic history of men or the existential history of the individual. The New Testament did not close the window which apocalyptic had opened for it towards the wide vistas of the cosmos and beyond the limitations of the given cosmic reality.

III

The Resurrection and the Future of Jesus Christ

1. Gospel and Promise

When we come to the question of the view of the revelation of God in the New Testament, then we discover the fact, already familiar from the Old Testament, that there is no unequivocal *concept* of revelation. What the New Testament understands by revelation is thus again not to be learned from the original content of the words employed, but only from the event to which they are here applied. The event to which the New Testament applies the expressions for revelation imparts to them a peculiar dynamic which is messianic in kind and implies a history of promise. The general impression could be described in the first instance by saying that with the cross and resurrection of Christ the one revelation of God, the glory of his lordship which embraces righteousness, life and freedom, has begun to move towards man.[1] In the gospel of the event of Christ this future is already present in the promises of Christ. It proclaims the present breaking in of this future, and thus *vice versa* this future announces itself in the promises of the gospel. The proclamation of Christ thus places men in the midst of an event of revelation which embraces the nearness of the coming Lord. It thereby makes the reality of man 'historic' and stakes it on history.

The eschatological tendency of the revelation in Christ is manifested by the fact that the revealing word is εὐαγγέλιον and ἐπαγγελία in one. J. Schniewind has rightly described ἐπαγγελία in Pauline theology as the 'complement' of εὐαγγέλιον.[2] The gospel of the

---

1 H. Schulte, *Der Begriff der Offenbarung im Neuen Testament* (Beiträge zur Evangelischen Theologie 13), 1949, p. 23.

2 *TWNT* TI, p. 575, art. 'ἐπαγγελία' by J. Schniewind and G. Friedrich.

revelation of God in Christ is thus in danger of being incomplete and of collapsing altogether, if we fail to notice the dimension of promise in it. Christology likewise deteriorates if the dimension of the 'future of Christ' is not regarded as a constitutive element in it.

But how is 'promise' proclaimed in the New Testament as compared with the Old Testament history of promise? How is the future horizon of promise asserted in the New Testament as against the views of the Hellenistic mystery religions?

The approach to Christology has been sought in Christian dogmatics along different lines. We here select two basic types as illustrations of the problem.

Since the shaping of Christian dogmatics by Greek thought, it has been the general custom to approach the mystery of Jesus from the general idea of God in Greek metaphysics: the one God, for whom all men are seeking on the ground of their experience of reality, has appeared in Jesus of Nazareth – be it that the highest eternal idea of goodness and truth has found its most perfect teacher in him, or be it that in him eternal Being, the Source of all things, has become flesh and appeared in the multifarious world of transience and mortality. The mystery of Jesus is then the incarnation of the one, eternal, original, true and immutable divine Being. This line of approach was adopted in the Christology of the ancient Church in manifold forms. Its problems accordingly resulted from the fact that the Father of Jesus Christ was identified with the one God of Greek metaphysics and had the attributes of this God ascribed to him. If, however, the divinity of God is seen in his unchangeableness, immutability, impassibility and unity, then the historic working of this God in the Christ event of the cross and resurrection becomes as impossible to assert as does his eschatological promise for the future.

In modern times the approach to the mystery of Jesus has often been from a general view of the being of man in history. History has always existed, ever since man existed. But the actual experiencing and conceiving of the existence of man as historic, the radical disclosure of the historic character of human existence, came into the world with Jesus. The word and work of Jesus brought the decisive change in man's understanding of himself and the world, for by him man's self-understanding in history was given its true expression as an understanding of the historic character of human existence. Instead of a general question of God and a general idea of God, which finds its true expression in Jesus and is thus verified by him, what is here presupposed is a general concept of the being of man, a general questionableness of human existence, which finds its true expression in Jesus and is thus verified by him.

Both approaches to the mystery of Jesus set out from the universal, in order to find its true expression in the concrete instance of his person and his history. Neither of these approaches to Christology, to be sure, *need* bypass the Old Testament, but their way does not necessarily lie through it. The approach of Jesus to all men, however, has the Old Testament with its law and its promise as a necessary presupposition. It is therefore a real question whether we do not have to take seriously the importance for theology of the following two propositions:

1. It was *Yahweh*, the God of Abraham, of Isaac and of Jacob, the God of the promise, who raised Jesus from the dead. Who the God is who is revealed in and by Jesus, emerges only in his difference from, and identity with, the God of the Old Testament.

2. *Jesus was a Jew*. Who Jesus is, and what the human nature is which is revealed by him, emerges from his conflict with the law and the promise of the Old Testament.

If we take these starting points seriously, then the path of theological knowledge leads irreversibly from the particular to the general, from the historic to the eschatological and universal.

The first proposition would mean, that the God who reveals himself in Jesus must be thought of as the God of the Old Testament, as the God of the exodus and the promise, as the God with 'future as his essential nature', and therefore must not be identified with the Greek view of God, with Parmenides' 'eternal present' of Being, with Plato's highest Idea and with the Unmoved Mover of Aristotle, not even in his attributes. Who he is, is not declared by the world as a whole, but is declared by Israel's history of promise. His attributes cannot be expressed by negation of the sphere of the earthly, human, mortal and transient, but only in recalling and recounting the history of his promise. In Jesus Christ, however, the God of Israel has revealed himself as the God of all mankind. Thus the path leads from the *concretum* to the *concretum universale*, not the other way round. Christian theology has to think along *this* line. It is not that a general truth became concrete in Jesus, but the concrete, unique, historic event of the crucifying and raising of Jesus by Yahweh, the God of promise who creates being out of nothing, becomes general through the universal eschatological horizon it anticipates.[3] Through the raising of Jesus from the dead the God of the promises of Israel becomes the God of all men. The Christian proclamation of this God will accordingly always move within a horizon of general truth which it projects ahead of it and towards which it tends, and will claim in advance to be general in character and generally binding, even if its own universality is of an eschatological kind and does not come of abstract argument from the particular to the general.

If on the other hand theology takes seriously the fact that Jesus was a Jew, then this means that he is not to be understood as a particular case of human being in general, but only in connection with the Old Testament history of promise and in conflict with it. It is through the event of the cross and resurrection, which is understandable only in the context of the conflict between law and promise, that he becomes the salvation of all men, both Jews and Gentiles. It is the Christ event that first gives birth to what can be theologically described as 'man', 'true man', 'humanity' – 'neither Jew nor Greek, neither bond nor free, neither male nor female' (Gal. 3.28). Only when the real, historic and religious differences between peoples, groups and classes are broken down in the Christ event in which the sinner is justified, does there come a prospect of what true humanity can be and will be. The path leads here from the historic and unique to the universal, because it leads from the concrete event to the general in the sense of eschatological direction. Christian proclamation will consequently here again move within the horizon of general truth and make the claim to be universally binding. It will have to expound this claim in contra-distinction to other kinds of general anthropological concepts of *humanitas*, precisely because its own general concept of humanity has an eschatological content. It will not be able, for example, to set out from the fact that man is the being which possesses reason and language, and then go on to verify this aspect of his being by means of the event of justification, but it will set out on the

---

1 The trend is expressed in the New Testament in the ἐφάπαξ, in which the thoughts of being once for all in history and of being universally eschatologically binding intermerge. Cf. E. Käsemann, 'Das Problem des historischen Jesus', in *Exegetische Versuche und Besinnungen* I, 1960, pp. 200f. (ET by W. J. Montague: *Essays on New Testament Themes* [Studies in Biblical Theology 41], 1964, pp. 30f.).

contrary from the event of justification and calling, and then go on in face of other assertions as to the nature of man to uphold this event which makes man, theologically speaking, true man.

2. The God of the Promise

When we take this approach to Christology into consideration, then it is peculiarly significant that in the New Testament God is known and described as the 'God of promise'. He is the θεὸς ἐπαγγειλάμενος (Heb. 10.23; 11.11, and frequently elsewhere). The essential predicate of God accordingly lies in the statement: Πιστὸς ὁ ἐπαγγειλάμενος, 'faithful is he that promised'. His essence is not his absoluteness as such, but the faithfulness with which he reveals and identifies himself in the history of his promise as 'the same'. His divinity consists in the constancy of his faithfulness, which becomes credible in the contradiction of judgment and grace. The word which reveals God has thus fundamentally the character of promise and is therefore eschatological in kind. It is grounded upon the event of God's faithfulness and open towards it. It sets us on a path whose goal it shows and guarantees in terms of promise. It places the one who receives it in a position of insurmountable antithesis and hostility to the existing reality of this world. It gives ground for hope and criticism, and expects us to endure in hope.

The result of this is a knowledge of God fundamentally different from the knowledge of the θεὸς ἐπιφανής in the surrounding world of the epiphany religions, of the Hellenistic mystery religions and finally of Greek metaphysics, even if in actual fact signs of syncretism are to be seen everywhere in the New Testament. The life, work, death and resurrection of Jesus are therefore not described after the pattern of the appearance of epiphany gods, but in the categories of expectation that are appropriate to the God of promise. Jesus is no θεῖος ἀνήρ, no divine man, although ideas of this kind are employed at many levels in the tradition. The gospels are not cult legends, but offer historical recollections under the auspices of eschatological hope, although traits of the cult legend are also to be found. The language of Christian mission is not the language of gnostic revelation,[4] although this type of language, too,

---

4 Cf. G. Bornkamm, *Studien zu Antike und Urchristentum*, 1959, pp. 128ff. The Pauline proclamation is to be distinguished from the revelatory speeches of

is used on occasion. 'Thus although Christianity stands in the midst of the religious life of its time, epiphany faith can influence it in the first instance only as a formal element in its presentation. For it stands under the protection of the Old Testament thought of God, which expects God to act uniquely and comprehensively upon the world.'[5]

The word ἐπαγγελία has its roots in Hellenistic usage.[6] There it is generally used of promises, vows and pledges which men make to their gods. That God is the 'God who promises' is here obviously unknown. Linguistically speaking it appears to have no previous history in the Old Testament, although it is actually only in the Old Testament traditions that a previous history exists. 'It was through Judaism that ἐπαγγελία received its peculiar character as revealing word of God in the history of salvation.'[7] Here a theology of the promises of God was developed – and that, too, both in the rabbinical Torah theology and in the apocalyptic traditions. While in the former case promise means the promised reward of the righteous and is bound up with righteousness in the sense of the Torah, in the latter case it is used in the context of election and law to describe the 'future world' as opposed to this world, which is not able to bear what is promised to the righteous. In both traditions God is recognized as the God who promises, and whose faithfulness guarantees the fulfilment.

Just as for rabbinism and apocalyptic the figure of Abraham as the example of righteousness becomes the focal point of the interest in the promise, law and righteousness of God, so also Paul sets this figure in the centre of his exposition of gospel and promise.[8] Yet

---

θεῖοι ἄνθρωποι, who present themselves as the commissioners or representatives of some deity, bring news from heaven, summon to repentance and promise salvation. Their characteristic mark is the 'hierophantic style' of their message. The style of Pauline preaching, on the contrary, is more like the style of the Cynic and Stoic diatribe, although he obviously understood himself and his preaching not as delivering Stoic wisdom, but spoke in apocalyptic expectation as a 'precursor of the end of the world' (cf. E. Käsemann, *ZTK* 60, 1963, p. 80).

5 H. Schulte, *op. cit.*, p. 66. A similar conclusion is arrived at by Elpidius Pax, *Epiphaneia. Ein religionsgeschichtlicher Beitrag zur biblischen Theologie* (Münchener Theologische Studien), 1955.

6 I am here following the article 'ἐπαγγελία' in *TWNT*.

7 *TWNT* II, p. 578.

8 Cf. C. Dietzfelbinger, *Paulus und das Alte Testament* (Theologische Existenz heute, NF 95), 1961; E. Schlink, 'Gesetz und Paraklese', in *Antwort: Festschrift für K. Barth*, 1956, pp. 323ff.; U. Wilckens, 'Die Rechtfertigung Abrahams nach

his reason for going back to Abraham as the 'father of the promise' in contrast to Moses and the law lies in the fact that for Paul the Christ event is not a renewal of the people of God, but brings to life a 'new people of God' made up of Jews and Gentiles. His quarrel with the Jewish Christians is concerned, to be sure, with law and gospel, but it is really centred on the promise. If for him Christ is the 'end of the law' (Rom. 10.4), yet he does not see him as the end of the promise, but on the contrary as its rebirth, its liberation and validation.

Paul links the traditional Abrahamitic promises with the promise of life and obviously understands 'life' no longer in the context of possessing the land, being fruitful and multiplying, but as 'quickening of the dead' (Rom. 4.15, 17). As in Judaism, so also he, too, is certain that God keeps his promises. Yet the ground of this assurance is new: because God has the power to quicken the dead and call into being things that are not, therefore the fulfilment of his promise is possible, and because he has raised Christ from the dead, therefore the fulfilment of his promise is certain. Lack of assurance in, or doubt of, God's will to fulfil it is therefore robbing God of his glory. Unbelief is doubt of God 's truthfulness, of his omnipotence and his faithfulness (Rom. 4.20). Unbelief does not let God be God, for it doubts the dependability of God which guarantees his promises. Paul manifestly sees the concrete form of such unbelief in the theology of Torah, righteousness, in which the power of the promise towards its fulfilment is bound to the fulfilling of the law. If, however, the promise of God is bound to the law, then the promise is invalidated: it then depends no longer on the power of the God who has promised, but on the power of the man who obeys. But the wrath of God will be revealed upon all who leave the law unfulfilled or transgress it. Hence law and promise are mutually exclusive, just as glorying in the works of the law and glorying in the God who justifies sinners and quickens the dead are mutually exclusive. The law does not have within it the power of the promised life and of the resurrection, but exposes life to death and leads it to death. The law does not have within it the power of justification, but the power to expose sins and to make them exceeding sinful. For the promise has in the form of

Röm. 4', in *Studien zur alttestamentlichen Überlieferung*, 1961, pp. 111ff.; G. Klein, 'Röm. 4 und die Idee der Heilsgeschichte', *EvTh* 23, 1963, pp. 424ff.; E. Jüngel, 'Das Gesetz zwischen Adam und Christus', *ZTK* 60, 1963, pp. 42ff.

the law been made of no effect. Just as for Paul the justification of the godless and the life that comes of the raising of the dead belong together, so also for him the righteousness of faith and the validation of the promise in the raising of Christ belong together. 'If they which are of the law be heirs, faith is made void, and the promise made of none effect' (Rom. 4.14). But if, on the contrary, the promise is set in force by God, then it confers righteousness by faith. 'Therefore it is "of faith", that it might be by grace; to the end the promise might be sure (βεβαίαν) to all the seed; not to that only which is of the law, but to that also which is of the faith of Abraham; who is the father of us all' (Rom. 4.16). Promise would no longer be the promise of God, who quickens the dead and calls into being what is not, if it had anything to do with the law. 'If the inheritance be of the law, it is no more of promise' (Gal. 3.18). If we sought to attain the inheritance of the promise through fulfilling the law, then we should lose this inheritance, for by the promise God showed himself to Abraham as gracious (Gal. 3.18). The true heirs of the promise and children of Abraham are therefore those who are partakers of the promise in faith in Christ (Gal. 3.29). For by the gospel the Gentiles become partakers of the promise in Christ (Eph. 3.6).

It is plainly recognizable how the gospel in its antithesis to the law is here related to the promise. Paul does not use Abraham as an example by which to illustrate his new understanding of righteousness by faith, but the struggle for the inheritance of Abraham as between the gospel of the raising of the crucified Christ and the Torah is concerned with the 'power of the promise'. If Christ is the 'end of the Torah' (Rom. 10.4), yet he is there for Israel 'for the sake of the truth of God, to confirm the promises made unto the fathers' (Rom. 15.8). If the true heirs of Abraham, the father of the promise, are those in whom the Abrahamitic promise gives proof of itself in the Christ event in the power of the God who justifies men and creates life out of death, then that is the end of the Jew's precedence over the Gentile in the history of salvation. What was promised to Israel is now valid for all believers, both Jews and Gentiles. The promise is no longer exclusive, but becomes inclusive. It becomes universal. This universalizing of the promise comes of its being liberated from the confining grip of the law and the election of Israel. If in the power of God, as seen in the raising of the Crucified and, as a result of that, in the justification and calling of the godless, the promise has become unconditional – of grace and not of the law – then it has also become unrestricted and is therefore valid 'without distinction'. If the Christ event thus contains the validation ($\beta\epsilon\beta\alpha\acute{\iota}\omega\sigma\iota\varsigma$) of the promise, then this means no less than that through the faithfulness and truth of God the promise is made true in Christ – and made true wholly, unbreakably, for ever and for all. Nothing more stands in the way of its fulfilment, for sins are forgiven in him (Heb. 9.15). Between this once-for-all validation of the promise and its fulfilment in the glory of God there stands only the dependability of God himself. Hence the promise now determines the existence of the recipient and all he does and suffers. It is not that *vice versa* the fulfilling of the promise is determined by the existence and behaviour of the recipient.

The gospel has its inabrogable presupposition in the Old Testament history of promise. In the gospel the Old Testament history of promise finds more than a fulfilment which does away with it; it finds its future. 'All the promises of God in him are yea, and in him Amen' (II Cor. 1.20). They have become an eschatological certainty in Christ, by being liberated and validated, made unconditional and universal. The history of promise which the gospel presupposes is not annulled. The Israel which comes into view with the presupposed promise is not paganized,[9] but on the contrary it has disclosed to it in the gospel the future and the certainty of its own promises. The Christ event can be understood as a reversal of the history of promise: the first will be last. It is not that the Gentiles will come and worship when Zion is at the last redeemed from its shame, but Israel will come when the fulness of the Gentiles have become partakers of the promise in Christ (Rom. 9–11). Thus the gospel is not to be understood as antiquating the promises of Israel or even putting an end to them. In the ultimate, eschatological sense of these promises it is in fact identical with them.

On the other hand, the gospel itself becomes unintelligible, if the contours of the promise are not recognized in itself. It would lose its power to give eschatological direction, and would become either gnostic talk of revelation or else preaching of morals, if it were not made clear that the gospel constitutes on earth and in time the promise of the future of Christ. The gospel is promise and as promise it is an earnest of the promised future. 'The divine word in Christ is

---

9 Against G. Klein, *op. cit.*, p. 436.

new solely because its fulfilment can no longer be endangered or abolished, as was once the case, but has become incontestable; and it is unique, despite all its varied earthly movement and manifold testimony and despite its prolepsis in the Old Testament, because in Christ it not only reveals anew the one eschatological salvation, but in addition also conclusively guarantees the realizing of that salvation. As such it is already present and apprehensible in history, yet solely in the form of promise, i.e. as pointing and directing us towards a still outstanding future.'[10]

3. Paul and Abraham

How are we to regard the connection between gospel and promise, and thus in a wider sense also the relation between the New and the Old Testaments? Two radically opposed conceptions suggest themselves: the continuity can be understood in terms of a view of history as history of salvation,[11] or the discontinuity can be understood in terms of an existentialist interpretation of the gospel.[12] Both methods employ concepts of history with which it is barely possible to comprehend the manifold perspectives in which Paul expounds the gospel's relation to law and promise.

A view of the *continuity* in terms of the history of election or of salvation, whatever its precise form, understands the gospel as the fulfilment of the history that has preceded it. The event of Christ accordingly cannot be taken by itself as an isolated fact. It always requires the witness of the history which it fulfils, if its significance as an event of universal eschatological salvation is to be intelligible. It is only by the witness of the Old Testament 'scripture' that the gospel shows the Christ event to be the fulfilment of the history of God's election. This is done not only by taking the saving events of the New Testament as the clue to the exposition of the Old Testament, but also *vice versa* by taking the saving events of the Old Testament as the clue to the understanding of the event of Christ. It is true of course that Paul set the Old Testament promise

---

10 E. Käsemann, *Das wandernde Gottesvolk*, 4th ed. 1961, pp. 12f.

11 This is best shown by U. Wilckens' essay, 'Die Rechtfertigung Abrahams nach Röm. 4', *op. cit.*

12 This emerges most clearly in G. Klein's reply to Wilckens, 'Röm. 4 und die Idee der Heilsgeschichte', *op. cit.*

to Abraham in a universal eschatological context: the 'land' has become the world, and his 'seed' has become all nations.[13] But this reinterpretation must prove itself to be a true interpretation of what was to be interpreted. The Christian interpretation of Abraham must make the claim that 'this beginning of the history of election in the promise of God and the faith of Abraham' points '*in essence* to its end as its fulfilment'.[14] The result of this is on the one hand a view of the fulfilment in the Christ event in terms of 'history of election', and secondly, an 'essential' view of the meaning of this history, i.e. a view which is arrived at in the light of its end and which 'in truth' underlies the story of Abraham. The Christ event thus has its place in a definite history: it is the fulfilment of that history and as such reveals its essence and truth. Christian faith is grounded in history, itself stands in history, and trusts in history. Faith and history belong together. Faith is not a possibility which is severally, and to that extent generally, open to individuals, but is due to a definite history of election and is concrete trust in future divine action.

What is here asserted as a continuity in the history of election and salvation form Abraham to Christ is no doubt noetically accessible only from the standpoint of the Christ event. The exposition and appropriation of the promise to Abraham in Christian faith cannot, however, present itself as insight into an 'essentially' coherent chain from Abraham to Christ. Christian faith is not a view of the essence of history underlying the temporal and concrete statements of the Old Testament tradition. The 'newness' of the New Testament is not to be seen merely in the disclosing of the essence and truth of the Old Testament. The continuity cannot be defined merely in terms of an essence of history which becomes apparent in the light of its end.

An existentialist interpretation of the *discontinuity*, on the other hand, takes 'history' out of the light of the promise and sets it in the light of the law. History here becomes the epitome of existence under the law – of the fact that man must understand himself from

---

13 Whereas U. Wilckens speaks of an extension of the promise to Abraham in Pauline exegesis (*op. cit.*, p. 124), the tendency elsewhere is apparently to speak of a 'Pauline reduction' of the Abrahamitic promises to the fact of the promise having been given to Abraham, with little regard to its content. Cf. C. Dietzfelbinger, *op. cit.*, pp. 7ff.

14 U. Wilckens, *op. cit.*, p. 125.

his works and, in analogy thereto, from established, demonstrable complexes of history. 'History' is here understood as a genealogical force. It becomes the epitome of transience and degeneration. It becomes the realm of the things that are ready to man's hand, calculable, objectively demonstrable, at his disposal. All views of history which provide surveyable complexes thus belong in principle to the realm of deficient, objectifying thought. Understanding oneself from history is therefore synonymous with man's understanding of himself from the world. If history is understood in this way in the light of the law, then faith and history never belong together; on the contrary, faith lies 'athwart' history and destroys every kind of historic continuity, including that which is understood in terms of the history of election and salvation. Faith brings liberation from history and is itself the eschatological crisis of history in the individual. The element of continuity between Abraham and the believer is accordingly not to be regarded as a 'product of historic development', but can only be understood as 'a retrospective projection of faith',[15] which is not demonstrable by historical science and must therefore itself again be an object of faith.

But now, in this antithesis of history and faith, faith is dialectically anchored to a negative concept of history from which it must repeatedly distinguish itself. On the other hand, history is dialectically anchored to a subjectivistic concept of faith, as a result of which it must repeatedly be seen in terms of the above-mentioned identification of legalistic and objectifying thought. It is easy to see how strongly the modern positivistic concept of history prevails in this identification of legalistic and objectifying thought. The result of this concept is that the searching, knowing and objectifying subject frees itself from the power of history, of genealogy and of tradition by means of this reflection, and withdraws into the objectively incomprehensible background of a transcendental subjectivity and spontaneity. What a thus subjectified faith sees in history, must then become an 'expression' of faith itself. What a faith understood in such terms has to say of Abraham, becomes a 'projection' of faith – a projection which, because it is unprovable, faith believes. This, however, makes it unintelligible why Paul does not use the figure of Abraham merely to illustrate his own view of righteousness by faith, but enters into a dispute with Jews and

Jewish Christians over the inheritance of Abraham. In this antithesis to 'history' as such, which then includes automatically also
the Old Testament history of promise, it becomes as impossible
to say what is 'new' in the New Testament as to say what is 'new'
in gnosticism. But when the 'old' is thus defined in the light of
our antithesis to history that is seen as the realm of the objective,
demonstrable and disposable, then the 'new' becomes nothing else
but faith in the form of immediate subjectivity, of pure, subjective
conception from the realm of the indisposable. When we see it in
this light, the 'new' is not very new – not at least as compared with
the ecstatic gnostic passion for newness. The Old Testament is not
then regarded as being historic testimony to the promise and as
such having present relevance along with its fulfilment in the New
Testament, but it can be presented by a transcendentally understood faith in Christ only in terms of antithesis, as a thing we have
always left beneath us.

Now it is no doubt true that Paul rejects the idea of the Jews'
genealogical connection with Abraham being in itself soteriological.
Yet what he puts in its place is hardly a picture of Abraham as
projected by Christian faith, but he manifestly regards Abraham
and his promise as forming both theologically and materially a
necessary bone of contention with Torah Judaism. Projections of
faith which are undemonstrable and have to be believed are not
things one can contend about. A view of the essence of history, too,
is really only a thing one either can or cannot see. Paul, however,
deals 'objectively' with Abraham and his promise, in the sense that
he understands them as an object of contention in necessary proceedings against the Jews. Thus it is really a question of the correct
exposition of the Abrahamitic promise as between the claims of
the Torah and the claims of the gospel. The continuity with the
Abrahamitic promise can therefore be taken neither as a product
of historic development nor as a retrospective projection of faith.
The continuity of the promise to Abraham exists according to Paul
where the promise is eschatologically validated. If Paul is concerned
in this sense with the 'object' of the promise to Abraham, then his
exposition and appropriation of it is neither a dictate of the historic
development nor a creation of his believing phantasy. His gospel
does not derive by necessity from the essence of the history of election, but neither does the promise to Abraham appear in his gospel
by chance. Because his gospel proclaims the promise as validated

in the event of Christ, it starts the traditional promise to Abraham off on a new history. The promise finds in the gospel its eschatological future, while the law finds its end. The 'newness' of the gospel is thus not 'totally new'. It proves its newness by asserting itself against the old, against human nature in the context of law, sin and death, and thereby bringing about the 'oldness' of the old. It proves its eschatological newness, however, by using the previously proclaimed promise of God as the means of its explication. Paul rediscovers the promise to Abraham in the gospel of Christ and therefore recalls along with the gospel of Christ the promise to Abraham as well. The history of law and gospel takes its bearings from the theological problem of the past. The history of promise and gospel, however, takes its bearings from the eschatological problem of the future. Without the relating of the gospel to what was promised in advance, it loses its own bearing on the eschatological future and threatens to transform itself into gnostic talk of revelation. Without relation to the promise in the gospel, faith loses the driving-power of hope and becomes credulity.

Because the gospel presents itself as validation of the promise of the God of Abraham by the same God, it must enter into a judicial process with Judaism concerning the future of the promise, while on the other hand it must bring Gentiles to hope in the God of promise. It has then the Old Testament at its side neither as a historic documentation of its fulfilment nor as a history of examples of human failure in the things of God. Just as the promise is validated in the gospel, so also the Old Testament, inasmuch as it is witness to the history of the promise, is validated and renewed in the New Testament.

Formally speaking, between the promise to Abraham that is witnessed at many levels of the Old Testament and the gospel of Christ that is witnessed in the New Testament, there takes place a 'word-history',[16] a history of tradition or the history of the working of the traditional hope. This history of word and tradition is materially determined by that future which is announced and promised in the transmission and constantly new reception of the promise. That is why Paul apparently sees the continuity as being given in the 'scripture', whose meaning and goal he finds in the present hope (Rom. 15.4). What the scripture that was 'written

---

16 So E. Jüngel, ZTK 60, 1963, p. 46.

before our time' offers must therefore contain possibilities and a future to which present hope can be directed. The exposition and presentation of what was written 'aforetime' must accordingly pay attention to that in it which is promised, open, unsettled and points to the future. Because the gospel directs men to the future of eschatological salvation, it has its presupposition in the promises that were issued and written aforetime, and along with the future of Christ it presents also the future of what was aforetime promised (Rom. 1.2).[17] It links on to promises that have been issued but not yet fulfilled and takes them up into itself. This is a process belonging to the sphere of the history of the promise. The promise which was promised aforetime is not interpreted in terms of the history of salvation, nor is it taken as an opportune occasion for a new projection of faith, but it is validated. Something thereby happens to it – something the New Testament understands as eschatologically 'new' – but this new thing does happen to it. Remembering the promise issued aforetime means asking about the future in the past. It is dominated by that expectation which is made possible by the eschatological validation and liberation of the promise. The promise to Abraham is called to mind in order to proclaim the gospel of Christ to Jews and Gentiles and to call them into the new people of God. The calling to mind is thus a necessary part of the proclamation of the gospel. In this way of calling to mind past promises and in this hope in the form of remembrance we are no longer presented with the alternative between a complex of saving history which is a product of history, and unprovable retrospective projections of faith which are products of subjective faith. We take the past promises up into our own eschatological future as disclosed by the gospel and give them breadth. We do not interpret past history. We do not emancipate ourselves from history altogether, but we enter into the history that is determined by the promised and guar-

---

17 E. Jüngel, *op. cit.*, p. 45: 'To the past there belongs, as compared with the gospel, on the one hand the promise and on the other hand the law. The promise belongs to the past as the historic presupposition of the gospel – and that, too, in the sense that the gospel makes the promise the presupposition of *itself* (cf. Rom. 1.2). Since the promise has its future in the gospel and has its own time because of this future, I call the mode in which the promise belongs to the past as compared with the gospel *the anticipation* of the gospel (*das Zuvor des Evangeliums*). Because the law has its end in the gospel and is made past because of this end, I call the mode in which the law belongs to the past as compared with the gospel *the antecedent* of the gospel (*das Vorher des Evangeliums*).'

anteed *eschaton*, and we expect from it not only the future of the present but also the future of the past.

4. Fulfilment Ecstasy in Primitive Christianity and the *eschatologia crucis*

The promissory character of the gospel can be seen not only from the language used especially by Paul and in Hebrews. It shows itself still more plainly in the conflicts in which Paul was involved with various tendencies in primitive Christianity. As long as Christianity remained within the sphere of Judaism with its apocalyptic outlook and its expectation of the Messiah, it was only natural that it should take an eschatological view of the Christ event and of the gospel. Only, here the Christians also remained within the bounds of the Jewish expectations and understood themselves as the 'renewed people of God' and maintained the gospel as the 'renewed covenant' of Israel. It was only the move into the Gentile world that compelled them to a new understanding of the gospel. The gospel shows itself effective by justifying the godless and calling the Gentiles to the God of hope. The Church which thereby arises and consists of both Jews and Gentiles, can therefore no longer be understood as the 'renewed people of God' but now only as the 'new people of God'. This crossing of the frontiers of Israel on to Hellenistic soil, however, brought with it problems of considerable magnitude. If it was here no longer possible to understand the Church as a Christian synagogue, then it was a short step on the other hand to the misunderstanding of the Church as a Christian mystery religion. The question arises, what it was that prevented Christianity from presenting itself to the Hellenistic world as a Christian mystery religion. What was it in its inheritance that proved resistant to an assimilation of this kind?

The view of the Christian faith as a mystery religion takes palpable form for us in that ecstatic Hellenistic fervour with which Paul finds himself embroiled in Corinth.[18] Yet the various hymns and fragments of confessions in the Pauline and deutero-Pauline epistles also show that similar ideas presumably lay at the root of the whole Christian outlook where it came within the influence of the

---

18 I am here following E. Käsemann's studies in exegetical theology.

Hellenistic mystery religions. It is generally a question here of the influence exerted upon Christianity by the epiphany religion of the time, of which it can be said: 'Since the man of myth lives only for the present, epiphany is for him already fulfilment. Eschatological thinking is foreign to him.'[19] The influence of this kind of piety shows itself not only as a formal element in the self-presentation of Christianity on Hellenistic soil, but quite certainly extends also to the understanding of the event of Christ. The Christ event can here be understood in a wholly non-eschatological way as epiphany of the eternal present in the form of the dying and rising Kyrios of the cultus. Then, however, the place of the scriptural authentication κατὰ τὰς γραφάς is taken by the cultic epiphany as proof of its own self in a timeless sense. Baptism into the death and resurrection of Christ then means that the goal of redemption is already attained, for in this baptism eternity is sacramentally present. The believing participant is transposed from the realm of death, of constraining forces and of the old aeon of transience into the eternally present realm of freedom, of heavenly life and of resurrection. All that now remains for him on earth is to exhibit his new, heavenly nature in freedom. In the sacramental and spiritual presence of Christ, resurrection from the dead is already imparted to the receivers and is eternally present to them. The earthly body and the things of the world fade away to become for them an unreal semblance, in the disregarding of which they must give proof of their heavenly freedom.[20] 'Among these Gentile Christians, as I Corinthians amply shows, there is a total view of the tradition at work within a framework of ideas which is not – as with Paul himself – that of the primitive Christian eschatology of the early Jewish tradition, but manifestly that of Hellenistic ideas of epiphany. As a result of this, all religious thought and experience is so strongly oriented towards the ever present event of the coming of the Spirit as the epiphanous presentation of the exalted Kyrios, that the content of the eschatologically oriented tradition is included within this total view.'[21]

---

19 Elpidius Pax, *op. cit.*, p. 266.

20 Schniewind, 'Die Leugner der Auferstehung in Korinth', in *Nachgelassene Reden und Aufsätze*, 1952, pp. 110ff.; E. Käsemann, 'Zum Thema der urchristlichen Apokalyptik', *ZTK* 59, 1962, p. 277.

21 U. Wilckens, 'Der Ursprung der Überlieferung der Erscheinung des Auferstandenen', in *Dogma und Denkstruktur*, 1963, p. 61.

What is the relation between this Christian mystery religion, which we have here only roughly outlined, and the primitive Christian apocalyptic expectations that were kindled by the riddle and the open question of the Easter appearance of Jesus? Did the original apocalyptic already contain the conditions of its possible transformation into terms of the epiphany piety of Hellenistic mystery religion? Did Hellenistic mystery religion in its Christian form still remain what it originally was?

It is plain that the ecstasy of Christian mystery religion has its presupposition in an apocalyptic ecstasy which was a feature of primitive Christianity, and which thought to perceive in the experience of the Spirit the fulfilment of long awaited promises. This non-Hellenistic, apocalyptic ecstasy, which arose from the consciousness of living in the age of the fulfilment of the divine promises, was then certainly able later on to identify this fulfilment with the timeless epiphany of the eternal presence of God. It was theologically able to take the original, temporal and teleological statements about the fulfilment of promises and translate them into timeless types of the presence of the eternal. It was therefore also able *vice versa*, in face of the Greek search for the eternal present in the mystery cults, to offer the cult of Christ as the true presence of the eternal. Thus it is a reciprocal process, whose result could be a 'presentative eschatology' on the one hand, but also on the other hand a 'presence of eternity'. The ecstatic eschatology of fulfilment could present itself in Greek terms, and the Greek idea of the presence of eternity could offer itself as a fulfilment of eschatological expectations. Thus even the Christian mystery religion still retained the appeal of finality and uniqueness, even when the explicit connection with the old eschatological hopes for the future was lost. Yet the temporally final (*das Endzeitliche*) now became the conclusively final (*das Endgültige*), and the conclusively final became the eternal.[22] In the light of this process of transformation it is possible

---

22 This transformation has been very acutely perceived by H. von Soden. Cf. *Urchristentum und Geschichte* I, 1951, p. 29: 'Christianity was of course originally a message of the end of the world, of the new, heavenly aeon, and to that extent was critical of all culture. Yet it was just the strictly transcendental view of the new aeon, as a renewal that was to be miraculously brought about by God, that caused the critical attitude towards the old, existing aeon to be in practice extremely conservative. The existing order of things, as being the *temporally* final order, was felt to be historically speaking the *conclusively* final order. ... It is extremely important to be clear about this most peculiar view in

to understand the early Church's passion for absoluteness; for with the departure from the eschatological categories of expectation the Church did not by any means turn itself into a relative body among the existing religions and cults, but took its confession of the one God, which could then be formulated in the terms of Greek metaphysics, and combined it quite definitely with a passionate assertion of the final and unique revelation of the one and only God in Christ. This process of transformation, which has often been described, took place not so much on the ground of an eschatology that had been abandoned because of the delayed parousia of Christ and the disappointed hopes of his nearness, as rather on the ground of an ecstasy of fulfilment which took the *eschaton* that was to be expected and transformed it into the presence of eternity as experienced in cultus and in spirit. It was not so much disappointed hopes but rather the supposed fulfilment of all hopes that led the acute Hellenization of Christianity but also to the acute Christianizing of Hellenism. 'Expectation of the nearness of Christ and his parousia has now become meaningless, because all that apocalyptic still hoped for appears to be already realized.'[23]

What are the consequences of this view of presentative eschatology as the presence of eternity? The event of promise, which is what the life and teaching, dying and raising of Jesus were held to be, now becomes an event of redemption, which can be subsequently repeated in the cultus in the form of a mystery drama. The sacramental event bestows participation in the dying and rising of the God. The solemn representation regarded the raising of Jesus as his enthronement as exalted Kyrios and took it to be already completed and therefore now awaiting only representation. 'In place of the hidden Lord of the world, who in truth is as yet only designated as such and whose return in glory to assume earthly power is still awaited by the Church, we have the Lord who now already reigns over all forces and powers and thus over the world hitherto dominated by them.'[24] With this change from the apocalyptic of the promised and still outstanding lordship of Christ to the cultic

---

early Christianity of the temporally final as the conclusively final, in other words the transformation of the temporally final into the conclusively final, of the transient into the immutable; and thus to be clear that the eschatological revolution necessarily worked out as a most conservative force. ...'

23 E. Käsemann, *ZTK* 59, 1962, p. 278.
24 *Ibid.*, p. 274.

presence of his eternal, heavenly lordship there goes at the same time also a waning of theological interest in the cross. The resurrection of Jesus is regarded as his exaltation and enthronement and is related to his incarnation. To be sure, his humiliation even to the cross can be understood as the perfecting of his incarnation, by means of which he draws all things into the sphere of his lordship, yet the cross is in this way made only a transitional stage on his way to heavenly lordship. The cross does not remain until the fulfilment of the *eschaton* the abiding key-signature of his lordship in the world. If his resurrection is understood in this sense as his heavenly enthronement, then the sacramental event which represents him in the cultus becomes a parallel to his incarnation and is taken as an earthly adumbration and accomplishment of his heavenly lordship, his heavenly life in the realm of the things that are earthly, transient and split up into a multitude of forces.

History thus loses its eschatological direction. It is not the realm in which men suffer and hope, groaning and travailing in expectation of Christ's future for the world, but it becomes the field in which the heavenly lordship of Christ is disclosed in Church and sacrament. In place of the eschatological 'not yet' (*noch nicht*) we have a cultic 'now only' (*nur noch*), and this becomes the key-signature of history *post Christum*. It is understandable that this disclosure of the eternal, heavenly lordship of Christ can then be regarded as a continuation of his incarnation. Here the transient continues in the light of the intransient things of heaven, the mortal continues in the light of the immortal things of heaven, and what is split up into multiplicity is transfigured in the lordship of the divinely one. A future expectation which is expressed sacramentally and in terms of salvation history takes the place of that of earthly eschatology: the Church gradually permeates the world with heavenly truth, with powers of heavenly life and with heavenly salvation. The world is led by the one Church to the Christ who is one with the one God, and is thus brought to unity and salvation. The eschatological expectation of what has 'not yet' happened becomes a noetic expectation of the universal disclosure and glorification of what has already happened in heaven. The old apocalyptic dualism which distinguished the passing aeon from the coming aeon is transformed into a metaphysical dualism which understands the coming as the eternal and the passing as transience. Instead of citizens of the coming kingdom we have a people redeemed from heaven. Instead of the citizens of the passing aeon we have those that are earthly and of the world. And finally, the cross becomes a timeless sacrament of martyrdom which perfects the martyr and unites him with the heavenly Christ.

With these few examples we can let the matter rest. The trend towards early Catholicism and the life and thought of the ancient Church is plain. The ecstasy of eschatological fulfilment in the Christ event is the presupposition for this process of the transformation of Christianity into an ecstatic form of Hellenistic mystery religion and into an ecumenical world Church. This form of 'presentative eschatology', this religion of the presence of the eternal whose eschatological determination is now only subliminal, can be called an *eschatologia gloriae*, if it is still possible to comprehend it in eschatological categories at all.

In this context Paul's passionate polemic against Hellenistic ecstasy in Corinth acquires an abiding significance, as do also his correctives to that Hellenistic type of Christian theology which afterwards became standard. His criticism clearly has two focal points. For one thing, there is an 'eschatological proviso'[25] which he maintains against this fulfilment ecstasy. It consists of the so-called 'relics of apocalyptic theology' which assert themselves in his view of the resurrection of Christ, of the sacrament, of the presence of the Spirit, of the earthly obedience of the believer, and of course in his future expectations. And secondly, there is his theology of the cross, in which he opposes the ecstasy that abandons the earth on which that cross stands. There is a profound material connection between these two starting points of his criticism. We shall therefore call the basis of his criticism the *eschatologia crucis*, meaning by this both objections in one.

When Bultmann interprets Paul by seeing the heart of Pauline theology in Paul's anthropological and existentialist interpretation of the peculiarity of presentative eschatology, then he has undoubtedly discovered an important modification of the theology of the eternal present, but not really a fundamental alternative to it. Presentative eschatology can appear equally well both in mythological dress and in existentialist interpretation. The 'presence of eternity' can be expressed both in the language of world-picture and myth, and can also be stated in paradoxical terms as a *nunc*

25 E. Käsemann, *ZTK* 59, 1962, p. 279.

aeternum in the history of existence. If Pauline criticism consisted merely in this transposition, then it would certainly contain an important modification of the theology of the Hellenistic church, but not a truly transforming corrective. But now, the polemic in which Paul attacks Hellenism is marked both by a new recognition of the significance of the cross of Christ and also by a new recognition of a truly futurist eschatology, and thus becomes a criticism of presentative eschatology as such.[26] 'The apostle's anti-ecstatic struggle, however, is in the last and deepest analysis fought out in the name of apocalyptic.'[27] This does not refer to mere repetitions or tiresome relics of late Jewish apocalyptic in Paul, but means his own apocalyptic, which is kindled by an eschatology of the cross and is therefore hostile to every eschatological ecstasy of fulfilment.

Against the uniting of the believer with the dying and rising Lord of the cultus after the fashion of the mysteries Paul asserts an eschatological distinction: baptism is the means of participation in the Christ event of the crucifixion and death of Christ. Fellowship with Christ is fellowship in suffering with the crucified Christ. The baptized are dead with Christ, if they are baptized into his death. But they are not already risen with him and translated into heaven in the perfect tense of the cultus. They attain participation in the resurrection of Christ by new obedience, which unfolds itself in the realm of the hope of resurrection. In the power of the Spirit who raised Christ from the dead, they can obediently take upon them the sufferings of discipleship and in these very sufferings await the future glory. 'Participation in the resurrection is spoken of not in the perfect, but in the future tense.'[28] Christ is risen and beyond the reach of death, yet his followers are not yet beyond the reach of death, but it is only through their hope that they here attain to participation in the life of the resurrection. Thus resurrection is present to them in hope and as promise. This is an eschatological presentness of the future, not a cultic presence of the eternal. The believer does not already in the cultus and in spirit find full participation in the lordship of Christ, but he is led by hope into the tensions and antitheses of obedience and suffering in the world. The life of everyday accordingly becomes the sphere of the true service of God (Rom. 12.1ff.). Inasmuch as call and promise point the believer on

---

26 E. Käsemann, *ZTK* 54, 1957, p. 14.
27 E. Käsemann, *ZTK* 59, 1962, p. 279.
28 *Ibid.*

the way of obedience in the body and on earth, earth and the body are set within the horizon of the expectation of the coming lordship of Christ. 'The reality of the new life stands or falls with the promise that God remains faithful and does not abandon his work.'[29] Hence the trials of the body and the opposition of the world are not understood as signs of a paradoxical presence of the eternal but are accepted in terms of seeking after, and calling for, the coming freedom in the kingdom of Christ. This is not 'now only' the sphere of transience, in which the believer has to demonstrate his heavenly freedom, but it is the reality in which the Church along with the whole creation groans for its redemption from the powers of annihilation in the future of Christ and earnestly awaits it (Rom. 8.18ff.). The imperative of the Pauline call to new obedience is accordingly not to be understood merely as a summons to demonstrate the indicative of the new being in Christ, but it has also its eschatological presupposition in the future that has been promised and is to be expected – the coming of the Lord to judge and to reign. Hence it ought not to be rendered merely by saying: 'Become what you are!', but emphatically also by saying: 'Become what you will be!'

The believer is given not the eternal Spirit of heaven, but the eschatological 'earnest of the Spirit' – of the Spirit, moreover, who *has* raised Christ from the dead and *will* quicken our mortal bodies (Rom. 8.11). For the word which leads the believer into the truth is promise of eternal life, but not yet that life itself. The observance of this eschatological distinction manifests itself also in the apostle's Christology. If in I Cor. 15.3–5 he takes over a primitive Christian tradition of the resurrection kerygma, yet his expositions of it in the verses that follow are nevertheless original. He extends the picture into the future and shows what is to be expected because with the resurrection of Christ it is held in prospect and has been made a certainty (I Cor. 15.25): 'He *must* reign, till he hath put all enemies under his feet.'[30] This shows that in the future possibilities

---

29 E. Käsemann, 'Paulus und der Frühkatholizismus', *ZTK* 60, 1963, p. 83.

30 Paul's eschatological thinking always combines the perfect tense of the raising of Jesus with the future tense of the eschatological future. Both are seen in a context in which each is the ground of the other. The primitive Christian confession, 'that Jesus died and is risen', is thus expounded in a way totally different from the mystery cult of the dying and rising God. The Christ event is presented within the framework of an eschatological expectation of what is to come, and the future expectation is grounded in the Christ event. I Thess. 4.14

there is an element of necessity in the sense that they can be relied on and are to be expected. The tendencies and latent implications in the resurrection event are drawn out into the future opened up by it. With the raising of Jesus all has not yet been done. The end of death's domination is still outstanding. The overcoming of all opposition to God is still outstanding in that future reality of which Paul says that 'God will be all in all' (I Cor. 15.28). Finally, even the coming world lordship of Christ over all his enemies can once again be eschatologically surpassed, in that not even his lordship is in itself the eternal presence of God, but has an eschatologically provisional character in which it serves the sole and all-embracing lordship of God.

When these perspectives are borne in mind, then it becomes clear that the Easter appearances of the risen Christ are not covered by the theological answer that he is the presence of the eternal, but require the development of a new eschatology. The resurrection has set in motion an eschatologically determined process of history, whose goal is the annihilation of death in the victory of the life of the resurrection, and which ends in that righteousness in which God receives in all things his due and the creature thereby finds its salvation. It is only from the standpoint of a presentative eschatology or a theology of the eternal present that the eschatological and anticipatory thinking displayed by Paul in I Cor. 15 can be regarded as a relapse into outmoded apocalyptic mythology. Yet it is not by an existentialist interpretation of the religion of the eternal present that the mythology of that religion is overcome, but only an eschatology of promise can overcome its mythical and illusionary view of the world and of human existence, because it alone takes the trials, the contradictions and the godlessness of this world seriously in a meaningful way, because it makes faith and obedi-

---

('if we believe *that* Jesus *died* and *rose* again, even so them also which sleep in Jesus *will* God bring with him') is as typical of this as is the exposition of the confession of I Cor. 15.3–5 in I Cor. 15.20ff. In all this, the connection between the resurrection of Jesus and the future which is expected is neither uniformly apocalyptic nor uniformly christological, but mutually complementary: If there is no resurrection of the dead, then neither is Christ risen. If Christ is risen, then the dead will rise and Christ 'must' reign over all his enemies, including also death. It is not a δεῖ ('must') in terms of salvation history, but one that discloses the future necessity and future tendency inherent in the event of the resurrection of Jesus. That is why it is linked not to the expectation of a fate, as in apocalyptic, but to the Kyrios title of Jesus. Cf. U. Wilckens, 'Der Ursprung der Überlieferung ...', in *Dogma und Denkstruktur* 1963, pp. 55ff.

ence possible in the world not by regarding the contradictions as of no account, but by enabling us to believe and obey on the ground of our hope in the overcoming of these contradictions by God. Faith does not come to its own in becoming radically unworldly, but by hopeful outgoing into the world it becomes a benefit to the world. By accepting the cross, the suffering and the death of Christ, by taking upon it the trials and struggles of obedience in the body and surrendering itself to the pain of love, it proclaims in the everyday world the future of the resurrection, of life and the righteousness of God. The future of the resurrection comes to it as it takes upon itself the cross. Thus the eschatology of the future and the theology of the cross are interwoven. It is neither that futuristic eschatology is isolated, as in late Jewish apocalyptic, nor does the cross become the mark of the paradoxical presence of eternity in every moment, as in Kierkegaard. The eschatological expectation of the all-embracing lordship of Christ for the corporeal, earthly world brings the clear perception and acceptance of the distinction of the cross and the resurrection.

Finally, it should be noticed that Paul is not so much concerned with a compromise between presentative and futuristic eschatology, that is, with a compromise between apocalyptic and Hellenism. Rather, the content of the Hellenistic idea of the presence of the eternal is futurized by him and applied to the still outstanding *eschaton*. That all-embracing truth in which the creature comes into saving harmony with God, that all-embracing righteousness in which God receives his due in all things and all becomes well, that glory of God in whose reflected light all things are transfigured and the hidden face of man disclosed – all this is set by Paul within the realm of hope in that future to which faith looks forward on the ground of the raising of the crucified Lord. The fulness of all things from God, in God and to God lies for him in the still outstanding fulfilment of the promises guaranteed in Christ. 'Eternal presence' is therefore the eschatological, future goal of history, not its inmost essence. Creation is therefore not the things that are given and lie to hand, but the future of these things, the resurrection and the new being.

God is not somewhere in the Beyond, but he is coming and as the coming One he is present. He promises a new world of all-embracing life, of righteousness and truth, and with this promise he constantly calls this world in question – not because to the eye of hope it is as nothing, but because to the eye of hope it is not yet what it has the prospect of being. When the world and the human nature bound up with it are called in question in this way, then they become 'historic', for they are staked upon, and submitted to the crisis of, the promised future. Where the new begins, the old becomes manifest. Where the new is promised, the old becomes transient and surpassable. Where the new is hoped for and expected, the old can be left behind. Thus 'history' arises in the light of its end, in the things which happen because of, and become perceptible through, the promise that lights up the way ahead. Eschatology does not disappear in the quicksands of history, but it keeps history moving by its criticism and hope; it is itself something like a sort of quicksand of history from afar. The impression of general transience that comes of looking back sorrowfully upon the things that cannot endure, has in actual fact as such nothing to do with history. Rather, that transience is historic which comes of hope, of exodus, of setting out towards the promised, not yet visible future. The reason why the Church of Christ has here no 'continuing city' is, that it seeks the 'city to come' and therefore goes forth without the camp to bear the reproach of Christ. The reason for its here having no continuing city is not that in history there is nothing that continues at all. In the eyes of Christian hope the epithet 'transient' belongs not only to the things which we generally feel are destined to pass away, but it sees as transient those very things which are generally felt to be always there and to cause the transience of all life, namely, evil and death. Death becomes transient in the promised resurrection. Sin becomes transient in the justification of the sinner and the righteousness for which we have to hope.

It is neither that history swallows up eschatology (Albert Schweitzer) nor does eschatology swallow up history (Rudolf Bultmann). The *logos* of the *eschaton* is promise of that which is not yet, and for that reason it *makes* history. The promise which announces the *eschaton*, and in which the *eschaton* announces itself, is the motive power, the mainspring, the driving force and the torture of history.

5. The 'Death of God' and the Resurrection of Christ

Christianity stands or falls with the reality of the raising of Jesus
from the dead by God. In the New Testament there is no faith that
does not start *a priori* with the resurrection of Jesus. Paul is clearly
taking over a basic form of the primitive Christian confession when
he says in Rom. 10.9: 'If thou shalt confess with thy mouth the Lord
Jesus, and shalt believe in thine heart that God bath raised him
from the dead, thou shalt be saved.' The confession to the person
of Jesus as the Lord and the confession to the work of God who
raised him from the dead belong inseparably together, although the
two formulae do not coincide but mutually expound each other. A
Christian faith that is not resurrection faith can therefore be called
neither Christian nor faith. It is the knowledge of the risen Lord
and the confession to him who raised him that form the basis on
which the memory of the life, work, sufferings and death of Jesus
is kept alive and presented in the gospels. It is the recognition of
the risen Christ that gives rise to the Church's recognition of its
own commission in the mission to the nations. It is the remembrance of his resurrection that is the ground of the inclusive hope in
the universal future of Christ. The central statements of the primitive Christian missionary proclamation are therefore: 1. 'God has
raised the crucified Jesus from the dead' (Acts 2.24; 3.15; 5.31; I
Cor. 15.4; and frequently elsewhere). 2. 'Of this we are witnesses.'
3. In him is grounded the future of righteousness for sinners and
the future of life for those subject to death. The fact, the witness
and the eschatological hope belong together in the Easter kerygma.
It is true that in the different angles of approach adopted in more
detailed study of the circumstances, ideas and expectations they
can be distinguished, but they cannot be separated from each other.
The question, 'What can I know of the historical facts?' cannot
here be separated from the ethical and existential question, 'What
am I to do?' and from the eschatological question, 'What may I
hope for?' – just as the other questions in turn cannot be isolated.
Only when concerted attention is given to these three questions
does the reality of the resurrection disclose itself.

   When the question of the reality of the resurrection is raised
today, then it mostly takes the form: *Is* he risen? In what modus
of *esse* is the reality of the resurrection to be understood? *Is* he
risen in the sense of a reality accessible to 'historical science'? *Is* he

risen in the sense of a reality belonging to the history of ideas and traditions? Is he risen in the sense of a reality that affects our own existence? Is he risen in the sense of a wishful reality of human longings and hopes?

The question of the reality of the resurrection of Christ can thus be asked in the light of a number of very different views of reality that are possible today. Hence it is not only the nature of the reality of the resurrection that stands in question, but also the reality on the basis of which the question of the reality of the resurrection is shaped, motivated and formulated.

We shall therefore have to try first of all to discover the point of approach at which the answer to the question of the reality of the resurrection of Christ can become plain. This approach cannot be by any single question within the context of those that can be asked on the basis of reality today, but it can only be a question which embraces the whole modern experience of the world, of self and of the future – a question which we ourselves constitute with our whole reality. If the question of the reality of the resurrection is tied down, say, to the question of the relevance and significance of this piece of church teaching, or to the question of the historical probability of the fact of Jesus' resurrection, or to the question of its real meaning for heart and conscience, or to the question of the hopes it may possibly contain, then the situation out of which the question arises and towards which it is directed is tacitly left as it was and simply taken for granted. It might well be, however, that the recognition of the reality of the resurrection calls this very situation in question.

Now of course it is difficult to find a single designation for the situation out of which the question of the reality of the resurrection of Christ can arise one way or another today. Yet it is no accident when this situation is interpreted by expounding the statement of Hegel and Nietzsche:

'God is dead.'

For that is not merely a statement of philosophical metaphysics or of theology, but is one which also seems to lie at the foundations of modern experience of self and the world and to provide the ground for the atheism that characterizes the methods of science. All possible questions as to the reality of the resurrection which are asked in such a way as to define this reality in 'historical' or 'existentialist' or 'utopian' terms, have their ground in the a-theistic form of the historian's view of history, of man's view of himself, and of his utopian view of the future. In none of these ways of dealing with reality does the idea of God thrust itself upon us as necessary. It has become partly superfluous, partly optional – at all events in its traditional theological and metaphysical form. Hence the proclamation of the raising of Jesus from the dead by God has also become partly superfluous, partly optional, as long as 'God' is understood as something that is known to us from history, from the world or from human existence. Only when along with the knowledge of the resurrection of Jesus the 'God of the resurrection' can be shown to be 'God' in terms of the 'death of God' that has become familiar to us from history, from the world and from our own existence – only then is the proclamation of the resurrection, and only then are faith and hope in the God of promise, something that is necessary, that is new, that is possible in an objectively real sense.

The origin of the impression that 'God is dead' gives some indication of this. The early romantic poet Jean Paul in his nightmare vision, 'Die Rede des toten Christus vom Weltgebäude herab, dass kein Gott sei' ('Address by the Dead Christ from the Heights of the Cosmic System to the Effect that there is no God'), placed this statement appropriately on the lips of the risen and returning Christ.[31] He himself wished only to give an idea of how it would feel if atheism were true – yet he had a greater effect than any other upon the romanticist nihilism of modern times. His marks are found in Stifter, Keller, Dostoievsky and Nietzsche. Heine's *Mönche des Atheismus*, the martyrs in F. Schlegel's *Diktatur des Nichts*, and also Dostoievski's *The Possessed*, were all influenced by him.[32] The setting of Jean Paul's piece is the hour of the Last Judgment. The Christ who is awaited by the dead comes and proclaims: 'There is no God. I was mistaken. Everywhere is only stark, staring nothing, the death rigour of infinity. Eternity lies in chaos, gnaws at it and turns self-ruminant.' This vision is like a commentary on I Cor. 15.13ff. Hence it is significant that the message, 'There is no God', is proclaimed in terms of despair of the hope of resurrection. It is

31 Cf. the text in G. Bornkamm, *Studien zu Antike und Urchristentum*, 1959, pp. 245ff.
32 W. Rehm, *Experimentum medietatis, Studien zur Geistes- und Literaturgeschichte des 19. Jahrhunderts*, 1947, now partly reprinted in *Jean Paul – Dostojewski. Zur dichterischen Gestaltung des Unglaubens*, 1962.

plain that for Jean Paul the reality of God and the hope of resurrection depend on each other both for faith and for unbelief.

Hegel in 1802 described the 'death of God' as the basic feeling of the religion of modern times and saw in it a new interpretation of Good Friday: 'The pure notion, however, or infinity as the abyss which engulfs all being, must take the infinite pain – which till now was historic only in culture and in the form of the feeling upon which the religion of modern times rests, the feeling that God himself is dead (that feeling which was merely empirically expressed, so to speak, in Pascal's words: "la nature est telle qu'elle *marque* partout un *Dieu perdu* et dans l'homme et hors de l'homme") – and designate it purely as an element, but also no more than an element, of the highest idea, and so give a philosophical existence to that which, as could also happen, was either a moral demand for sacrifice of empirical being or else the concept of formal abstraction, and thereby restore to philosophy the idea of absolute freedom, thus taking absolute suffering, or the speculative Good Friday which was otherwise historical, and restoring it in nothing less than the "full truth and stringency of its godlessness, out of which stringency alone – because the cheerful, more unfathomable and more individual aspects of the dogmatic philosophies and of the nature religions must disappear – the highest totality can and must rise again in all its seriousness and from its deepest foundation, as also all-embracingly, and in the most cheerful freedom of form' (*Glauben und Wissen*, in *op. cit.*, pp. 123f.). Hegel meant by this that modern atheism and nihilism, which causes the disappearance of all dogmatic philosophies and all nature religions, can be understood as a universalizing of the historic Good Friday of the god-forsakenness of Jesus, so that it becomes a speculative Good Friday of the forsakenness of all that is. Only then does resurrection, as a resurrection of the totality of being out of nothing, and only then does the birth of freedom and cheerfulness out of infinite pain, become a prospect necessary to all that is. If the modern a-theistic world thus comes to stand in the shadow of Good Friday, and Good Friday is conceived by it as the abyss of nothingness that engulfs all being, then there arises on the other hand the possibility of conceiving this foundering world in theological terms as an element in the process of the now all-embracing and universal revelation of God in the cross and resurrection of reality. Then the stringency of the world's god-forsakenness is not in itself enough to ruin it, but its ruination comes only when it abstracts the element of the expending and death of God from the dialectical process of God and fastens on that. The romanticist nihilism of the 'death of God', like the methodical atheism of science (*etsi Deus non daretur*), is an element that has been isolated from the dialectical process and is therefore no longer engaged in the movement of the process to which it belongs. From the theological standpoint one thing at least is unforgettably plain in Hegel – that the resurrection and the future of God must manifest themselves not only in the case of the god-forsakenness of the crucified Jesus, but also in that of the god-forsakenness of the world.[33]

This speculative dialectic even in the very matter of God or the highest idea had already eluded the grasp of Kierkegaard. Kierkegaard returned to the dualism of Kant and radicalized it. The age of infinite reflection no longer allows of any objective certainty in regard to the being or the self-motion of objects. Doubt and criticism do away with all mediation of the absolute in the objective. Thus all that remains is, in irreconcilable dialectic, the paradoxical antithesis of a theoretical atheism and an existential inner life, of objective godlessness and subjective piety. The inner life of the immediate and unmediated relationship of existence and transcendence goes hand in hand with contempt for outward things as absurd, meaningless and godless. Kierkegaard's 'individual' falls out of the dialectic of mediation and reconciliation and falls back upon pure immediacy. His 'inner life' is, even to the extent of verbal parallels, the 'unhappy consciousness' of Hegel's *Phenomenology of Mind*, only isolated from Hegel's dialectic and abstracted from its movement. When the unhappy consciousness of the 'beautiful soul' fastens upon itself and seeks in its own inward immediacy all that is glorious along with all that is transcendent, then at the same time it fastens down the world of objects to rigid immutability and sanctions its inhuman and godless conditions. Since no reconciliation between the inward and the outward can be hoped for, it is also pointless to expend oneself on the pain of the negative, to take upon oneself the cross of reality. The god-forsakenness and absurdity of a world that has become a calculable world of wares and techniques can now serve only as a negative urge towards the attaining of pure inwardness. This dialectic that has frozen into an eternal paradox is the mark of romanticism and of all romanticist theology.

A different exposition of the statement, 'God is dead', appears in Nietzsche and Feuerbach. 'God is dead! God stays dead! And it is we who have killed him! ... Is not the greatness of this deed too great for us? Must we not ourselves become gods, if we are to appear worthy

---

33 For an exposition cf. G. Rohrmoser, *Subjektivität und Verdinglichung*, 1961, pp. 83ff.; K. Löwith, 'Hegels Aufhebung der christlichen Religion', in *Einsichten: Festschrift für G. Krüger*, 1962, pp. 156ff.

of it? There was never a greater deed – and whosoever is born after us belongs because of this deed to a history higher than any history was till now!' [F. Nietzsche, *Die fröhliche Wissenschaft*, No. 125.] Here the death of God is ascribed to man, who has killed him, not to God's expending of his own self. God's death is the exaltation of man above himself. History, which man takes into his own hands, is built upon the corpse of God. The cross becomes the symbol of the victory of man over God and himself. 'Dead are all gods: let us now see the superman live.' When the feeling of the modern age that God is dead is thus based on saying that we have killed him, then this is in very close proximity to Feuerbach's abolition of God through which man is said to come to himself. Only, Nietzsche is thinking of an event and of a new destiny given to our being, and not merely of a re-subjectifying of religious objectifications. The result is not man's coming to himself in his sensual presence and immediacy, but man's self-transcendence and his rising beyond himself. Yet even here in Nietzsche the place which for meta-physical thinking would belong to God, as being the place of effective cause, is now no longer experienced in the passivity of the human sub-ject, but in his activity (M. Heidegger, *Holzwege*, 1957, pp. 236ff.). The 'world' is the projection and object of our subjectivity. It is conse-quently 'disenchanted' to become the material for possible changes. It is no longer able to reconcile our subjectivity with itself. The all-powerful self becomes abstract identity. This new self-transcendence in the experi-ence of being able to dominate the world is, to be sure, the end of all cosmological metaphysics and theology, but not by any means the end of metaphysics as such, for it contains a metaphysic of subjectivity. Its 'atheism' is merely theoretic atheism in regard to the world of objects. The subject, on the other hand – that *fundamentum inconcussum* which is so certain of itself in all human activity – arrogates to itself all the traditional divine predicates of metaphysics and theology (*causa sui* in Feuerbach and Marx, transcendence in Nietzsche). If Christian faith is given its theological home in this subjectivity, then it inevitably becomes a *creatrix divinitatis*, a god-creating and god-venturing force. This faith – mysticism becomes the necessary complement of the math-ematics which man uses to prescribe to the world its laws. This means, however, that here, too, we have an exposition of the statement, 'God is dead', which returns in the end to those antitheses in the modern consciousness which Hegel's dialectic was meant to reconcile. Hegel had addressed himself both to the banishing of God from the world on the part of mathematics and to the corresponding rise of man to the throne of immediate subjectivity, and had sought to understand and accept both of these as elements in the process of the self-movement of absolute Spirit. The following sentences, in which Feuerbach characterizes Hegel's solution and seeks to reduce it *ad absurdum*, give much food for theological thought: 'Hegel's philosophy was the last great attempt to restore a lost and ruined Christianity by means of philosophy – whereby, as is general in recent times, the *negation* of Christianity *is identified with Christianity itself*. This contradiction is obscured and hidden from sight in Hegel only by turning the negation of God, or atheism, into an objective determination of God – God is defined as a process, and atheism as an element in this process. But just as the faith that is reconstructed on the basis of unbelief is no true faith, because it is constantly entrammelled with its opposite, so the God who reconstructs himself on the basis of his own negation is no true God, but on the contrary a self-contradictory, atheistic God' (*Grundsätze der Philosophie der Zukunft*, 1843, §21).

Here it becomes plain that Feuerbach knows only the God of dogmatic philosophy and nature religion, for it is only this God who in his abstract identity can be reduced to man. Christian faith, however, constantly rises on the ground of the conquest of unbelief and has the latter always at its side to vex it. The risen Christ is and remains the crucified Christ. The God who in the event of the cross and resurrection reveals himself as 'the same' is the God who reveals himself in his own contradiction. Out of the night of the 'death of God' on the cross, out of the pain of the negation of himself, he is experienced in the resurrection of the crucified one, in the negation of the negation, as the God of promise, as the coming God. If 'atheism' finds its radical form in the recognition of the universal significance of Good Friday, then it is a fact that the God of the resurrection is in some sort an 'a-theistic' God. This is presumably also what Dietrich Bonhoeffer means – in Hegel's sense, and not in Feuerbach's – when he writes: 'And we cannot be honest unless we recognize that we have to live in the world *"etsi deus non daretur"*. And this is just what we do recognize – before God! ... God would have us know that we must live as men who manage our lives without him. The God who is with us is the God who forsakes us. ... Before God and with God we live without God. God lets himself be pushed out of the world on to the cross. He is weak and powerless in the world, and that is precisely the way, the only way, in which he is with us and helps us.'[34] Only, the god-forsakenness of the cross cannot,

---

34 *Widerstand und Ergebung*, 1951, pp. 241f.; ET by R. H. Fuller: *Letters and Papers from Prison* (1953), 3rd ed. revised by F. Clarke, 1967, p. 196.

as in Hegel, be made into an element belonging to the divine process and thus immanent in God. A theology of the dialectical self-movement of absolute Spirit would then be only a modification of the dialectical epiphany of the eternal as subject. Hegel attempted to reconcile faith and knowledge – but at the price of doing away with the historicity of the event of revelation and understanding it as an eternal event. 'For concept cancels time.' But the cross – the hiddenness of God and the independence of man – is not at once 'done away with' in the *logos* of reflection and of consciousness, but is taken up for the time being into the promise and hope of a still outstanding, real *eschaton*, which is a stimulus to the consciousness but is not resolved into the believing consciousness. The cross is the mark of an eschatological openness which is not yet closed by the resurrection of Christ and the spirit of the Church, but remains open beyond both of these until the future of God and the annihilation of death. When it is precisely Nietzsche's 'frantic man' who cries incessantly, 'I seek God', then that surely points in this direction. It is one thing whether the 'death of God' leads to the enthronement of deified man, and quite another thing whether the 'death of God' causes us, on the ground of our preview of resurrection in the raising of Christ, to ask, seek and hope for resurrection, life, kingdom and righteousness and thus, through this asking, seeking and hoping and the criticism, opposition and suffering that result from them, gives the world that has established itself upon the corpse of God its proper setting in the historic process of the future of the truth. The world is then not engulfed in the abyss of nothingness, but its negative aspects are taken up into the 'not yet' of hope. The world is not stabilized in eternal being, but is 'held' in the 'not yet being' of a history open towards the future.

6. The Historical Question of the Resurrection of Christ and the Questionableness of the Historical Approach to History

The first question regarding the reality of the resurrection of Christ will always be concerned with the fact which is reported and proclaimed by the Easter witnesses. Since this fact is reported as an event – namely, as the 'raising of Jesus from the dead by God' – the question as to the reality of this event will in the first instance take the form of a historical question. Even if the witnesses did not attempt after the fashion of ancient chroniclers or modern historians only to report what happened, yet they did speak of a fact and an event whose reality lay for them outside their own consciousness and their own faith, whose reality was indeed the origin of their consciousness in remembrance and hope. They did not merely wish to tell of their own new self-understanding in the Easter faith, but in that faith and as a result of it they reported something also about the way of Jesus and about the event of the raising of Jesus. Their statements contain not only existential certainty in the sense of saying, 'I am certain,' but also and together with this objective certainty in the sense of saying, 'It is certain.' They did not merely proclaim that they believe, and what they believe, but therewith and therein also the fact they have recognized. They are 'selfless witnesses', so to speak.[35] Hence it is not by any means self-evident that the point of their statements is the new self-understanding of faith.[36] Rather, the Easter narratives themselves compel us to ask about the reality of the event of which they tell. It is not their own faith, nor the demand for faith or offer of faith bound up with their proclamation, that constitutes the reality underlying their statements, but it is solely the reality of the fact declared and proclaimed that must correspond with their declarations and their proclamation. It would be foreign to the intention of the Easter texts themselves, if the 'point' of their statements were to be sought solely in the birth of faith. There can thus be no forbidding the attempt to go behind their kerygma and ask about the reality which underlies their statements and makes them dependable and credible.[37]

Now these questions as to the certainty of the reality which underlies the proclamation of the resurrection and makes it legitimate

---

35 For this expression cf. H. G. Gadamer, 'Zur Problematik des Selbstverständnisses', in *Einsichten. Festschrift für G. Krüger*, 1962, p. 84.

36 Cf. R. Bultmann, *Das Verhältnis der urchristlichen Christusbotschaft zum historischen Jesus*, 1960, p. 27 (ET: 'The Primitive Christian Kerygma and the Historical Jesus' in *The Historical Jesus and the Kerygmatic Christ*, ed. and trans. C. E. Braaten and R. A. Harrisville, 1964, p. 39); H. Conzelmann, 'Jesus von Nazareth und der Glaube an den Auferstandenen', in *Der historische Jesus und der kerygmatische Christus*, 1961, p. 191: 'The appearances of the risen Lord are of course understood as taking place in space and time, that is, in the world. But the question is, what is the *point* of the appearances and consequently of recounting them. ... The point of the statement is simply to affirm the salvation of God as the end of worldly being.'

37 This has rightly been emphasized by von Campenhausen, Grass, Pannenberg, Wilckens and others.

and credible have all, ever since the collapse of the orthodox way of asserting the truth, taken the form of historical examination. This is in harmony with the texts, in so far as they themselves speak of an event which can be dated. But it is alien to the texts if, and in so far as, the historical form of the question implies a definite anterior understanding of what is historically possible, and one which since the birth of the modern age does not coincide with the understanding which these texts themselves have of the historically possible as being the divinely possible. The concept of the historical, of the historically possible and the historically probable, has been developed in the modern age on the basis of experiences of history other than the experience of the raising of Jesus from the dead – namely, since the Enlightenment, on the basis of the experience of man's ability to calculate history and to make it. The controversy between the disciples and the Jews was concerned with the question: has God raised him from the dead according to his promises, or can God according to his promises not have raised him? The modern controversy on the resurrection, however, is concerned with the question whether resurrection is historically possible. If, as has frequently been pointed out,[38] it is true that the experiences of history on the basis of which the concepts of the historical have been constructed have nowadays an anthropocentric character, that 'history' is here man's history and man is the real subject of history in the sense of its metaphysical *hypokeimenon*, then it is plain that on this presupposition the assertion of the raising of Jesus by God is a 'historically' impossible and therefore a 'historically' meaningless statement. Yet even on this presupposition there is point in asking 'how far and with what degree of probability the actual facts and the actual course of events can still be ascertained',[39] even if that brings us to the limits of the historical as these are prescribed by the presupposed view of historic fact as such. Enquiries conducted in the light of the modern concept of the historical lead neither to the fundamental provability of the resurrection nor to fundamental historical scepticism. But they prevent theology from postulating 'historical' facts on dogmatic grounds, and they prevent theology from abandoning the ground of history altogether in despair.

---

38 K. Löwith, *Meaning in History*, 1949.

39 Hans von Campenhausen, *Der Ablauf der Osterereignisse und das leere Grab*, 1952, p. 7.

Neither the historian nor the theologian can allow methods based on the principle that what must not be cannot be.

But now, the historian who enquires into the reality of the resurrection of Jesus is confronted in the biblical texts not only by realities of history, but also with a different outlook on the experience and significance of history, which sets the event here recounted in a different light. The experience of history which is expressed in the historical approach is here confronted not merely by events which are more or less well testified, more or less imaginatively embellished, but this experience of history is confronted also by a different experience of history. Hence the historical question as to the reality of the resurrection of Jesus also recoils upon the historical enquirer and calls in question the basic experience of history which is the ground of his historical enquiry. The historical question as to the historicity of the resurrection of Christ is thereby expanded to include the questionability of the historical approach to history as such. For in the historical question of the resurrection, the texts which tell of the resurrection of Jesus have always a historical view of the world also brought to bear on them. This latter must be subjected to questioning in the process of understanding, as surely as the proclaimed resurrection of Jesus is subjected to historical questioning. Let us therefore now consider the way the historical question as to the resurrection of Jesus recoils upon the questioner.

It is generally acknowledged that historical understanding nowadays is always analogical understanding and must therefore always remain within the realm of what is understandable in terms of analogy. This method of analogy in historical understanding had been ontologically grounded by E. Troeltsch in the 'correlation which exists between all historical processes'. 'For the means by which criticism becomes possible at all is the application of *analogy*. The analogy of that which happens before our eyes ... is the key to criticism. The illusions, ... the formation of myths, the deceptions, the party spirit, which we see before our eyes, are the means of recognizing such things also in the tradition. Agreement with normal, usual, or at least variously attested, happenings ... as we know them, is the mark of probability for happenings which the critic can recognize as really having happened or can leave aside. The observation of analogies between past events of the same kind makes it possible to ascribe probability to them and to interpret the unknown aspects of the one on the basis of the known aspects of the other. The omnipotence thus attaching to analogy implies, however, the basic similarity of all historical events, which is not, of course, identity ... but presupposes that there is always a common core of similarity, on the basis of which the differences can be sensed and perceived.'[40] If historical understanding and historical criticism thus depend on the postulate and presupposition of a fundamental similarity underlying all events, then historical understanding and historical criticism manifestly depend on a specific view of the world. In this view of the world, much as in Greek cosmology, it is presupposed that a 'common core of similarity' underlies all the changes and chances of history and that 'all things are eternally related at heart'. In terms of this core of similarity, however, the historic now becomes only accidental. Historic events become understandable when they are conceived as *'manifestations'* of this common core of similarity. This, however, is to put an end to their nature as events and to abandon the historic character of history in favour of a metaphysic which sees all historical things in terms of substance. In L. von Ranke and the great historians of romanticism this core was felt to be pantheistic: all ages and all events follow each other in meaningful succession 'in order that what is not possible to any of them individually may happen in *all*, in order that the whole fulness of the spiritual life breathed into the human race by the deity should come to light in the course of the centuries'.[41] For H. von Sybel the similarity acquired a mechanistic appearance: 'The presupposition by which the certainty of knowledge stands or falls is the regulation of all development by absolute laws, the common unity in the constitution of all earthly things.'[42] So, too, in W. Dilthey's philosophical hermeneutic of the history of the expressions of human life, historical understanding rests on the presupposed similarity of the underlying, unfathomable life. To be sure, there is no hard and fast nature of man which exists as a self-identical factor anterior to history and independent of it. 'The human type melts in the process of history.'[43] But the fact that

---

40 E. Troeltsch, 'Ueber historische und dogmatische Methode' (1898), *Gesammelte Schriften* II, pp. 729ff. (esp. p. 731).

41 Quoted according to C. Hinrichs, *Ranke und die Geschichtstheologie der Goethezeit*, 1954, p. 168.

42 *Über die Gesetze historischen Wissens*, 1864, p. 16.

43 *Werke* VIII, p. 6, cf. also VII, p. 278 and O. F. Bollnow's comment, *Die Lebensphilosophie*, 1958, p. 41.

human existence in itself has a hermeneutic structure proves to be the abiding core that motivates the history of man's expressions of his life and expositions of his self. From the depths of his creative unfathomableness man must ever again seek and find himself, ever again form and determine himself, and it is this that constitutes that common core of similarity which makes historical understanding possible and also necessary.

In face of this basing of historical understanding on a metaphysical definition of the core, the substance or the subject of history, Christian theology finds itself in grave difficulties as it seeks to reflect upon the proclamation of the resurrection. In face of the pantheistic definition of the nature of history, according to which the eternal idea does not delight to present itself wholly in an individual, it becomes impossible to regard a person and an event in history as absolute.[44] In face of the positivistic and mechanistic definition of the nature of history as a self-contained system of cause and effect, the assertion of a raising of Jesus by God appears as a myth concerning a supernatural incursion which is contradicted by all our experience of the world. And finally, in face of the philosophy of life with its definition of the creative ground of life that manifests and objectifies itself in history, the Easter texts can be taken only as expressions of the life acts of a faith which is in itself unfathomable.

A theology of the resurrection can try several ways of solving the problem of history thus presented to it. If, as is plain from the above few references, the risen Lord does not fit in with our concept of the historical,[45] it is possible to grant that the report of the raising of Jesus by God is 'unhistorical' and to look around for other ways for modern, historically determined man to approach to and appropriate the reality of the resurrection.[46] Yet in so doing, the whole realm of our knowledge of history and our dealings with it is abandoned to historical expositions of the world. If the reality of the resurrection cannot be comprehended by the historical means of the modern age, neither is the modern intellectual way of dealing with history theologically comprehensible for faith. The *fides quaerens intellectum* must then give up all claim to an

44 D. F. Strauss, *Das Leben Jesu* II, 1835, p. 734.
45 Cf. O. Weber, *Grundlagen der Dogmatik* II, 1962, p. 83.
46 Cf. my essay, 'Exegese und Eschatologie der Geschichte', *EvTh* 22, 1962, pp. 40f.

intellectus fidei in the realm of history. This is primarily done by theology's leaving aside the historical question as to the reality of the resurrection and concentrating on the second question – the question of the character of witness and of claim that attaches to the proclamation of the Easter faith. It then leaves the knowledge of history to all possible kinds of pantheistic or atheistic principles and concentrates on the personal encounter, the non-objectifiable experience or the existential decision, to which the Easter kerygma leads. 'Thus we are simply asked whether we believe that in such things (visionary Easter experiences) God acts in the way they themselves believe and in the way the proclamation asserts.[47] The word 'simply' here plainly recommends the leap from mediating, objectifying, historical knowledge to personal decision. The resurrection of Christ is then to be grasped neither mythically nor historically but 'only in the category of revelation'.[48] But then the message of the resurrection is left hanging in the air, and so also is the existence affected by it, without it being possible to understand the need for the proclamation and the necessity for decision in face of it at all.

Another possibility is, that we no longer regard the historical method and its view of history as being final and inescapable in its substantio-metaphysical form, and thus veer off into the subjective decision of faith, but that we seek new ways of further developing the historical methods themselves in such a way 'that they become adequate to grasp the *whole* of history in all its variety'.[49] Such an extension of the historical approach to history and the historical mediation of it can have an eye to the other side of the analogical process in historical understanding. For indeed the cognitive power of a comparative understanding need not lie merely in recognizing only the similar and common elements amid the dissimilarities in historical events and expressions of life, but can also be directed towards observing what is dissimilar and individual, accidental and suddenly new, in the similar and the like.[50] A one-sided interest in the similar, ever-recurring, typical and regular, would level

---

47 R. Bultmann, *TLZ* 65, 1940, col. 246.

48 K. Barth, *Die Auferstehung der Toten*, 1924, pp. 79f., ET by H. J. Stenning: *The Resurrection of the Dead*, 1933, pp. 145f.

49 R. Rendtorff, 'Geschichte und Ueberlieferung', in *Studien zur Theologie der alttestamentlichen Überlieferungen*, 1961, p. 94, n. 39.

50 W. Pannenberg, 'Heilsgeschehen und Geschichte', *Kerygma und Dogma* 5, 1959, p. 266.

down the really historic element, which lies in the contingent and new, and would thus end up by losing the feeling for history altogether. The method of understanding by comparison can thus be expanded in the direction of bringing to light the incomparable, hitherto non-existent and new. To be sure, it comes to light only in the comparison. But if we are to set eyes on it in this comparison, then we must divest ourselves of all hard and fast presuppositions about the core or the substance of history and must regard these ideas themselves as provisional and alterable. But if, as compared with the historical methods that are interested in the regular and the similar, Christian theology were to manifest merely a supplementary interest in the individual, contingent and new, then that would be only an interesting variant in the historical picture of history as a whole, yet one that would be possible and conceivable also without a theology of the resurrection. The rediscovery of the category of the contingent does not in itself necessarily involve the discovery of a theological category.[51] For the raising of Christ involves not the category of the accidentally new, but the expectational category of the eschatologically new. The eschatologically new event of the resurrection of Christ, however, proves to be a *novum ultimum* both as against the similarity in ever-recurring reality and also as against the comparative dissimilarity of new possibilities emerging in history. To expand the historical approach to the extent of taking account of the contingent does not as yet bring the reality of the resurrection itself into view. It is quite possible to overcome the anthropocentric form of historical analogy, but this does not necessarily give the latter a theological character. Only if the whole historical picture, contingency and continuity and all, could be shown to be in itself not necessary but contingent, should we come within sight of that which can be called the eschatologically new fact of the resurrection of Christ. The resurrection of Christ does not mean a possibility within the world and its history, but a new possibility altogether for the world, for existence and for history. Only when the world can be understood as contingent creation out of the freedom of God and *ex nihilo* – only on the basis of this *contingentia mundi* – does the raising of Christ become intelligible as *nova creatio*. In view of what is meant and what is promised when we speak of the raising of Christ, it is there-

---

51 *Ibid.*, p. 277; cf. H. G. Geyer's criticism in *EvTh* 22, 1962, p. 97.

fore necessary to expose the profound irrationality of the rational cosmos of the modern, technico-scientific world. By the raising of Christ we do not mean a possible process in world history, but the eschatological process to which world history is subjected.

Finally, theology has the possibility of constructing its own concept of history and its own view of the tale of history on the basis of a theological and eschatological understanding of the reality of the resurrection.[52] Then the theology of the resurrection would no longer be fitted in with an existing concept of history, but an attempt would have to be made, in comparison with and contra-distinction to the existing views of history, to arrive at a new understanding of history with the ultimate possibilities and hopes that attach to it on the presupposition of the raising of Christ from the dead. In conflict with other concepts of history, an *intellectus fidei resurrectionis* must then be developed which makes it possible to speak 'Christianly' of God, history and nature. The resurrection of Christ is without parallel in the history known to us. But it can for that very reason be regarded as a 'history-making event' in the light of which all other history is illumined, called in question and transformed.[53] The mode of proclaiming and hopefully remembering this event must then be presented as a mode of historical remembrance which is wholly governed by this event both in content and in procedure. It is not that from the hopeful remembrance of this event we then derive general laws of world history, but in remembering this one, unique event, we remember the hope for the future of all world history. Then the resurrection of Christ does not offer itself as an analogy to that which can be experienced any time and anywhere, but as an analogy to what is to come to all. The expectation of what is to come on the ground of the resurrection of Christ, must then turn all reality that can be experienced and all real experience into an experience that is provisional and a reality that does not yet contain within it what is held in prospect for it. It must therefore contradict all rigid substantio-metaphysical definitions of the common core of similarity in world events, and therefore also the corresponding historical understanding that works with analogy. It must develop a historical understanding which works

---

52 R. R. Niebuhr, *Resurrection and Historical Reason*, 1957. Cf. L. Landgrebe's comment in 'Philosophie und Theologie', *Neue Zeitschrift für systematische Theologie* 23, 1963, pp. 3ff.

53 L. Landgrebe, *op. cit.*, pp. 10f.

with eschatological analogy as a foreshadowing and anticipation of the future. The raising of Christ is then to be called 'historic', not because it took place *in* the history to which other categories of some sort provide a key, but it is to be called historic because, by pointing the way for future events, it *makes* history in which we can and must live. It is historic, because it discloses an eschatological future. This assertion must then give proof of itself in conflict with other concepts of history, all of which are ultimately based on other 'history-making' events, shocks or revolutions in history.

Here of course there arises an objection in the form of the question whether such theological statements are universally binding. If the modern, historical approach to history is taken as the only one that is possible, honest and binding today, then the view of reality and history which is presupposed by it has to be accepted as inevitable also for theological thought. This view of reality is then 'imposed upon us by our place in history'.[54] In the society in which Christians and non-Christians live together, it is the axiom within the framework of which alone we are able and willing to 'understand'. If according to this now universally binding and universally recognized view of reality, scientifically and historically speaking, the gods are silent – or hearing them is optional and left to the individual's discretion – then a theology of the resurrection can be developed only at a point which is not affected by this view of reality and comes under the aegis of the individual's subjectivity – which, however, means only in that realm of human subjectivity and inwardness which is set free by the rationalizing of the world and the historicizing of history. A theology of the resurrection can then no longer speak of facts of the resurrection, in terms of a metaphysic of history, but in terms of a metaphysic of subjectivity it can certainly still speak of an Easter faith for which 'resurrection of Jesus' is merely an expression of faith, and one that can be left behind in the course of history. In this form the resurrection faith that makes no assertions of the resurrection fits in exactly with the modern world's view of reality and is in a sense the ultimate religion of our society. If theology on the other hand strives to attain a theological view of history and a revolution in the historical way of thinking, then there is justification for the objection that theology

---

54 This is F. Mildenberger's objection, *EvTh* 23, 1963, pp. 5, 274.

is thereby driven into the ghetto of an esoteric church ideology and can no longer make itself intelligible to anyone else.[55]

But the Church – including theology – is neither the religion of this or that society, nor yet is it a sect. It can neither be required to adapt itself to the view of reality which is generally binding in society at the moment, nor may it be expected to present itself as the arbitrary jargon of an exclusive group and to exist only for believers. As the church is engaged with its surrounding society in a struggle for the truth, so theology, too, has a part in the mission of the church. It must engage with views of history and historical world-views in a struggle for the future of the truth and therefore also in a battle for the reality of the resurrection of Jesus. If in contesting and exploding the modern historical concepts of reality we are wrestling for the mysterious reality of the resurrection of Jesus, then that is no mere wrangle about a detail of the distant past, but this reality becomes the ground for questioning also the historical means of attaining certainty about history. It is a struggle for the future of history and for the right way of recognizing, hoping and working for that future. It is a battle for the recognition of the mission of the present, and for the place and the task of human nature in it.

The point of the historical debate on the resurrection of Christ was never merely historical. Thus the specialist's question as to the historical reality of the resurrection – 'what can I know?' – points him on to the neighbouring questions, 'what am I to do?' and 'what may I hope for? What future horizon of possibilities and dangers is opened up by past history?' To put the question of the resurrection in exclusively historical terms is to alienate the texts of the Easter narrative, as we have seen. These, however, as we have seen, alienate the historian from that context of experience of the world in which he seeks to read the texts. All real understanding begins with such alienations.

---

55 F. Mildenberger, *EvTh* 23, 1963, p. 275.

7. The Approach of Form-Criticism to the Easter Narratives and the Questionableness of its Existentialist Interpretation

The critical examination of the resurrection narratives in regard to their historical correctness, which has been usual since the Enlightenment, has been transformed, and largely also supplanted in scholarly interest, by form-critical examination of the narratives.[56] The form-critical approach no longer asks about the historically accessible events which the accounts relate and which possibly made the accounts necessary, but it enquires into the kerygmatic motives which shaped the accounts, and examines their place in the life and conduct of specific societies. It argues from the forms to the life of the society, and from the life of the society to the forms. The real subject of the accounts is then not the matter to be recounted but the social life which finds its expression in them. The form-critical method is originally a sociological method. From its standpoint the Easter texts present themselves primarily as kerygma, as proclamation by the Church in faith and to faith. The texts are found to exist in a specific tradition of proclamation in which, according to the circumstances, the addressees and the opponents, they could be very freely varied in the various stages of the tradition and could to a certain extent be theologically enriched and transformed according to the new situations. The discovery of such kerygmatic transformations in particular elements of the tradition and in the history of the forms in which they are stated in worship, instruction, exhortation, polemic, etc., brought out an abundance of new insights. The question of the underlying events in which they have their ground was not thereby discarded, yet there was a decisive shift in the centre of the researcher's interest. It was no longer a question of the historicity of the statements in the old sense of historical criticism, but it was now a historical question of the motives and forms of the statements themselves, and of the changes undergone by these motives and forms. Yet the insight into the fact that in these texts we have to do not with historical reports but with testimonies of faith on the part of the primitive Christian Church, is also a historical insight.

---

56 Cf. E. Fascher, *Die formgeschichtliche Methode*, 1924.

The important question for theology arises only when the results of the form-critical analyses of the primitive Christian message are removed from their own historic ground and theologically grounded in a different reality from that of which they speak, when the enquirer has no desire at all to know how things really were, but only how the believers saw them and how they represented them in terms of their faith, when the texts are no longer taken as statements about a reality, but are understood only as expressions of the Church's faith. Do these pieces of witness and of proclamation have their ground in a new self-understanding of the existence of the witnesses and proclaimers? Is the kerygmatic character of these statements grounded in a revelational commission which can no longer be grasped historically? The form-critical approach clearly provided the possibility of conceiving these statements as grounded elsewhere than in the reality of the events to be proclaimed – the possibility of understanding them no longer as 'statements about' something, but as 'expressions of' personal or corporate faith. This change of subject has come about through the alliance between form-critical research and dialectical theology, especially in existentialist interpretation since the twenties.

If the reality of the resurrection is not to be conceived as a historically accessible reality, then it can of course still become real for man in another sense of the word 'reality'. It can be reality for man in the sense in which he is real to himself. It is not from a historical detachment that he becomes aware of his own existential reality, but only in the immediate experience of himself as a reality that has constantly to come about anew. Similarly, the resurrection of Christ then no longer confronts him in the doubtful image of historical tradition and historical reconstructions, but then, in the Easter faith of the disciples and in the proclamation, the resurrection of Christ becomes for him a reality which affects him in the questionableness of his own existence and faces him with a decision. Doubtful as the resurrection may appear from the objectifying standpoint of historical science, it is yet in all closeness and immediacy that the Easter faith of the disciples encounters man in the claim of the proclamation and in the decisive question of faith. The Easter faith of the disciples presents itself as a possibility of existence which we can repeat and re-echo in the questionableness of our own existence. Only in being thus immediately involved by the preaching of faith today, only in beholding the Lord today, only in today obeying his absolute claim, in which salvation is disclosed for today, do we then discover the reality of the resurrection.[57] The 'reality' of the resurrection encounters us as word of God, as kerygma, to which we can no longer put the question of its historical legitimacy, but which asks us whether or not we are willing to believe.[58] The message which proclaims Jesus as the risen Lord must convince 'our heart and conscience'. It must speak of his resurrection in such a way that the latter no longer appears as a historical or mythical event, but as 'a reality that concerns our own existence'.[59]

Here the question of the 'reality' of the resurrection is raised in a way different from that of the historian. The questioner is not concerned to arrive at a historically assured picture of that event, but the question which he puts to the Easter narratives is the questionableness of his own historic existence. He does not stand outside history, in order to survey its correlations, but he stands with his own existence and decisions in the midst of history. His interest in history is therefore identical with his interest in his own historic existence. Hence in this encounter with the Easter texts he will seek an existentialist exegesis in which the exposition of history and the exposition of himself correspond. If, however, the radical questionableness of his own historic existence provides the angle from which he approaches the kerygma of the resurrection, then his question is no longer as to 'whether the resurrection once took place in terms of possible analogies in world history, but is directed towards the understanding of human existence which comes to expression in these narratives.[60] The place of the substantio-metaphysically conceived common core of similarity in all events, which makes analogical understanding possible, is taken by a similarity in the historic character of human existence, which is conceived in terms of fundamental ontology and makes understanding possible between one existence and another in encounter. That the resurrection actually took place is not thereby denied, but does not lie within the field of interest. That God is not percep-

57 Cf. H. Conzelmann, *op. cit.*, p. 196.

58 R. Bultmann, *Kerygma und Mythos* I, 3rd ed. 1954, p. 46 (ET p. 41).

59 R. Bultmann, *TLZ* 65, 1940, col. 245. Cf. H. Grass' comment in *Ostergeschehen und Osterberichte*, 2nd ed. 1962, pp. 268ff.

60 Cf. here the hermeneutic principles developed by R. Bultmann in *Glauben und Verstehen* II, p. 232 (ET by J. C. G. Grieg, *Essays Philosophical and Theological*, 1955, pp. 258f.).

tible apart from faith, certainly need not mean that he does not exist apart from faith, nor yet that 'God' is merely an 'expression' for believing existence, but this question of whether God and his action exist *extra nos* does not lie within the field of our interest. Of vital interest to our existence, on the other hand, is the Easter faith of the witnesses, and the understanding of existence which emerged in primitive Christianity as a new possibility for human existence. This view of 'reality' as an event which concerns existence, or an event that happens 'to heart and conscience', can then also lead to a new mode of historical understanding. 'The Easter event of the resurrection of Christ is not a historical event; the only thing that can be grasped as a historical event *is the Easter faith of the first disciples.*' This historical statement is wholly in accord with the theological statement that the Easter faith has no interest in the historical question. 'For the historical event of the rise of the Easter faith means for us what it meant for the first disciples, namely, the self-manifestation of the risen Lord, the act of God in which the redemption event of the cross is completed.'[61] This, however, is to shift the 'reality' of the resurrection from something that happens to the crucified Jesus to something that happens to the existence of the disciples. The act of God is then the rise of the Easter faith, in so far as this Easter faith understands itself as brought about by the self-manifestation of the risen Lord. The 'reality' of the resurrection is then no longer a reality about Jesus, but is identical with the reality of kerygma and faith in a 'today' which cannot be historically authenticated but is ever and again without past or future.

It is an undeniably true insight that the Easter narratives are not meant to be 'narratives', but to be proclamation directed to faith, and that the reality of the resurrection of Jesus is inseparably bound up with the witness of universal missionary proclamation; but it is an insight that can lead in the way just indicated to no longer enquiring into the historical legitimacy of this proclamation, but putting in place of that an existential verification of it to heart and conscience or to a historic self-understanding in terms of a general historic questionableness of human existence. The transition from form-critical research to existentialist interpretation often proceeds by the following stages:

---

61 R. Bultmann, *Kerygma und Mythos* I, p. 47 (ET p. 42).

1. The place of the question, 'What do the accounts in substance say?', is taken by the question, 'Who speaks in these accounts?'

2. Once it has been established that the Church in these accounts and in the forms assumed by them is expressing its relation to Jesus, there follows the further question, 'How does the Church understand its relation to Jesus?'

3. Once the Church's christological conceptions of Jesus have been established, the next question is, 'How does the Church understand itself?' Then its understanding of Christ is grounded in its understanding of faith, and its understanding of faith is grounded in its self-understanding and is understood as an expression of the self-understanding that is sought by all men. Christology is then the variable, anthropology the constant.

Just as the historical question presupposes a historical approach which sets the proclamation of the resurrection in the alien light of a mere report about the events, so too the question as to the self-understanding announced and expressed in it presupposes an approach from the angle of the general questionableness of human existence, which also sets these texts in an alien light. This whole approach in terms of 'reality' as a reality which concerns existence leaves out of account the fact that these texts speak of God and his action on Jesus, and purposely so speak – that they speak of the world and the future and certainly do not mean all this merely as an 'expression' of a new self-understanding. The existentialist interpretation examines the texts in order to find the 'meaning' of what they say, and takes it for granted from the start that this meaning is existential truth and not factual truth. This is today no doubt a 'meaningful' way of appropriating what was then proclaimed, but is not at all in harmony with its own original intention. On the other hand it is not by any means self-evident that 'understanding' today must take place only in the context of 'self-understanding' of our own particular existence. This is as far from being self-evident as is the modern custom of defining the reality of the world in terms of a hard and fast 'world picture' and projecting our age's concept of a world picture back into ages which had a completely different relation to the world.

The Easter reports in the New Testament proclaim in the form of narrative, and narrate history in the form of proclamation. The modern alternative, reading them either as historical sources or as kerygmatic calls to decision; is foreign to them, as the modern distinction between factual truth and existential truth is also foreign to them. The question therefore arises whether the insights of form-criticism into the fact that, briefly speaking, it was not archivists but missionaries who shaped this tradition, would not have to be combined again in a new way with the intention of the historical question which enquires about the events which this proclamation brings to expression. If the reality of the resurrection of Jesus is transmitted and mediated to us only in the form of missionary proclamation, and this form of transmission and mediation manifestly belongs to the reality of the resurrection itself, then it must be asked whether the inner compulsion to this kind of statement and communication is not grounded in the peculiarity of the event itself. For it cannot really be accounted for as supplement or accident. The reality which stands behind the proclamatory reports must plainly be of such a kind that it *compelled* proclamation to all peoples and the continual formation of new christological conceptions. The commission and authorization to this universal mission must then be a constitutive part of the very event of which this mission tells. If we no longer ask merely *how* the Church preached and to what changes the form of its proclamation was subjected, but *why* it spoke as it did and what provoked its proclamation, then we are on the road to raising the historical question in a new way and seeing the existential truth of faith as grounded in the factual truth of what is to be believed. The question is then no longer whether this proclamation is correct in the 'historical' sense, but whether and how the proclamation is legitimated and necessarily called to life by the event of which it speaks. We cannot then merely embark on a historical examination of the past that once was, nor yet merely provide an existentialist interpretation of present claims, but we must enquire into what is open, unfinished, unsettled and outstanding, and consequently into the future announced by this event. If in this event there lies something which has not yet been realized and strains after a particular future, then it is understandable that this event cannot be spoken of in historical detachment in the form of a report on a process complete in itself, but it can be spoken of only in the form of remembrance and hope. If this event of the raising of Jesus can be rightly understood only in conjunction with his universal eschatological future, then the only mode of communication appropriate to this event must be missionary proclamation to all peoples without distinction – a mission which knows itself in the service of the promised future of this event. Only missionary proclamation does justice to the historical and eschatological character of this event. It is, in the light of this event, the only appropriate way of experiencing history, historic existence and historic expectation.

What unites our present age with past ages in history is, to the extent that we have here a 'historic' relationship, not a common core of similarity nor a general historic character attaching to human existence as such, but the problem of the future. The meaning of each several present becomes clear only in the light of hopes for the future. Hence a 'historic' relationship to history will not seek merely to illumine the factual sequences of events and their laws, nor merely to explore past possibilities of existence in order possibly to repeat them, but will search the reality of the past for the possibilities that lie within it. Unborn future lies in the past. Fulfilled past can be expected from the future. Positivistic historicism reduces history to realities that can be dated and localized, without noticing the realm of future possibilities that surrounds these realities so long as they are 'historic' realities. We have here a process of exclusion and abstraction which the historian can and must employ in order to reach plain conclusions, but he must also always be clear that his picture is painted in perspective. The existentialist interpretation on the other hand seeks the existential possibilities attaching to past existence in order to repeat and re-echo them, yet without noticing that they are made possible by events which institute history and provide the gateway to the historic character of existence. This, too, is a process of exclusion and abstraction which the interpreter must employ in order to reach conclusions, but he, too, must always be clear that his picture is painted in perspective. Beyond both historicism and existentialism stands the attempt to find the ground of historic phenomena neither in a positivistic system of laws nor in the historic character of human existence, but to see them in their significance for the future.[62] This does not mean that the future, and indeed eschatological, significance of historic phenomena is confined within the framework of a teleology of universal history. Nor does it mean that the future of historic phenomena is exhausted in a present summoned to responsibility by the future. 'Meaning' (*Bedeuten*) is

---

62 This third possibility is indicated by R. Bultmann himself in *Glauben und Verstehen* III, 1960, pp. 113ff., 148f.

something which strains and stretches towards that which it seeks to indicate (*be-deuten*), to announce and to pre-figure, and which is not yet present in all its fullness. We know historic phenomena in their own peculiar historic character only when we perceive their meaning for 'their' future. Only in that light do we then also attain to a perception of their meaning for our future and to the perception of our meaning for their future.

In this sense the event of the raising of Christ from the dead is an event which is understood only in the *modus* of promise. It has its time still ahead of it, is grasped as a 'historic phenomenon' only in its relation to *its* future, and mediates to those who know it a future towards which they have to move in history. Hence the reports of the resurrection will always have to be read also eschatologically in the light of the question, 'What may I hope for?' It is only with this third question that our remembrance and the corresponding historical knowledge are set within a horizon appropriate to the thing to be remembered. It is only in the light of this question that the historic character of existence and the corresponding self-understanding are set within a horizon appropriate to the history which provides the ground of, and the gateway to, the historic character of existence.

8. The Eschatological Question as to the Future Horizon of the Proclamation of the Risen Lord

Experience and judgment are always bound up with a *horizon* of openness towards reality, in which a thing comes to view and can be experienced and in which judgments become meaningful. A horizon of this kind contains a certain anterior knowledge of that which we learn. It is not a closed system, but includes also open questions and anticipations and is therefore open towards the new and the unknown.[63] Horizons of this kind can come from our traditions, and they can also arise from the context of our own experience and our familiarity with the world. They can arise out of the incalculable significance attaching to specific experiences we

---

63 We are here adopting the concept of 'horizon' as developed in the phenomenology of Edmund Husserl. Cf. E. Husserl, *Erfahrung und Urteil*, 1939, pp. 26ff.; L. Landgrebe, *Der Weg der Phänomenologie*, 1963, pp. 181ff.; H. G. Gadamer, *Wahrheit und Methode*, 1960, pp. 286ff., 356ff.

have undergone, and they can also have their source in ideas of our own which we use for the purpose of attaining to knowledge of history. Without a horizon of this kind, and in abstraction from it, no event can be experienced and stated.

In the resurrection narratives experience and judgment manifestly take place within a decidedly *eschatological horizon* of expectations, hopes and questions about the promised future. The very designations 'raising', 'resurrection', etc., contain a whole world of memories and hopes. Thus the resurrection narratives do not stand directly within a cosmological horizon of questions as to the origin, meaning and nature of the world. Nor do they stand directly within an existentialist horizon of questions as to the origin, meaning and nature of human existence. Nor, finally, do they stand directly within a general theological horizon of questions as to the nature and appearance of the deity. They stand directly within the special horizon of prophetic and apocalyptic expectations, hopes and questions about that which according to the promises of this God is to come. What is spotlighted in the resurrection appearances is therefore expounded in terms of the earlier promises, and this exposition in turn takes place in the form of prophetic proclamation of, and eschatological outlook towards, the future of Christ which was spotlighted in these appearances. Christian eschatology arose from the Easter experience, and Christian prophecy determined the Easter faith. But Christian eschatology expounded and expressed the Easter experiences in recalling and taking up the earlier promises and – in regard to Jesus himself – in recalling and taking up what had earlier been promised and proclaimed. The Easter appearances are bound up with this eschatological horizon, both in that which they presuppose and call to mind and also in that which they themselves prefigure and provoke. The question of the divinity of God, the question of the worldliness of the world and the question of the human nature of man are not thereby rendered irrelevant, but in the light of the Easter appearances they are set within a peculiar horizon, both in regard to the way they are asked and also in regard to the point at which the answer is sought. To the extent that the earlier promises become general and universal in the resurrection event, these questions concerning the universal become relevant. But to the extent that this universality and generality appears in the Easter event in eschatological form, i.e. in hope and in looking forward, the questions are asked in a different way, and they are no longer answered on the basis of experience of the world, of man's experience of himself, or of the concept of God, but on the basis of the event of the resurrection and within the eschatological horizon of this event.

Christian eschatology differs from Old Testament faith in the promise, as also from prophetic and apocalyptic eschatology, by being Christian eschatology and speaking of 'Christ and his future'.[64] It is related in content to the person of Jesus of Nazareth and the event of his raising, and speaks of the future for which the ground is laid in this person and this event. Christian eschatology does not examine the general future possibilities of history. Nor does it unfold the general possibilities of human nature in its dependence on the future. It is therefore right to emphasize that Christian eschatology is at heart Christology in an eschatological perspective.[65]

While it is true that in the Easter experiences the modes of experiencing the 'revelation of Jesus Christ', and the forms of communicating it, incorporate apocalyptic ideas and hopes from the tradition of late Judaism, yet it is equally true that the content of this revelation breaks the bounds of late Jewish apocalyptic. For what God made manifest, according to the statements of the Easter narratives, was not the course of history, not the secrets of the higher world of heaven, not the outcome of the future world judgment, but the future of the crucified Christ for the world.[66] Christian eschatology or eschatological Christology is therefore not to be understood as a special case of general apocalyptic. Christian eschatology is not Christianized apocalyptic. The adoption of apocalyptic ideas and apocalyptic hopes in the Easter narratives and in the Easter theology of the primitive Church is plainly eclectic. Specific memories are aroused by this event and are recalled along with the Easter proclamation, while others are dropped. Particular ideas of God's revelation of the end are used, yet the *Weltanschauung* of late Jewish apocalyptic and its attitude to life are not restored as a whole. 'Resurrection from the dead' does,

---

64 Cf. E. Thurneysen's happy phrase, 'Christ and his future' – 'Christus und seine Zukunft', *Zwischen den Zeiten* 9, 1931, pp. 187ff.

65 W. Kreck, *Die Zukunft des Gekommenen. Grundprobleme der Eschatologie*, 1961, pp. 120ff.

66 Cf. U. Wilckens, *Der Ursprung der Überlieferung der Erschseinung des Auferstandenen*, 1963, pp. 63ff.

to be sure, also belong to the apocalyptic expectations of God's revelation of the end, but certainly not in every case and not even centrally. When, however, Jesus is described as 'the firstfruits of them that slept', then that goes beyond the bounds of apocalyptic inasmuch as it means that the raising of the dead has already taken place in this one case for all, and that the raising was performed not on one faithful to the law but on one who was crucified, and consequently future resurrection is to be expected not from obedience to the law but from the justification of sinners and from faith in Christ. The central place of the Torah in late Jewish apocalyptic is thus taken by the person and the cross of Christ. The place of life in the law is taken by fellowship with Christ in the following of the crucified one. The place of the self-preservation of the righteous from the world is taken by the mission of the believer to the world. The place of the Torah shining in the light of the fulness of divine glory is taken by the ἀποκάλυψις κυρίου, the judgment seat of Jesus Christ before whom all things will be revealed. It is not that the secrets of what awaits world history and the cosmos at the end of time are disclosed in advance according to a heavenly plan – 'what shall befall thy people in the latter days' (Dan. 10.14) – but the universal future of the lordship of the crucified Christ over all is spotlighted in the Easter appearances. Yet the Old Testament, prophetic and apocalyptic expectation of a universal revelation and glorification of God in all things is still maintained. Thus the adoption and recalling of apocalyptic ideas and apocalyptic expectations does not by any means lead to levelling down the uniqueness of the Christ event, but it becomes possible to state the eschatological 'once for all' by means of recalling the earlier promises.

The Christian hope for the future comes of observing a specific, unique event – that of the resurrection and appearing of Jesus Christ. The hopeful theological mind, however, can observe this event only in seeking to span the future horizon projected by this event. Hence to recognize the resurrection of Christ means to recognize in this event the future of God for the world and the future which man finds in this God and his acts. Wherever this recognition takes place, there comes also a recalling of the Old Testament history of promise now seen in a critical and transforming light. Christian eschatology, which seeks to span the inexhaustible future of Christ, does not set the event of the resurrection within a framework of apocalyptic and world history. Rather, it examines the inner *tendency* of the resurrection event, asking what rightly can and must be expected from the risen and exalted Lord. It enquires about the mission of Christ and the *intention* of God in raising him from the dead. It recognizes as the inner tendency of this event his future lordship over every enemy, including death. 'For he *must* reign ...' (I Cor. 15.25). It recognizes as the outer tendency, or as the consequence of this tendency, its own mission: 'The gospel *must* be published among all nations' (Mark 13.10).[67] Christian eschatology speaks of the future of Christ which brings man and the world to light. It does not, on the contrary, speak of a world history and a time which brings Christ to light, nor yet of man whose good will Christ brings to light. It is therefore out of the question to classify the resurrection event among the events of world history and apocalyptic and to give a date for his future or his coming again. It is not that 'time' brings his day and it is not that history proves him right, but he guides time to his day. The return of Christ does not come 'of itself', like the year 1965, but comes from himself, when and as God will according to his promise. It is therefore also out of the question to eternalize the openness of the Christian hope towards the future. There is an end to the openness of Christian existence, for it is not openness for a future that remains empty, but it presupposes the future of Christ and finds in that future its fulfilment.

One could say that Christian eschatology is the study of the tendency of the resurrection and future of Christ and therefore leads immediately to the practical knowledge of mission. In that case it is false to lay down the alternative: either apocalyptic calculation of the times and apocalyptic belief in a final destiny, or else the ethic of hope. The speculative interpretation of history on the part of cosmic apocalyptic is not simply replaced by a moral eschatology. To be sure, alternatives of this kind do appear in many sayings: Ye know not when the end cometh, therefore watch and pray. Nevertheless, experiences of history are important for Christian eschatology. These are the experiences involved in relation to Jesus and his mission – namely, persecution, accusation, suffering and martyrdom. The Revelation of John and also the Little Apocalypse of Mark 13 show that what we have here is not merely apocalyptic speculations

---

67 Cf. also the corresponding, eschatologically determined ἀνάγκη or compulsion to preach in Paul, I Cor. 9.16, and E. Käsemann's comment *ZTK* 56, 1959, pp. 138–154. esp. 152f.

or moral appeals, but an eschatological grasp of that history which is to be expected, and is experienced, in martyrdom in the mission of Christ. Thus the experiential content of Christian eschatology is not that 'world history' which is arrived at by exploring and comparing great events of world history and stringing them together in a temporal succession to form an apocalyptic system of universal history; rather, it comprises the experiences which are undergone in the course of the mission undertaken in world history 'to all peoples'. The Christian consciousness of history is not a consciousness of the millennia of all history, in some mysterious knowledge of a divine plan for history, but it is a missionary consciousness in the knowledge of a divine commission, and is therefore a consciousness of the contradiction inherent in this unredeemed world, and of the sign of the cross under which the Christian mission and the Christian hope stand.

The Easter appearances of Christ are manifestly phenomena of vocation. That is why the knowledge of Jesus Christ and the knowledge of his mission and future coincide in them. That, too, is why self-knowledge and the knowledge of being called and sent into his future also coincide. The horizon within which the resurrection of Christ becomes knowable as 'resurrection', is the horizon of promise and mission, beckoning us on to his future and the future of his lordship. It is only in this context, on this basis and for this reason, that these other questions arise concerning the future of world history. Hence they arise in the form of the question as to the destiny of 'Israel and the nations', and are answered at that cardinal point in history constituted by the crucifixion of Christ by Jews and Gentiles and his resurrection for Jews and Gentiles. They are answered within the horizon of the mission of Christ and the mission of the Jewish and Gentile church.

It is only in this context, too, that the question of 'true human nature' arises – the question of what makes man to be true man – and is answered by the disclosure of a way, a promise and a future in which 'the truth' comes to man and he himself is brought into the truth. Communion with Christ, the new being in Christ, proves to be the way for man to become man. In it true human nature emerges, and the still hidden and unfulfilled future of human nature can be sought in it. This is an openness of human existence towards the world and towards the future – an openness grounded, manifested and kept alive by that openness of the revelation of God which is announced in the event of the resurrection of Christ and in which this event points beyond itself to an *eschaton* of the fulness of all things. The openness of Christian existence is not a special case of general human openness. It is not a special form of the *cor inquietum*, the restless heart that is part of man's created makeup. Rather, the historic and history-making *cor inquietum* of man arises from the *promissio inquieta*, and clings to it and is dependent on it. The resurrection of Christ goes on being a *promissio inquieta* until it finds rest in the resurrection of the dead and a totality of new being. Through the knowledge of the resurrection of the crucified the contradiction that is always and everywhere perceptible in an unredeemed world, and the sorrow and suffering caused by that world, are taken up into the confidence of hope, while on the other hand hope's confidence becomes earthly and universal. Any kind of docetic hope which leaves earthly conditions or corporeal existence to the mercy of their own contradictoriness and restricts itself to the Church, to the cultus or to believing inwardness, is therefore a denial of the cross. The hope that is born of the cross and the resurrection transforms the negative, contradictory and torturing aspects of the world into terms of 'not yet', and does not suffer them to end in 'nothing'.

9. The Identity of the Lord who Appears as Risen with the Crucified Christ

How are the cross and resurrection of Jesus, that is to say, the historical and eschatological notes, combined with each other in the Easter proclamation?

None of the Easter narratives goes back any further than to the appearance of the risen Lord. Nowhere is the actual process of the raising of Jesus described in a historicizing or mythological way. What actually happened between the experience of his crucifixion and burial and his Easter appearances, is left in the darkness of the still unknown and still hidden God. Yet this event that took place between the two experiences of the cross of Jesus and his living appearance was already very early described as 'raising from the dead'. It is covered by a term for which there is no basis in experience hitherto and elsewhere. That is to say, it is described as something for which there are no analogies in the history we know,

but only apocalyptic promises and hopes that where death is concerned God will give proof of his divinity at the last. 'Raising of the
dead' is an expression which looks expectantly towards the future
proof of God's creative power over the non-existent. What 'resurrection of the dead' really is, and what 'actually happened' in the
raising of Jesus, is thus a thing which not even the New Testament
Easter narratives profess to know. From the two mutually radically
contradictory experiences of the cross and the appearances of
Jesus, they argue to the event in between as an eschatological event
for which the verifying analogy is as yet only in prospect and is
still to come. That is, they use the term 'raising' to express not only
a judgment about something that happened to Jesus, but at the
same time also an eschatological expectation. This expectation is
fulfilled in Jesus' own case in the experiences of the cross and of the
appearances, and yet it still remains an expectation and a hope that
precedes our own experience of being raised.

Now there is more to be said about the process of the raising
of the crucified than merely that it is an eschatological mystery
and that the assertions of the disciples have to be believed. The
disciples' proclamation that he was raised from the dead does not
arise from peculiar powers of imagination or from a unique kind
of inspiration, but it arises from, and is made necessary by, the
comparing of the two contradictory experiences which they have
of Christ. The experience of the cross of Jesus means for them the
experience of the god-forsakenness of God's ambassador – that
is, an absolute *nihil* embracing also God. The experience of the
appearance of the crucified one as the living Lord therefore means
for them the experience of the nearness of God in the god-forsaken
one, of the divineness of God in the crucified and dead Christ – that
is, a new totality which annihilates the total *nihil*. The two experiences stand in a radical contradiction to each other, like death and
life, nothing and everything, godlessness and the divinity of God.
But how can it be possible to identify both experiences in one and
the same person without resolving either the one experience or the
other and making it of no account?

If this process of identification is to be made intelligible, then we
must surely start from the fact that in the Easter appearances we
have not merely dumb visions, but at the same time, and at bottom
no doubt first and foremost, so-called auditions as well. This is
indicated by the fact that these visions were entirely a matter of

vocatory visions. Without the speaking and hearing of words it would have been unlikely – indeed impossible – to identify the one who appeared with the crucified Jesus. Without words spoken and heard the Easter appearances would have remained ghostly things. The appearances – for such things also exist elsewhere in the history of religion – would have been taken as hierophanies of a strange, new heavenly Being, if they had not been coupled with the speaking of the one who appeared here. The phenomenon of primitive Christian ecstasy shows that this possibility of understanding the Easter appearances as hierophanies of a new, divine spiritual Being was one that lay very close to hand. Moreover, it is surely a fact that the appearances themselves hardly provided the possibility of identifying the one who appeared with the one who was crucified. This possibility will therefore have to be looked for in what is said by the one who appeared. What he said must have contained something in the nature of a self-identification ('It is I'). In that case the self-identification of the one who appears in the glory of the promised divine life with the one who was crucified can be regarded as an act of the self-revelation of Jesus. The fundamental event in the Easter appearances then manifestly lies in the revelation of the identity and continuity of Jesus in the total contradiction of cross and resurrection, of god-forsakenness and the nearness of God. That is why the whole New Testament can assert that the disciples at Easter did not see a new heavenly Being of some kind, but Jesus himself. The Lord who is believed and proclaimed at Easter therefore stands in continuity with the earthly Jesus who had come and been crucified – a continuity which must repeatedly be sought and formulated anew and can never be surrendered. The sole bridge of continuity between the primitive Christian proclamation and the history and proclamation of Jesus himself is *via* the raising of the one who was crucified. This is a continuity in radical discontinuity, or an identity in total contradiction. The enigma of this mysterious identity between the crucified and the risen Christ is manifestly the driving force in the christological controversies of primitive Christianity. In all its repeatedly obvious questionableness it is really the constant factor in the christological controversies. The following possibilities arising here are erroneous:

1. The earthly, crucified Jesus is completely swallowed up in the heavenly being of the risen and exalted Lord. The memory of his words and his death is so overrun and choked out by visions of

his present heavenly being, that the harshness of the godlessness of Good Friday is no longer noticed. This tendency led to Docetism.

2. The Easter appearances are taken merely as divine confirmation of the claims of the dead prophet, so that while his words certainly go on working, yet he himself does not. Then the 'resurrection' is merely the legitimation and interpretation of the historical. The line of continuity runs from the words of the dead Master to the proclamation of the Church which carries on what he said. His death is so to speak cancelled out by the divine confirmation in the Easter appearances. The abiding continuity is then of a direct and repetitive kind and bypasses the cross and resurrection in favour of Jesus' understanding of himself or of existence. Then the Easter appearances are not signs of something new that happens to Jesus, but mean the birth of faith in Jesus' message. This tendency led to Ebionitism.

3. Jesus Christ, crucified yesterday, risen today, is in both modes of his appearing the 'same'. Then cross and resurrection are merely two modes of being, which belong to his one, eternal, and in itself unchangeable person. His earthly death and his risen life then become relative to the one substance of his person, which in itself would stand beyond death and life. This view, as suggested above all by the Christology of the ancient Church, perceives neither the deadliness of his death nor the startling newness of his resurrection. This tendency led to Modalism.

With an eye on these ideas we shall have to say that the identity of Jesus can be understood only as an identity *in*, but not above and beyond, cross and resurrection – that is, that it must remain bound up with the dialectic of cross and resurrection. In that case the contradictions between the cross and the resurrection are an inherent part of his identity. Then the resurrection can neither be reduced to the cross, as showing its meaning, nor can the cross be reduced to the resurrection, as its preliminary. It is formally a question of a dialectical identity which exists only through the contradiction, and of a dialectic which exists in the identity.

The apocalyptic expression 'raising from the dead by God' introduces a verb form into the adjectival qualifications of the person as 'crucified' and 'risen'. In the act of raising by God, Jesus is identified as the crucified one who is raised. In that case the point of identification lies not in the person of Jesus, but *extra se* in the God who creates life and new being out of nothing. He is then wholly dead and wholly raised. For this kind of thinking, the self-revelation of Jesus in his appearances includes the revelation of the divinity and faithfulness of God. In that case we must say that in this event which is experienced in the crucifixion and the Easter appearances, God confesses to God and reveals his faithfulness. Then, however, this event which is revealed in the cross and the Easter experiences points back to the promises of God and forwards to an *eschaton* in which his divinity is revealed in all. It must then be understood as the eschatological coming to pass of the faithfulness of God, and at the same time as the eschatological authentication of his promise and as the dawning of its fulfilment. It is a logical consequence of this, that then the future of Christ is not only awaited in his universal glorification, but that his lordship is subordinated to the eschatological revelation of the divinity of God in all that is and in all that is not, as Paul suggests in I Cor. 15.28. What happened between the cross and the Easter appearances is then an eschatological event which has its goal in future revelation and universal fulfilment. It points beyond itself, and even beyond Jesus, to the coming revelation of the glory of God. Then Jesus identifies himself in the Easter appearances as the coming one, and his identity in cross and resurrection points the direction for coming events and makes a path for them. The Lord who appears as risen is not then recognized as one who is eternalized or clothed in heavenly glory, but he appears in the foreglow of the coming, promised glory of God. What happened to him is understood as the dawn and assured promise of the coming glory of God over all, as the victory of life from God over death. Cross and resurrection are then not merely *modi* in the person of Christ. Rather, their dialectic is an open dialectic, which will find its resolving synthesis only in the *eschaton* of all things. If, on the other hand, cross and resurrection are seen as distinctions in the eternal person of Jesus, then what happened between the cross and Easter is not understood as a revelation of the divinity of God in face of death, and is no longer taken as a creative act of God, but is understood as the αὐτοβασιλεία of Jesus: the crucified has arisen. Moreover, he has arisen without any special interference on God's part, because he is himself God. This view, however, turns Easter into the birth of a new cultic Kyrios, and can assert itself only with the greatest difficulty over against the real experience of the existing lordship of death and the powers of annihilation over men.

The fact that the one who appears is heard to speak contains, if we would sum up the Easter narratives, not only the element of self-identification, but also a constant note of mission and promise. The appearances of the risen Lord were experienced by those involved as a commission to service and mission in the world, but not as blissful experiences of union with the divine Being appearing here. The commission to apostolic service in the world was held to be *the* word of the risen Lord. His appearances were vocatory appearances by which the men involved were set to follow the footsteps of the mission of Jesus. By the revelation of the risen Lord the men involved were identified with the mission of Jesus and thus placed in the midst of a history which is instituted and determined by the mission of Jesus and by his future as revealed and made an object of hope in the fore-glow of Easter. The perceiving of the event of resurrection which took place in him thus led by logical necessity to a perception of their own mission and their own future. This is really intelligible only when the mystery of the person of Jesus and of his history in the cross and resurrection is grasped from the standpoint of his mission and in the light of God's future for the world, which his mission serves. Only when his history is thus seen as determined by the *eschaton*, and only when our own consciousness of history takes the form of a consciousness of mission, can the raising of Jesus from the dead be called 'historic'. His enigmatic identity in the contradiction of cross and resurrection has therefore to be understood as an eschatological identity. The titles of Christ which are used to express it anticipate his future. They are therefore not hard and fast titles which define who he was and is, but open and flexible titles, so to speak, which announce in terms of promise what he will be. They are therefore at the same time also dynamic titles. They are stirred and stirring ideas of mission, which seek to point men to their work in the world and their hope in the future of Christ.

10. The Future of Jesus Christ

If we now ask what the future of the risen Christ contains by way of promise and expectation, then we discover promises whose content is already lit up in certain outline by the prophetic expectations of the Old Testament, but whose form is determined by the words, the suffering and the death of Christ. The future of Christ which is to be expected can be stated only in promises which bring out and make clear in the form of foreshadowing and prefigurement what is hidden and prepared in him and his history. In this case, too, promise stands between knowing and not knowing, between necessity and possibility, between that which is not yet and that which already is. The knowledge of the future which is kindled by promise is therefore a knowledge in hope, is therefore prospective and anticipatory, but is therefore also provisional, fragmentary, open, straining beyond itself. It knows the future in striving to bring out the tendencies and latencies of the Christ event of the crucifixion and resurrection, and in seeking to estimate the possibilities opened up by this event. Here the Easter appearances of the crucified Christ are a constant incitement to the consciousness that hopes and anticipates, but on the other hand also suffers and is critical of existence. For these 'appearances' make visible something of the eschatological future of the Christ event, and therefore cause us to seek and search for the future revelation of this event. Thus knowledge of Christ becomes anticipatory, provisional and fragmentary knowledge of his future, namely, of what he will be. All the titles of Christ point messianically forward in this sense. On the other hand, knowledge of the future has its stimulus nowhere else than in the riddle of Jesus of Nazareth. It will thus be knowledge of Christ in the urge to know who he is and what is hidden and prepared in him.

If, however, we take the *absconditum sub cruce* as *latency* and the *revelatum in resurrectione* as *tendency*, if we enquire about the *intention* of God in the mission of Jesus, then we light upon what was promised beforehand. The *missio* of Jesus becomes intelligible only by the *promissio*. His future, in the light of which he can be recognized as what he is, is illuminated in advance by *the promise of the righteousness of God, the promise of life as a result of resurrection* from the dead, and *the promise of the kingdom of God* in a new totality of being.

11. The Future of Righteousness

Righteousness means 'being in order', standing in the right relationship; it means correspondence and harmony and is to that extent akin to 'truth'. But righteousness also means 'being able to stand', having subsistence, finding a basis on which to exist, and is to that extent akin to existence as such. Righteousness in the Old Testament does not mean agreement with an ideal norm or with the *logos* of eternal being, but describes a historic communal relationship which is founded on promise and faithfulness. When Israel praises the righteousness of God, then it thankfully remembers his faithfulness to his covenant promises as it has taken practical shape in the history of Israel. Yahweh's righteousness is his faithfulness to the covenant. That is why his righteousness 'happens', and why one can 'tell' it and trust in it for the future and expect 'salvation' from this righteousness. In trusting in God's faithfulness to this covenant, and in living in accordance with his covenant in promise and statute, men do right by God and are set right. They are set right not only in relation to God, but also in their mutual relationships and in relation to things.[68] This history of the divine righteousness is manifestly recognized not only in Israel's own history and not only in human history, but in the history and the destiny of the whole of God's creation. By the righteousness of God is meant the way in which in freedom he remains true to his statutes, his word and his works and gives them subsistence. The righteousness of God requires everything that owes its existence to the action of God, that is, the whole creation. The righteousness of God is the essence of its stability and the ground of its subsistence. Without his justice and faithfulness nothing can exist, but everything is swallowed up in nothingness. Hence God's righteousness is universal. It is concerned with the justification of life and with the ground of the existence of all things. If we expect the righteousness of God to set man right with himself, with his fellows and with the whole of creation, then it can become the summary expression for a universal, all-inclusive eschatology which expects from the future of righteousness a new being for all things. The righteousness of God

---

68 G. von Rad has shown how the righteousness of God became for Israel the summary expression of the right relationship between God and man, man and fellow man, man and world. Cf. *Theologie des Alten Testamentes* I, 1958, pp. 368ff. (ET 1962, pp. 370ff.).

then refers not merely to a new order for the existing world, but provides creation as a whole with a new ground of existence and a new right to life. Hence with the coming of the righteousness of God we can expect also a new creation.

In the New Testament the divine righteousness is accordingly understood by Paul as God's faithfulness in communal relationships, as an event brought about by God, and as an event from which there arises a new creation and new life. Paul sees this divine righteousness as revealed in the gospel (Rom. 1.17) and grasped in faith. It is the christological gospel of the cross and of the raising of Christ by God. In this event divine righteousness is revealed for the unrighteous and justification of life (Rom. 5.18) for those who, both in a juridical and in an ontological sense, cannot stand before the wrath of God. It is the eschatological gospel, which imputes this divine righteousness 'that must be hoped for' (Gal. 5.5) as now already present and as savingly at work in the wrath of God that is now being revealed. It is, finally, the universal gospel, which is oriented towards the new creation that fulfils all things, sets them right with God and so gives them status and being.

Divine righteousness 'happens' here, and the gospel reveals it by proclaiming the event of the obedience of Jesus even to the death of the cross, by proclaiming the event of his surrender to this death, and by proclaiming his resurrection and his life as the coming of the divine righteousness to the unjust. The realization and revelation of a new divine righteousness for sinners thus becomes the mystery of Jesus Christ which is disclosed in the promise of the gospel: 'delivered for our offences, and raised again for our justification' (Rom. 4.25). 'He hath made him to be sin for us, who knew no sin; that we might be made the righteousness of God in him' (II Cor. 5.21). Thus there takes place in him reconciliation of the unreconciled by God. It is important here to see that this divine righteousness has its ground both in the event of the cross and in that of the resurrection, that is, both in his death and in his life. A one-sided theology of the cross would attain only to the gospel of the *remissio peccatorum*, but not to the *promissio* of the new righteousness whose life is grounded in his life and whose future consists in the future of his lordship. 'In that he died, he died unto sin once (ἐφάπαξ): but in that he liveth, he liveth unto God. Likewise reckon ye also yourselves to be dead indeed unto sin, but alive unto God through Jesus Christ our Lord' (Rom. 6.10–11). The divine righteousness which is here revealed finds its measure not in the sin it forgives, but in that new life in the glory of the risen and exalted Christ which it promises and to which it points.

Along with this goes the fact that since the gospel of divine righteousness has its ground in the dying and living of Jesus, sin and death are seen together. 'The wages of sin is death; but the gift of God is eternal life through Jesus Christ our Lord' (Rom. 6.23, cf. I Cor. 15.55ff.). Sin is therefore to be understood as unrighteousness, as having no ground and no rights, as being unable to stand. This includes both being lost in revolt against God and in falsehood, and also dying and being swallowed up in nothingness. The divine righteousness which is revealed in the cross and resurrection of Jesus accordingly embraces both reconciliation with God and justification of life. It embraces forgiveness of guilt and annihilation of the destiny of death. It embraces reconciliation and redemption of the mortal body. It takes place in the pledge of reconciliation and the promise of quickening. Since Jesus' resurrection and his exaltation to be Lord is not yet the consummation of his lordship, but the ground and guarantee of his liberating and remedial lordship over all, so the divine righteousness is present in faith and in baptism, yet in such a way that it is engaged in a process which will be completed only at the parousia of Christ. In this process we have the divine righteousness here always as a gift that is pledged, disputed and subject to testing, that is, we have it in terms of promise and expectancy.[69] Then, however, the promised divine righteousness sets us on a path whose tension and whose goal it announces. It is this eschatological differentiation in the revelation of Christ in gospel and promise that forms the ground of the historic and ethical statements in which Paul speaks of 'grace reigning through righteousness' (Rom. 5.21), of the 'ministration of righteousness' (II Cor. 3.9, cf. Rom. 6.13), and of 'submission unto righteousness' (Rom. 10.3). Divine righteousness is not merely a gift that has been made manifest, but means also the power of the Giver which is at work in the life of the believer. That is why the man who is justified begins to suffer under the contradiction of this world with which he has a bodily solidarity, for he must in obedience seek the divine righteousness in his body, on earth, and in all creatures.

---

69 Cf. E. Käsemann, 'Gottesgerechtigkeit bei Paulus', ZTK 58, 1961, p. 368.

If the divine righteousness of God means that in communal relationships he is faithful to his promise and to the work of his hands, then justification has finally not only the sense that the unjust is given a right to stand before God and to endure in his judgment, but it has contrariwise also a theological sense – namely, that in this event God attains his rights over against his creation. Luther, in his Lectures on Romans in 1516, had sought to interpret this as a reciprocal event of *justificatio Dei activa et passiva*: justification means that God justifies man by grace and that man acknowledges God's justice in confessing his sins, so that in this reciprocal event not only the sinner but God, too, is given his rights.[70] If this insight of Luther's is detached from the framework of the *humilitas* Christology in which he formulated it, then it can be said that because the divine righteousness is gift and power and the communion of faith with Christ is both a dying with Christ to sin and also a living under his lordship with an outlook towards his future, therefore the event of justification is the earnest and promise of an all-inclusive setting to rights on God's part. If in the justification of the sinner God attains to his rights, then this justification is the beginning and foreshadowing of his sole lordship. The divine righteousness which is latent in the event of Christ has an inner trend towards a totality of new being. The man who is justified follows this trend in bodily obedience. His struggle for obedience and his suffering under the godlessness of the world have their goal in the future of the righteousness of the whole. Thus this struggle is a fragment of, and a prelude to, the coming divine righteousness, for it already gives God his due, and in it already God attains to his rights over his world.

Thus in the New Testament, too, we shall have to understand divine righteousness as promise. In this promise the promised

---

70 M. Luther, *Vorlesung über den Römerbrief 1515/16*, ed. J. Ficker, 1908, II, p. 65. Cf. H. J. Iwand's comment on this in *Glaubensgerechtigkeit nach Luthers Lehre*, 4th ed. 1964, pp. 11ff. This new insight on Luther's part in seeing in the event of justification not only the forgiveness of sins and the right of the godless to life before God, but *vice versa* also the judicial realization of God's right to lordship, has been regained for New Testament theology today by E. Käsemann. Cf. 'Neutestamentliche Fragen heute', *ZTK* 54, 1957, pp. 13f.; 'Gottesgerechtigkeit bei Paulus', *ZTK* 58, 1961, pp. 367ff. Only with this new insight is it possible to do away with the individualization of the event of justification in the revelation of the divinity of God, and only where that happens does the *justificatio impii* come to stand within the eschatological horizon of the *resurrectio mortuorum* and the *creatio ex nihil*.

object is offered in the present, and yet it is grasped in the believing hope which makes man ready to serve the future of the divine righteousness in all things.

12. The Future of Life

Expectation of life and recognition of death are immediately bound up together in love. It is only in the things a man loves that he can be hurt, and it is only in love that man suffers and recognizes the deadliness of death. What sort of expectation of life and what sort of experience of death were quickened by the promises of Israel?

It is a widely established and surprising fact that 'Yahwism turned with a special intolerance against all forms of the cult of death'.[71] 'It is surprising that for long the Jews had no thoughts or dreams about the last agony. They were as much a this-worldly people as the Greeks, and yet their life was incomparably more vigorously determined by future goals.'[72] In this enigmatic fact that Israel's religion of promise clings with obstinate exclusiveness to the historic and this-worldly fulfilment of the promises, we have the presupposition for understanding the resurrection of Christ as the resurrection of the crucified one and not as a symbol for the hope of immortality and for the resigned attitude to life that goes along with it.

All dead things represent for Israel the acme of uncleanness. All pollutions of this kind involve exclusion from the service of God. It is true that the temptation to necromancy did exist in Canaan. Yet the very rejection of it by Israel shows plainly that the religion of promise must abjure all sacral communication with the dead. The dead are cut off from God and from living communion with him. Because God and his promise are life, the real bitterness of death lies not merely in the loss of life, but also in the loss of God, in god-forsakenness.[73] For life means giving thanks and praise in the presence of God. But in death there can be no giving of praise, and therefore no thanksgiving either and no harmony with God. Being able to praise God and being no longer able to praise him are here

---

71 G. von Rad, *Theologie des Alten Testamentes* I, p. 275 (ET p. 276).
72 E. Bloch, *Das Prinzip Hoffnung* II, 1959, p. 1323.
73 G. von Rad, *op. cit.* I, p. 386 (ET pp. 388f.).

THE RESURRECTION AND THE FUTURE OF JESUS CHRIST

synonyms for the antithesis of life and death.[74] Death cuts man off
from God by separating him from his promises and his praise. Not
only our physical end, but also sickness, exile and oppression can
cut us off from the life of praise and from the promised life and
thus be understood as death. We have our life in praising God,
hoping in him and giving thanks to him. Death therefore means
that we are far from God and he from us.

On this ground it becomes understandable that the Greek doctrine of universal transience in the outward world and of the
essential immortality of the true being of the soul hardly gained
any admittance in Israel, but that the hopes of resurrection on the
other hand certainly did find a place on the periphery of the Old
Testament and in the apocalyptic of late Judaism. This expectation of the resurrection of the dead is found in its Israelite form
neither in an anthropological context – as a hope for man beyond
death – nor in a cosmological context – in recognition of immortal
substances in which man participates – but in a theological context – in expounding the power of the God of promise, whom even
death cannot rob of his due but who must attain his due beyond
death. Thus according to Ezek. 37.11 the people of the promise can
now recognize itself only in the picture of dead bones, i.e. of hope
that has come to nothing, and is then given to hear the prophetic
message of a new promise of life by Yahweh: 'Behold, I will cause
breath to enter into you, and ye shall live' (Ezek. 37.5). This is a
new promise of life, for it is no longer attached to the condition of
a possible repentance, but promises a creative act of Yahweh upon
his people beyond the bounds of the temporal and the possible. It
therefore acquires the form of a promise that has no conditions and
no presuppositions, a promise of life from the dead on the ground
of a creative act of Yahweh *ex nihilo*. Thus in Israel the idea of
'raising of the dead' is formulated in the first instance within the
framework of the religion of promise: it is not a case of natural
reanimation, but of the fulfilling of Yahweh's promises of life in the
dead bearer of the promise. It is not until the apocalyptic writers
that 'raising of the dead' is understood in universal terms, in the
sense that even beyond death this God will achieve his judgment
and his due in both righteous and unrighteous. This is entirely in

---

74 *Ibid.* I, p. 367 (ET p. 370): 'Praising and not praising stand over against
one another like life and death: praise becomes the most elementary "mark of
being alive".'

harmony with the development of the Israelite confession to God the Creator and to his faithfulness as Creator. The late Israelite ideas of *creatio ex nihilo* and *resurrectio mortuorum* mark the eschatological extremities of the religion of promise.[75]

It has rightly been said: 'Should we not see this theological vacuum, which Israel zealously kept free from any sacral concepts, as one of the greatest theological enigmas in the Old Testament? The prediction that God will prepare a resurrection from the dead for his own people is found only peripherally.'[76] This 'vacuum' caused by the absence of religious ideas and hopes against death makes it possible on the one hand to experience in all its undisguised harshness the deadliness of death as compared with the promised life received from the promise of God. It can be filled on the other hand only by a hope which makes possible a whole-hearted, unrestricted and unreserved assent to life, to the body and to the world, and which yet extends beyond death. The hope of resurrection does not overcome the deadliness of death by regarding living and dying as mere summary expressions for the transience of all things and as such unimportant, but by proclaiming the victory of praise and therewith of life over death and over the curse of god-forsakenness, by announcing the victory of God over the absence of God.

What is the significance of the death and resurrection of Jesus Christ in the context of these expectations?

In the context of these expectations of life, his death on the cross implies not only the end of the life which he had, but also the end of the life which he loves and in which he hopes. The death of Jesus was experienced as the death of him who had been sent as the Messiah of God, and therefore implies also the 'death of God'. Thus his death is experienced and proclaimed as god-forsakenness,

---

75 W. Zimmerli, '"Leben" und "Tod" im Buch des Propheten Ezechiel', in *Gottes Offenbarung*, 1963, p. 191. Zimmerli points out how closely Ezek. 37 approaches the priestly narrative of the creation and how the prophet's conditional promises of life – 'return, and ye shall live' – are anchored in God's promise of life which unconditionally embraces the beginning (creation) and end (resurrection of the dead) of the history of the people of God. Cf. also Christoph Barth, *Die Errettung vom Tode in den individuellen Klage- und Dankliedern des Alten Testamentes*, 1947; Robert Martin-Achard, *De la mort à la resurrection d'après l'Ancien Testament*, 1956, and K. Koch's review in *Verkündigung und Forschung*, 1960/2, 1/2, pp. 57–60.

76 G. von Rad, *op. cit.* II, p. 362 (ET p. 350).

as judgment, as curse, as exclusion from the promised life, as reprobation and damnation.

In the context of these expectations of life, his resurrection must then be understood not as a mere return to life as such, but as a conquest of the deadliness of death – as a conquest of god-forsakenness, as a conquest of judgment and of the curse, as a beginning of the fulfilment of the promised life, and thus as a conquest of all that is dead in death, as a negation of the negative (Hegel), as a negation of the negation of God.

It is then understandable, further, that Jesus' resurrection was not seen as a private Easter for his private Good Friday, but as the beginning and source of the abolition of the universal Good Friday, of that god-forsakenness of the world which comes to light in the deadliness of the death of the cross. Hence the resurrection of Christ was not understood merely as the first instance of a general resurrection of the dead and as a beginning of the revelation of the divinity of God in the non-existent, but also as the source of the risen life of all believers and as a confirmation of the promise which will be fulfilled in all and will show itself in the very deadliness of death to be irresistible.

To recognize the event of the resurrection of Christ is therefore to have a hopeful and expectant knowledge of this event. It means recognizing in this event the latency of that eternal life which in the praise of God arises from the negation of the negative, from the raising of the one who was crucified and the exaltation of the one who was forsaken. It means assenting to the tendency towards resurrection of the dead in this event of the raising of the one. It means following the intention of God by entering into the dialectic of suffering and dying in expectation of eternal life and of resurrection. This is described as the working of the Holy Spirit. The 'Spirit' is according to Paul the 'life-giving Spirit', the Spirit who *'raised up* Christ from the dead' and *'dwells* in' those who recognize Christ and his future, and *'shall* quicken their mortal bodies' (Rom. 8.11).

The 'Spirit' in question here does not fall from heaven and does not soar ecstatically into heaven, but arises from the event of the resurrection of Christ and is an earnest and pledge of his future, of the future of universal resurrection and of life. 'And as the power of the "flesh" is manifested in the fact that it binds man to the transitory, to that which in reality is always already past, to death, so the power of the Spirit is manifested in the fact that it gives the believer freedom, opens the way to the future, to the eternal, to life. For freedom is nothing else than being open for the genuine future, letting oneself be determined by the future. So Spirit may be called the power of futurity.'[77] Yet the difference between past and future emerges for the Spirit of faith not in the *punctum mathematicum* of the present, and not in an airy *nunc aeternum*, but in that historic event of the raising of the crucified Christ in which the power of transience and the deadliness of death are conquered and the future of life is opened once and for all. Christ did not rise into the Spirit or into the kerygma, but into that as yet undetermined future realm ahead of us which is pointed to by the tendencies of the Spirit and the proclamations of the kerygma. This realm of the future which lies before us cannot be turned into mere 'futurity' by reflecting solely on its relation to existence, but it is the future of Jesus Christ and can therefore be inferred only from the knowledge and recognition of that historic event of the resurrection of Christ which is the making of history and the key to it. The 'Spirit' who 'mortifies the things of the flesh' and gives freedom for the future is not an eternal event, but arises from a historic event and discloses eschatological possibilities and dangers. As a reminder of Christ he is also the promise of his future, and *vice versa*. Hence he leads us into the 'fellowship of the sufferings of Christ', into conformity to his death, into the love which exposes itself to death because it is upheld by hope. Hence, too, he leads into the future of that glorification of Jesus Christ on which depends the future and glorification of humanity and of all things. 'As he was crucified through weakness, yet liveth by the power of God, so we also are weak in him, but we shall live with him by the power of God' (II Cor. 13.4). Thus the Spirit is the power to suffer in participation in the mission and the love of Jesus Christ, and is in this suffering the passion for what is possible, for what is coming and promised in the future of life, of freedom and of resurrection. The Spirit subjects man to the tendency of the things which are latent in the resurrection of Jesus and which are the intended goal of the future of the risen Lord. Resurrection and eternal life are the future that is promised, and thereby make obedience possible in the body. In all our acts we are sowing in hope. So, too, in love and obedience we are sowing for the future of the resurrection of the body. In obedience, those

---

77 R. Bultmann, *Theologie des Neuen Testamentes*, 1953, p. 331 (ET pp. 334f.).

who have been quickened by the Spirit are on the way towards the quickening of the mortal body.

Just as the urge of promise is towards fulfilment, as the urge of faith is towards obedience and sight, and as the urge of hope is towards the life that is promised and finally attained, so the urge of the raising of Christ is towards life in the Spirit and towards the eternal life that is the consummation of all things. This eternal life here lies hidden beneath its opposite, under trial, suffering, death and sorrow. Yet this its hiddenness is not an eternal paradox, but a latency within the tendency that presses forwards and outwards into that open realm of possibilities that lies ahead and is so full of promise. In the darkness of the pain of love, the man of hope discovers the dissension between the self and the body.[78]

---

78 The interpretation of σῶμα and corporeality in R. Bultmann (*Theologie des Neuen Testamentes*, pp. 191ff., ET pp. 195ff.) seems to be too one-sidedly personalistic. For him, σῶμα means man, 'the person as a whole'. 'He is called σῶμα in so far as he can make himself the object of his own actions, or experiences himself as the subject of something that happens or that he suffers. Thus he can be called σῶμα in so far as he has a relation to himself' (p. 192, cf. ET pp. 195f.). 'Man does not *have* a σῶμα, but he is σῶμα' (p. 191, ET p. 194). The former thesis no doubt aptly represents what modern philosophic anthropology calls the 'ex-centric position' of man. The second thesis, however, cancels out the dialectic of the ex-centric position of human nature. 'He neither *is* only body, nor *has* he only a body. Every claim upon his physical existence demands a balance between being and having, without and within' (H. Plessner, *Lachen und Weinen*, 3rd ed. 1961, p. 48). Bultmann sees the fact of man's 'having a relation to himself' as providing the possibility of 'being one with himself or being estranged from himself, at odds with himself' (p. 192, ET p. 196). The σῶμα πνευματικόν can therefore be understood as a reconciliation of the dualism in man between self and self (p. 195, ET p. 199). In harmony with this view of corporeality as the relation of man to himself, G. Ebeling finds that in faith man comes 'to himself' and attains to agreement with himself (*Theologie und Verkündigung*, pp. 84ff.; ET, pp. 83f.). But now, man's relation to himself is not identical with his relation to his body. His corporeal, physical and social existence is not identical with 'existence' in the sense of the relation to himself. The two belong together in such a way that according as man acquires in reflection a consciousness of his self and his subjectivity, so he attains to an objective consciousness of the world and assumes a detached attitude to the corporeal, social and cosmic 'world around him' as belonging to the world of objects. 'To become man is to be raised to openness towards the world through the spirit' (M. Scheler, *Die Stellung des Menschen im Kosmos*, 2nd ed. 1949, p. 41). The thing man becomes conscious of as his corporeality is not his 'self', but is rather the very thing from which he succeeds in differentiating himself. The fact that through the spirit, through consciousness and through reflection man can differentiate himself from himself, that he is able to objectify himself, constitutes the ambiguity of his existence: he can neither be himself without having himself, nor

In the struggle for obedience and for what is due to God in the body he discovers the contradiction of the flesh and his subjection to the hostile powers of annihilation and death. In beginning to hope for the triumph of life and to wait for resurrection, he perceives the deadliness of death and can no longer put up with it. The corporeality which thus comes to the fore in hope is plainly the starting point for the solidarity of the believer with the whole of creation which, like him, is subjected to vanity – in hope. This corporeality, for the redemption of which the man of hope waits because it has not yet taken place, is the existential starting point for the universality that marks the Christian hope and for the as yet undetermined character of what is hoped for. The hope of the redemption of the body and the hope of the redemption of all creation from vanity are one. Hence it is on this hope of the redemption of the body that the universality which belongs to the Christian hope depends. On the other hand, in the contradictions of the body, in the painful difference between what he hopes and what he experiences, the man of hope perceives that his hoped-for future

---

have himself without being himself, he achieves neither complete distinction and objectivity in regard to himself, nor complete identity. If the promise of justification gives him a prospect of reconciliation and identity, then it cannot mean only the reconciliation of man with himself, but must also mean the redemption of his corporeality and of the world that has become to him a world of objects. Hence through the promise and the Holy Spirit he perceives not only his own reconciliation, but along with it at the same time also the unreconciled and unredeemed character of the body that is subject to death and of the world that is subject to the powers of godlessness. His reconciliation in the Spirit does not yet reconcile him with his body and his world in such a way that he would see these as the 'world around him', in such a way that like the animals (or the angels) he could attain to harmony with his environment amid existing things. E. Käsemann is therefore right when he asserts against Bultmann that 'body' for Paul is not in fact the relation of man to himself, but is that piece of world which we ourselves are and for which, as a gift of the Creator, we are responsible. 'For the apostle it means man in his worldliness, that is, in his ability to communicate' (*ZTK* 59, 1962, p. 282). If the perceiving of his corporeality is grounded for man in his being raised to openness towards the world through the spirit, if his corporeality is not his 'self' but that from which he can differentiate himself, then the perceiving of corporeality, of socialness and of worldliness becomes one. Then the perceiving of his unredeemed corporeality is the starting point for the perceiving of man's solidarity with the whole unredeemed creation. And in this context there also finally comes to light the existential character of all man's objective statements. Objective statements are not by any means statements that are oblivious of self and of existence, but are grounded in the existential raising of man to openness towards the world through the spirit. This calls for a re-check on demythologizing and existentialist interpretation.

is still outstanding. Hence it is on the difference between hope and bodily reality that the wide open, future character of the Christian hope depends. The cosmic ideas of Christian eschatology are therefore not by any means mythological, but reach forward into the open realm of possibilities ahead of all reality, give expression to the 'expectation of the creature' for a *nova creatio*, and provide a prelude for eternal life, peace and the haven of the reconciliation of all things. They bring to light not only what future means in man's 'openness towards the world', but also what future means in the world's 'openness towards man' (cf. the relation of correspondence between the 'expectation of the creature' and the 'liberty of the children of God' in Rom. 8.20ff.).

In the light of the differences which the hope of resurrection and of reconciled, perfect life finds in the existing reality of man and the world as at present experienced, and which it reveals in all their negativity, the positive side of the future for which it hopes for man and the world, for spirit and body, for Israel and the nations, can be expressed in the first instance as negation of the negative. The 'new heaven and new earth, wherein dwelleth righteousness' (II Peter 3.13), the promise that 'God shall wipe away all tears from their eyes; and there shall be no more death, neither sorrow, nor crying, neither shall there be any more pain' (Rev. 21.4), the face unveiled in the glory of God (II Cor. 2.18) and the body glorified by the Spirit of the resurrection (I Cor. 15.35ff.) – these are representations and pictures of this kind, in which the future is re-'pre'-sented and 'pro'-mised[79] in contrast to the experiences of a negative present. These ideas and pictures are fragments from a life that has been unmasked in all its flaws by hope and is therefore one of suffering. The book of Revelation is the book of the martyrs. These ideas and pictures may well be conditioned by their time – they are, and must be, if they would be critical of their time – yet they are used with the intention of expressing something which goes completely beyond the *status quo* and sets things on the move.

---

79 [The somewhat curious orthography is an attempt to convey something of the author's intention in hyphenating *vor-stellen* ('represent') and using the antiquated form *vorheissen* for *verheissen* ('promise'). The stress laid on the syllables *pre* and *pro* (in German *vor*) is meant to suggest that representation and promise have literally to do with *advance* conceptions about things to come. – Translator.]

As long as 'every thing' is not 'very good', the difference between hope and reality remains, and faith remains irreconciled and must press towards the future in hope and suffering. Thus the promise of life through the resurrection of Christ also brings us within the tendency of the Spirit who quickens men in suffering and whose goal is the praise of the new creation. This is something like 'progressive revelation' or 'self-realizing eschatology', only it is a case of the *progressus gratiae* itself. It is not objective time that brings the progress. It is not human activity that makes the future. It is the inner necessity of the Christ event itself, the tendency of which is finally to bring out in all things the eternal life latent in him and the justice of God latent in him.

13. The Future of the Kingdom of God and of the Freedom of Man

The real heart of eschatology, and the basic concept which it constantly employs with varying content, is doubtless to be found in the promise and expectation of what is known as the 'kingdom of God' and the 'lordship of God'. It is plain that even in the early days of Israel, the hope which has its ground in the promise is directed towards the lordship of Yahweh. It is in his real, historic lordship that his glory manifests itself. It is in the faithful and powerful fulfilment of his promises that he manifests himself as himself, as God and Lord. Bound up with the expectation of the lordship of God is the expectation that his people, mankind, and all that he has made will attain to salvation, peace, happiness, life – in a word, to what it was truly meant to be. Faith in his lordship finds its expression in the confession that Yahweh is king (Judg. 8.23). If we go back to the nomadic period of the Israelite tribes, then we find the idea that Yahweh is the Leader who goes before his people, that he rules them by leading them as a shepherd, issuing commands, giving counsel and announcing his will for the future.[80] Thus his lordship does not mean in the first instance a worldly kingship over the natural world around man, but leadership towards the lands of promise, and thus a historic lordship which shows itself in unique, unrepeatable, startlingly new, purposeful events.

---

80 Cf. M. Buber, *Königtum Gottes*, 2nd ed. 1936.

God's lordship originally means lordship in promise, faithfulness and fulfilment. Life under his lordship then accordingly means the historic life of the nomad in breaking new ground and in obedient readiness to face the future – a life that is received in promise and is open to promise. It is only in controversy with the nature religions and theophanous ideas of the world in Palestine, and in the context of the development of belief in creation and of the prophetic eschatology, that the idea of God's lordship becomes universal, and that this universality of the lordship of the one God is at the same time understood eschatologically. The praises of God's royal lordship over all things, the ideas of his coming, his justice and judgment upon earth, are all related to the God who is on the march with Israel, the God of the promise and the exodus. Thus the ideas of universal theophany can be supplemented by ideas from the nature religions, and yet these latter can at once be set in an eschatological framework on the ground of the historic religion of promise.

In the idea of the lordship of God two elements are combined: remembrance of his historic lordship and confidence in it, and expectation of his universal lordship in which the world and all nations and things become his universe, his kingdom and his praise.

It is not possible to distinguish the two by making the first a matter of narrow nationalism and the second one of universal cosmic faith. Rather, the universal expectation has its ground in remembering the particular historic reality of his sovereign action in Israel. After the breakdown of Israel's historic independence, the expectation of the divine lordship was represented in rabbinic theology in the obedience of the legally righteous, while in apocalyptic theology it was futurized by means of speculations about world history, and his coming was delegated to events in the course of world history. This shows the impossibility of conceiving the promise of divine lordship in both historic and eschatological terms without its being given new content from experience.

In the New Testament the βασιλεία is obviously a central concept – especially in the synoptic tradition, and here indeed at all levels of the tradition. In particular, the message and acts, miracles and parables of Jesus before Easter are described as 'the kingdom of God'. Jesus proclaims the messianic kingdom of God. The peculiar feature of his proclamation of the kingdom lies in the fact that nearness to, entry into, and inheritance of, the kingdom are bound by him to the decision of the hearers and their attitude to his own person. The future of the divine lordship is immediately bound up with the mystery of his own presence.

This can be understood in the sense that as the last prophet of the coming kingdom he gives men's decision in face of his message the character of the final, and in this sense eschatological, decision.

It can also be understood as a transformation of the kingdom of God tradition. Then Jesus has surmounted the apocalyptic question as to the appointed times and historic circumstances of the arrival of the kingdom 'by concentrating on what the announcement of the kingdom means for existence'.[81] By proclaiming his hour as the last hour of decision, Jesus himself demythologizes the apocalyptic pictures of the kingdom for the sake of existential actualization. 'The eschatological proclamation and the ethical demand both point man to the fact that he is brought before God and that God is at hand; both point him to his Now as the hour of decision for God.'[82] In that case, however, the peculiar feature of Jesus' message of the kingdom would lie in an existential ethicizing of it, in favour of which all ideas of cosmological apocalyptic fade out of the picture. But this alone gives the primitive Christian Church no reason, and hardly even a right, to continue his proclamation. The reason and the right of the Christian Church to carry on his proclamation, and for its part even to transform it, surely lies in the event which gave it cause to remember Jesus' words and actions at all and to proclaim him as Lord of all the world – namely, in the Easter appearances of the risen Lord. The Easter appearances, however, were recognized and proclaimed within a horizon of apocalyptic expectation: resurrection as an eschatological event – Jesus as the firstfruits of the resurrection. The understanding of Jesus which results from the event of the raising of the crucified one by God was necessarily connected in the Church's mind with its remembrance of the understanding of God and his kingdom which results from the words and acts of Jesus.[83] The note of eschatolog-

---

81 H. Conzelmann, Art. 'Reich Gottes', in *RGG*[3] vol. V, col. 915.

82 R. Bultmann, *Theologie des Neuen Testamentes*, p. 20 (ET p. 21).

83 For what follows cf. the discussion on kingdom of God and Son of Man: P. Vielhauer, 'Gottesreich und Menschensohn in der Verkündigung Jesu', *Festschr. f. G. Dehn*, 1957, pp. 51ff.; H. E. Tödt, *Der Menschensohn in der synoptischen Überlieferung*, 1959 (ET by D. M. Barton: *The Son of Man in the Synoptic Tradition*, 1965); E. Schweizer, 'Der Menschensohn', *Zeitschrift für NT Wissenschaft* 50, 1959, pp. 185ff.; P. Vielhauer, 'Jesus und der Menschensohn', *ZTK* 60, 1963, pp. 133ff. (now also in *Aufsätze zum Neuen Testament* [Theol. Bücherei

ical decision in his proclamation of the imminent lordship of God was therefore necessarily transferred to the note of eschatological decision in the message of the crucified and risen Lord. With this, however, the proclamation of the divine lordship acquired a new apocalyptic character and could be bound up with the messianic titles of Christ, such as Son of Man, which are found in apocalyptic. This constitutes a discontinuity between Jesus' message of the kingdom and the Church's christological message of the kingdom, as it is aptly expressed in the remark of Albert Schweitzer: Jesus proclaimed the kingdom, and the Church proclaimed – him. Yet this discontinuity exists rightly. The Church has not to 'carry on Jesus' self-consciousness or self-understanding, but to proclaim who he *is*. This, however, can be seen only in the light of the end, i.e. of the cross and of the Easter appearances as the foreshadowing of his eschatologically still outstanding goal and end. The Church's statements are based not on Jesus' self-understanding, but on that which happened to him in the cross and the resurrection. His death and resurrection mark the discontinuity between the historical Jesus and primitive Christian Christology. His identity, however, which lies in the fact that he who here appears as risen is the one who was crucified and no other, forms at the same time the bridge to the historical Jesus and provides the ground and occasion for the historical remembrance of Jesus' message and acts. This remembrance may be clouded in the gospel tradition of primitive Christianity by many an enthusiastic concern for resurrection and the Spirit, yet the Easter Christophanies are the only adequate ground for remembering and calling to mind his proclamation, just as his cross is the only adequate ground for not forgetting his promise of the kingdom in face of the so-called delay of the parousia of the kingdom. There is no need here to subject the gospel narratives to the verdict of being imaginative backward projections of the resurrection faith. They remember Jesus on the ground of the expectations for his future which are aroused by the resurrection appearances, and present the earthly Jesus of the past in the light of the hopes for his future which become possible with Easter. These hopes are no doubt a strong motive for historical remembrance and also for

---

31], 1965, pp. 135ff.). The latter's systematic observations on the problem how far it is true that Jesus did not understand himself as the expected Son of Man, but that the Church rightly did so (*ZTK* 60, pp. 173f.), provide our starting point here.

historical discoveries. The key to what he 'in fact' was and is, is provided not by his self-understanding, whatever that may have been, but by the understanding of his future which Easter makes credible and enables us to hope for. It is not the remembrance of the dead Master in the light of his death, but the experience of Easter, that makes it necessary to identify Jesus. It is only the enigmatic, dialectical identity of the risen Lord with the crucified Christ that compels the acceptance of a continuity between the primitive Christian Christology and the message of Jesus himself. The 'self-consciousness' of Jesus does not compel men to remain conscious of him, but their consciousness of Jesus – as fashioned by the resurrection appearances – is certainly compelled to raise the question of its own continuity with Jesus' consciousness.

But if the raising of Jesus from the dead is thus a constitutive part of the Christian message of the kingdom, then it is hardly possible any longer for the latter to be concentrated on its 'meaning for existence' and existentially ethicized, but then it is essential to take the universal horizon of hope and promise embracing all things and develop it just as widely as apocalyptic had done – not in the same way, but in the same cosmic breadth. Hence we ought not to speak only of divine *lordship*, meaning by this the eschatological subjection of man's existence to the absolute demand, but we should also speak again of the *kingdom* of God, and so bring out the all-embracing eschatological breadth of his future, into which the mission and the love of Christ lead the man of hope.

If the Easter appearances of Jesus as perceived within the eschato-logical horizon of expectation are the occasion for remembering and taking over Jesus' message of the kingdom, yet they are at the same time also the occasion for the transforming of this message of the kingdom. The future which remained open in Jesus' message of the kingdom is confirmed by his resurrection appearances, assured in anticipation as the dawn of his parousia, and can now be called *his* future. At the later levels of the synoptic tradition a christological understanding of the kingdom of God asserts itself, inasmuch as the idea of the kingdom of Christ, or of the Son of Man, is devel-oped on the lines of the Jewish idea of the messianic kingdom. This, however, brings with it a change in the idea of the kingdom of God itself. To be sure, it still retains its bearing on the present decision for new obedience, but this call which summons men to new life in obedience finds support and prospect in the resurrecting act of God.

The sole Lord of the kingdom is the God 'who has raised Jesus from the dead' and therein shows himself to be the *creator ex nihilo*. His kingdom can then no longer be seen in a historic transformation of the godless state of man and the world. His future does not result from the trends of world history. His rule is his raising of the dead and consists in calling into being the things that are not, and choosing things which are not, to bring to nothing things which are (I Cor. 1.28). This makes it impossible to conceive the kingdom of God in deistic terms of salvation history, as a result of world history or of a divine plan for the world. It also makes it impossible to conceive the kingdom of God 'without God' and to resolve 'God' himself as the 'highest Good' into the ideal of the kingdom.

Finally, the enigma of the Easter appearances – understood in the Hellenistic church as 'exaltation' – also led to regarding Jesus as the exalted cultic Kyrios and extolling his kingdom as his hidden heavenly lordship. Thus whatever the horizon within which the ideas were formed, it was always the interpretation of the resurrection of the crucified one which became determinative for the understanding of the promise of the kingdom of God.

In the very different views which thus arose, we note the following characteristics:

1. The experiences of the cross and of the resurrection appearances of Jesus give a new stamp to the message of the kingdom of God. His cross and resurrection in a certain sense 'distort' his own open picture of the future and the coming of the kingdom of God. But at the same time, and for this reason, the lordship of God assumes the concrete form of this event of the raising of the crucified one. In this event the kingdom of God is not only christologically 'distorted' (*verstellt*), but concretely represented (*vorgestellt*). If Jesus has been raised from the dead, then the kingdom of God can be nothing less than a *nova creatio*. If the risen Lord is the crucified Christ, then the kingdom is *tectum sub cruce*. The coming lordship of God takes shape here in the suffering of the Christians, who because of their hope cannot be conformed to the world, but are drawn by the mission and love of Christ into discipleship and conformity to his sufferings. This way of taking into consideration the cross and resurrection of Christ does not mean that the 'kingdom of God' is spiritualized and made into a thing of the beyond, but it becomes this-worldly and becomes the antithesis and contradiction of a godless and god-forsaken world.

2. The experience of the cross and resurrection of Jesus brings not only a christological understanding of the 'kingdom of God', but also in a new sense an eschatological understanding of it. Because of their experiences of the cross and of Easter, the oldest churches did not live in a 'time of fulfilment', but in earnest looking forward to the future. To be sure, it was possible for the experiences of Easter and of the Spirit to give occasion for an eschatology of fulfilment in the Spirit, as a result of which the experiences of the cross and of the contradiction of reality appeared to be overcome in the Spirit. Only, the realism of the earthly cross of Jesus and of the contradiction everywhere perceptible in an unredeemed world in the course of the Christian mission showed this religious or cultic docetism to be an error. Thus particularly in Paul an eschatological view of the still outstanding kingdom of God asserted itself over against all eschatological and cultic enthusiasm. If the raising of Jesus from the dead provides the ground for a new kind of hope in the kingdom, then the promised future cannot lie simply in the very fact of the giving of the Spirit, but the 'Spirit' himself becomes the 'earnest' of the still outstanding future and therefore 'strives' against the 'works of the flesh'. If the kingdom of God implies the raising of the dead, then it is a new creation, and then the 'exalted Lord' cannot be understood as one of several cultic lords or as the 'true cultic Lord', but only as the *Cosmocrator*. The lordship of the risen and exalted Christ, as it was understood in the Hellenistic church's Christology of exaltation, is from the eschatological standpoint itself provisional and serves the final goal of the sole lordship of God, in which all things become new. Then, however, the christological understanding of the message of the kingdom does not distort Jesus' message of the kingdom, but makes it universal, opens it to embrace a totality of new being. The Easter appearances are then made the occasion for expecting the lordship of God over death and the righteousness of God in all transient things. If the kingdom of God begins as it were with a new act of creation, then the Reconciler is ultimately the Creator, and thus the eschatological prospect of reconciliation must mean the reconciliation of the whole creation, and must develop an eschatology of all things. In the cross we can recognize the god-forsakenness of all things, and with the cross we can recognize the real absence of the kingdom of God in which all things attain to righteousness, life and peace. Hence the kingdom of God can mean no less than

resurrection and new creation, and hope in the kingdom can be satisfied with no less than this. Because of this universality, the new hope of the kingdom leads us to suffer under the forsakenness and unredeemedness of all things and their subjection to vanity. It leads us to a solidarity with the anxious expectation of the whole creation that waits for the liberty of the children of God (Rom. 8.22), and thus it perceives in all things the longing, the travail, and the unfulfilled openness for God's future. Thus the kingdom of God is present here as promise and hope for the future horizon of all things, which are then seen in their historic character because they do not yet contain their truth in themselves. If it is present as promise and hope, then this its presence is determined by the contradiction in which the future, the possible and the promised stands to a corrupt reality. In the Reformers it was said that the kingdom of God is *tectum sub cruce et sub contrario*. This was intended to mean that the kingdom of God is here hidden beneath its opposite: its freedom is hidden under trial, its happiness under suffering, its right under rightlessness, its omnipotence under weakness, its glory under unrecognizability. Here the kingdom of God was seen in the form of the lordship of the crucified one. This is a true insight, and one that cannot be relinquished. Only, the kingdom of God does not end in the paradoxical form of a presence of this kind. Its paradoxical hiddenness 'under the contrary' is not its eternal form. For indeed it is only the resurrection hope and the mission of Christ, the hunger for righteousness in all things and the thirst for true life, that first lead to the suffering, the weakness, the rightlessness and the unrecognizability. The contradiction does not result automatically from man's experiences with history, with sin and death, but it results from the promise and the hope which contradict these experiences and make it no longer possible to put up with them. If the promise of the kingdom of God shows us a universal eschatological future horizon spanning all things – 'that God may be all in all' – then it is impossible for the man of hope to adopt an attitude of religious and cultic resignation from the world. On the contrary, he is compelled to accept the world in all meekness, subject as it is to death and the powers of annihilation, and to guide all things towards their new being. He becomes homeless with the homeless, for the sake of the home of reconciliation. He becomes restless with the restless, for the sake of the peace of God. He becomes rightless with the rightless, for the sake of the divine right that is coming.

The promise of the kingdom of God in which all things attain to right, to life, to peace, to freedom, and to truth, is not exclusive but inclusive. And so, too, its love, its neighbourliness and its sympathy are inclusive, excluding nothing, but embracing in hope everything wherein God will be all in all. The *pro-missio* of the kingdom is the ground of the *missio* of love to the world.

It is the ground of the outgoing of the spirit in bodily obedience, because and in order that the 'inward' may become the 'outward' reality become rational and reason real – as Hegel put it, and as it can be theologically understood if by reason we understand the Spirit of God as the 'earnest' which causes the longing for a reality filled with the Spirit and brought about by the Spirit (Rom. 8.23 and I Cor. 15.42ff.).

14. Summary and Review

We now proceed to sum up by attempting a review of the method we have here followed.

1. Christian eschatology speaks of 'Christ and his future'. Its language is the language of promises. It understands history as the reality instituted by promise. In the light of the present promise and hope, the as yet unrealized future of the promise stands in contradiction to given reality. The historic character of reality is experienced in this contradiction, in the front line between the present and the promised future. History in all its ultimate possibilities and dangers is revealed in the event of promise constituted by the resurrection and cross of Christ. We took the promise contained in this event, in the sense of that which is latent, hidden, prepared and intended in this event, and expounded it against the background of the Old Testament history of promise, perceiving at the same time the tendencies of the Spirit which arise from these insights. The *promissio* of the universal future leads of necessity to the universal *missio* of the Church to all nations. The promise of divine righteousness in the event of the justification of the godless leads immediately to the hunger for divine right in the godless world, and thus to the struggle for public, bodily obedience. The promise of the resurrection of the dead leads at once to love for the true life of the whole imperilled and impaired creation. In expounding the promises in the Christ event in terms of latency and tendency,

we discovered a historic process of mediation between subject and object, which allows us neither to assign the future of Christ to a place within some system of world history and of the history of salvation, and thereby make this event relative to something that is foreign to it, acquired from other experiences and imposed upon it from without, nor yet to reflect the future of Christ into the existentialistic futurity of man. The history of the future of Christ and the historic character of the witnesses and missionaries condition each other and stand in a correlation of *promissio* and *missio*. The Christian consciousness of history is a consciousness of mission, and only to that extent is it also a consciousness of world history and of the historic character of existence.

2. We have employed in various ways the concept of 'progressive revelation'. It derives from Richard Rothe and Ernst Troeltsch, and means in both writers that the impulse of the Christian spirit in the history of the West links up again and again with the spirit of the modern age and produces progressively better views of the world and of life. The progressive development of the kingdom of the Redeemer is the constantly progressing revelation of that kingdom's absolute truth and perfection. 'Progressive revelation' here means that the revelation becomes progressive in the progress of the human spirit, or that the progress of the human spirit can be interpreted as the self-movement of absolute Spirit. Similar conclusions can be reached when it is thought possible to deduce the direction and future of the Christ event from a comprehensive chain of historic events before and after this event. The Christ event is then given its place in a historic chain that results from fate, or providence, and from the course of the facts of world history. If, however, the promise of the future of Christ arises from the resurrection of the one who was crucified, then the promise enters into such a contradiction to reality that this contradiction cannot be classified within a general dialectic of history such as can be deduced from other processes. It can be classified within the sphere of world history and history of salvation only by diminishing the contradiction in question. Only then can it be resolved in a dialectic of world history. If, however, the event of the raising of the one who was crucified is recognized to be *creatio ex nihilo*, then it is not a case here of possible changes in existing things, but of all or nothing., Then it becomes clear that this world 'cannot bear' the resurrection and the new world created by resurrection. The

dialectic which would seek to bear this contradiction must be of an apocalyptic kind. The reconciling synthesis of cross and resurrection can be expected and hoped for solely in a totality of new being. The theology of saving history does indeed perceive the process of promises and events, but not the contradiction in which the promise stands to reality, and hence not the unmasking of the godless world in the cross of Christ. Only when we see the progressive, eschatological driving forces in the contradictory event of the cross and resurrection itself, do the true problems arise. The revelation – i.e. the appearances of the risen Lord – does not acquire its character of progressiveness from a reality foreign to it, from the mysteriously continuing history after Easter, but itself creates the progress in its process of contradiction to the godless reality of sin and death. It does not become progressive by 'entering into' human history; but by dint of promise, hope and criticism it makes the reality of man historic and progressive. It is the revelation of the potentiality and power of God in the raising of the one who was crucified, and the tendency and intention of God recognizable therein, that constitute the horizon of what is to be called history and to be expected as history. The revelation of God in the cross and resurrection thus sets the stage for history, on which there emerges the possibility of the engulfing of all things in nothingness and of the new creation. The mission on which the man of hope is sent into this advance area of universal possibilities pursues the direction of the tendency of God's own action in omnipotently pursuing his faithfulness and his promise. The man of hope who leaves behind the corrupt reality and launches out on to the sea of divine possibilities, thereby radically sets this reality of his at stake – staking it on the hope that the promise of God will win the day.

3. When we speak of the 'future of Jesus Christ', then we mean that which is described elsewhere as the 'parousia of Christ' or the 'return of Christ'. Parousia actually does not mean the return of someone who has departed, but '*imminent* arrival'.[84] Parousia can also mean presence, yet not a presence which is past tomorrow, but a presence which must be awaited today and tomorrow. It is the 'presence of what is coming towards us, so to speak an arriving future'.[85] The parousia of Christ is a different thing from a reality that is experienced now and given now. As compared with

---

84 Thus A. Oepke in *TWNT* V, p. 863.
85 Paul Schütz, *Parusie – Hoffnung und Prophetie*, 1960, p. 78.

what can now be experienced, it brings something new. Yet it is not for that reason totally separate from the reality which we can now experience and have now to live in, but, as the future that is really outstanding, it works upon the present by awaking hopes and establishing resistance. The *eschaton* of the parousia of Christ, as a result of its eschatological promise, causes the present that can be experienced at any given moment to become historic by breaking away from the past and breaking out towards the things that are to come.

Now this parousia of Christ is also described as *revelation of Christ*, as ἀποκάλυψις τοῦ κυρίου. But how have we then to understand the future of Christ? Can his expected future then still be conceived in the expectational category '*novum*'? Does his future then bring something new, or merely a universal repetition of what has already happened in the history of Jesus Christ? Is the future of Christ then merely an *unveiling* of what has already happened in Jesus once and for all? Or does it contain something which has not yet happened?

According to Karl Barth the future of Christ is mainly only a matter of *unveiling*: 'Christ's coming again ... is described in the New Testament as *the* revelation. He will be revealed, not only to the Church but to everyone, as the Person He is. ... In full clarity and publicity the "it is finished" will come to light. ... What is the future bringing? Not once more a turning-point in history, but the revelation of that which is. It is the future, but the future of that which the Church *remembers*, of that which has already taken place once and for all. The Alpha and the Omega are the same thing.'[86]

Similarly, Walter Kreck declares: '[What is expected is] precisely the coming of *the* Lord who is proclaimed and believed to have come. The fulfilment, to be sure, can at bottom be nothing else but the unveiling of that which is already reality in Jesus Christ, but this very unveiling is nevertheless now looked forward to and awaited as future.'[87] Here it is somewhat clearer than in Barth that revelation is understood as promise, and that the revelation of Christ is also conceived as the fulfilment of the promise of Christ. But if this is followed up consistently, then the expression 'unveiling' for

---

86 K. Barth, *Dogmatik in Grundriss*, 1947, pp. 158f. (ET: *Dogmatics in Outline*, 1949, pp. 134f.).

87 W. Kreck, *Die Zukunft des Gekommenen*, 1961, p. 100.

revelation must be dropped, and in its stead revelation must be conceived as an event that takes place in promise and fulfilment. The revelation of Christ cannot then merely consist in what has already happened in hidden ways being unveiled for us to see, but it must be expected in events which fulfil the promise that is given with the Christ event. This Christ event cannot then itself be understood as fulfilling all promises, so that after this event there remains only the sequel of its being unveiled for all to see. 'In Christ all the promises of God are yea and Amen' (II Cor. 1.20), i.e., in him they are confirmed and validated, but not yet fulfilled. Therefore the Christian hope expects from the future of Christ not only unveiling, but also final fulfilment. The latter is to bring the redeeming of the promise which the cross and resurrection of Christ contains for his own and for the world. What, then, does the future of Christ bring? Not a mere repetition of his history, and not only an unveiling of it, but something which has so far not yet happened through Christ. The Christian expectation is directed to no other than the Christ who has come, but it expects something new from him, something that has not yet happened so far: it awaits the fulfilment of the promised righteousness of God in all things, the fulfilment of the resurrection of the dead that is promised in his resurrection, the fulfilment of the lordship of the crucified one over all things that is promised in his exaltation. The visible and painful experience of the unredeemed state of the world is not for Christians, as for Jews, an argument against belief in the Messiah's having come, but constitutes the burning question in their prayers for the future of the Redeemer who has come. It is not because it is doubtful whether Jesus is the Christ, but because in him our redemption is confirmed, that Christians groan along with all creation under the unredeemed state of the world and long to see the universal fulfilment of his redeeming and saving acts. But if they know the Redeemer and expect the future of redemption in his name, then neither can the unredeemed state of this world of death become for them, after the fashion of Plato, a part of the insignificant world of appearance in which it is now only a matter of the demonstrating and unveiling of redemption. To be sure, the Alpha and the Omega are the same as far as the Person is concerned: 'I am Alpha and Omega' (Rev. 1.8). But they are not the same where the reality of the event is concerned, for 'it doth not yet appear what we shall be' (I John 3.2) and 'the former things' are not yet passed away, nor are 'all things' yet become new. Thus we must expect something new from the future. But if this future is expected as the 'future of Jesus Christ', then it is not expected from someone new or from someone else. What the future is bringing is something which, through the Christ event of the raising of the one who was crucified, has become 'once and for all' a possible object of confident hope. Faith in Jesus as the Christ is not the end of hope, but it is the confidence in which we hope (Heb. 11.1). Faith in Christ is the prior of the two, but in this faith hope has the primacy.

IV

Eschatology and History[1]

1. Criticism and Crisis

The modern consciousness of history is a consciousness of crisis, and all modern philosophy of history is in the last analysis a philosophy of crisis.[2]

Modern man's epochal experience of history is grounded in the experience of infinitely new and overwhelming possibilities which cannot be mastered by the customary methods of his traditions. They are new possibilities for good or for evil, for progress or for irrevocable disaster. Yet these new possibilities of a new future are always experienced in the first instance as the crisis and collapse of the hitherto known and familiar possibilities with their traditional institutions and ways of life and methods of coping with it. History overflows the banks of tradition, as it were. The dams of tradition and order everywhere begin to burst. They are no longer a match for the new experiences of history and can therefore no longer present themselves as self-evident. They become antiquated, or can be conservatively maintained only with great difficulty. They no longer possess for man the old, unquestioned obviousness of institutionalized modes of conduct. Hence they become the object of reflection and criticism, and man is thrust out into a world that is unprotected, frightening and uncertain. He finds himself in a crisis

---

1 For this chapter cf. my essays 'Exegese und Eschatologie der Geschichte' *EvTh* 22, 1962, pp. 31ff., and 'Verkündigung als Problem der Exegese', *Monatsschrift für Pastoraltheologie* 52, 1963, pp. 24ff.

2 G. Mann, 'Grundprobleme der Geschichtsphilosophie von Plato bis Hegel', in *Der Sinn der Geschichte*, 1961, pp. 13f.; H. Heimpel, 'Geschichte und Geschichtswissenschaft', *Vierteljahrshefte für Zeitgeschichte*, 1957, vol. 1, p. 15: 'Since Herder the historical sense has meant reflection on imperilled order.' Cf. also R. Koselleck, *Kritik und Krise. Ein Beitrag zur Pathogenese der bürgerlichen Welt*, 1959; E. Rosenstock-Huessy, *Die europäischen Revolutionen*, 1931.

in which his existence is at stake and he is under the pressure of a vital decision. Thus it is in terms of crisis that history becomes perceptible to him, and historical criticism of his traditions is the offspring of this consciousness of crisis.

All reflection on 'history' by historians, sociologists and philosophers of history on the continent of Europe in the nineteenth century has behind it the earthquake of the French revolution and before it the incalculable consequences of that event.[3] In this revolution the edifice of the old institutions collapsed, and its metaphysical stabilization with it. In it the things which were taken for granted and commonly accepted in the cultural and spiritual realm, and which made it possible to live a protected life, were lost. With it there came an awareness of the totally historic character of life as the total criticalness of man's world. 'Crisis' has ever since become the theme of historical research and the basic concept of reflection on the philosophy of history. Hegel applied the new concept of 'crisis' together with its new experimental content to the whole of the past. He knew that 'thus the movement and unrest continues. This is the conflict, the difficulty, the problem which confronts

---

3 I. Kant, *Der Streit der Fakultäten*, 1798 (Philosophische Bibliothek 252, p. 87): 'A phenomenon of this kind *can never again be forgotten*, because it has disclosed in human nature a predisposition and capacity for improvement, such as no politician could have thought up on the basis of the course of things so far.' F. Schiller, *Über die ästhetische Erziehung des Menschen*, 1793/4: 'A question which was otherwise answered merely by the blind right of the stronger has now, it seems, been brought before the judgment seat of pure reason, and whoever is capable of putting himself at the centre of the whole and projecting his individuality to become typical of the species, may regard himself as coadjutor on this judgment-seat of reason, in that as a man and a citizen of the world he is at the same time also a party and sees himself more or less closely involved in the result.' G. W. F. Hegel, *Vorlesungen über die Philosophie der Weltgeschichte*, Werke XI, p. 557: 'As long as the sun has stood in the firmament and the planets have revolved around it, it had never been known for man to stand on his head, that is, on his mind, and to construct reality according to his thoughts. Anaxagoras had been the first to say that *nous* rules the world, but only now has man reached the stage of recognizing that thought should rule the reality of the spirit. So this was a glorious dawn.' J. G. Fichte, *Briefwechsel* I, pp. 349f. (ed. H. Schulz, 1925): 'My system (the doctrine of science) is the first system of freedom. As that nation (France) sets man free from his outward chains, so my system sets him free from the fetters of things as such, from their outward influence, and represents him as in first principle an independent being.' F. Schlegel, *Athenäumsfragmente*, No. 222: 'The revolutionary desire to realize the kingdom of God is the elastic point of all progressive culture and the beginning of modern history' (quoted according to K. Löwith, *Abhandlungen*, 1960, p. 157).

history and which it has in future to solve.'[4] Ranke thought it possible to achieve a conservative mastery of this revolutionary crisis by restoring the balance between the great powers of Europe, and believed in reconciliation with the old traditions.[5] Jakob Burckhardt sought amid the anxiety for the future of the West in its continuing crises the 'standard by which to measure the rapidity and strength of the particular movement in which we live'.[6] Johann Gustav Droysen asked what is the 'direction of the flowing movement' in which all things are engaged from the viewpoint of history.[7] The 'call' of the nineteenth century for the study of history and the absolutely vital necessity of that call, dates from the French revolution. 'History' has ever since been experienced as a *permanent state of crisis*, or as permanent, irresistible and unrestrainable revolution. Historians and philosophers of history, whether conservative or revolutionary, have therefore concentrated on the spiritual, political and social mastering of this continual crisis. Historical science and the philosophy of history have been compelled to make 'history' comprehensible, in order to make it possible to control the chaos, the catastrophes and the crises, and therewith history as such. The place of a world-orientation in terms of cosmology and metaphysics has since been taken by an orientation of the present in terms of the philosophy of history. It was precisely the collapse of historic continuity that gave rise to that apotheosis of 'history' which led to the religion of history in the messianic movements of the nineteenth century.

Now the sense for history, the interest in history and the necessity to understand history always arise in critical times of unrest, in which new possibilities that were hitherto unknown and unsuspected begin to dawn on the horizon. If we are to understand the new present and to be able to live in it, then we must concern ourselves with the past, whether to bring the new experiences into harmony with the traditions of the past or to rid ourselves of the burden of the past and become free for the new present. The

---

4 Werke IX, p. 563; J. Ritter, *Hegel und die französische Revolution* (AGFNRW 63), 1957, pp. 15ff.; H. Marcuse, *Vernunft und Revolution*, 1962, pp. 15ff.

5 C. Hinrichs, *Ranke und die Geschichtstheologie der Goethezeit*, 1954.

6 J. Burckhardt, *Weltgeschichtliche Betrachtungen*, ed. W. Kaegi, 1947, pp. 59, 250ff. (ET: *Reflections on History*, 1943, p. 25).

7 J. G. Droysen, *Historik*, 4th ed. 1960, p. 358: 'Beginning and end are hidden from the finite eye. But its scrutiny can discover the direction of the flowing movement.'

experience of such crises has been in the background of the great thinkers on history ever since Augustine's *City of God*. Since the French revolution, however, history has been understood entirely in terms of crisis. The latter can no longer be restricted to the political or the social field, but has the tendency to become total and to make every realm of life uncertain. The crisis becomes one of universal world history and affects the whole existence of man and his world. That is why the interpretations of this crisis are likewise of a total and totalitarian kind.[8] It has therefore become absolutely necessary to consider in terms of world history all the realms of life which are involved in this crisis of history – and this is still necessary even when it is evident that all such interpretations in terms of universal history have so far broken down in face of this crisis, because they have not provided a synoptic view of the crisis, but have themselves been an immanent part of it and have therefore only furthered it and served to extend it. Every crisis throws up the question of the historic future. For when the whole existing situation is in a state of crisis, it becomes obvious that the future can no longer arise automatically out of the past, that it can no longer be the natural repetition and continuation of the past, but that something new must be found in it. This means that for the present a decision has to be made which finds no precedent in the past and for which traditional custom no longer provides any rule. On this decision depends the form of the future, and this decision derives its form from a vision of the future which is hoped for or feared, to be sought or to be avoided. This, however, means that the decision which is forced upon the present must arise from our dream of the future. Criticism of the existing situation makes the existing situation a thing of the past and frees us to face the crisis of present decision. From the standpoint of history such criticism is always bound up with the utopian outlook which examines the possibilities and tendencies of things to come, anticipates them, and incorporates them in the present decision.[9] As the criticism

---

8 J. L. Talmon, *The Origins of Totaletarian Democracy*, 1952; *Political Messianism; The Romantic Phase*, 1960.

9 This is shown particularly clearly by R. Koselleck, *op. cit.*, pp. 133ff., 208ff.: The Enlightenment's criticism of the existing situation is combined with hopes of a 'belle révolution' (Voltaire), a 'révolution totale' (Mercier) and a permanent revolution (Rousseau). 'Nous approchons de l'etat de crise et du siècle des révolutions', said Voltaire. The Illuminati, the Freemasons and the Enlighteners base this criticism, and their expectation of the great crisis, upon utopian

is born of the crisis, so also are the utopian ideas. This connection between utopia and criticism can be seen particularly clearly in the century which paved the way for the crisis. Everywhere in the eighteenth century the criticism of absolutism, the criticism of churches and orthodoxies that have become historical institutions, the criticism of a class-ridden society, is combined with powerful utopian ideas of the nation of mankind, of the kingdom of God and of the new natural state of man, and is exercised in the service of these ideas. In its feeling for the philosophy of history the Enlightenment emphatically no longer combines its criticism, as earlier movements in history had done, with a retrospective dream, with regeneration, reform, renaissance or reformation of the corrupt present, but with the category of the new – new age, new world, *novum organon*, *scienza nuova*, progress, final age. The criticism of the present is no longer exercised in the name of the origin and in the name of the need to restore the original golden age, but in the name of a future that has never yet been. Since 1789 the land of 'utopia' no longer lies somewhere beyond the seas, but by means of the belief in history and the idea of progress it is shifted to the future which is possible and is to be expected or desired. The utopian dream has thus become a part of the philosophy of history and moved into the realm of practical philosophy. For the first time, history is subjected to the influence of an apocalyptic millenarianism and an apocalyptic enthusiasm of spirit, for which the end is other than the origin, and the goal greater than the beginning, and the future more than all the past. A criticism that has roots of this kind, however, precipitates a crisis which sets all that has been hitherto, and all that is, 'under the shadow' of collapse. The coming of this crisis can no longer mean only the collapse of the *ancien régime*, can no longer imply only the *fin de siècle*, but sets at stake everything that man's being means for him in home,

---

ideas of the harmony of the universe, the abrogation of states and classes and the disappearance of churches in the humanist kingdom of moral religion. If, as has been rightly observed, German Idealism is the theory of the French revolution, or at least the philosophical answer to the challenge of this crisis, then it is understandable that German Idealism begins as the 'theory of the present age' and is concerned to grasp in thought its age, the revolutionary crisis – and that means history. Then it is also understandable why in Herder, Schiller, Kant, Fichte, Novalis, E. M. Arndt and Hegel the criticism of the spirit of the age is combined with utopian ideas of the kingdom of God, of world citizenship and the rational state, of the invisible church, etc.

state, world and nature. Thus the identification of this crisis which began with the French revolution and – closely related to it – the industrial revolution, everywhere employs apocalyptic pictures. This kind of world history means the world judgment. This kind of freedom confronts mankind with the 'fury of disappearing'. For revolutionary thinkers this crisis brings the kingdom of God or the kingdom of freedom and humanity palpably near. In this sense a political messianism seizes the new possibilities. For conservative thinkers like de Bonald, de Maistre, and later de Tocqueville and Jakob Burckhardt, this crisis sounds the trumpet of the Last Judgment. Both take this crisis as the prelude to the final battle.

For Saint-Simon 'revolution' meant 'crisis'. 'L'espèce humaine', he wrote in 1813, 'se trouve engagée dans une des plus fortes *crises* qu'elle ait essuyée depuis l'origine de son existence.'[10] This concept of crisis also emerges as early as Rousseau, but in Saint-Simon and Auguste Comte it is new. 'It means revolution, but by penetrating beyond the political foreground of the latter, it opens a view of historic and social reality in its totality. In other words, when Saint-Simon speaks of crisis, he means – and is the first to mean – *history* in a completely modern sense.'[11] The aim of comprehending the revolution historically, politically and sociologically is for Saint-Simon and Comte: 'Terminer la révolution'. 'It is time to complete the vast intellectual operation begun by Bacon, Descartes and Galileo. ... This is the way to put an end to the revolutionary crisis which is tormenting the civilized nations of the world.'[12] Once the circumstances, laws and origins of revolution can be thoroughly understood, then it becomes calculable and also avoidable. By means of 'social physics' the revolutionary upheavals in society become calculable and their laws are understood, just as the phenomena of nature are by modern natural science. Comte's 'philosophie positive' acquires from this background a thoroughly messianic tenor. Scientific knowledge of the world and of history will supplant the now useless epoch of metaphysics and the still older epoch of theology. World phenomena are calculable because

---

10 N. Sombart, 'St Simon und A. Comte', in A. Weber, *Einführung in die Soziologie*, 1955, p. 87. Cf. also J. L. Talmon, *Political Messianism*, pp. 35ff. on Saint-Simon.

11 J. L. Talmon, *op. cit.* (cited from the German translation, *Politischer Messianismus*, 1963, p. 88).

12 *The Political Philosophy of Auguste Comte*, translated by Harriet Martineau, 1853, vol. 1, p. 16.

of the laws of their interconnection. Scientific and socio-technical civilization will become the third and last world epoch. The crises become controllable, wars avoidable. The age of eternal peace is coming, in which the really sovereign knowledge is in the hands of the sociologists. In this age there will still be endless progress in the perfecting of science and technology, but there will be no more radical alternatives and no revolutionary changes. And now, if revolution is 'crisis' and crisis means 'history', then the 'ending of revolution' by means of historical science and the 'ending of crisis' by means of sociology means no less than a comprehensive 'ending of history' through scientific knowledge of it and through its technical controllability. The 'end of history' thereby acquires palpable, because creatable and attainable, nearness. The 'loss of history' (Alfred Heuss), the 'farewell to history' (Alfred Weber), the immanent 'perfectibility of history' (Hans Freyer) through scientific enlightenment and technical manipulation, become inevitable. The enigmatic chaos of history comes to an end where it is abrogated by knowledge of history and by its controllability.

The 'science' of history, too, which arises in the shadow of revolution and the permanently smouldering crisis, acquires a positivistic, apocalyptic sense. Again and again in the nineteenth century we are told that the science of history liberates us from history. 'The historical consciousness shatters the last fetters which philosophy and natural science were unable to break. Man is now completely free' (Dilthey).[13] 'A historical phenomenon, once fully and completely known and resolved into a problem of epistemology, is for the man who knows it dead. ... History conceived as pure science, and become sovereign, would be a sort of winding up and settlement of the life of mankind' (Nietzsche).[14] 'For the historic examination of any construction of human thought always serves to liberate us from it' (W. Herrmann).[15] Historical science thus becomes an instrument for the mastering of history. It confers on man freedom from history. History as science thereby acquires a tendency to do away with history as remembrance. This kind of historicism as a

13 W. Dilthey, *Gesammelte Schriften* VIII, p. 225.

14 F. Nietzsche, *Vom Nutzen und Nachteil der Historie für das Leben*, Kroner 37, 1924, p. 12.

15 W. Herrmann, *Verkehr des Christen mit Gott*, 3rd ed. 1896, p. 42. Similarly A. Eichhorn, *ZTK* 18, 1908, p. 156: critical historical research is particularly concerned 'that by means of history we should become free men as far as tradition is concerned'.

'science of crisis', and in that sense the remedy against crises, has thus the tendency to destroy the interest in history and the feeling for it. The result of the historicizing and rationalizing of history is then to abolish history and leave human social life bereft of all historic character. In this sense scientific historicism stands in the service of the mystico-messianic idea of the 'end of history' and is itself a factor in the 'ending of history'.

This motif of the historical probing and investigation of historic phenomena is understandable against the background of total crisis that comes into view with the French revolution. Yet it is equally understandable that in the age of historical perfection, in the second half of the nineteenth century, the question was raised as to the price of mastering the crisis in this way. Nietzsche's book *Vom Nutzen und Nachteil der Historie für das Leben*, 1874, leaves us with the question of that 'unhistorical' element of 'atmosphere' or 'horizon' within which alone life goes on. The historical outlook leaves the future without roots, because it destroys our illusions and robs things of the atmosphere in which alone they can live and in which alone they acquire potentialities. 'All living things need to have an atmosphere, a mysterious nimbus, around them; if we rob them of this covering, if we condemn a religion, an art, a genius to be like a star circling without any atmosphere, then we ought not to be surprised at its quickly drying up and becoming hard and unfruitful. This is simply true of all great things, "which never yet succeeded without a certain amount of illusion".'[16] The question now arises as to the historic character of history, which the historian obscures in his search for facts and laws. If the revolutionary crises in human society are ended by positivistic investigation of the facts, then it is a question whether that does not also mean the ending and petrifying of the liveness of human life and the movements of the world process. It is a question whether the ending of the historic crisis which is achieved in this way is not itself a highly critical undertaking. For while an 'ending of history in history' does solve the crises in the observable realm, yet the undertaking as a whole is itself exposed to a much more tremendous crisis. Whatever crises may arise within the scientific, technical world, they can be rationalized. But the scientific, technical universe itself becomes an inestimable, irrational force, of which we can no longer have a

---

16 *Op. cit.*, p. 60.

comprehensive view because we are no longer able to look beyond it to a possibly different future.[17] Thus it becomes an important question whether the concept of history which identifies 'history' with 'crisis' is adequate, and whether the science of history which resolves history into knowledge does justice to the historic character of history and to the – possibly – historic character of its own knowledge.

THE 'SOLVED RIDDLE OF HISTORY'

2. The Historical Method[18]

Ever since the fundamental methodical approach to man's experience of the world by Petrus Ramus and René Descartes and its success in the natural sciences, every effort has been directed towards applying a methodical treatment also to the experiences of history and to the process of acquiring knowledge of history. The question of the historical method therefore applies not only to the technical ways in which the historian works, but also, and more comprehensively, to the peculiarity of historical knowledge and the scientific character of historical research. Without 'method' no assured knowledge can be attained. Historical methodology therefore embraces principles for historical research and principles for the critical control of their results. Since the natural sciences in the nineteenth century had not been content to collect and collate experimental results but had gone on to construct an exact and verifiable system of the laws of nature, and since exact 'science' in general meant 'natural' science, it was necessary to raise the question as to the scientific character of historical research and as to the general laws of the course of history. Although the peculiar character of the methods of the human sciences has been emphasized since the end of the nineteenth century by W. Dilthey, yet certain minimum requirements from the concept of science associ-

---

17 This inversion was perceived especially by Max Weber. The 'disenchantment' and rationalization of the world and its history by modern science presents us with a meaningless irrationality of independent, arbitrary 'conditions' which now govern human behaviour. Cf. K. Löwith, 'Max Weber und Karl Marx', in *Gesammelte Abhandlungen zur Kritik der geschichtlichen Existenz*, 1960, p. 26.

18 *Geschichte*, Fischer-Lexikon 24, 1961, ed. W. Besson, pp. 78ff.

ated with natural science have been introduced also into the science of history:

(a) The science of history is not art, fiction or legend, but the concept of truth which underlies it is that of a verifiable truth of fact. The statements of historical science must be able to prove their historical correctness by reference to sources that can be verified by anyone at any time, and thus by reference to verifiable events. History is not 'legends and acts' (Bertram) but, in so far as it seeks assured knowledge, it depends on the verifiable agreement between statement and fact.

(b) The historical correctness of our knowledge of history, however, presupposes that our insights are controllable. The fact that they are bound to the sources and to the criticism of the sources means that they are bound to the controllability of their statements by reference to the reality of which the historian speaks and which he seeks to know.

(c) This controllability, however, presupposes that historical objects can in principle be reconstructed. Historical knowledge is dependable only when it can be verified at any time by anyone who will make the methodical effort. But if it is to be verifiable, it must always be possible to reconstruct the materials and the authoritatively documented events. This reconstructability of the facts thus becomes the methodological mark of the facts as facts. This is what distinguishes the science of history from legend and lively remembrance, from statements of experience and encounter.

(d) Historical science, too, works with definite hypotheses, plans, approaches and outlooks, by means of which the events are illumined and perceived as events. But now, whereas the constructions of natural science use experiment to extort an answer from nature and to let us see and understand it, historical objects are always already bound up with interpretations and outlooks in which the knowledge of them is transmitted. The historian's first task must therefore be to read the witnesses of history as 'sources', and to date, localize and trace back to the 'historical facts' the objects which are mediated by manifold processes of interpretation, bias and touching up. The historical facts thus ascertained become the starting point for subjecting the witnesses, interpretations and traditions to the criticism of the historical consciousness. Thus the historical method is in the first instance applied critically to the traditions and the historical sources. This sort of destructive criticism of the traditions of an event, however, is itself always bound up with the historian's own power of picturing and imagining how things may 'in fact' have been, and is thus always combined with reconstruction. Such reconstructions of the actual course of events, in turn, are for their part also drafts, hypotheses and standpoints which must be verified by reference to the sources. Hence historical criticism has always a link with historical imagination, whether that of the sources or our own. This means that historical criticism is always bound up with historical heuristics.

The methodical treatment of the experience of history must 'objectify' historic reality. The historical approach must regard past history in that historical detachment in which it can be objectively examined. It has to establish historic reality and must therefore presuppose that this reality is established fact, no longer subject to change. This, understandably enough, becomes more difficult the more it is a question of 'contemporary history'. For here the object is not firmly established but is still in a state of flux. Here the historical observer does not stand over against history, but in the midst of the events, and exerts an influence on these events themselves by means of his historical diagnosis. At bottom, all history is 'contemporary history'. The historian's object is thus engaged in a twofold movement which 'derives first from the process character of all past life, and secondly from the continual change in the man who contemplates history and is himself subject to historic development'.[19] For this reason the old saying is true, that 'history has constantly to be rewritten'. The historic character of the historical observer is the point at which there constantly takes place the decisive process of the translating of 'present' into 'object', of historic present into historical object, of a history that is in a state of flux and open to the influence of our own knowledge and decision into the retrospective contemplation of a history that has come to a standstill. The historical, objectifying relation to past history is therefore itself one that is highly historic and that makes history.

---

19 *Geschichte*, Fischer-Lexikon, p. 80.

3. Historical Heuristics

The historical method does not only work with destructive criticism of past pictures of history, in order to investigate the 'bare' facts, but must itself approach the source material with its own problems and plans. While historical criticism in the name of fact does attack the interpretations of fact in the sources, yet the facts themselves cannot possibly be known and stated without other interpretations. In the science of history, the facts are not the first datum, but the last product of a process of abstraction that moves from the traditional interpretations to what is today generally and unquestioningly taken to be 'objectivity'.[20] 'Fact' is the substratum interpretatively mediated by the sources and traditions. The natural scientist in his experiments must isolate his object, eliminate factors which do not enter into the question and disregard other problems, if he is to attain to unequivocal results. This is very difficult in the case of historical objects, because here we have always to do with highly complicated structures whose isolation destroys the fact of their being so multifariously conditioned. Thus historical science, according as it isolates a single fact from its manifold context and reduces its questions to one problem only, must take care at the same time to move on again from the isolated and individual facts to the wider context and from the one angle of approach to the complex of other problems. Thus the individual fact can be known and evaluated only along with the general, and the general only along with the individual. The positivistic separation of fact and meaning is not one which is possible in principle, and can be asserted only when our own interpretation of what we call 'fact' remains naive, uncritical and unconscious. When Max Weber asserts that rational science 'disenchants' the world, and that the full understanding of the facts ceases where the value-judgment begins, then that is true where the value-judgment is subsequently appended in order to introduce values into a world that rests on other facts, but not where the value judgment is already included within the field of judgment in which the illumination of the facts itself takes place – and within that field it is always already given.

---

20 Cf. E. Rothacker, *Die dogmatische Denkform in den Geisteswissenschaften und das Problem des Historismus*, Abhandlungen der geistes- und sozialwissenschaftlichen Klasse der Akademie der Wissenschaften 6, Mainz 1954, p. 55.

When historical science moves on from isolated, individual facts to more general statements embracing historic processes, then there arises the *problem of the forming of historical concepts*.[21] It is necessary to make use of concepts of a generalizing and typifying kind. These concepts acquire their binding force from the standpoint and perspective of the moment, and therefore cannot claim to reflect the historic processes as such, but are heuristic modes of contemplating historic processes, and means of explaining and understanding them. They require to be confirmed by the object, and are therefore constantly open to question.

One such means is the 'historical law'. An event becomes explicable when its causes can be seen. This connection between cause and effect, however, presupposes that the plane of being on which cause and effect are connected is the same. History must then be social history or political history or cultural history, i.e. the substance of the history must be determined, if we are to be able to present a chain of cause and effect of this kind. This, however, can be demonstrated only in things of uniform character and in repetitions and in definite processes in history which have a definite, automatic character. Apart from these, historic processes are so complex that, for one thing, we cannot discover all the conditions which cause them, but always only a selection of them. Single causes can be asserted in history only by discarding or disregarding other connections. And in the second place, historical causality lacks the characteristic of reversibility.[22] We can certainly argue from effects to causes, but hardly ever from causes to effects. Hence the really historic factor lies in the concept of possibility rather than in that of necessity: we never find all the possibilities turned into unequivocal necessities. Thus the concept of causality too, can have only heuristic significance.

Another conceptual means of grasping connections is the discovering of 'tendencies'. This concept has been familiar in German historical writing since Ranke. But it is applied also in the historico-dialectical materialism of Georg Lukács and Ernst Bloch.[23] It means that the stringency of the causality of natural science is renounced and the transition in historic movements is described

21 R. Wittram, *Das Interesse an der Geschichte*, 1958, pp. 33ff.

22 *Geschichte*, Fischer-Lexikon, p. 83.

23 G. Lukács, *Geschichte und Klassenbewusstsein*, 1923; E. Bloch, *Das Prinzip Hoffnung*, 1959.

not as a transition from *causa* to *effectus*, but from possibility to reality. What stands between possibilities and realized realities is not a causal necessity, but tendency, impulse, inclination, trend, specific leanings towards something, which can become real in certain historic constellations. Ernst Topitsch thinks this expression obscures 'the tricky problem of the relationship between act, value and independent evolution'. R. Wittram thinks this expression can be completely void of any relation to an objective teleology and can mean only an 'impulse' within the working of a concrete historical event.[24] For G. Lukács and E. Bloch, 'tendency' means something that mediates between the real, objective possibilities and the subjective decisions, and to that extent places the historical 'facts' within the stream of the historical process and sets the subjective decisions of the historical observer within this same process. Then, however, the intention in employing the heuristic medium of exploring 'tendencies' is surely to discover a directional trend on the part of history which is teleological as a whole.

E. Rothacker has recommended as a means towards the grasping of historical complexes the concept of 'style'. 'What is called "historical thinking" in the emphatic and passionate use of the term has indeed its primary aim not in the establishing of facts, but in grasping as congenially as may be the appearances of the immanent *logos*, the styles in which these facts arrange themselves.'[25] This concept, to be sure, has its roots in the history of art and is appropriate to an aesthetic view of things. When transferred to historic complexes, however, it means the anthropological and sociological connection of acts and events with their 'environment' in the experiences of the moment and in the current views of life. What is meant is the 'style of living', the *façon de vivre*, the *façon d'agir*. Just as animals have their specific kind of 'environment' of vitally necessary openness towards the world, so also men live in a cultural 'environment' consisting of modes of experience, customs of living, institutions and expectations of life, in which they perceive history and act historically. In his search for facts the historian shatters this horizon of interpretation and experience that belongs to the history of any given moment, whereas the truth is, that the facts and acts became 'historic' only in their particular contempor-

---

24 R. Wittram, *op. cit.*, p. 44.
25 *Op. cit.*, p. 23.

ary 'environment' in the world of language, law, *Weltanschauung*, views of life, religious ideas and economic forms.

In much the same way the concept of 'structure' attempts to grasp the social institutions in which history was accepted and mastered at a given moment, by seeing them as the world of the orders and expressions of life that exercised their influence on history.[26] This framework of ideas leads on to the history of 'forms'. Form-critical historiography is likewise sociologically oriented in enquiring into the institutional grounding of statements in the life of historic groups and societies, and in examining not so much the individual statement as once made, but rather the '*Sitz im Leben*' provided for the statements by religion law, culture, politics and art.

Lastly, the concept of the '*understanding of existence*' is also a heuristic medium of this kind.[27] Here the phenomena of past history are interpreted and brought to consciousness on the basis of the possibilities of man's understandings of existence. The heuristic model consists in 'situation' and 'decision', in challenge and response, and past history shows how history was experienced and responsibility received by the human subject and how possibilities of existence were thereby discovered, grasped or destroyed. The historian is then not so much interested in the events themselves and their causal or tendentious connections with other events, but rather in the historic character of the several existences that have been, and in the possibilities of human existence.

Thus the range of historical concepts extends from the 'facts' to the possibilities of existence, from 'objectivity' – in the sense of the exact natural sciences – to the unmistakable uniqueness of human subjectivity and spontaneity. We have here selected only a few typical examples. 'All general historical concepts have a certain fluidity,' as R. Wittram rightly observes.[28] They are heuristic concepts whose applicability has repeatedly to be checked in detail. The flexibility, however, in which they resist fixed metaphysical systematizing and logical unequivocalness, has its ground not only in the limited historic perspective of the observer who uses them in order to shed light on an enigmatic reality. It has its ground also in the fact that unequivocal and eternally established reality is not yet

---

26 F. Braudel, as quoted by Wittram, *op. cit.*, p. 44.

27 M. Heidegger, *Sein und Zeit*, 8th ed. 1957, pp. 382ff. (ET by J. Macquarrie and E. Robinson: *Being and Time*, 1962, pp. 434ff.).

28 R. Wittram, *op. cit.*, p. 43.

there to be conceived. The concept of 'nation', or 'class', or 'culture' etc., is not a standing category in which we can ascertain the history of the nation, the history of the class struggle, or the history of culture, but the real meaning of 'nation', 'class', 'church' etc., is itself in a state of historic flux, historically disputed and therefore engaged in historic transformation. If the basic idea of historicism is that the essence of a thing is to be grasped from its historic development, and that the result of the historical process is decided only within the historical process itself, then the 'land of the realized, absolute concept' is not to be reached by way of abstraction from the particular to the general, nor yet by way of a comprehensive review of the past, but then this land is the as yet undiscovered fore-land of history, which can be reached from within history only in the form of fragmentary anticipations. It is not due merely to the defective range of the human mind that history remains dark to it, but this is due to history itself, which has not yet reached its end and therefore cannot yet be resolved into historical knowledge, or only in a proleptic, fragmentary way.

4. Historiology

The question of historical heuristics leads of itself to the problem of the philosophy of history. 'In criticism, history of itself becomes philosophy of history' (F. C. Baur).[29] But how can a philosophy of history be possible in the Greek sense of knowledge and of science? If 'the essence of history is change' (J. Burckhardt),[30] yet 'change' is the direct opposite of 'essence'. 'Philosophy of history' therefore appeared to J. Burckhardt to be a centaur, a contradiction in terms, 'for history co-ordinates, and hence is unphilosophical, while philosophy subordinates, and hence is unhistorical.'[31] Nevertheless all the general historical concepts by means of which we

---

29 F. C. Baur, as quoted by Koselleck, *op. cit.*, p. 6.

30 *Weltgeschichtliche Betrachtungen*, ed. W. Kaegi, 1947, p. 72.

31 *Ibid.*, p. 43 (ET p. 15). Nevertheless, ... the *logos*: 'We, however, shall start out from the one point accessible to us, the one eternal centre of all things – man, suffering, striving, doing, as he is and was and ever shall be. Hence our study will, in a certain sense, be pathological in kind. The philosophers of history regard the past as a contrast to and preliminary stage of our own time as the full development. We shall study the *recurrent*, *constant* and *typical* as echoing in us and intelligible through us' (p. 45, ET p. 17).

endeavour to understand historic complexes are bound up with definite approaches to the illuminating of reality and are therefore part and parcel of a philosophical knowledge of the world as history. If the general endeavour of human reason is towards the abolition of chance, as Wilhelm von Humboldt has said, then this endeavour is intensified in that philosophy of history which sees the experience of history as the experience of crisis and of permanent revolution. The 'nightmare of history' loses its nightmare character where it is comprehended. It is comprehended, however, where sense, an immanent *logos*, can be found in the chaotic movements of history, where necessity and dependence can be discovered in the contingent. Then history is 'comprehended', and where history is 'comprehended' in this way, there it ceases to be 'history'.

Let us take a look at this – often unconscious – transition from historical heuristics to philosophy of history in one or two specific historians.

(*a*) Even Ranke was constantly in search of a 'general bond' of history. Ranke as a historian is usually commended for turning his back on the *a priori* constructions in the speculations of German Idealism on world history, in order to address himself to the objects of history themselves in their vast abundance as these are empirically accessible to historical science. Nevertheless Ranke, too, is bound to definite speculative presuppositions in his historiography.[32] Thus in his *Deutsche Geschichte im Zeitalter der Reformation* he observes: 'We may perhaps say that the ages succeed each other precisely in order that what is not possible to any of them individually may happen in all, in order that the whole fulness of the spiritual life breathed into the human race by the deity should come to light in the course of the centuries.'[33] According to this, spiritual life has been 'breathed into' mankind by the deity, and that too in its 'whole fulness' as the deity itself is infinite, and can therefore come 'to light' in the ages of history only in successive stages. It is true that the laws according to which it gradually emerges are obscure to us, greater and more mysterious than we think,[34] yet it is nevertheless possible to have an inkling of the divine order of things, for this 'divine order' is '*identical*

---

32 C. Hinrichs, *Ranke und die Geschichtstheologie der Goethezeit*, 1954, pp. 161ff.

33 Quoted *ibid.*, p. 162.

34 *Ibid.*, p. 164.

with the succession of the ages'.[35] Hence Ranke describes it by the use of historical concepts like 'tendencies' and 'forces'. 'Here are forces, and spiritual forces at that, life-producing, creative forces, themselves life, here are moral energies which we see developing. ... They flourish, take possession of the world, assume outward expression in the greatest variety of forms, attack, restrict and over-power each other: in their interrelation and succession, in their life, their passing away or their reanimation, which then embraces ever greater fulness, deeper significance, wider compass, lies the mystery of world history.'[36] The basic philosophical picture underlying this interpretation of the 'mystery of world history' is manifestly the neoplatonic, panentheistic picture of the age of Goethe. The 'idea', 'God', the 'sun' or the 'source', does not contain within it for Ranke any dialectical principle that is immanent to it, as for Hegel, but it emanates, while itself always remaining extra-worldly in its unchanging, unchangeable being. Its emanations become manifest in the stream of historic phenomena and movements, in the inter-play and succession of forces and tendencies, of moral energies and epochs. Each of these stands in an immediate relationship to the highest idea. Hence every epoch is *'immediately* related to God, and its value does not at all depend on what emerges from it, but lies in its own existence, in its own self', as it is put in the *Berchtesgadener Vorträge.*[37] 'The ideas which form the ground of human conditions never contain perfectly within them the divine and eternal source from which they spring.'[38] And yet according to Ranke the 'inner necessity of the succession' must not by any means be overlooked. To be sure, no final goal can be stipulated for world history. 'To stipulate a definite goal for it (world history) would be to darken the future and fail to recognize the limitless sweep of the move-ment of world history.'[39] Nevertheless there does exist for Ranke

---

35 *Ibid.,* p. 168.

36 *Ibid.,* p. 174. The quotations are from *Die grossen Mächte.*

37 *Ibid.,* p. 165

38 Quoted in C. Hinrichs, *Ranke und die Geschichtstheologie der Goethe-zeit,* p. 165. Cf. also *Die grossen Mächte,* 1955, pp. 3f. and 43: 'There is no doubt that for the historian inestimable value attaches also to the contempla-tion of the single moment in its truth, of the particular development in and for itself; the particular contains the general within it.' ... But it contains the general within it in such a way that 'from isolation and pure elucidation there (will) emerge true harmony'.

39 F. Meinecke, 'Deutung eines Rankewortes', in *Zur Theorie und Philoso-phie der Geschichte,* 1959, pp. 117ff.

a goal. The goal of the developments and entanglements of history is, that the 'whole fulness' of the spirit breathed into mankind, the infinite multiplicity which is provided for in the one divine idea, should come to light in the succession of the epochs. It is not that the idea will at last stand realized and revealed, but the totality of world history, of which there can here be no comprehensive view, will reveal, as a sum of the partial manifestations of the idea, the fulness of the divine being. 'For Ranke, development consists in the succession of a series of forms of manifestation of the one idea, all of equal standing, which have their value in themselves and whose infinite fulness, taken all together, would supply the revelation of the whole.' This is world history in terms of 'teleology without a *telos*', as G. Masur has called Ranke's view of history and historiography. Thus for Ranke history is a process, but its meaning is not contained in the end result. God appears in history, but does not resolve himself into it. The historian's task is to reconstruct the life of the past – and indeed to reconstruct it in that harmony which is already given in the facts of history as a whole.

Thus Ranke had a 'vision of the whole', a basic view belonging to the philosophy of history and a faith belonging to the theology of history. He shares this with the age of Goethe. Yet he was modest and discreet enough not to construct history according to this conception and not to dismiss the inexplicable with the remark that it is really not good for the facts (Hegel). He brings his 'idea' on the scene only at particular turning points in history and – though this indeed is decisive – in the constructing of his historical concepts.

(*b*) In a similar way Ferdinand Christian Baur, thanks to whom historical criticism and historical thinking have become imperative for Protestant theology, attempted to comprehend history as a universal whole.[40] For him, historical criticism leads of necessity to the question of the 'real truth of history'. 'What higher task can history have at all than the ever more profound examination of the historic complex of all the phenomena that form its given object? ... But for that reason its endeavours are very naturally also directed towards one end: by every means at its command, both by the examination of individual phenomena, and also by

---

40 Cf. E. Käsemann's introduction to the new edition of *Historisch-kritische Untersuchungen zum Neuen Testament*: F. C. Baur, *Ausgewählte Werke*, ed. K. Scholder, vol. 1, 1963; and E. Wolf's introduction to F. C. Baur, *Ausgewählte Werke*, ed. K. Scholder, vol. II, 1963.

the classifying of individual phenomena under the higher view-points from which they first receive their firm place in the whole, it seeks also to penetrate what still confronts it as a solid, closed mass, in order to resolve it and make it fluid, and to draw it into the general stream of historic development in which, in the infinite concatenation of causes and effects, one thing is always the presupposition of the other, everything together upholds and maintains itself, and the only thing that would have to remain for ever uncomprehended is that which could claim in advance to stand in the midst of history outside the context of history.'[41] If, however, the 'context of history' is understood in this way, then on grounds of the philosophy of history – not of historiography – 'miracle' or 'overspringing' must be eliminated. For 'in the end the only view which can be maintained is the one which brings unity, coherence and rational consistency into our *Weltanschauung*, into our view of the gospel history, into our consciousness as a whole'. 'It is always in the context of the whole, in which it can be ascribed its specific place, that a historical truth first receives its firmness and stability.'[42] Thus for F. C. Baur, historical criticism inevitably leads on to historical speculation,[43] for historical criticism cannot and must not lead to atomizing the facts, as in the Enlightenment, but for Baur it must in effect mean an understanding of the individual in the whole. '"Critical historical" means that no single feature is made absolute or negated, but each is understood as a transitional link in the chain of immanent historic progress and thus of the total self-realization of the revelation of the spirit or the idea.'[44] This historical criticism is only the reverse side of historical speculation. But what becomes of 'history' when historical speculation subjects it to a total vision of this kind?

1. History becomes a 'given object confronting us'.

2. The individual 'events' of history are understood as historic 'appearances' of a comprehensive whole.

3. Historic 'moments' are taken as 'elements' in the movements of a total complex of history.

---

41 *Epochen der kirchlichen Geschichtsschreibung*, quoted according to E. Wolf, *op. cit.*, p. IX.

42 *An Dr K. Hase. Beantwortung des Sendschreibens der Tübinger Schule*, 1855, quoted according to E. Wolf, *op. cit.*, p. XI.

43 E. Käsemann, *op. cit.*, p. XIX.

44 E. Käsemann, *op. cit.*, p. XIX.

4. The complex of history is given 'rational consistency' as 'an infinite concatenation of causes and effects'.

5. 'History' becomes a summary term for reality in its totality for the self-contained movement of a universal whole in which 'everything together upholds and maintains itself'.

6. History thus becomes the field of the manifestation of a spiritual whole. It becomes the 'eternally clear mirror in which the spirit regards itself, contemplates its own image'. In history the spirit realizes and manifests itself. In the science of history it is received back again. Thus the speculative view of history as the world of the manifestation of the spirit is in complete accord with the principle of the subjectivity of the spirit that becomes conscious of itself in historical reflection. The critical historical method, historical speculation on history as a whole, and the re-subjectifying of the spirit in the knowledge of history go together and mutually condition each other.

Here, however, there arises the question whether a critical historical method and a historical speculation of this kind still understands 'history' as being 'historic' at all, or whether in this process of knowing and comprehending history the historic character of history is not resolved into a non-historic Greek *logos*. History is turned into a self-supporting cosmos. The riddle of history is solved by means of Platonic philosophy, Hegelian dialectic and pantheistic ideas. History becomes the totality of the changing, self-transforming epiphanies of the eternal present. It is not possible to see how this can be a way of 'using the ruthless application of historical criticism to repeat in a changed situation the Reformers' decision for "*sola fide*".[45]

(*c*) For Johann Gustav Droysen, the 'realm of the historical method' is 'the cosmos of the moral world'.[46] To see this moral world in its development and growth, in its successive movements, is to see it as history. This already shows at the start what Droysen takes to be the substance whose historic manifestations are to be historically examined. His 'cosmos of the moral world' is expounded in a world

---

45 Against G. Ebeling, 'Die Bedeutung der historisch-kritischen Methode', in *Wort und Glaube*, 1960, p. 45 (ET 'The Significance of the Critical Historical Method', in *Word and Faith*, 1963, p. 56) and F. Gogarten, *Verhängnis und Hoffnung der Neuzeit*, 1958, p. 154, whose theses K. Scholder, in the preface to the above mentioned new edition of F. C. Baur's works, quotes as putting significant questions to the work of F. C. Baur.
46 J. G. Droysen, *Historik*, 4th ed. 1960, p. 345.

history of moral teleology. The place of the principle of causality is taken by the principle of moral entelechy. The mystery of the movements of history is illumined in the light of their goals. 'From observing the progress in the movement of the moral world, from recognizing its direction, from seeing goal after goal fulfilled and revealed, the contemplation of history argues to a goal of goals, in which the movement is perfected, in which all that moves and motivates this world of men and makes it hasten restlessly on becomes rest, perfection, eternal present.'[47] 'All development and growth is movement towards a goal which seeks to attain its fulfilment in the movement.'[48] 'The highest goal, which unconditionally conditions all others, motivates them all, embraces them all, explains them all, the goal of goals is not to be empirically discovered.'[49] 'Beginning and end are hidden from the finite eye. But its scrutiny can discover the direction in which the movement flows. Bound though it is to the narrow limits of here and now, it beholds the whence and the whither.'[50] Thus 'the self-certainty of our personal being, the pressure of our moral obligations and desires, the longing for perfection, unity, eternity' adds 'to the other "proofs" of the existence of God the one that for us proves most'.[51] The certainty thus acquired of a highest goal of goals that gives meaning to things, is what Droysen calls a 'theodicy of history', without which history would lapse into the meaninglessness of a cyclic movement that merely repeats itself. Thus for 'history' Droysen holds fast to the belief in God's wise ordering of the world, which embraces the whole human race; and 'in taking this faith, "that is an undoubting confidence of things not seen", and striving to spell it out in terms of knowledge ... therein and therein alone does it know itself to be a science'.[52]

In Droysen the relation between history and philosophy of history is especially interesting. The movements of history are movements within the framework of the 'cosmos' of the moral world. The place of the causal cosmos of the natural sciences, however, is taken by a teleological cosmos which has its culminating point of metaphys-

47 *Ibid.*, p. 345.
48 *Ibid.*, p. 356.
49 *Ibid.*, p. 356.
50 *Ibid.*, p. 358.
51 *Ibid.*, p. 356.
52 *Ibid.*, p. 373.

ical unity in the highest final goal, the goal of all goals. This is manifestly the entelechy-cosmos of Aristotelian metaphysics. The latter is combined with the postulates of Kant's practical reason, with the need to presuppose belief in 'God and a future world'. The eschatology of Christian hope is transposed into the teleology of the moral reason. The *eschaton* is turned into the *telos* of all *tele* – rest, perfection, one flock and one shepherd, one nation of mankind, one full royal freedom of moral man, a new heaven and a new earth, return of the whole creation to God.[53] Neoplatonic *logos* speculation and the Hegelian dialectic of the coming to itself of absolute Spirit supply the further description of this *eschaton/ telos*.

Here, too, the riddle of history is resolved. The man who is engaged in moral action knows himself on the way to the final solution. Our last quotation, however, shows plainly that the question as to the meaning or meaninglessness of history is decided in a 'pre-scientific' way, as R. Wittram observes, yet not in an unscientific pre-scientificness but, as Droysen says, in the foundations and motive causes of the science of history – namely, in that believing hope in the as yet unseen future which presses for knowledge and which calls for the historical science that 'strives after' knowledge. This would mean that the range of the historic consciousness, of historic remembrance and historic knowledge is always as wide as the extent to which the historic consciousness of mission, in hope for the future and assurance of faith, anticipates an *eschaton* of ultimate goals and aims. The historical consciousness of history has the possibilities and limitations of its perception prescribed by a historic consciousness of mission which accepts the future in responsibly embracing its aims and goals. If this missionary consciousness is formulated in moral terms, as in Droysen, then the realm of the historical method becomes the cosmos of the moral world. It is significant that for this moral teleology Droysen can, to be sure, take over the biblical promises of the new humanity, the liberty of the children of God, the perfection of all historic, finite movements in the 'eternal present', but not the cardinal point of Christian eschatology – the resurrection of the dead.

(*d*) For Wilhelm Dilthey, history is a human science and the human sciences rest on the relationship between life, expression

---

53 *Ibid.*, p. 357 n. 11.

and understanding. 'The summary expression for all that meets us in experience and understanding is life as a complex embracing the human race.'[54] Everywhere in history we find expressions of life, conditions of life, objectifications of the one, unfathomable life. 'Each *individual expression of life represents* in this realm of objective spirit (*viz.*, in the sense of the objectification of life) something *common* to all.'[55] All expressions of life stand in a sphere of community, and are understandable only in such a sphere. The 'basic fact' of man's world is 'life', and the 'essence of history' is therefore to be seen in the idea of the 'objectification of life'.[56] 'It is life of all kinds in the most varied relationships that constitutes history. History is merely life, seen from the standpoint of the whole of mankind as forming one complex.'[57] Over against Hegel's starting point in the 'absolute Spirit' Dilthey sets the 'reality of life': 'In life the totality of the psychic complex is at work.' Hence he understands 'objective spirit' not from the standpoint of 'reason', but as a live unity of expressions of life and objectifications of life. The historic 'chain of effects' accordingly does not consist for him in the causal chain of nature, but in the structure of the life of the soul which produces values and realizes aims. The life that springs from unfathomable sources becomes intelligible to us in the endless historic objectifications of that life, so far as we ourselves have part in it. The understanding of historic expressions of life presupposes the grounding of our own life in the unfathomable stream of life, and stands in mutual interaction therewith. We understand what we experience, and can experience what we understand. 'We are first of all historic beings, before we are observers of history, and only because we are the former do we become the latter.'[58] Thus mental science or the science of life, as it grows in understanding, broadens the horizon of the things that are common to all life, and

---

54 *Gesammelte Schriften*, 192ff., vol. VII, p. 131. On Dilthey's work cf. G. Misch, *Lebensphilosophie und Phänomenologie*, 2nd ed. 1931; E. Rothacker, *Einleitung in die Geisteswissenschaften*, 1920; H. Plessner, *Zwischen Philosophie und Gesellschaft*, 1953, pp. 262ff.; O. F. Bollnow, *Dilthey*, 2nd ed. 1955, and *Die Lebensphilosophie*, 1958.

55 *Gesammelte Schriften*, VII, p. 146.

56 VII, p. 147: 'It is through the idea of the objectification of life that we first acquire an insight into the essence of history. ... Whatever aspect of its character the spirit puts into its expressions of life today, stands there tomorrow as history.'

57 VII, p. 276.

58 VII, p. 278.

draws near to the unfathomable, infinite whole that is history. The recognition of the finitude and relativity of all historic manifestations of life does not then lead us to relativism, but sets us free for the unfathomably creative activity of life itself. 'This tangle of torturing, enrapturing questions, of intellectual delights and the pains of insufficiency and contradiction – this is the enigma that is life, the unique, dark frightening object of all philosophy ... the face of life itself, ... this sphinx with the body of an animal and the face of a man.'[59] True as it is that history is here taken up into the sphere of a philosophy of life and regarded as the fulness of the finite objectifications and manifestations of infinite life, yet it is equally true that for Dilthey this can also be combined with a goal: 'Man's capacity for development, the expectation of future, higher forms of human life – that is the mighty wind that drives us on.'[60]

Here, too, historic 'events' are interpreted in terms of a primary substance that is the inexhaustible source of history – in this case 'life' – and in the light of the unfathomable life process they become 'objectifications' of something. All events, ideas and movements in history have at bottom something in common, which manifests itself in them all and makes it possible to understand them and accept them as an enrichment of our own life. The 'riddle of history' is not rationally solved. History is not subjected to a general formula of mathematics. But the riddle of history is identified as the riddle of life, whose solutions are manifested in fragmentary, finite, supersedable form in the relations and objectifications of life. Life, unfathomable as it is, is perennial. The relations and objectifications of life change. History becomes intelligible when it is related to an underlying foundation, to some eternally springing, eternally driving source, to the *hypokeimenon* of 'life'. Then 'history' is the history of life, and in so far as 'life' is mind, the science of history is a human science. Its knowledge and understanding of past history is a knowledge and self-understanding of the similar in the different. Here, too, history becomes a totality and, in the immensurable whole of this totality, 'life' becomes epiphanous.

---

59 VIII, p. 140. Cf. M. Landmann, *Der Mensch als Schäpfer und Geschöpf der Kultur*, 1961. The 'anarchy of thought' and the 'relativity of values' which are so much feared in historism are changed by Landmann into the positive form of the inexhaustible fulness of creative power: 'Multiplicity of Knowledge as a Source of Creative Power', pp. 72ff.

60 H. Nohl, postscript to W. Dilthey's *Die Philosophie des Lebens*, Philosophische Texte, ed. H. G. Gadamer, 1946, p. 98.

(e) Martin Heidegger sets out from the view of history contained in Dilthey's philosophy of life.[61] Yet for him the 'basic weakness' of thus seeing history in terms of the philosophy of life lies in the fact that 'life' itself has not been taken as an ontological problem. For him, 'life' is 'essentially accessible only in Dasein'. By 'Dasein' is meant exclusively the being of man or – later – that in which man finds and has being. This means that for him the place of 'unfathomable life' is taken by Dasein as disclosed to a phenomenological analysis. History has its roots no longer in the creative unfathomability of life, but in the historic character, or 'historicality', of Dasein. 'Historicality, as a determining character, is prior to what is called "history" (events of world history). Historicality stands for the state of Being that is constitutive for Dasein's "happening" as such; and only on the basis of such "happening" is anything like "world history" possible or can anything belong historically to world history.'[62] This means that the origin and the essence of history are to be sought in the finitude, temporality and historical character of the existence of man. Dasein is finite, for it extends between birth and death. To the temporal extension of Dasein belongs death. '*Authentic Being-towards-death – that is to say, the finitude of temporality* – is the hidden basis of Dasein's historicality.'[63] Human Dasein is 'Being-towards-death' as the inevitable possibility of existence. 'Only Being-free *for* death gives Dasein its goal outright and pushes existence into its finitude. Once one has grasped the finitude of one's existence, it snatches one back from the endless multiplicity of possibilities which offer themselves as closest to one ... and brings Dasein into the simplicity of its *fate*.'[64]

If the essence of history is seen in the 'historicality' of Dasein as such in terms of this analysis, then that means turning our backs on the multiplicity of things and events, and no longer examining the course of history and its reality as such, but asking what essentially makes it possible. 'In the existential analysis we cannot, in principle, discuss what Dasein *factically* resolves in any particular case.'[65]

61 Cf. W. Müller-Lauter, 'Konsequenzen des Historismus in der Philosophie der Gegenwart', *ZTK* 59, 1962, pp. 226ff.

62 M. Heidegger, *Sein und Zeit*, pp. 19f. (ET p. 41).

63 *Ibid.*, p. 386 (ET p. 438).

64 *Ibid.*, p. 384 (ET p. 435).

65 *Ibid.*, p. 383 (ET p. 434).

The analysis supplies only a formal structural context which provides the conditions for the various several events.

What is the view of history that comes of thus grounding history in the fundamental 'historicality' of Dasein? Like Dilthey, when in terms of the philosophy of life he interpreted history as a mental science and a science of life, so also Heidegger's existentialist interpretation of history as a science is aimed at demonstrating its ontological derivation from the historic character of Dasein itself, and seeks to construct the idea of history from the 'historicality' of Dasein. This, however, is to lay down not only the historic character of the historical subject, but also a new description of the historical object. Heidegger makes a very precise distinction between what is 'primarily historic' and what is 'secondarily historic'.[66]

The historian's primary and authentic object lies not in the individual occurrence, or in 'laws' which govern the sequence of events, but in 'the possibility which has been factically existent. ... The central theme of historiology is the *possibility* of existence which has-been-there.'[67] Thus in the science of history, 'historicality' in the authentic sense of the term 'understands history as the "recurrence" of the possible, and knows that a possibility will recur only if existence is open for it fatefully, in a moment of vision, in resolute repetition'.[68] This means that historical science becomes a return to the possibility (that was), a repetition of the possibility and a re-echoing of the possibility. Historical science 'will disclose the quiet force of the possible with all the greater penetration the more simply and the more concretely having-been-in-the-world is understood in terms of its possibility, and "only" presented as such'.[69] '*Repeating is handing down explicitly* – that is to say, going back into the possibilities of the Dasein that has-been-there. The authentic repetition of a possibility of existence that has been – the possibility that Dasein may choose its hero – is grounded existen-

66 *Ibid.*, p. 381 (ET p. 433): 'We contend that what is *primarily* historic is Dasein. That which is secondarily historic, however, is what we encounter within-the-world – not only the things ready-to-hand, in the widest sense, but also the environing Nature as "the very soil of history". Entities other than Dasein which are historic by reason of belonging to the world are what we call "world-historic".

67 *Ibid.*, p. 395 (ET p. 447).
68 *Ibid.*, pp. 391f. (ET p. 444).
69 *Ibid.*, p. 394 (ET p. 446).

tialistically in anticipatory resoluteness.[70] Thus the historian will examine past history in search of its underlying understandings of existence, and from the understandings of existence he will extract the possibilities of Dasein and present them as possibilities for today's ability to exist – in order that Dasein may choose its hero. Thus historical science once more becomes 'tradition' – viz., handing down of possibilities of existence that have been.

The secondarily historic, on the other hand, has its roots in the inauthentic historicality of Dasein. In its flight from death it loses itself in general terms of 'they' and of world history, and is dissipated in the multiplicity of all that occurs from day to day. It understands Being without further differentiation in the sense of mere presence-at-hand and becomes historically blind to the possibilities. It therefore retains and receives only the 'actual' that is left over from the world history that has been, 'the leavings, and the information about them that is present-at-hand'. It 'evades choice'. 'Loaded down with the legacy of a "past" which has become unrecognizable, it seeks the modern.'[71] To that extent historical study of this kind seeks to estrange Dasein from its authentic historicality.

It was Heidegger's distinction between authentic and inauthentic study of history which first gave rise to that dualism that splits man's relation to history into objectifying contemplation and immediate encounter, into factual positivism and existentialist interpretation of the past possibilities of existence, in order then 'to interpret the movements of history as possible ways of understanding human existence, thus demonstrating their relevance today'.[72]

But now, it transpires that when real history is grounded in the formal structure of the historicality of Dasein, this tends to obscure the fact that the movements, individualities and complexes of history have really happened.[73] Historical relativism, to be sure,

---

70 *Ibid.*, p. 385 (ET p. 437).

71 *Ibid.*, p. 391 (ET pp. 443f.).

72 R. Bultmann, *Das Urchristentum*, 2nd ed. 1954, p. 8 (ET p. 12). On this dualism cf. H. Ott, *Geschichte und Heilsgeschichte in der Theologie R. Bultmanns*, 1955; J. Moltmann, 'Exegese und Eschatologie der Geschichte', *EvTh* 22, 1962, pp. 38ff. This contrasting of critical historical examination and kerygmatic interpretation, especially where it is sharpened by means of the antithesis of law and gospel, is not in harmony with the primarily and secondarily historic in Heidegger, but represents a subjectivistic exposition of the history of existence.

73 W. Müller-Lauter, *op. cit.*, p. 254 n. 1. Similarly also C. von Krockow, *Die Entscheidung*, 1958, pp. 131f.

is surmounted when the possibility of history is ontologically grounded in the historicality of Dasein. This historicality is itself not subject to history, but comes of Dasein's eternally being given thematic and problematical character by death. But this also means losing sight of history as such. 'The intended surmounting of historism becomes an unintended surmounting of history.'[74] What happens here in the name of 'historicality' and in the work of existentialist interpretation of history is again the annihilation of history. The riddle of history is the historicality of Dasein, and man knows himself in his historicality to be the solution. In his 'resoluteness' he cuts the Gordian knot. But to surmount historicism in this way is to lose history itself.

(f) To sum up the results of this brief review of the philosophy of history that emerges from historical heuristics, we find that the definition, comprehension and understanding of history inevitably brings about at the same time an abrogation, a negation and annihilation of history. When the primary question is that of the origin, substance and essence of history, then the concrete movements, changes, crises and revolutions which constitute history are related to some factor that does not change, always exists and has equal validity at all times. The science and philosophy of history are here striving to combine the Greek *logos* with our modern experiences of reality, and our modern experiences of crisis with the Greek *logos*.

It has often been rightly emphasized that 'history' was fundamentally foreign to Greek thought. Greek thought was primarily in search of the ever existent, the unchanging, ever true, ever good and ever beautiful. 'History', however, is that which rises and passes, unstable and transient, and as such shows no signs of anything that is perpetual and abiding. For that reason it was not possible to discover in the accidental *pragmata* of history any *logos* of eternal, true Being. It was not possible to 'know' history, and at bottom there was in history nothing worth knowing either. This idea of *logos* and knowledge, of truth and essence, plainly has its ground in the religion of ancient Greek belief in the gods and the cosmos. Thucydides, the historian of the Peloponnesian war, shows profound insights into the nature of men and forces and their typical features, but he, too, searches for what is abiding and unchanging

---

74 W. Müller-Lauter, *op. cit.*, p. 253.

in this war. 'He is a man void of hope, and therefore void of wide perspectives.'[75] He portrays a self-contained picture of 'a history', but does not ask about 'history'. He lacks the sense for change and newness, because there can be no divine sense in the changing and the suddenly new. What makes divine sense would require to have the dignity of being constant and abiding.

On the other hand it has been emphasized that the concept of history is a creation of Hebrew prophecy. 'For the Greek mind, historical science is synonymous with knowledge as such. Thus for the Greeks history is and remains related merely to the past. The prophet on the other hand is a seer. His seer's eye fashioned the concept of history as the being of the future. ... Time becomes future ..., and the future is the primary content of this reflection on history. In place of a golden age in the mythological past, the eschatological future puts a true historical existence on earth.'[76] This has its ground in the fact that for Jews and Christians history means history of salvation and history of the divine promise. The 'divine' is not seen as that which is ever existent in constant and abiding orders and self-repeating structures, but is expected in the future from the God of the promises. The changes of history are not 'the changing', as measured in terms of the abiding, but they contain the possible, as measured in terms of the promise of God. 'History' is not a chaos into which the observer must bring divine order and eternal *logos*, but history is here perceived and sought in the categories of the new and the promised. The place of dispassionate observation and contemplation or review is therefore taken by passionate expectation and by participation in forward-moving mission. The place of the question as to the abiding essence and eternal origin of times past is taken by the historic question of the future and of the preparations for it and intimations of it in the past. The real category of history is no longer the past and the transient, but the future. The perception and interpretation of past history is then no longer archaeological, but futuristic and eschatological. Accounts of history then belong to the genus of prophecy – prophecy that looks back, but intends the future. If the meaning of history is expected from the future and conceived in terms of the

---

75 G. Mann, *Der Sinn der Geschichte*, 1961, p. 15. Cf. also K. Löwith, *Meaning in History*, 1949; E. Auerbach, *Mimesis*, 1946.

76 H. Cohen, *Religion der Vernunft aus den Quellen des Judentums*, 1919, p. 302.

mission of the present, then history is neither a tangle of necessities and laws nor a tumbling-ground for meaningless caprice. Future as mission shows the relation of today's tasks and decisions to what is really possible, points to open possibilities in the real and to tendencies that have to be grasped in the possible.

If, as we said at the beginning, modern historical study and the modern philosophy of history is 'philosophy of crisis', the very designation of 'history' as 'crisis' really already implies the use of the Greek *logos* for a 'philosophy' of history. For the word 'crisis' measures the uncomprehended new event by the standard of the traditional order of human life, which now finds itself in a crisis, is threatened by it, and must therefore be rescued, preserved or renewed. The expression 'crisis' is always related to 'order'. The 'crisis' calls the order in question and can therefore be mastered only by means of a new order. It then remains unnoticed that this event, which is perceived as a 'crisis', contains on the other hand also the 'new'. Philosophy of history as a philosophy of crisis has therefore constantly a conservative character. Historical science as an anti-crisis science therefore fell back on the Greek *logos* with all its cosmological implications, and on the Roman concept of *ordo* with all its political and juridical implications. If, however, the new factor is perceived in the crisis, and history is not regarded as a crisis of the existing order but is expected in the category of the future, then the horizon of illumination and expectation will have to be totally different. Philosophy of history as a philosophy of crisis has the aim of annihilating history. An eschatology of history, however, which revolves around the concepts of the new and the future, of mission and the front line of the present, would be in a position to take history as history, to remember and expect it as history, and thus not to annihilate history but to keep it open.

5. Eschatology of History – Philosophic Millenarianism

It was the theological evaluation of 'time' resulting from the expectation of the arrival of the promised future of God in terms of Jewish and Christian messianic thought, that first opened the Greek mind for the problem of history and for the philosophic idea of a purposeful, irreversible and unrepeatable process of history. 'Just as space with its closed bounds and its fulness of forms is the sphere of truth for the Greeks, so that of Israel is the open, formless stream of time. In the former case we have the circle of the cosmos returning upon itself, in the latter the straight line of creation pressing on to infinity; in the former the world of seeing and contemplating, in the latter that of hearing and learning; in the former image and resemblance, in the latter decision and action. ... In space is presence and remembrance, in time danger and hope. ... Over against the spatial goal of perfection stands the goal of redemption to be attained in time.'[77] The combining of both spheres of truth and both ways of thinking in the manifold encounters between Jewish and Christian messianic ideas and Greek thought in the course of the history of Christianity brought about the decisive transition in Greek thinking from the static to the dynamic, from substance to function, from the eternal present of Being to the open possibilities of the future, from the metaphysical glorification of the cosmos to the sense of mission that transforms the world. The transition which arose from such encounters can be particularly clearly seen in the philosophy of history in the nineteenth century. If in the last chapter we saw modern historiography and modern philosophy of history in the light of the Greek *logos* and noticed in them a subliminal annihilation of history, yet they can also be read from the standpoint of historic eschatology.

Since the time of Herder's *Ideen zur Philosophie der Geschichte der Menschheit* ('Ideas on the Philosophy of the History of Mankind'), Kant's *Ideen zu einer allgemeinen Geschichte in weltbürgerlicher Absicht* ('Ideas on a Universal History, with a Cosmopolitan Intent'), Schiller's *Was heisst und zu welchem Ende studiert man Universalgeschichte?* ('What is Universal History and to what End is it studied?'), and finally Hegel's *Philosophy of History*, all historians and thinkers on history have possessed a *sense of mission*, a belief in a history that is meaningful and a faith in the great task of mankind. Whether this goal is governed by the 'vision of eternal peace' in the cosmopolitan state or, as in national histories, by the 'mission of Prussia' (Treitschke), the 'mission of France' (Jules Michelet) or the mission of Panslavism, everywhere a secular messianism becomes the dominating philosophical and political idea in the view of history. Historiography and philosophy of history become necessary where the foreground is occupied by the mission

---

77 M. Susman, *Das Buch Hiob und das Schicksal des jüdischen Volkes*, 2nd ed. 1948, pp. 16f.

of a nation, or by world redemption or the doctrine of a revolution that is now due or the doctrine of a vitally necessary restoration. The messianic outlook becomes political and motivates men's
thoughts on history. This in itself has already brought a fundamentally new element into the view of history in modern times as
compared with Greek historiography.

It also means, further, that modern views of history can no longer
renounce the governing idea of a *universal history or world history*.
Speculations on world history and discussions about history as a
whole, and about the whole as history, first became possible as a
result of Christianity's sense of mission, and have therefore not
ceased to be possible even where Christianity is no longer the
centre of this mission.

Finally, it can be said that only where a knowledge of mission
supplies the sense of a future and a purpose, and only so long as that
is so, and only where this knowledge finds its goal in a universal
horizon that embraces the whole world, and only so long as that is
so, is there room for the concept of growth in time, of the uniqueness of events and of a meaningful future that is to be expected and
sought – in a word, for a historic concept of history. That is why
the Dutch historian Jan Huizinga can say that the future is the real
category of historic thinking.[78] And that is why Ernst Bloch is right
when he insists that 'the nerve of the true historical concept is and
remains the new'.[79]

The concept of history that is marked by future expectations, a
sense of mission and the category of the new can, of course, also
make history obscure. It depends on the nature of the future that
is expected in each particular case, and on the source from which
the mission emerges and the object at which it aims. Yet 'history'
here remains the epitome of possible danger and possible salvation.
'History' does not become, in the sense of the Greek *logos*, the
epitome of reality in its totality or of the universe. To understand
and embrace history in the front-line of the present in terms of hope
and forward-moving mission can therefore be dangerous as well
as salutary in its effects. For where this way of perceiving history
is concerned, Hölderlin's saying is true: 'Where there is danger,
the salutary also grows' – as is also its reverse: where the salutary

---

78 Cf. A. A. van Ruler, *Die christliche Kirche und das Alte Testament*, 1955,
p. 36 n. 11.
79 E. Bloch, *Das Prinzip Hoffnung* II, 1959, p. 1626.

grows, there danger grows also (E. Bloch).[80] The would-be rescue for the sake of which everything else is abandoned, and which then fails, plunges everything into infinite danger of forsakenness and meaninglessness. To expect and seek a deliverance which does not embrace all that is and all that is not yet, has disastrous results when everything is staked upon it. To abandon ourselves and all existing reality to the unstable seas of history always has point only when there is a prospect of new land. If these prospects prove to be illusions, then our loss is doubled. If there are no prospects at all, then history, too, becomes pointless. But if the experience of reality as history has once arisen and the breakthrough to history has once taken place, then there can be no return to non-historic faith in the ever existing and eternally abiding cosmos. The understanding of history, of its possibilities for good and evil, of its direction and its meaning, lies in the field of hope and can be acquired only there.

If from this standpoint we take another look at modern historiography and modern philosophy of history, then we shall notice that the real problem in their concepts of history is not the problem of the particular and the general, not the problem of the idea and its appearances, and so on, but the question of the relation of history to the 'end of history'. Kant remarked in his philosophy of history that philosophy, too, can have its 'millenarianism'.[81] His remark draws our attention to the fact that every understanding of history on the basis of an already existing and ascertained totality of the idea or of the primary substance or of life, and every resolution of history into knowledge, is in search of the 'end of history', and that the aporia of the philosophy of history is to be seen in its having to seek this 'end of history' *in* history. Modern philosophy of history has in fact the character of a philosophic, enlightened millenarianism: the 'ending of history in history' is, as in the old religious millenarianism, its goal. It has, further, the character of eschatological spirit mysticism. Joachim di Fiore's historico-theological idea of a third empire of the spirit has haunted and inspired the nineteenth-century view of history since Lessing. History is the 'developing God', as it was said in the age of Goethe from Herder on. Knowledge of history therefore imparts a share in the God who

---

80 E. Bloch, *Verfremdungen* I, 1962, p. 219.

81 I. Kant, *Ideen zu einer allgemeinen Geschichte in weltbürgerlicher Absicht*, as in the edition, *Zur Geschichtsphilosophie (1784–1798)*, ed. A. Buchenau, Berlin, 1947, p. 24.

is becoming spirit. The idea that a third age of the – scientific – spirit will clear up the crises of history and in this way resolve enigmatic history into understood history, constituted for Lessing and Kant, for Comte and Hegel and their followers, the hidden basis for a new orientation of the world, and one that was fundamentally no longer 'metaphysical', but 'historical'. Thus wherever the philosophy of history lays down an 'essence of history', its statements, although formulated in the sense of Greek cosmology, have an eschatological character involving the 'end of history'. All the 'general bonds' or trends which historiography finds in history have therefore an eschatological tenor.

But if 'history' becomes a new concept for the 'universe' or for 'reality in its totality', then this is to coin a new concept of the cosmos and no longer take a 'historic' view of history. If reality is engaged in history, then that means precisely that it has not yet become a rounded whole. The 'whole world' would be the sound world, the perfect world, which bears its truth within itself and can demonstrate it of itself. Only as long as the world is not yet sound and whole, only as long as it is open towards its truth and does not yet possess it, can we speak of 'history'. Only as long as reality itself is involved in the difference between existence and essence, only as long as human nature is experienced in terms of the difference between consciousness and being, is there such a thing as history and is there any need for knowledge of the future, for a sense of mission and for present decision.

But what does knowledge of history mean in that case, and what is then the point of historiography?

6. Death and Guilt as Driving Forces of the Historical Outlook

Efforts towards a knowledge of history which take seriously this historic character of history will begin with Friedrich Nietzsche's protest against historism in the name of life. 'All living things can be healthy, strong and fruitful only within a surrounding horizon.'[82] Historism, an excess of which stifles life, has its ground according

---

82 *Vom Nutzen und Nachteil der Historie für das Leben*, Kröner 37, 1924, p. 5.

to Nietzsche in the mediaeval *memento mori* and in the 'hopeless-ness which Christianity cherishes in its heart towards all coming ages of earthly existence'.[83] The historical outlook, 'when it reigns unrestrainedly and draws all its conclusions, leaves the future with-out roots, because it destroys our illusions and robs existing things of the atmosphere in which alone they can live'.[84] For 'life' means having a horizon, and to have a horizon means to be borne by hope into the realm of the future and the possible. This is the 'plastic power of life' which is undermined by the historical outlook and an excess of the historical outlook. If, however, it is really in the name of Nietzsche's *'memento vivere'* that we would take up and con-sider past history, then this 'life' would have to be a match for the 'death' which has made past history irretrievably past. The under-standing of 'life' on the basis of which Nietzsche enquires into the 'historical outlook's advantages and disadvantages for life' cannot assert itself against the death that makes all things historic, or can do so only by dint of forgetting and of appealing to 'life's youth'. For this reason his protest against historism is no match for the lat-ter and its consequences. The historian's impression is correct: 'To me the great historic events of the past always seem like frozen cat-aracts – pictures that have stiffened in the cold of vanished life and keep us at a distance. ... We shiver with cold as we contemplate the greatness of – fallen empires, perished cultures, burnt-out passions, dead minds. ... When we take these things seriously, then we can have a feeling that we historians are engaged in a curious business: we dwell in the cities of the dead, encompass shadows, censure the departed.'[85] Only the question remains, why we do it and why we do not rather flee the shadowy realm of the past. Underlying all history, in the sense of an attempt at scientific knowledge, is what has been called 'history as memory'.[86] It is true that our faculty of remembering matters of history is always selective. Remem-bering and forgetting are interwoven in each other. It is true that our faculty of remembering matters of history is conditioned by the imagination. The thing we remember changes its colours in the image of memory. Where these memories of history are con-cerned, 'history as a science' has a twofold consequence: history as

---

83 *Ibid.*, pp. 68f.
84 *Ibid.*, pp. 56f.
85 R. Wittram, *Das Interesse an der Geschichte*, 1958, pp. 15f.
86 A. Heuss, *Der Verlust der Geschichte*, 1959, pp. 13ff.

a science may well turn the 'memory' into a known, historic fact by destroying it, but from its own standpoint it cannot possibly reverse the process and by its own means create new memories, unless it were to cancel itself (A. Heuss).[87] In regard to 'history as memory', however, and to the extent that it is present as such, historical science has a task of criticism and purification. It has the 'task of combatting innocent forgetfulness and guilty legend' (H. Heimpel).[88] In this sense R. Wittram has called *guilt* the 'secret motor which keeps the movement going, mostly hidden, always at work, the real *perpetuum mobile* of world history'.[89] Memories of the kind that are experienced as 'guilt' 'force themselves upon us'. They compel the present to define its position towards them, for in everything that is remembered as guilt there lurks something which is not yet over and done with, whose implications are not yet grasped, whose significance is not yet plain. When what has been, or has happened, is seen as 'guilt', then the present enters into proceedings which have not yet found their end and their solution. The past becomes determinative for the burdens and tasks of the present. To such proceedings Hegel's remark does not apply: 'As the idea of the world it (philosophy) appears only after reality has finished the process of its formation and completed itself. ... When philosophy paints one of life's figures as grey as grey can be, then that figure has grown old and the greyness cannot be a means of rejuvenating it but only of recognizing it.'[90] Once processes in history and particular figures in life have become old, then a detached historical consideration of them is *possible* – only, then it is no longer *necessary*. Processes of this kind that are complete in themselves completely lack anything to stimulate the onset of memory. If, on the other hand, history is not yet at an end and the individual figures in its life are not yet completed, then to behold it with the eyes of Minerva's owl is not *possible*, but then, on the contrary, to perceive the open possibilities, the tendencies and directions in this process of things is *necessary*. For then it is not a case of frozen cataracts of dead facts, but of an open *fieri*, of something that is in process of becoming, in an open process of decisions

---

87 *Ibid.*, p. 53.

88 H. Heimpel, *Der Mensch in seiner Gegenwart*, 1954, pp. 163f.

89 R. Wittram, *op. cit.*, p. 17.

90 *Grundlinien der Philosophie des Rechts*, 4th edition, ed. Hoffmeister, 1955, Vorrede 17.

and hopes. Then the science of history will not be able merely to present historical 'findings', but will have to be conscious of the fact that in all its presentations it also 'finds' and in all its ascertainings it also 'as-certains'. To this extent the science of history stands in the service of life and of the – as yet unfounded – righteousness of life in the past.

This is true not only in regard to 'history as memory' of guilt, but also in regard to death, which is always the hardest, and therefore also the most certain fact of past history. It is not merely guilt, but ultimately *death* that makes the past irretrievably past. What was, does not return. What is dead, is dead. Now if history were the history of death, then historical science would be the history of death as grasped by man, and as such would be death to all living memory. Then, however, it would again remain an open question what is the real motive of the interest in history, if all history were history of death, if history did, to be sure, include much that is in flux and in process of development, and yet the dead remained dead. Then there would at this point be no *fieri*, but only a fact – and a bare, uninterpretable fact at that. It would be the end of the interest in history and of its usefulness for life, for death would here be found to constitute a perpetual and eternal factor in the shape of an annihilating nothingness. But now, the peculiar thing is, that the historian can and must deal with the dead. 'The dead are dead; but we awake them, we have dealings with them – "eye to eye", as Ranke put it; they demand the truth from us.'[91] This business of dealing with the history of the dead must therefore be motivated by something that reaches beyond death and makes death, too, a passing thing – otherwise historical science would have no motive and would fall to pieces in face of death. Walter Benjamin in his 'Theses on the Philosophy of History' has declared: 'The gift of fanning the spark of hope in the past belongs only to the historian who is convinced that *even the dead* are not secure against the enemy if he wins. ... The Messiah comes not only as Redeemer; he comes also as the Conqueror of Antichrist.'[92] This, however, would mean that hope of the resurrection of the dead, and fear of Antichrist or annihilating nothingness, is alone able to awake hopes in the field of past history, and so to keep history in remembrance and thus, finally, to make history as a science a live possibility. In this sense

91 R. Wittram, *op. cit.*, p. 32.
92 W. Benjamin, *Illuminationen*, ed. T. W. Adorno, 1961, p. 270.

Otto Weber, too, rightly declares: "'History" as an intended object of research, or as the realm in which the present situation originated, is always a process that represents in a manner of speaking a reawakening of the dead. Those who study history (*wer Geschichte* "*treibt*") "make" of the "history of death" a "history of life".'[93] The historian's re-awakening of the dead, even if, and precisely because, it takes place only 'in a manner of speaking', means anticipating eschatology and projecting upon history the last act of history. The 'reason in history' has a messianic light and shows things with all their flaws laid bare and ready for redemption – or else it has no light that historically illuminates history.

How, in this light, can history be experienced and known?

It will no longer be possible to regard the past only archaeologically and take it merely as the origin of the particular present. The past will have to be examined in regard to its own future. All history is full of possibilities – possibilities that have been profited by and not profited by, seized and blocked. In this perspective it appears full of interrupted possibilities, lost beginnings, arrested onsets upon the future. Past ages will thus have to be understood from the standpoint of their hopes. They were not the background of the now existing present, but were themselves the present and the front-line towards the future. It is the open future that gives us a common front with earlier ages and a certain contemporaneity, which makes it possible to enter into discussion with them, to criticize and accept them. That is why past positions in history and the traces of vanished hopes can be taken up once more and awakened to new life. The dialectic of past happening and present understanding is always motivated by anticipations of the future and by the question of what makes the future possible. Future is then found in the past and possibilities in what has been. The unfinished and promising character of past ages is borne in mind. The dualism of which we have spoken, in which the positivist historian strives to discover the facts of the past while the existentialist interpreter endeavours to find the existential possibilities in past existence,

---

93 O. Weber, *Grundlagen der Dogmatik* II, 1962, p. 108. [*Geschichte treiben* ('to study history') could also literally mean 'to drive history', and is therefore here held to suggest that the historian himself is the driving-force that brings dead history to life. We have attempted to reproduce the wordplay by transferring it to the principal clause, where 'make of' is of course used in the sense of understanding, but could also mean literally making. – *Translator.*]

fails to recognize how closely fact and possibility are interwoven in history, how much new possibilities of existence depend on historic events and how full historic events are of possibilities. Only in the process of reconciliation between originally undivided subject-object constellations, when men's decisions are a response to really given possibilities and new real possibilities give rise to new decisions, do future prospects and ordered ends emerge. This is a thing historical positivism cannot see, because its own horizon is taken to be final and therefore cannot be subjected to questioning in recognition of other horizons. It is a thing an existentialist interpretation can bring out only in the realm of man's existence as in quest of itself, but not in the universal realm of all being as open to the future.

7. The Peculiarity of the Historian's Universal Concepts

What happens in this context to the historian's universal concepts, as employed by the historical method which must always also generalize? The philosophical presupposition for a knowledge of history cannot then lie in a metaphysic of being, of the idea, of unfathomable life, or of God. As long as our reality has not yet 'completed' itself and not yet become a rounded whole, a metaphysic of the historical universe in the sense of the Greek *logos* is impossible. All the historian's universal concepts therefore prove to be elastic concepts which themselves belong to history and make history. But the fact that they are not inherently absolute does not mean that they are adequately designated by the term 'relative'. The place of a universal metaphysic of history is taken by a mission aimed at the universal which is future and not yet present. The universal concepts, themselves belonging to history, which are used by historians in an effort to grasp what man is, what the world is, and so on, arise only supposedly and only wrongly from abstraction. In actual fact they contain the note of prophecy and of mission towards the future land of the 'realized generic concept'. They always contain a futuristically anticipated eschatology. In their abstractness the truth which the general concepts seek to grasp is manifested in a manner which is – literally – *pro*-visional in view of the openness of reality. The universals in the metaphysic of history are neither real nor merely verbal, but constitute tendencies in the potential. They mark provisionalities in the fore-land of the mission in history. They are therefore not relative in the sense of historical relativism, but they are surpassable in the sense that the process of history itself is open. What 'world' history is, is decided by what is desired, hoped for and re-pre-sented as the one, future world. What the history of 'mankind' is, is decided by what mankind one day should be and will be. Both are directly related to present mission. Thus there exist only histories on the way to world history, but there is not yet a world history. The lines on which these histories are on their way *towards* world history are all maintained by the consciousness of having a mission towards world history.

Jakob Burckhardt has said of the historian's business: 'Actually, we should have to live in a constant intuition of the world as a whole. Only, this would require a superhuman intelligence, superior to the temporally successive and spatially limited and yet at the same time engaged in constant contemplation of it and complete sympathy with it.'[94] He was not thereby declaring the contemplation of world history to be senseless, but rather indicating the dialectical position of man towards history. Man neither stands *above* history, so that he could survey the world as a whole, nor does he stand wholly *within* history, so that he would have no need to ask about the totality and goal of history and this very question would be pointless. Always he stands both *within* history and also *above* history. He experiences history in the modus of being and in the modus of having. He *is* historic and he *has* history. He must be able to detach himself from history as an investigator and spectator, in order to experience it in the modus of having. He must identify himself with it as a hearer and actor, in order to experience it in the modus of being. He can neither abrogate himself in his survey of history and turn into nothing but an enormous eyeglass, nor can he enter into history without thought and reflection and turn into nothing but a minute decision. He stands both in history and above it and must conduct his life and his thinking in this dialectical and ex-centric position. He is like a swimmer moving in the stream of history – or it may be, against the stream – but with his head out of the water in order to get his bearings and above all to acquire a goal and a future. The concepts and ideas which he can form about historic complexes are therefore historic

---

94 J. Burckhardt, *op. cit.*, p. 372.

in a twofold sense: they are acquired in the process of history, and they reach ahead towards future, possible land, to that extent keeping the movement of history on the move. They are concepts which are conditioned by history, but which also condition history. They are moved and mobile concepts of movement. They seek not to bear the train of history, but to carry the torch before it. For that reason they have necessarily the character of pre-supposition, of postulate, of draft and of anticipation. And for that reason they are not so much generic concepts for the subsuming of known reality as rather dynamic functional concepts whose aim is the future transformation of reality.

8. The Hermeneutics of Christian Mission

1. The Proofs of God and Hermeneutics

Among the presuppositions of a rational Christian theology, hermeneutic reflections on the principles of the understanding of biblical texts have today replaced the old proofs of God which once, as *theologia naturalis*, constituted the prolegomena for what Christianity says of God. This, however, is not by any means the end of these proofs of God which demonstrated the existence and nature of God, as well as the universal necessity of raising the question of God, from a reality known or accessible to all men. On the contrary, they recur in all their conceivable forms in the hermeneutic reflections in which the anterior understanding and the terms of reference for the exposition and preaching of the biblical witness to God and his actions are formulated today. G. Ebeling rightly observes: *'The understanding of what the word "God" means has its place within the sphere of radical questionableness.'*[95] It is therefore the business of a comprehensive analysis of reality to take account of that radical questionableness of reality which provides the general presupposition for the special, Christian questions and statements in theology. In the radical questionableness of reality there appears the problem of transcendence, or simply the *question* of God, in face of which the Christian affirmation of God must prove and authenticate itself. This has much in common with

---

95 G. Ebeling, *Wort und Glaube*, 1960, pp. 364f. (ET p. 347).

the enterprise of the classical proofs of God, even if it is here no longer the existence and nature of God that is demonstrated, but the necessity of raising the question of God. What the name 'God' means, can be intelligibly shown only when it is related to a radical, and therefore necessary, questionableness of reality. 'God' is what we are asking about in and with this questionableness of reality.

The traditional proofs of God can be divided into three major groups: 1. the *proofs of God from the world*, from the cosmos or the history of reality, 2. the *proofs of God from human existence*, from the soul or from the self-consciousness of man's necessary ability and obligation to be a self, 3. the *proofs of God from 'God'*, the proofs of the existence of God, or of the quest of God, from the concept or name of God. 'God' can be sought and understood as what we are asking about in the questionableness of reality as a whole, or in the question of the unity, the origin and the wholeness of reality. 'God' can be understood as what we are asking about in what every man can himself experience as the questionableness of human existence as distinct from the things of the world. 'God' can be understood as what is to be sought and asked about in addressing ourselves to the concept, the name or the self-revelation of God. Rational Christian theology can be cosmo-theology or historico-theology, can be ethico-theology or existential theology and can be onto-theology. These are to begin with the three possibilities in terms of which it can make itself and its business intelligible. These three possibilities have their corresponding results in the principles of hermeneutics, of exegesis, and of the scientific treatment which that involves in our dealings with history and with the historic witness of the Bible. These three possibilities present themselves also for the formulating of the universal theological concepts by means of which the God of the Bible can be understood, proved and proclaimed as the God of all men.

(*a*) We begin with the *proof of God from existence*, since it is so generally employed in hermeneutics today that it is hardly consciously recognized any more as a 'proof of God'. When G. Ebeling says that the radical questionableness 'seems to arise at a totally different point from where the usual so-called proofs of God placed it', namely, 'not with the question of the *primum movens* or such like, but with the problems relating to personal being',[96] then

---

96 *Ibid.*, p. 367 (ET p. 349).

this alternative merely shows how strong the tendency is today to understand by the 'proofs of God' only the theoretic reason's cosmological proofs of God, and then to confine oneself to the proof of God from existence – an extended and deepened form of Kant's moral proof of God. The proof of God from the existence proper to every man is to the effect that 'God' is what is asked about in the questionableness of human existence, limited as it is by death and therefore finite, resting on decisions and therefore historic. The affirmation of the existence of God accordingly cannot be understood as a universal, theoretical and objective truth, but only as an 'expression of our existence itself'.[97] For it is obviously not feasible 'to think of God as a principle of the world in the light of which the world and with it also our existence would become intelligible'.[98] God can be grasped only when men grasp their own existence. The existence of man, however, is historic, i.e. the historic character of man's being is what makes him able to be. Thus God can be grasped only where man chooses himself as his own possibility. Both things happen together in the one act of faith. The question which causes man to ask about God and causes him in asking to know very well who God is, is the question which in his historic existence he himself is. 'If his existence were not motivated (whether consciously or unconsciously) by the enquiry about God in the sense of the Augustinian "*Tu nos fecisti ad Te, et cor nostrum inquietum est, donec requiescat in Te*" ("Thou hast made us for thyself, and our heart is restless until it rests in thee"), then neither would he know God as God in any manifestation of him.'[99] This phenomenon is revelation's point of reference. In it lies the anterior understanding, the universal *theologia naturalis* with which every man has to do and by reference to which alone God's revelation can show itself to be the revelation of God.

The basic principles of hermeneutics automatically result from this. 'In the light of this insight we shall in each instance interpret the historical source as a genuine historic phenomenon, i.e. in the light of the presupposition that in each instance a possibility of human existence is grasped and expressed in it.'[100] The sense of historical science, or exegesis as the case may be, can then no longer

---

97 R. Bultmann, *Glauben und Verstehen* I, p. 32.
98 *Ibid.*
99 *Ibid.* II, p. 232 (ET p. 257); *Kerygma und Mythos* II, p. 192 (ET p. 192).
100 *Glauben und Verstehen* I, p. 119.

lie in reconstructing a piece of the past and assigning it a place in the great complex of relationships that is called history (= world history).[101] The sense of historical science or exegesis then lies in an existentialist interpretation which examines the texts in search of their understanding of existence and interprets the biblical texts in the light of the dominating question of God, of God's revelation, and that means of the truth of human existence as a present possibility of existence. The principles of an understanding exposition result from the presupposed hermeneutic structure of human existence itself. If the motivating question about God is identical with man's question as to the authenticity of his own existence, then the existentialist interpretation can present itself as a true historic and true theological interpretation of the biblical texts. It finds the point of its enquiry in the question as to the understanding of human existence expressed in scripture, because the ground for this question has been supplied to it by the proof of God from existence.

To this the critic must object that man's self-knowledge cannot by any means be arrived at today in antithesis to knowledge of the world, that the historic character of human existence cannot by any means be arrived at without an understanding of the situation in world history, but invariably both can only be arrived at together.[102] Instead of the antithesis between world and self there is in reality always a correlation. For this reason the historic character of a past understanding of existence can be understood only in the context of the 'great complex of relationships' that is called history or world history. The questionability of human existence always stands in a context in which it is conditioned by the questionability of historic reality as a whole. The proof of God from existence has always an eye to the proof of God from the world. An understanding of God can therefore be acquired only in the correlation between understanding of self and understanding of the world, between understanding of history and of 'historicality' – otherwise the intended divinity of God would not be universal.

---

101 *Ibid.*, p. 123.

102 I agree here with W. Pannenberg's criticism, *ZTK* 60, 1963, pp. 101ff., except that in place of the primacy of the world-God relationship I set the correlation of the world-God relationship and the world-existence relationship. It is neither possible to explain human nature as a piece of world, nor is the world synonymous with man's 'being-in-the-world'.

The historic character of believing existence does not by any means already constitute the authenticity of human existence itself, but it is the way to, the witness of, and the mission towards, that authenticity and truth of human nature which lies in the future, is accordingly still outstanding, and is at stake in the mission of Christian faith. The interpretation of all history in the light of the perpetual historic character of human existence does, to be sure, surmount a specific form of positivist historism, but like the latter it also brings the disappearance of the real movements, differences and prospects in history.

Augustine's 'restless heart' is not a universal human presupposition for the Christian understanding of God, but is a mark of the pilgrim people of God and a goal of the Christian mission to all men. It is only in the light of the biblical understanding of God that human existence experiences itself as being moved by the question of God.

(b) The *proof of God from the world* has had no further influence on theology since Kant's critique. Yet, if the reality of the world as a whole is understood in a new way no longer as a cosmos but as universal history, it can be classed alongside the proof of God from existence and can likewise become a source for the stating of hermeneutic principles. 'God' is here experienced on the basis of the world.[103] 'God' is here what is asked about in the question of the one origin, the unity and wholeness of all reality. With the question of the unity and wholeness of reality, the question of God is also given. If, on the other hand, there is no support for the idea of God, then there is no support for the question of the wholeness of reality either. Thus God can be spoken of only in the context of the perception of the unity of all reality. But now, this unity of reality can no longer be understood as a cosmos in the sense of Greek monotheism, since in Greek cosmic faith the accidental events of history were meaningless and therefore remained of no account. But if reality in its totality of continuity and contingency is understood as history, then the structures of the biblical idea of God become visible. The idea of God in the witnesses of the divine history in Israel and Christianity makes it necessary to understand reality as a whole as history. This means, first, that 'world history'

---

103 W. Pannenberg, *op. cit.*, p. 101 n. 18; *Dogma und Denkstruktur*, 1963, pp. 108f. and n. 28.

becomes the most comprehensive horizon for what Christianity says of God. It means, secondly, that such a comprehensive understanding of reality in its totality, since it is itself historic, can only be formulated in each several instance in the context of the present experience of reality as a whole. It is therefore itself historically open and provisional in view of that end of history in which the wholeness of reality will come to light.

For hermeneutics, this results in the principle that the texts which come to us from history are not to be examined merely in regard to the possibilities of existence in the several existences that have been, but have to be read in terms of their historical place and their historical time, in terms of their own historical connections before and after. The connection between then and now does not result from the perpetual finitude and historicality of human existence, but from the context of universal history which links the past with the present. The temporal, historical difference between then and now is not bridged by tracing past and present possibilities back to human existence as such, but is preserved, and yet at the same time also bridged, by the context of events that joins them both together. 'That is to say, the text can be understood only in the context of the comprehensive history which joins the past with the present – and indeed not merely with the present that today exists, but with the future horizon of present possibilities, because the meaning of the present becomes clear only in the light of the future.'[104] 'Only a conception of the course of history which does in fact join the past situation with the present and with its future horizon can provide the comprehensive horizon in which the limited present horizon of the expositor and the historical horizon of the text blend together.[105] 'Then' and 'now' are united while still preserving their peculiarity and their difference, when they 'become elements in the unity of a context of history which embraces them both'.[106] Since this comprehensive context of history can be expressed in the midst of history only in terms of a finite, provisional and therefore revisable perspective, it remains fragmentary in view of the open future.

---

104 W. Pannenberg, 'Hermeneutik und Universalgeschichte', *ZTK* 60, 1963, p. 116.

105 *Ibid.*

106 *Ibid.*

Here it is considered necessary to give expression to 'God' in the totality of reality, and yet at the same time it is admitted to be impossible to comprehend an as yet unfinished and therefore historic reality as a 'totality'. It would therefore be better to abandon the intentions of the cosmological proof of God. As long as the reality of the world and of man in it is not yet 'whole', but its totality is historically at stake, there can be no proof of God from it. The 'comprehensive context of history' which joins 'then' and 'now', the historical horizon and the present future horizon, is not the context of an interrelated chain of events, but is a context of the history of mission and promise. The horizons do not already 'blend together' in the question as to the connection between the events of then and now, but only in the question of the intended future then and now. It is because the inadequate present raises the question of the future that past intentions, hopes and visions of the future are called to mind. In reformations and revolutions past positions towards the future are taken up. It is not only a case of the future of the present but, if this future is to be universal and eschatological, always a case also of the future of the past and the future of the dead. It is not that a 'context of history' merely 'unveils' the truth of all reality[107] but the compiling of history 'leads', and intends to lead, to the truth of reality. The future horizon about which the present asks cannot be understood as a horizon within which to interpret the hitherto existing reality of the world in world history hitherto, but only as a horizon of promise and mission towards a new, future reality, in which everything attains to truth, to rest and to authenticity. The 'sense of the present', which is disclosed only in the light of the future, does not lie in assigning the present its place in the course of history hitherto, but its 'sense' lies in its promise and its task, its break-away from the reality that has been and is, to a new reality. The wholeness and unity of reality which is sought in terms of universal history does not result from the simple course of the world process which, one day at the last, will make reality a rounded whole, but the 'wholeness' and 'unity' of reality must, as compared with all existing reality, be a new reality in which all things become new and whole. The saved world which will prove God 's divinity is one our thoughts and hopes do not yet reach at the point where we have thought history to its end, but

---

107 W. Pannenberg, 'Hermeneutik und Universalgeschichte', *ZTK* 60, 1963, p. 119 n. 37.

only where God 'will be all in all'. This, in biblical terms, is the ἀνακεφαλαίωσις τῶν πάντων in which even the dead are not secure but return and rise again. It is a new reality, which does not put the finishing touch to the reality of history up to then, but so to speak rolls it up. That is why there is sense in asking about the future of past people and things – not merely in order to bring the light of understanding into the dark field of history, but in order to 'kindle in the past the spark of hope'.

(c) The *proof of God from 'God'* is the ontological proof of God. It derives from Anselm of Canterbury. It was not rejected by Kant, but it was Hegel who first made it once more the foundation of the concept of God. It is no accident that Kart Barth, in the book on Anselm (1931) which is so important for his own theology, took it up in a new form and combined it with his own concept of the self-revelation of God. This proof of the existence of God from the concept of God – 'something beyond which nothing greater can be conceived' – or from the name or self-revelation of God, does not assert that on the ground of what we can learn of the reality of the world, or on the ground of what we can ourselves experience of the reality of existence, we must necessarily conceive of God or ask about God if we are to be able to make clear the truth about the world and about human nature. It says merely that whoever conceives of God must necessarily also conceive of his existence. It has its presupposition not in a specific world-picture or a specific understanding of human nature, but in the fact that man – even the godless man – 'hears', that he makes room in his mind for the concept of God and has God's name, or his self-revelation in his name, proclaimed to him. It is not necessary to conceive of God, but if we do conceive of him, then we must conceive of him as necessary. God is known only through 'God'. Only in his light do we see light.

According to the hermeneutic principles which this involves, all exegesis of historical Bible texts must have its source in the undemonstrable event of the happening of that word in which God is known through God, in which God himself speaks and reveals himself. This to be sure, in contrast to the possibilities so far discussed, is a 'starting point in the indisposable',[108] but nevertheless implies hermeneutic and historical consequences. In the preface to the first edition of his *Romans* in 1919, Karl Barth still expressed

---

108 G. Eichholz, 'Der Ansatz Karl Barths in der Hermeneutik', in *Antwort, K. Barth zum 70. Gerburtstag*, 1956, p. 63.

these consequences in Platonic terms: 'But my whole attention was directed towards looking *through* the historical to the Spirit of the Bible, who is the eternal Spirit. ... The understanding of history is a continuing, ever more honest and ever more urgent conversation between the wisdom of yesterday and the wisdom of tomorrow, which is one and the same.'[109] In the preface to the second edition in 1921 it is said that we should conscientiously determine what stands in the text, and reflect upon it, i.e. wrestle with it until the wall between the first century and our own becomes transparent, until Paul speaks there and man hears here, until the conversation between text and reader is concentrated wholly on the substance (which cannot be any different there and here!). 'In seeking to understand I must advance to the point where it is wellnigh only the riddle of the *substance* that confronts me, and really no longer the riddle of the *text* as such, where I therefore wellnigh forget that it is not I who am the author, where I have understood him wellnigh so perfectly that I can let him speak in my name and can myself speak in his name.'[110] But what is the 'substance' that could bring about this blending together of text and reader, author and hearer? What was then called 'substance and text' is in Barth later 'Word and words'. Before all our methods of appropriating what is said in the text, and before all blending together of the horizons then and now, there stands in Barth the great event 'that God himself speaks', that the 'substance' of the texts is this word in which God reveals himself and proclaims or proves himself. Only this event – that God proves himself in the word he speaks to man, and thus the proof of God from God takes place in God 's word – can be the ultimate goal of all historical and theological exegesis and bring about the blending together of times and persons. This would mean, for 'history', that the presupposition and goal of exegesis is not to be seen in the historic character of existence, nor in a universal historical context, but that the problem of the biblical stories and words lies in the fact of the history of God in Christ for men having taken place. This history is to be grasped neither in historical or universal historical terms, nor in terms of the history of existence, but is only to be repeated as the kerygmatic history of God for men. The goal of exegesis is therefore neither a

---

109 Now in *Anfänge der dialektischen Theologie* I, ed. J. Moltmann, 1962, p. 77.

110 *Ibid.* I, p. 112.

believing self-understanding nor an orientation in terms of universal history, but is proclamation. The 'word of God' in the words urges us on from the exegesis of the 'words' to the proclamation of the word. Thus the place of the hermeneutic key provided by the historic character of existence is here taken by the 'history of God *for* men'. The place of the word-character of existence is taken by the sovereignty of the divine word.

As with the other proofs of God, so too the ontological proof is really a piece of anticipated *eschaton*. For that 'God proves himself through God', and that 'God is God', must undeniably imply that 'God is all in all' and that he proves his divinity in all that is and all that is not. Of this omnipotent divinity of God, however, the only sign we have here in history is the foreglow of the raising of Christ from the dead. That God is God accordingly cannot be the eternal source and background of the proclamation of Christ, but must be the promised, but as yet unattained, future goal of Christian proclamation. Barth's very expressions in their originally Platonic terms of the 'eternal Spirit' and the eternally self-identical 'substance' of the Bible show a tendency towards uneschatological, and then also unhistorical, thinking which is still to be met even in the later terms of the word of God and his self-revelation. 'The Word' in 'the words' can, rightly understood, only have an apocalyptic sense and mean the 'Word' which here in history is only to be witnessed to, only to be hoped for and expected, the 'Word' which God will one day speak as he has promised. That exegesis should lead to proclamation if it rightly follows the intentions of the text, cannot be grounded in the transcendent background of the self-revelation of God, but only in the fact that the once-for-all event of the resurrection of Christ leads to an eschatological, missionary necessity of the proclamation to all peoples. This is possible only within an eschatological horizon, but not on the ground of an eternal self-revelation of God. An onto-theological argument for the proclamation can lead to levelling down the different historic tasks and horizons of Christian mission in the ages of history.

2. *Mission and Exposition*

All proofs of God are at bottom anticipations of that eschatological reality in which God is revealed in all things to all. They assume this reality as already present and as immediately perceptible to every man. The hermeneutic principles developed from them take the presence of God which can be demonstrated, experienced or perceived from the world, from existence or from the proclaimed name of God – were it even only because of the necessity of asking about him – and make it the point of reference for the exposition and appropriation of the historic witness of the Bible.

A 'natural theology' of this kind, however, in which God is manifest and demonstrable to every man, is not the presupposition of Christian faith, but the future goal of Christian hope. This universal and immediate presence of God is not the source from which faith comes, but the end to which it is on the way. It is not the ground on which faith stands, but it is the object at which it aims. It is only on the ground of the revelation of God in the event of promise constituted by the raising of the crucified Christ that faith must seek and search for the universal and immediate revelation of God in all things and for all. The world which proves God's divinity, and the existence which is necessarily exercised by the question of God, are here sketches for the future on the part of Christian hope. They are anticipations of the as yet unattained future land in which God is all in all. They are anthropological and cosmological sketches on the part of Christian faith, in which the God of Jesus Christ is 'imputed' or given over to all men and all reality as the God of all men and of the whole of reality. This is possible, as long as reality and the people in it are on the move in history. It is necessary, in order to outline the universal future horizon of Christian mission. Without such sketches, which involve the whole of reality and shed a meaningful light on the existence and determination of all men, Christianity would become a sect and faith would become a private religion. Such interpretations of the whole of reality and of authentic human nature, however, remain 'sketches', whose goal is the universe and the human nature that are promised and will be. They are historic and subject to change, and always depend upon the movement of the Christian mission. *Theologia naturalis* is at bottom *theologia viatorum*, and *theologia viatorum* will always concern itself with the future *theologia gloriae* in the form of fragmentary sketches.

(a) The Hermeneutics of the Apostolate

The real point of reference for the exposition and appropriation of the historic Bible witness, and the one that is their motive and driving force, lies in the mission of present Christianity, and in the universal future of God for the world and for all men, towards which this mission takes place.

The key to the hermeneutics of the historic witness of the Bible is the 'future of scripture'. The question as to the correct exposition of the Old and New Testament scriptures cannot be addressed to the 'heart of scripture'. The biblical scriptures are not a closed organism with a heart, or a closed circle with a centre. On the contrary, all the biblical scriptures are open towards the future fulfilment of the divine promise whose history they relate. The centre of the New Testament scriptures is the future of the risen Christ, which they announce, point forward to and promise. Thus if we are to understand the biblical scriptures in their proclamation, their understanding of existence and their understanding of the world, then we must look in the same direction as they themselves do. The scriptures, as historic witnesses, are open towards the future, as all promises are open towards the future. In this sense R. Bultmann is right when he declares: 'It is not at all "in themselves", nor yet as links in a causal chain, that events or historical figures are historic phenomena. They are such only *in their relationship to the future*, for which they have significance and for which the present has responsibility.'[111] 'Thus it is true also of scripture that it is what it is only in relation to its history and its future.'[112] Only, this 'future of scripture' does not yet lie in the several readers' own present, but in that which gives the momentary present its orientation towards a universal, eschatological future. Hence present perception of the 'future of scripture' takes place in that mission which plays its part in history and in the possibilities of changing history. The biblical witness is witness to a historic forward-moving mission in the past, and hence in the light of the present mission it can be understood for what it really is.

The point of reference and the aim in the exposition of the biblical witness is not something universal which lies at the bottom

111 R. Bultmann, *Glauben und Verstehen* III, p. 113.
112 *Ibid.*, p. 140.

of history or at the bottom of existence and keeps everything moving, but the concrete, present mission of Christianity towards the future of Christ for the world. One could also say that the point of reference in true, historic and eschatological exposition of the Bible is the reconciliation of the godless, if the reconciliation of the godless is understood to mean also the calling of the heathen to participation in the historic mission of Christianity. The link between coming history and past history is provided in the light of this forward-moving, historic mission. The connection between then and now in the history of tradition is a connection in the history of promise and of mission, for tradition, as Christians understand it, means mission that moves forwards and outwards. The word-event in which past events are brought to expression means the event of being called to the future of salvation in Christ and to the present labour of hope in the service of reconciliation. It is only in mission and promise, in the charge committed and the prospect opened, in the labour of hope, that the 'meaning of history' is grasped in a historic way and one that keeps history moving. The link between past history and coming history is not then supplied on the ground of an abstractly ascertained substance of history, nor yet on the ground of the perpetual 'historicality' of human existence. The missionary direction is the only constant in history. For in the front-line of present mission new possibilities for history are grasped and inadequate realities in history left behind. Eschatological hope and mission thus make men's reality 'historic'. The revelation of God in the event of promise reveals, effects and provokes that open history which is grasped in the mission of hope. It takes the reality in which men live together and establish themselves, and makes it a process of history – namely, a judicial process concerning the truth and righteousness of life.

The human nature of man becomes historic inasmuch as the determination of man comes to light in historic mission.

The reality of the world becomes historic inasmuch as in this mission it is seen to be the field of the missionary charge and is examined in search of real possibilities for the world-transforming missionary hope.

God is revealed in this mission as the God who calls and promises. He proves his existence not in terms of man's already existing question about God, not in terms of the question as to the unity of the existing world, nor yet by means of the concept of God, but he proves his existence and his divinity by making possible the historic and eschatological possibilities of mission.

Thus the questions of true human nature, of the unity of the world and of the divinity of God are removed from the sphere of an illusionary *theologia naturalis*. These questions are raised, and answered, in the midst of the movement of mission. They are questions of the *theologia viatorum*.

(b) The Humanizing of Man in the Missionary Hope

The dominant question of all anthropology – who or what is man? who am I? – does not arise in the biblical narratives from comparing man with the animals or with the things of the world. Nor does it arise simply *coram Deo*, as Augustine and the Reformers affirmed. Rather, it arises in face of a divine mission, charge and appointment which transcend the bounds of the humanly possible. Thus Moses (Ex. 3.11) asks in face of his call to lead the exodus of the Israelites from Egypt: 'Who am I, that I should go unto Pharaoh, and that I should bring forth the children of Israel out of Egypt?' Thus, too, Isaiah (Isa. 6.5) in face of his call recognizes himself to be personally guilt-laden in the midst of a guilt-laden people: 'Woe is me! for I am undone; because I am a man of unclean lips, and I dwell in the midst of a people of unclean lips.' Thus Jeremiah in face of his call recognizes what he is and what he was: 'Ah, Lord God ! behold, I cannot speak: for I am a child' (Jer. 1.6). Self-knowledge here comes about in face of the mission and call of God, which demand impossibilities of man. It is knowledge of self, knowledge of men and knowledge of guilt, knowledge of the impossibility of one's own existence in face of the possibilities demanded by the divine mission. Man attains to knowledge of himself by discovering the discrepancy between the divine mission and his own being, by learning what he is, and what he is to be, yet of himself cannot be. Hence the answer received to man's question about himself and his human nature runs: 'I will be with thee.' This does not tell man what he was and what he really is, but what he will be and can be in that history and that future to which the mission leads him. In his call man is given the prospect of a new ability to be. What he is and what he can do, is a thing he will learn in hopeful trust in God's being with him. Man learns his human nature not from himself, but from the future to which the mission leads him. What man is, is told him, only by history, declared W. Dilthey. We can here accept this statement, if we add: the history to which the missionary hope leads him. The real mystery of his human nature is discovered by man in the history which discloses to him his future. In this very history of missionary possibilities which are as yet unknown and as yet unlimited, it comes to light that man is not an 'established being', that he is open to the future, open for new, promised possibilities of being. The very call to the possibilities of the future which are as yet obscure, makes it clear that man is hidden from himself, a *homo absconditus*, and will be revealed to himself in those prospects which are opened up to him by the horizons of mission. The mission and call do not reveal man simply to himself, with the result that he can then understand himself again for what he really is. They reveal and open up to him new possibilities, with the result that he can become what he is not yet and never yet was. This is why according to Old and New Testament usage men receive along with their call a new name, and with their new name a new nature and a new future.

Now in the Old Testament such calls and commissions are particular and contingent. They relate to a single people and a few prophets and kings. They contain specific historic charges. Hence they do not yet provide any clue to the human nature of man as such. In the New Testament, however, mission and call are directed 'without distinction' to Jews and Gentiles. The call to hope and to participation in the mission here becomes universal. The gospel call contains the summons to the eschatological hope of final and universal salvation. The gospel call is here identical with the reconciliation of the godless and with the instituting of believing obedience among all men. If, however, the gospel summons all men to the hope and the mission of the future of Christ, then it is possible in the light of this particular event to reflect also on the general structures of human nature. For indeed the believer does not understand himself as the adherent of a religion which is one possibility among others, but as being on the way to true humanity, to that which is appointed for all men. That is why he cannot present his truth to others as 'his' truth, but only as 'the truth'. The concrete humanity disclosed by the Christian mission must therefore enter into debate with the universal definitions of humanity in philosophic anthropology, and for its part also outline general structures of human nature, in which the future of faith shines as a foreglow of the future of all men. The gospel call is addressed to all men and promises them a universal eschatological future. It is delivered 'in all openness' and must therefore also assume open responsibility for its hope for the future of man. A Christian anthropology will always insist that a general, philosophic anthropology understand human nature in terms of history and conceive its historic character in the light of its future. What man is in body and soul, in partnership and society, in the domination of nature, is disclosed in its reality only from the direction of the life he lives. Human nature first becomes really determinable in the light of the determination to which it is on the way. The comparison with nature and with the animals, or the comparison with other men in the present and in history, does not yet bring out what man's nature is, but only the comparison with the future possibilities which are disclosed to him from the direction of his life, from his *intentio vitalis*. Man has no subsistence in himself, but is always on the way towards something and realizes himself in the light of some expected future whole. Man's nature is not sub-sistent, but ex-sistent. It becomes intelligible not on the ground of an underlying *substantia hominis*, but only from the perspectives in which he lives and which derive from his direction in body and soul. Man is 'open towards the world' only in that he is directionally open to determination and to the future. In other words, the *natura hominis* first emerges from the *forma foturae vitae*. It is in process of developing in the light of this 'shape of the future life', and its success in attaining to it is staked on history. Hoping in the promised new creation by God, man here stands in *statu nascendi*, in the process of his being brought into being by the calling, coaxing, compelling word of God.

A missionary exposition of the biblical witness to man's history and mission will therefore agree with the existentialist interpretation in enquiring about the new possibilities which entered the world through Israel and Christianity. It, too, will have to present these past existential possibilities as possibilities of the present understanding of existence. But it will interpret these existential possibilities as new possibilities for man's future. It will not interpret the phenomena of past history on the ground of the possibilities of human existence, but on the contrary, it will interpret the new possibilities of human existence on the basis of the 'phenomenon' of God's promise and mission and of the 'phenomenon' of the resurrection and future of Christ. It will be able to open up to man today new possibilities, prospects and goals through its exposition of that event which paves the way for the eschatological future. To this end it is necessary to take man in his selfhood along with, and not in abstraction from, the present constellation of human society, in order to subject the whole of present human reality to the future of Christ and to the possibilities of the mission that moves towards his future. The whole present situation must be understood in all its historic possibilities and tasks in the light of the future of the truth.

(c) The Historifying of the World in the Christian Mission

It is not mere *theoria*, in its investigation of the divine nature of the world as a cosmos, but it is only missionary practice, involved in history and bent on transformation, that first renders the world questionable in a historic way. Its questions are concerned not with the unity and wholeness of the world and with the order in a chaotic reality, but with the transformability of the world. For the eschatological hope shows that which is possible and transformable in the world to be meaningful, and the practical mission embraces that which is now within the bounds of possibility in the world. The theory of world-transforming, future-seeking missionary practice does not search for eternal orders in the existing reality of the world, but for possibilities that exist in the world in the direction of the promised future. The call to obedient moulding of the world would have no object, if this world were immutable. The God who calls and promises would not be God, if he were not the God and Lord of that reality into which his mission leads, and if he could not create real, objective possibilities for his mission. Thus the transforming mission requires in practice a certain *Weltanschauung*, a confidence in the world and a hope for the world. It seeks for that which is really, objectively possible in this world, in order to grasp it and realize it in the direction of the promised future of the righteousness, the life and the kingdom of God. Hence it regards the world as an open process in which the salvation and destruction, the righteousness and annihilation of the world are at stake. To the eye of mission, not only man is open to the future, full of all kinds of possibilities, but the world, too, is a vast container full of future and of boundless possibilities for good and for evil. Thus it will continually strive to understand world reality in terms of history on the basis of the future that is in prospect it will therefore not search, like the Greeks, for the nature of history and for the enduring in the midst of change, but on the contrary for the history of nature and for the possibilities of changing the enduring. It does not ask about the hidden wholeness by which this world, as it is, is intrinsically held together, but about the future *totum* in which everything that is here in flux and threatened by annihilation will be complete and whole. The totality of the world is not here seen as a self-dependent cosmos of nature, but as the goal of a world history which can be understood only in dynamic terms. The world thus appears as a correlate of hope. Hope alone really takes into account the 'earnest expectation of the creature' for its freedom and truth. The obedience that comes of hope and mission forms the bridge between that which is promised and hoped for and the real possibilities of the reality of the world. The call and mission of the 'God of hope' suffer man no longer to live amid surrounding nature, and no longer in the world as his home, but compel him to exist within the horizon of history. This horizon fills him with hopeful expectation, and at the same time requires of him responsibility and decision for the world of history.

The man who is summoned by the divine promise to the transforming of the world falls outside the sphere of Greek cosmic thinking. He has here 'no continuing city', for he seeks 'the coming city of God'. His thinking will therefore not subject reality to a metaphysical transfiguration in the light of the absolute. His thinking is not directed towards mediating between the multiplicity of beings and the one, eternal being.

His experience of reality as history in all its possibilities of change is not, on the other hand, conditioned by whether history can be made at the whim of the human subject. For him, the world can be changed by the God of his hope, and to that extent also by the obedience to which this hope moves him. The subject of the transformation of the world is for him therefore the Spirit of the divine hope. Thus his experience and his expectation of history is both opened up and tied down by the future promises of the God he believes. World reality therefore does not become for him, as in the modern age, the material for the exercise of duty or of technique. His thinking about the world does not adjust things to the human subject in his imagined needs or his arbitrary prescriptions. His thinking adjusts things to the coming messianic reconciliation. Hence both his world-transforming obedience and also his knowledge of, and reflection on, the world stand 'in the service of reconciliation'. He does not take being, as it is, and link it in metaphysical transfiguration with the absolute. He does not link things, as in technical positivism, with his own subjectivity. Rather, he adjusts being to the universal, rectifying future of God. Thus his mediation serves the reconciliation of the world with God. His understanding does not consist in contemplating things in search of their eternal ground. His understanding does not consist in practical reflections on the technical appropriation of things. His understanding consists in the fact that in sympathy with the misery of being he anticipates the redeeming future of being and so lays the foundation of its reconciliation, justification and stability. Thus Luther declares: '... a strange language and a new grammar. ... For his will is, because we are to be new men, that we should also have other and new thoughts, minds and understandings and not regard anything in the light of reason, as it is for the world, but as it is before his eyes, and take our cue from the future, invisible, new nature for which we have to hope and which is to come after this wretched and miserable nature. ...'[113] In this sense it is also possible to take up the concluding words of T. W. Adorno's *Minima Moralia, Reflexionen aus dem beschädigten Leben*: 'Philosophy, in the only form in which it can still be responsibly upheld in face of despair, would be the attempt to regard all things as they present themselves from the standpoint of redemption. Knowledge has no light save that which shines upon the world from the standpoint of redemption: all else exhausts itself in imitation and remains a piece of technique. Perspectives must be created in which the world looks changed and alien and reveals its cracks and flaws in much the same way as it will one day lie destitute and disfigured in Messiah's light. To attain such perspectives without arbitrariness or force, entirely out of sensitiveness towards things – that alone is the aim of thought.'[114]

In the field of the investigation and presentation of past history this would surely mean that the historian's aim can be neither a theodicy of history nor a self-justification of past or present history. The glory and misery of past ages do not require to contain the justification of God or of reason. Nor can they abide the positivistic dictatorship of present subjectivity. Rather, the 'earnest

---

113 *WA* 34, II, pp. 480f.
114 T. W. Adorno, *Minima Moralia*, 1962, pp. 333f.

expectation of the creature' seeks to come to expression in them
and to attain the prospect of freedom from the powers of annihilation. In the messianic light of hopeful reason the historian must
make manifest something of the 'cracks and flaws' in which past
ages earnestly expect their justification and redemption. Then there
is solidarity between the present and the ages of the past, and a certain contemporaneousness both in the historic alienation and in the
eschatological hope. This solidarity is the true core of similarity, on
the ground of which an analogical understanding becomes possible
over the ages. Only this solidarity in the earnest expectation which
groans under the tyranny of the negative and hopes for liberating
truth, takes historic account of history and performs among the
dead shades of history the service of reconciliation.

(d) The Tradition of the Eschatological Hope

Traditions are alive and binding, current and familiar, where,
and as long as, they are taken as a matter of course and as such
link fathers to sons in the course of the generations and provide
continuity in time. Where this unquestioned familiarity and trust-
worthiness becomes problematical, an essential element in the
traditions is already lost. Where reflection sets in and subjects the
traditions to critical questioning, with the result that the accepting
or rejecting of them becomes a conscious act, the traditions lose
their propitious force. It is not only when traditions are discarded,
but as soon as they are made consciously problematical, that the
character of tradition attaching to human life is abrogated. For the
traditions are then no longer the guardian and the subject of present
thought and action, but become the object of a kind of thinking
which in itself and in its roots is traditionless. They can then be
rejected by the revolutionary, or restored by the conservative. But
from the day that we speak 'conservatively' of tradition, we no
longer have it.[115]

The beginning and principle of the modern break with tradition
is the basing of assured knowledge upon the method of doubt since
Descartes. If the Western mind even up to modern times had been
fashioned by the texts of our traditions, now – beginning already
in the late Middle Ages – it develops from its own experience and

---

115 G. Krüger, *Freiheit und Weltverwaltung*, 1958, p. 223.

the methodical assimilation of its own experience. This is for Pascal the point at which the paths of theology and modern science divide: 'When we perceive this distinction clearly, then we shall lament the blindness of those who in physics allow the validity of tradition alone, instead of reason and experiment; we shall be horrified at the error of those who in theology put the arguments of reason in place of the tradition of scripture and the fathers.'[116] Theology can teach only on the ground of the word given in tradition. But in the realms in which truth is now sought in order to be the ground for human social life, traditions become the epitome of inherited prejudice – *idola*, as Francis Bacon put it. The place of the historic forms of the spirit which live in and from traditions is taken by the abstract self-assurance of the human mind: *sum cogitans*. For the human mind the *res gestae* of history are in principle no different from the *res extensae* of nature. Hence in the field of history, too, it will seek for methodically assured, critical historical experience. This non-historic concept of reason makes traditions into accidental truths of history and finds eternal truths of reason in itself. Past history, for it, is no longer called to mind in traditions, but is 'historicized' by means of scientific reflection. 'The historical relation to the past not only presupposes that the past in question is past, but has manifestly also itself the effect of confirming and sealing this non-actuality of what has been. Historical science has taken the place of tradition, and this means that it occupies that place and makes it ... impossible really to follow the ancients and thus to stand in their tradition.'[117] The historical reason is then well able to abolish traditions, but not to create new traditions. 'The pressure which tradition pre-consciously exercises on our behaviour is progressively diminished in history as a result of the advancing *science* of history.'[118]

This historical relation to history undoubtedly brings in the first instance a break with tradition whose full effects are as yet immeasurable. It is in the first instance a break with quite definite traditions of the West. The question is, however, whether we have here also a break with tradition as a characteristic feature of human

---

116 Pascal, *Œuvres* II, p. 133, quoted by J. Pieper, *Über den Begriff der Tradition*, 1957, pp. 10f.

117 G. Krüger, *op. cit.*, p. 216.

118 M. Scheler, *Die Stellung des Menschen im Kosmos*, 1927, p. 31. Cf. H. G. Gadamer's criticism in *Wahrheit und Methode*, 1960, p. 267.

existence as such. But with the beginning of the modern age the emancipated reason undergoes new experiences of history, which collapse the received edifice of tradition. The voyages of discovery to America and China bring a knowledge of peoples who cannot be classified in the classical Christian genealogies of mankind. The reason that has become sure of itself in reflection makes discoveries in nature, which antiquate the old world-picture. And finally, it produces in society new economic forms and modes of civil behaviour which destroy the traditional Christian ethic. The French revolution merely executed the testament of the Enlightenment, and was in its turn continued by the industrial revolution and our scientific technical civilization. The support of traditions and authorities, and the connection with the truth as received from of old, which was so essential for the traditional consciousness, have here no longer any constitutive significance. The place of quotation is taken by successful experiment and successful technique. As producer and consumer and in the traffic of everyday, man is the same everywhere, apart from his varied origins. Sciences and techniques thus become independent and indifferent towards the distinctions in historic origin.

These prospects have always led traditionalists, from romanticism to the present day, to paint nihilistic nightmare visions. 'If tradition were really entirely destroyed, if nihilism were complete, if there were nothing at all that still endures, the self-evident, common foundations of our human nature could no longer be appealed to at all.'[119] The self-existent world resolves itself into mere subjective views of the world, so that in the end nothing more would exist in itself and nihilism would be the end of the story.[120] Then we should find ourselves in an age 'which is overtaken by the loss of tradition altogether, as a disastrous fate, as a disappearance of support and security, as a vanishing of all that is enduring, as a suffocating emptiness and annihilation in the realm of spiritual life.'[121] This romantico-nihilistic argument for the necessary readmittance of

---

119 G. Krüger, *op. cit.*, p. 123, cf. also p. 94: '*It is due only to our inconsistency that we are still alive* – to the fact that we have not really silenced all tradition. But our life is becoming visibly more historic, more frail, more catastrophic. We are on the way towards the *radical impossibility of a meaningful, common life.* ... Under these circumstances it is vitally necessary to break with this paradoxical, restless epoch and *once more assent to tradition in principle.*'
120 R. Geiselmann, *Die heilige Schrift und die Tradition*, 1962, p. 81.
121 G. Ebeling, *Die Geschichtlichkeit der Kirche*, 1954, p. 36.

traditions, however, is not able to integrate the 'modern age' into the traditions of history, because it does not grasp the new kind of progressiveness in modern ways of thinking and working. It has regard only to the loss of origin, but does not see the gain of a possible future in the breakaway of the modern age. Hence the realm of history, which the modern age with its visions has opened up before us, must be restricted again by building dams against the overflowing charms of 'historicality'. This, however, is to make traditions a matter of form. It is not known what traditions are adequate to master the modern age's break with tradition, but it is recommended that thought and action should be marked by tradition as such.

The real mainspring of the emancipation of reason and society from the guardianship and dominance of tradition, however, lies in the eschatological, messianic passion of the 'modern age'. The 'old' was left behind, because the presence and prospect of the 'new' appeared to have come within reach. The hopes that had been bottled up by the old, classical traditions put forth new life and began to influence the future of history. 'Secularization' was no apostasy from the traditions and ordinances of Christianity, but meant in the first instance that Christian expectations were realized in the field of world history, and then that Christian hopes were outstripped by millenarianism. It was not that the 'horrors of history' overflowed the dams of the old traditions and their bonds, but that the hope that had been domesticated within them broke loose. The place of the accustomed traditions was taken by a messianism of varying content which set to work upon history. Hence we cannot set out from the assumption that the 'modern age' is really only a different age, and that the modern historical consciousness is nothing radically new, but merely constitutes a new element within that which has always determined man's attitude to the past.[122] We shall discover the element of tradition in historical thinking only when we take seriously the revolutionary and indeed millenarian elements in it. Hence we must ask: *which* traditions were broken down in the upheaval of the modern age, and what was the concept of tradition against which the revolutionary *ratio* has been able to prevail? What is the tradition of the Christian proclamation, and what does it demand of man? To this

---

122 H. G. Gadamer, *op. cit.*, p. 267.

end we shall have to make a very clear distinction between the ancient classical concepts of tradition and the Christian concept of tradition, both in regard to their different content and in regard to their different modes of procedure.

The anti-revolutionary, anti-rationalistic concept of tradition in romanticism everywhere shows itself to be a restoration of the ancient classical way of thinking about tradition. Here religion and participation in the divine are bound to the tradition that has existed unbrokenly from of old.

In the ancient way of thinking about tradition,[123] the passing ages are regenerated in the times of sacred festival. Each festival and each liturgical season brings once more the time of the beginning, the time of the origin, *in principio*. The profane time of the passing and flowing away of life is halted as it were in the times of festival. The world's time renews itself each year. With each new year it acquires its original holiness again. In the times of festival men periodically become contemporaries of the gods once more and live with them again as in the first beginning. History here means falling away from the origin and degenerating from the holiness of the beginning. Tradition means the bringing back of fallen life to the primaeval age and the first origin. Primaeval mythical events are here presented. For this conception of tradition, 'truth' is always bound up with 'the old'. The prerogative of tradition is expressed in the phrase 'from of old'.

Similarly, it is held in the classical way of thinking about tradition that the *antiqui*, the ancestors, the *majores*, οἱ παλαιοί οἱ ἀρχαῖοι, are 'near the beginning, prime, original'. Authority belongs to those 'who are better than we and dwell nearer to the gods'.[124] 'The ancients know the truth. If we discovered it, then we should have no need to trouble ourselves about the opinions of men.[125] 'A gift of the gods was brought down by a certain Prometheus in the bright glow of fire, and the ancients, who are better than we and dwell nearer to the gods, have transmitted this account to us.'[126] In the phrase πάλαι λέγεται, 'it was said of old', lies the proof of the truth. 'It has been handed down from those of early and primaeval

---

123 On this section cf. the studies of M. Eliade.
124 Plato, *Philebus* 16 c 5–9.
125 Plato, *Phaedrus* 274 c 1, quoted in J. Pieper, *op. cit.*, p. 22.
126 *Ibid.*

days that the divine surrounds the whole of nature.'[127] Thus, in this conception of tradition, revelation stands at the beginning. It is from this that the ancients who were before us and lived near the beginning acquire their authority. It is also this which gives the old its proved excellence and which requires its preservation. ἀνάμνησις brings to mind again the true, original nature of things. Tradition is then μνημοσύνη, keeping in memory. To this there belongs the mythical idea of the θησαυρός, the treasure of original truth which we have to guard, and of the *depositum*, the gift entrusted to our charge.

On the quotation from Plato's *Philebus*, Joseph Pieper observes: 'The most important thing about his remark, however, ... is that this remark of Plato's is largely identical with the answer which Christian theology for its part supplies to the same question. When we consider the elements of Plato's characterization of the ancients ... then we must surely ask whether there is any essential difference between Plato's description of the ancients on the one hand, and on the other hand the definition which Christian theology applies to the writer who is "inspired" in the strict sense of the word, the author of the holy book. The decisive feature in common is manifestly that both are conceived as the first recipients of a θεῖος λόγος, of a divine word.'[128] Yet is this really the case? Is the content of Greek tradition 'from of old' the same as the content of Christian proclamation? Are the apostles to be equated with Plato's primaeval ancients? Can the risen Christ be proclaimed in terms of the classical concept of tradition?

What tradition is, and how it comes about, all depends on the matter to be transmitted. The matter determines the tradition even to the extent of determining the process of tradition. In Israel it was not a primaeval mythical event that was handed down and called to mind *in principio*, but a historic event, and one which determined the nature, the life, the path and the history of Israel. When Israel remembered the 'days of ancient times' and the 'years of former generations', it was thinking not of a mythical, but of a historic past – namely, of the events of the exodus and the occupation of Canaan brought about by Yahweh. The men of old are not the primaeval ancients, but are the generation which received Yahweh's promises and experienced in history his acts of faithfulness. 'God' is here

---

127 Aristotle, *Metaphysics* 1074 b 1.
128 J. Pieper, *op. cit.*, pp. 23f.

not the 'primaeval one', but the God of Abraham, of Isaac and of Jacob. The content of the tradition that was constitutive for Israel was the great acts and promises of Yahweh which are unique and unrepeatable, and therefore at the same time also determine Israel's future. Because Yahweh's acts of promise in the past open up a future to Israel – and a historic future at that – therefore the Israelite conception of tradition is not only to be interpreted in terms of retrospective questions, but at the same time also looks forwards. Yahweh's faithfulness in the past is recalled and recounted to the 'children of the, future' (Ps. 78.6), in order that the 'people which shall be created' may praise Yahweh and recognize his lordship for their own present and future (Ps. 71.18; 102.18). Thus it is in order to awake confidence in Yahweh's faithfulness in the future that the historic experiences of former times are recounted. Yahweh's faithfulness is not a doctrine that has been received from the ancients of an early mythical age, but a history which must be recounted and can be expected. Thus this tradition comes from history, and its goal is future history. Now this goal itself can change in the course of Israel's history. Its aim is in the first instance the confident knowledge: such is Yahweh. As he was, so he will be. This implies an element of repetition, yet not of return to a mythical beginning, but of repetition in historic faithfulness and constancy. If the great prophets introduce the change which G. von Rad has called the 'eschatologizing of the way of thinking in terms of history', then we can find in them also an *eschatologizing of the way of thinking in terms of tradition*. Prophecy, too, proceeds to construct a tradition. Yet it is a construction of tradition in a new form. As the herald of history, the prophetic word rouses men to wait on history. 'I will bind up the testimony and seal the law among my disciples. And I will wait upon the Lord, that hideth his face from the house of Jacob, and I will look for him' (Isa. 8.16f.). The prophetic word is preserved and written down 'that it may be a witness for the time to come for ever and ever' (Isa. 30.8).[129]

To sum up the development of the conception of tradition in Israel, it may be said that as compared with the classical concept of tradition it has a strikingly firm, non-mythological reference to past and future history. Promises are transmitted, events of God's faithfulness are recounted, all pointing to the future which has not as

---

129 Cf. H. W. Wolff, *EvTh* 20, 1960, p. 220 n. 3.

yet come about. In this conception of tradition the future which is announced and promised increasingly dominates the present. This tradition of promise turns our eyes not towards some primaeval, original event, but towards the future and finally towards an *eschaton* of fulfilment. We do not drift through history with our backs to the future and our gaze returning ever and again to the origin, but we stride confidently towards the promised future. It is not the primaeval ancients who are near the truth and dwell nearer to the gods, but it is to future generations that the promises are given, in order that they may see the fulfilment.

As compared with the classical conception of tradition, the Christian tradition of Christian proclamation has in the first instance this much in common with the Old Testament understanding of tradition, (1) that here, too, the tradition is bound to, and binds us to, a unique, unrepeatable, historic event – namely, the raising of the crucified Christ – and (2) that the process of tradition is necessitated and motivated by the future horizon projected ahead of us 'once and for all' by this event. Neither the once-for-all event of the resurrection of Christ nor the eschatological future horizon of the Christian mission can be grasped by the ancient or the classical concept of tradition. Hence every formulation of the Christian tradition according to the standard of classical tradition – and since the days of anti-revolutionary romanticism such formulations have often arisen in Catholicism and frequently in Protestantism – is wrong. Both the Christian *tradendum*, or object to be transmitted, and the process of tradition in the Christian proclamation break these bounds.

(*a*) Christian proclamation begins with the raising of the crucified Christ and his exaltation to be Lord of the coming world of God. 'Christian tradition has existed ever since Easter, ever since there was a confession to the risen Lord and with it a Church.'[130] It can thus be said that Christian tradition was proclamation, and was transmitted in proclamation. Here we have a highly important distinction from the understanding of tradition both in classical and in rabbinical life. What distinguishes the proclamation of the gospel from tradition as it is there understood? Christian proclamation is not a tradition of wisdom and truth in doctrinal principles. Nor is it a tradition of ways and means of living according to the

---

130 E. Dinkler, *RGG*[3] VI, col. 971.

law. It is the announcing, revealing and publishing of an eschatological event.[131] It reveals the risen Christ's lordship over the world,
and sets men free for the coming salvation in faith and hope. As
proclamation, the gospel has to do with the advent of the coming lordship of Christ, and is itself an element in this advent. It
reveals the presence of the coming Lord. This is why in Paul the
proclamation of the gospel and the mission to the heathen in all
the world are not derived from those who were there at the start
and dwelt temporally nearer the divine, in other words from the
apostles, but directly from the exalted Lord (Gal. 1.2ff.; I Cor. 9.1;
I Cor. 15.8), in whose service he therefore knows himself to stand.
His gospel accordingly does not seek to transmit doctrinal statements by or about Jesus, but to disclose the presence of the exalted
and coming Lord. The process of the proclamation of the gospel,
or of the revelation of this mystery, is therefore not described in
the terminology of rabbinical tradition, but by new words like
κηρύσσειν and εὐαγγελίζεσθαι. 'Paul is no Christian rabbi who differs
from the teachers of late Judaism merely in regard to the content of
his tradition. Nor does his understanding of tradition result from
a mere spiritual refraction of the Jewish principle of tradition, but
it is something specifically new among the conceptions of tradition
in the first century of our era.'[132] It is in understanding his gospel
as the eschatological revelation of the exalted Lord that he gains
the freedom which, as has often been observed, he exercises over
against the primitive Christian tradition in doctrinal, confessional
and parenetic statements. This freedom does not, however, mean
indifference on the ground of personal inspiration. On the contrary,
the gospel which reveals the presence of the coming Lord requires a
continuity with the earthly Jesus which has constantly to be discovered anew – for otherwise a myth about some new heavenly being
threatens to take the place of Jesus of Nazareth and the gospel turns
into gnostic talk of revelation. Historical knowledge of Jesus must
therefore be constitutive for the faith which awaits the presence and
future of God in the name of Jesus. It is this identity of the exalted
Christ with the earthly Jesus which in the gospel and in the process
of its proclamation links the eschatological with the historical, the

---

131 K. Wegenast, *Das Verständnis der Tradition bei Paulus und den Deutero-paulinen*, 1961, p. 44.

132 K. Wegenast, *Das Verständnis der Tradition bei Paulus und den Deutero-paulinen*, 1961, p. 164.

apocalypse of the future with the memory of the past. Hence for his gospel, which, as he says, he received not from men but from the Lord, Paul requires the confirmation, and indeed the identification, of the Jerusalem tradition of Jesus and Easter (cf. I Cor. 15.3ff.). Not even this acceptance of historic tradition by Paul justifies the assumption that he understood his gospel one way or another in a traditional sense as tradition, but it plainly has christological grounds and thus means something new as compared with his inherited conceptions of tradition or with those existing elsewhere. The continuity of the risen Christ with the earthly, crucified Jesus necessitates the acceptance of the historic witness about him and about what happened to him. The Easter experiences of the raising of Jesus and his exaltation to be the coming Lord, however, shatter any straightforward continuity in the transmitting of the past. The fundamental process for the gospel is not a continuity which has to be created in the history of transience and which results in endurance through the course of time, but it is the raising of the crucified and dead Christ to eschatological life. The fundamental process is not the surmounting of transience by something that is abiding, but it is the anticipation of the goal of history in the raising of the dead, it is the advent of the coming salvation, life, freedom and righteousness in the resurrection of Christ. It is understandable that this process which the gospel reveals must have a formative and determinative influence extending even to the process of the proclamation. The process of Christian proclamation thus implies a Christology. It cannot be deduced from the general problem of history and continuance. The gospel would be put to the service of foreign gods and ideologies if in the sense of modern romanticism it were expected to provide anti-revolutionary, Western continuity and a rescue for decaying civilizations.

(b) If the Christ event affects the process of proclamation even to the extent of determining the way it takes place, what is then the nature of this process? Christian proclamation shares with the Old Testament tradition its orientation towards the future. Tradition is forward-moving mission, into the new situation of the promised future. The new aspect in the Christian proclamation, however, lies in its universal mission to all peoples. Christian 'tradition' is mission that moves forwards and outwards. It does not ride the line of the generations from father to son, but spreads outwards to all men. It is not through birth, but through rebirth, that faith is propagated. And once again this is brought out with special clarity in the apostolate of Paul. Ever since his 'conversion' he has known that he is sent to the Gentile mission (Gal. 1.15f.; Rom. 1.5). Proclaiming the gospel and going to the heathen coincide for him.[133] Both have their ground in his understanding of Christ. The God who has raised Jesus from the dead is the God who justifies the godless. Just as all men are subject to sin, so Christ is the reconciliation of the whole world with God. In raising him from the dead, God has appointed Jesus to be Lord and Reconciler of the whole world. In the light of his understanding of the lordship of Christ as being universal and coming without any preconditions, we can understand both the universally inclusive character of his proclamation and also its peculiar, eschatologically anticipatory orientation. There is a certain Old Testament framework here: in the establishment of the obedience of faith among the heathen there already begins to happen what according to the Old Testament promise is to happen only after Israel has received salvation. There begins the eschatological glorification of God in the world. The fact that the order of the Israelite hope is thus changed, however, has its ground in the work and message of Jesus himself: the divine sovereignty which has drawn near becomes a live issue in his gracious communion with publicans and sinners, it arrives in the raising of the crucified one and becomes effectual in the justification of the godless. What is the result of this for the process of Christian proclamation, for its 'tradition'? Christian tradition is then not to be understood as a handing on of something that has to be preserved, but as an event which summons the dead and the godless to life. The process and procedure of the Christian proclamation is the calling of the heathen, the justification of the godless, the rebirth to a living hope. This is a creative event happening to what is vain, forsaken, lost, godless and dead. It can therefore be designated as a *nova creatio ex nihilo*, whose continuity lies solely in the guaranteed faithfulness of God. This continuity is to be seen not so much in the unbroken succession of bishops, but rather in the *'homuncio quispiam e pulvere emersus'*, the 'little man of some kind fashioned from dust', as Calvin calls the presbyter.[134] The goal

---

133 F. Hahn, *Das Verständnis der Mission im Neuen Testament*, 1964, pp. 8off. (ET by F. Clarke: Mission in the New Testament, 1965, pp. 95ff.).

134 O. Noordmans, *Das Evangelium des Geistes*, 1960, p. 162, with a quotation from Calvin, *Institutio* IV.3.1.

towards which Christian proclamation pro-ceeds in the process of the justification and calling of the godless, provides another clear indication of this: it is not the finally perfect triumph of that which has been approved and preserved unbroken from of old, but the 'raising of the dead', and the triumph of the resurrection life over death to the glory of the all-embracing lordship of God.

Christian tradition is proclamation of the gospel in justification of the godless. It is made possible and necessary by the raising of the crucified Christ, inasmuch as the hope of the universal future of salvation for the world is therein guaranteed. It is thus identical with eschatological mission.

What significance does the above mentioned 'break with trad-ition' on the part of the modern age have for this tradition of Christian proclamation? What breaks down as a result of the emancipation of reason and society is the ancient and classical tradition in which the tradition of Christian proclamation was also embedded until modern times. Hence the tradition of Christian proclamation either collapses along with these traditions of the religious age, and is understood along with them as being now only a romanticist glorification of the past, or else it radically frees itself from this understanding of tradition. The Christian mission has no cause to enter into an alliance with romanticist nihilism against the revolutionary progressiveness of the modern age and to present its own tradition as a haven of traditionalism for a contemporary world now grown uncertain and weary of hoping. The emanci-pation of reason and society from their historic past is upheld in modern times by a millenarian enthusiasm. To this present world Christian proclamation must give an answer concerning its hope in the future of the crucified one (I Peter 3.15) by conveying to the godless justification and hope of resurrection. We cannot turn our backs on the open horizons of modern history and return to perpetual orders and everlasting traditions, but we must take these horizons up into the eschatological horizon of the resurrection and thereby disclose to modern history its true historic character.

V

Exodus Church

Observations on the Eschatological
Understanding of Christianity[1]
in Modern Society

1. Modern Society and the Cult of the Absolute

We now raise in a concluding chapter the question of the concrete form assumed by a live eschatological hope in modern society. Here the tide 'Exodus Church' is meant to focus attention on the reality of Christianity as that of the 'pilgrim people of God', as described in the Epistle to the Hebrews: 'Let us go forth therefore unto him without the camp, bearing his reproach. For here we have no continuing city, but we seek one to come' (Heb. 13.13f.). What does this mean for the social shape of Christianity in 'modern society' and for the task it has there to fulfil in the field of social ethics?

In this context we cannot speak simply of the 'Church' and mean by this the organized institution with all its public functions. Nor can we speak merely of the 'congregation' and thereby mean the company that gathers around the word and sacrament in divine service. We must follow the Reformation, and especially Luther, in speaking of 'Christianity' as represented in 'church' and 'congregation' and in Christians at their worldly callings. According to the Schmalkald Articles of 1537 'by the grace of God alone our churches are thus illumined and nurtured by the pure word and the right use of the sacrament and the knowledge of all kinds of stations and

---

1 'Christianity' in this chapter is used not in the usual English sense of 'the Christian faith', but means the whole body of believers in every aspect of their life. – *Translator.*

right works (*cognitione vocationum et verorum operum*)'.[2] This means, however, that Christianity must also continually present itself, and does de facto always present itself, in the weekday obedience and the worldly callings of Christians and in their social roles. This third insight on the part of the Reformation has receded unduly into the background in the movements of the modern evangelical church towards reform. From the standpoint of sociology this is understandable, for modern, emancipated society seems to offer no chance for peculiarly Christian obedience. But from the standpoint of theology it is unintelligible, for it is precisely at this point, at which it is a question of the Christian's call in our social callings, that the decision falls as to whether Christians can become an accommodating group, or whether their existence within the horizon of eschatological hope makes them resist accommodation and their presence has something peculiar to say to the world.

When in this context we speak of *modern society*, we mean the society that has established itself with the rise of the modern industrial system. We mean, in negative terms, not the state and not the family, but that sphere of public life which is governed by the conduct of business, by production, consumption and commerce – the realm in which the relations between man and man are determined by the things of the business world and by the business-like approach. Naturally, this social intercourse in terms of things and functions extends far into the spheres of political and family life, yet the reduction of all relationships to terms of things and facts does not have its origin in these spheres, but in the advancing possibilities of scientific, technical civilization. The society which is dominated by the modernity and progressiveness of this civilization has the peculiar characteristic of considering itself to be neutral towards matters of religion and questions of value and consequently emancipating itself from the control of history and tradition, whereby it also withdraws itself from the influence of religions and religious bodies. What are the social roles in which this modern society places faith, the congregation, the Church and finally Christianity?

Ever since classical times our Western societies had always had a definite, clearly outlined concept of religion. Since the rise of 'bourgeois society' and the 'system of needs' in industrial society,

---

2 *Die Bekenntnisschriften der evangelisch-lutherischen Kirche*, 2nd ed. 1952, p. 411.

however, modern society has emancipated itself from the classical concept of religion. The Christian Church can consequently no longer present itself to this society as the religion of society.

From the days of the Emperor Constantine until far into the nineteenth century the Christian Church, despite many reformations and despite many changes in society, had possessed a clearly defined character in public social life. The place and function of the Church were firmly established. Everyone knew what was to be expected of it. It was the rise of industrial society that first destroyed the old harmony between *ecclesia* and *societas*. From the standpoint of the history of religion, the former public claims of the Christian Church had their source in the public claims of the Roman state religion.[3] Beginning with Constantine, and then consolidated in the legislation of the Emperors Theodosius and Justinian, the Christian religion took over the social place of the old Roman state religion. The Christian religion became the *cultus publicus*. It became the protector and preserver of the *sacra publica*. According to the classical view of society, it is the supreme duty (*finis principalis*) of human *societas* to see that the gods are given their due veneration. Peace and prosperity depend on the favour of the national gods. The public wellbeing and enduring stability of the state depend on the blessing of the gods of the state. 'Religion' here has the sense of pious veneration for the powers in which the divine eternity of Rome is represented, and without which there can be no such thing as 'Rome' in the fullest sense.[4] When the Christian faith took the place of the Roman state religion, then of course the public state sacrifices ceased, yet their place was taken by the Christian prayers of intercession for the state and the emperor. Thus the Christian faith became the 'religion of society'. It fulfilled the supreme end of state and society. Hence titles of the Roman emperor-priest were transferred to the pope. State and society understood the Christian faith as their religion.

In the Protestant humanism of Melanchthon, too, without which the Reformation would presumably not have got moving, princes and magistrates were appealed to in the interests of society's religious duty as understood in the classical sense.[5] The highest goal

---

3 Cf. K. G. Steck, *Kirche und Öffentlichkeit* (Theologische Existenz heute, NF 76), 1960.

4 W. Kamlah, *Christentum und Geschichtlichkeit*, 2nd ed. 1951, p. 134.

5 R. Nürnberger, *Kirche und weltliche Obrigkeit bei Ph. Melanchthon*, 1937.

of society is the true veneration of God – so it is affirmed here also, though here to be sure in expounding the First Commandment in terms of the *usus politicus*. What is 'true veneration of God'? The answer was: the carrying out of the Reformation as a restoration of the true religion of the one God. A government which seeks to be religiously neutral and to restrict itself to the cultivation of peace and worldly wellbeing, was here, too, with the help of arguments from the classical view of society, represented as lunacy.

Thus the understanding of society in classical and pre-modern times always in itself implies a religious goal of society. Here we have the source of the images which are still employed today to describe the role of the Church in society: 'crown of society', 'healing centre of society', 'inner principle of the life of society'.[6] In its worship and its moral precepts, the human and material is raised to the plane of the divine, and the Eternal and Absolute stoops to the plane of earthly society. When today the 'loss of a centre' is lamented in a disintegrating society, then that is an expression of the longing for such a pre-modern, religious integration of men combined to form a society.

Modern society, however, acquired its nature and its power precisely through its emancipation from this religious centre. Hegel was one of the first to perceive the rise of the modern, emancipated society which destroys all the forces of tradition, and to analyse it, following the British national economy, as a 'system of needs'.[7] It is the society which emancipates itself in principle from all presuppositions in regard to the orders of human life as laid down by historic tradition, and finds its content solely in the constant and consistent nature of man's needs as an individual and their satisfaction by means of collective and divided labour. According to its own principles, it contains nothing but what is demanded by 'the ascertaining of *needs* and the satisfying of the *individual* by means of his labour and by means of the labour and satisfaction of the needs of *all the rest*'.[8] That means that this society, in contradistinction to all previous societies, restricts itself to such social relationships as

---

6 Thus Pius XII: 'As the life principle of human society the Church, drawing upon the deep sources of her inner riches, must extend her influence to every realm of human existence' ('Grundsätze der sozialen Neuordnung', originally broadcast in German, published in *Acta Apostolicae Sedis* 41, 1949, p. 462).

7 *Rechtsphilosophie*, §§188ff. Cf. J. Ritter, *Hegel und die französische Revolution*, 1957, pp. 36ff.

8 *Rechtsphilosophie*, §188.

bind individuals together in the satisfying of their needs by means of their divided labour. Men here associate themselves with each other necessarily only as the bearers of needs, as producers and consumers. Everything else that makes up a man's life – culture, religion, tradition, nationality, morals, etc. – is excluded from the necessary social relationships and left to each man's individual freedom. Social intercourse thus becomes abstract. It emancipates itself from the particular historic conditions from which we have come, and becomes irresistibly universal. 'The non-historic nature of society is its historic essence.'[9] The future and the progressiveness of this society bear no relation to its origin. This, however, makes social intercourse totalitarian. 'Need and labour, when exalted to such universality, thus form in themselves a tremendous system of community and mutual interdependence, a self-propelled system of dead creatures.'[10] 'Civil society ... is the tremendous power which seizes hold of man and demands from him that he work for it and make it the medium of all he is and does.'[11] Hegel sees in this the approach of the age of universal conformity, of mediocrity and the mass. But he differs from modern critics of culture in seeing also the other side of the dialectic. The general objectification of social intercourse in the modern world, and its reduction to a question of things and facts and functions, bring at the same time also a tremendous disburdening of the individual. Beyond the system of needs and of division of labour in civil society, the 'private person whose aim is his own interest'[12] necessarily becomes the citizen (citoyen) and subject of this society. The individual becomes the 'son of civil society'.[13] Thus the revolutionary idea of the freedom of all men which goes back to the French revolution comes to its own with the birth of modern working society from the industrial revolution. The latter is its necessary presupposition and the condition on which it becomes possible. 'It is precisely through its abstract, non-historic character that society gives free rein to subjectivity's right to particularity.'[14] In its emancipation from history, society finds its ground in the satisfying of needs through labour,

9 J. Ritter, op. cit., p. 41.
10 Jenenser Realphilosophie, ed. J. Hoffmeister, 1931, p. 239.
11 Rechtsphilosophie, §238 Zus.
12 Rechtsphilosophie, §187.
13 Rechtsphilosophie, §238.
14 J. Ritter, op. cit., p. 43.

and thus gives man free rein in all his other life relationships. All other life relationships are relieved of social necessity. It is only from the standpoint of need that we can speak of 'the concrete conception that is called man'.[15] In civil society man counts because he is man, and not because he is a Jew, Catholic, Protestant, German or Italian.[16] The modern subjectivity in which we today experience ourselves as individual and personal human beings, is a result of the disburdening of social intercourse by reducing it to terms of practical affairs.

Hegel's analyses thus make it clear that the age of increasing mass organization is at the same time dialectically also the age of individuality, and that the age of socialization at the same time became the age of free associations. Any critic of culture who attacks the age of mass movement, of objectification, of materialism, etc., and sees the salvation of culture in the regaining of personal humanity, accordingly fails to recognize the nature of modern society, and is himself moving within that dualism of subjectivity and objectification which is the basic principle of this very society.

'The society of conformity and mediocrity supplies the individual with a tremendous diversity of individual variations in matters of taste, evaluation and opinion, so that the most motley assortment of informal groupings weaves its way across the constant bureaucratic uniformity of the major organizations, and the age of a new uniformity of conduct is yet at the same time also the age of a peculiar unfolding of the things of the soul and the intellect.'[17] 'Conformity and individualization both have their roots in the fact that the social ties and relationships are becoming slacker and less binding, that ... while the mobility of industrial society facilitates accommodation to the model of uniform social behaviour, it is equally favourable towards the opportunity of reserving the private and personal sphere from social conventions and constraints.'[18] Hence the dilemma does not by any means consist in the fact that man, who is conditioned and claimed by modern social intercourse only in functions which only partially involve him, now encounters his fellow man only as a 'representative' of socially predetermined

---

15 *Rechtsphilosophie*, §190.
16 *Rechtsphilosophie*, §209.
17 A. Gehlen, 'Mensch trotz Masse. Der Einzelne in der Umwälzung der Gesellschaft', in *Wort und Wahrheit* 7/1952, pp. 579ff.
18 H. Schelsky, *Die skeptische Generation* (1957), 1963, p. 297.

roles. Rather, it lies in the question how man can endure, and even live in, the state of being torn between the rational objectification of his social life on the one hand and the free and infinitely variable subjectivity conferred on him on the other.

There arises also the further question whether everything that is thus dismissed from modern society's abstract bond of association, and left to the freedom of the subject, does not become functionless and necessarily fall to pieces, when it can no longer acquire any social relevance. This applies especially to religion and culture. Once bereft of social necessity, they threaten to become the playthings of inclination and the tumbling ground for varieties of unreal and ineffective beliefs and opinions.

Hegel, however, was able to recognize the movement of the spirit as acting precisely *in* this torn and divided state of objectification and subjectivity. It is not the romanticist's self-preservation from this tornness and his way of shutting himself off from it, but only self-emptying surrender to it that proves the power of the spirit.

What became of the Christian Church in its social significance as a result of this development in society? The result of this development was, that it lost the character of *cultus publicus* to which it had been accustomed for more than a thousand years. It became something which in its religious form it never was and which, moreover, from the theological standpoint of the New Testament it can never seek to be – namely, a *cultus privatus*. The cult of the Absolute is no longer necessary for the integration of this society. The Absolute is now sought and experienced only in our liberated, socially disburdened subjectivity. 'Religion' ceases to be a public, social duty and becomes a voluntary, private activity. 'Religion' in the course of the nineteenth century becomes the religiosity of the individual, private, inward, edifying. By giving free rein to religion and leaving it to the free unfolding of the personality in complete freedom of religious choice, modern society as a modern 'society of needs' emancipates itself from religious needs. This process was furthered by many revivalist and pietist movements within Christianity. There prevailed within it a pious individualism, which for its own part was romanticist in form and withdrew itself from the material entanglements of society. The Church thus slipped over into the modern *cultus privatus* and produced in theology and pastoral care a corresponding self-consciousness as a haven of intimacy and guardian of personality for a race that had developed a materialist society and felt itself not at home there. This certainly means that the Christian religion is dismissed from the integrating centre of modern society and relieved of its duty of having to represent the highest goal of society, but that is not by any means the end of it. On the contrary, society can assign to it other roles in which it is expected to be effective. While it is true that in these roles it has nothing more to do with the *finis principalis* of modern society, yet it can exercise dialectical functions of disburdening for the men who have to live in this society. This allows it infinite possibilities of variation, but they are the possibilities of self-propulsion and self-development within the bounds of the general social stagnation imposed on the Christian faith as being a matter of religion.

2. Religion as the Cult of the New Subjectivity

The first and most important role in which industrial society expects religion as the cult of the absolute to be effective, is undoubtedly that of providing the transcendental determination of the new, liberated subjectivity. The primary conception of religion in modern society assigns to religion the saving and preserving of personal, individual and private humanity. It is expected that the materialist industrial system must be supplied from 'somewhere or other' with a human foundation which is a match for this world of things that has swollen to such incalculable dimensions.[19] It is expected that 'the man of our day may once again become a vessel to receive the influx of transcendent forces'.[20] 'Islands of meaning' are sought in a world which, while it is certainly not meaningless, is nevertheless non-human. 'If it were possible ... to establish a humanity which was a match for the secondary system, then this secondary system would have restored to it the foundation which it has itself destroyed'.[21] Now as a result of the fact that all things and conditions can be manufactured by dint of technique and organization, the divine in the sense of the transcendent has disappeared from the world of nature, of history and of society. The world has become the material for technical reshaping by man. The gods of cosmological

---

19 H. Freyer, *Theorie des gegenwärtigen Zeitalters*, 1958, p. 243.
20 G. Mackenrodt, *Sinn und Ausdruck der sozialen Formenwelt*, 1952, p. 200.
21 H. Freyer, *op. cit.*, p. 244.

metaphysics are dead. The world no longer offers man a home and an abiding shelter.

Its place has been taken, however, by a 'metaphysic of subject-hood',[22] in which the world of objects is submitted to planning by the human subject. To be sure, the gods of cosmological metaphysics are dead. Rationalization has 'disenchanted' the world (Max Weber), and secularization has stripped it of gods. Yet this was possible only on the basis of the modern metaphysic of 'subjecthood'. The latter has disclosed to man his freedom over against the world as the possible work of his hands. In so doing it demands of man at the same time also responsibility for the world. The world is surrendered to the reason of man.

The saving of man's humanity in the midst of industrial culture is therefore seen in the cultivation and development of this metaphysic of 'subjecthood'. H. Schelsky advises us to reflect once more on an 'inwardness', on a 'spirituality' beyond the relationships that have been reduced to materialist terms. He sees this possibility of metaphysics in our technical scientific civilization as consisting in the mental attitude of 'constant metaphysical reflection'. 'This is the form in which the thinking subject constantly seeks to hasten ahead of his own objectification, and thus assures himself of his superiority to his own world process.'[23] 'However much of his reflection the subject may surrender to the mechanical process, he becomes only the richer thereby, because ever new powers of reflection flow to him from an inexhaustible and boundless inwardness.'[24] By means of this mental attitude of constant metaphysical reflection the subject manifestly reflects itself out of all its objectifications,

---

22 M. Heidegger, *Holzwege*, 1957, p. 237.

23 H. Schelsky, *Der Mensch in der wissenschaftlichen Zivilisation*, 1961, p. 45. Much the same already in 'Ist Dauerreflexion institutionalisierbar?', *Zeitschrift für evangelische Ethik* 1, 1957, pp. 135ff. and *Ortsbestimmung der deutschen Soziologie*, 1959, p. 105: 'It could be asked, what is the universal standpoint of man in our society, at which he stands beyond social constraint and thus over against society? The answer would be: the reflecting subjectivity which does not conclusively expand itself in any social fulfilment or does not suffer itself to be conclusively determined by any social force, the moral conscience which does not find in social reality any conclusive criterion for confirming or rejecting it, the religious faith which does not feel itself ultimately bound to any social reality, not even its own.'

24 G. Günther, 'Seele und Maschine', *Augenblick*, vol. 3/1, p. 16, quoted according to H. Schelsky, *Der Mensch in der wissenschaftlichen Zivilisation*, p. 45.

takes them back again into itself and its freedom, and gains from its own self an endless influx of new possibilities. All social realities are traced back again in the detachment of reflection and irony to the possibilities arising in the subject. It is plain that behind this advice for the saving of humanity there stands the concept of tran- scendental subjectivity found in early idealism and developed by Fichte. It is a question, however, whether this 'reflective philosophy of transcendental subjectivity', as it was already called by Hegel, does not separate the human subject in a romanticist way from relationships that have become petrified, abandon these latter to themselves in their meaningless, inhuman petrification, and seek to save the individual in himself.

In harmony with this romanticist metaphysic of subjecthood and this mental attitude of constant metaphysical reflection there then appears also the theology which takes the cult of the absolute that has become of no significance in our social relationships and culti- vates it as the transcendent background of modern existence. This is the theology which presents itself as 'doctrine of the faith' and finds the place of faith in the transcendental subjectivity of man. It is a theology of existence, for which 'existence' is the relation of man to himself as this emerges in the 'total reflection of man on himself'. This theology assigns faith its home in that subjectivity and spontaneity of man which is non-objectifiable, incalculable and cannot be grasped in his social roles. It localizes faith in that ethical reality which is determined by man's decisions and encounters, but not by the pattern of social behaviour and the self-contained rational laws of the economic circumstances in which he lives. In 'total reflection' on himself man becomes aware of a selfhood that is unmistakably his own, and in so doing he distinguishes himself from the modern world and sees it as a secularized world which is nothing but world. The self which here emerges, however, becomes the 'pure receiving' of the transcendent and divine.[25] The modern metaphysic of subjecthood with its consequences in the seculari- zation of the world must then be represented as a consequence of Christian faith, and Christian faith must be represented as the truth behind this metaphysic of subjecthood. Faith as the 'total reflection

---

25 F. Gogarten, *Der Mensch zwischen Gott und Welt*, 1952, pp. 181ff. ('Die Personalität. Christlicher Glaube als Reflexion'), esp. pp. 187ff. Here the distinc- tion must not be overlooked which Gogarten makes between idealist subjectivity and the personal character of faith.

of man on himself' (F. Gogarten) then presents itself as the truth and radicalization of the mental attitude of 'constant metaphysical reflection' (H. Schelsky). In this theology, Christian faith is transcendent as compared with everything meaningful that can be socially communicated. It is not provable – but its unprovability, so it is said, is its very strength – and consequently it is also irrefutable. Unbelief alone, as being the contrary decision, is its enemy. As constant reflection it cannot be given institutional form,[26] but is itself transcendence as compared with social institutions. It has primarily to do with the 'self-understanding' of the human subject in the technical world. It sees 'God' not as a God of the world or of history or of society, but rather as the unconditioned in the conditional, the beyond in the things of this world, the transcendent in the present.[27] The adjectives which are used to describe the peculiarity of this religious experience are all contrapuntally related to the objectified, material, non-human relationships of industrial society. It is a 'thing that happens or comes about again and again from instance to instance', an 'unexpectable event', 'openness for God's encounters' and readiness for self-transformation in God's encounters. Faith is the receiving of one's self from God. This places it in a position of radical loneliness, makes it 'individual', de-secularizes it in the midst of an organized society. This gives man the freedom 'to stride confidently through darkness and perplexity, and to venture and bear the responsibility for action in the loneliness of his own decision.'[28]

In the 'inability to make anything of the world of objects',[29] which is typical of existentialism, the Christian ethic is then reduced to the 'ethical demand'[30] to accept one's self and take responsibility

---

26 H. Schelsky, 'Ist Dauerreflexion institutionalisierbar?', op. cit.

27 R. Bultmann, 'Der Gottesgedanke und der moderne Mensch', ZTK 60, 1963, pp. 335ff. (ET by R. W. Funk in World Come of Age, ed. R. Gregor Smith, 1967, pp. 256ff.). Pp. 346f. (cf. ET p. 271): 'The concept of God which can find, can seek and find as a possibility of encounter, the unconditioned in the conditional, the beyond in the things of this world, the transcendent in the present, is the only one that is possible for modern man.'

28 R. Bultmann, Glauben und Verstehen III, 1960, p. 196.

29 E. Topitsch, 'Zur Soziologie des Existentialismus', in Sozialphilosophie zwischen Ideologie und Wissenschaft, 1962, p. 86.

30 K. Løgstrup, Die ethische Forderung, 1959, p. 232: 'There are no absolute, revealed demands, but only the one radical demand.' Cf. W. D. Marsch, 'Glauben und Handeln in der "technisch-organisatorischen Daseinsverfassung"', Monatsschrift für Pastoraltheologie 52, 1963, pp. 269ff.

for the world in general. But it is no longer able to give any pertinent ethical instructions for the ordering of social and political life. Christian love accordingly quits the realm of justice and of the social order. It is a thing that comes about in each several event of spontaneous co-humanity, in the I-thou relationship which is immediate and not objectively mediated. Justice, social order and political righteousness, once they have been rendered so void, must then be understood positivistically as pure organization, as matters of power and law. The 'neighbour' who is the object of Christian love is then the man who encounters us at any given moment, our fellow man in his selfhood, but he can no longer be known, respected and loved in his juridical person and his social role. Our 'neighbour' comes on the scene only in personal encounter, but not in his social reality. It is the man within arm's length or at our door who is our neighbour, but not man as he appears in the social and juridical order, in questions of aid to under-developed countries and race relationships, in social callings, roles and claims.

If, however, we now examine the dialectic of modern, dualistic society, it transpires that the metaphysic of subjecthood and the cult of the absolute in transcendental subjectivity are due to specific, modern social conditions. The 'category of individuality' is itself a product of society.[31] 'A personality is an institution in the form of a *single* instance.'[32] It is not as if modern, scientific technical civilization were only an objectification of the infinitely creative subjectivity of man. The modern subjectivity of man for its part also owes its freedom, its spontaneity and its infinite inward resources to the ways in which modern, materialist society relieves it of its burdens. A cultural saving of humanity by means of the cultivating and deepening of our subjectivity in constant metaphysical reflection, in art and religion, is romanticist escapism as long as social conditions are not changed. Where conditions are left as they are, this cultural saving of humanity automatically acquires the function of stabilizing these social conditions in their non-humanity, by providing the inner life of the heart with the things which it has to do without in the outside world.

A theology which settles faith in the 'existence' of the individual, in the sphere of his personal, immediate encounters and decisions, is a theology which from the viewpoint of sociological science

31 T. W. Adorno, *Sociologica* II, 1962, p. 100.
32 A. Gehlen, *Die Seele im technischen Zeitalter*, 1957, p. 118.

stands at the very place to which society has banished the *cultus privatus* in order to emancipate itself from it. This faith is in the literal sense socially irrelevant, because it stands in the social no-man's-land of the unburdening of the individual – that is, in a realm which materialist society has already left free to human individuality in any case. The existential decision of faith consequently hardly provokes the counterdecision of unbelief any longer, and is consequently not really engaged in a struggle with unbelief at all. What it actually does constantly provoke is its own non-committal character – namely, the now notorious attitude of refusing to take sides in disputes of faith that have long become socially irrelevant, the well known 'religion void of decision'.[33] The battle of faith is socially no longer necessary, since for social life it has no longer any binding character. The transcendent point of reference which is constituted by man's free subjectivity, and in view of which this proclamation addresses him, has already been socially neutralized before it can be made use of in the decision of faith. Hence this theology threatens to become a religious ideology of romanticist subjectivity, a religion within the sphere of the individuality that has been relieved of all social obligations. Nor does the appeal of its existential radicality prevent the Christian faith, as thus understood, being brought to social stagnation.

3. Religion as the Cult of Co-humanity

The second role in which modern society expects religion to be effectual consists in the transcendent determination of co-humanity as community.

Since the beginning of the industrial revolution the romanticist reaction to the conditions that seem to rob man of his humanity has clung again and again and in ever new forms to the idea of

---

33 Cf. H. O. Wölber's essay in sociographical evaluation, *Religion ohne Entscheidung*, 1959; also E. Stammler, *Protestanten ohne Kirche*, 1960. H. J. Iwand had as early as 1929 pointed to the self-abrogation of decision in the appeal for decision (*Deutsche Literaturzeitung*, 1929, col. 1228): 'The very act of confronting man with the decision also frees him from it, since thanks to this theoretical manipulation the decision for or against God stands like two possibilities before man, and in the end we have once more to resort after all to the urge of imperatives and the enticement of value-judgments, in order to prise man out of the neutrality in which we have artificially placed him.'

'community'. 'True human community is ... that between man and man; i.e. the community in which man finds himself by surrendering himself to the other.'[34] This form of complete disclosure of personal co-humanity in 'community' is then always set in a polemical relation to its antithesis in the concept of 'society': society is an artificial, arbitrary, organized arrangement between men for practical and businesslike purposes. The dominant factor in it is not the will to be a self, but rational purposefulness, convention, and a businesslike approach. It is pseudo-community and brings man merely to a semblance of existence. This kind of society is seen above all in the 'large industrial cities',[35] whereas community apparently means the idyllically conceived village conditions of pre-modern times.

This idea of community, which is held to promise the saving of culture from technical civilization, has its origins in the age of romanticism. It is found in the *Communist Manifesto* as the revolution's goal in a 'free association of free individuals', in that community of the future in which division of labour is abolished, in which man is the highest being in man's eyes, in which each can exchange 'love only for love, trust only for trust', which accordingly produces 'man with his all-embracing and profound mind' as its constant reality, in which the total loss of man in capitalist society is followed by the total recovery of man. This idea of community is found in detail in Ferdinand Tönnies[36] and through him inspired the youth movement and a vast array of community movements at the beginning of the twentieth century. It is found again in the sociologically critical and nationalistically revolutionary idea of the *community of nations*. Hans Freyer canvassed it in 1931 in his 'revolution from the right': industrial society, which rests on

---

34 So the very apt definition by R. Bultmann, 'Formen menschlicher Gemeinschaft', in *Glauben und Verstehen* II, p. 263 (ET: 'Forms of Human Community', *Essays Philosophical and Theological*, p. 292). In this essay Bultmann is apparently taking up the ideas of community advanced by F. Tönnies.

35 Cf. Rilke's poem quoted by R. Bultmann, *op. cit.*, p. 266 (ET p. 295):
The cities play us false ...
Nought of that broader real activity
That is your prize as further you mature
Occurs in them. ...
For a criticism of the romanticist criticism of large cities, cf. H. P. Bahrdt, *Die moderne Grosstadt* (Rowohlts deutsche Enzyklopädie 127), 1961.

36 F. Tönnies, *Gemeinschaft und Gesellschaft*, 8th ed., 1935 (reprinted 1963).

nothing but the calculation of matter and forces, has no solid foundation but hangs in the air. It has no vitality to give it a peculiar rationality of its own. It is a *perpetuum mobile* of material values, work quotas, commercial media and mass needs. The revolution from the left has come to a dead end in the trade unions and has already been merged into this industrial world. But where can man assert himself as man over against this system? 'The people is the antagonist of industrial society. The principle of the people against the principle of industrial society.' This story has not been played out, but the tide is rising in the village against the industrial city. Primaeval forces of history, decrees of the Absolute, flow to man once more from the people. In the life of the people, in the man of the people and in the people's state the 'earth' rises up as it were against the abstract, non-committed, inhuman system of industrial society. Man and earth find each other again. The principle of industrial society has become invalid, because there are men who are no longer defined by their social interest. The 'human emancipation of man', which Marx expected from the revolution of the proletariat, is here expected from the life of the people. 'Man is free when he is free amid his people, and this too in his *Lebensraum*. Man is free when he stands within a common will which carries on its history on its own responsibility.'

The idea of community, however, is found with socially critical and socially therapeutic intent also in Roman Catholic social teaching. According to *Mater et Magistra*, it is essential 'that the above mentioned groups present the form and substance of a true community, that is, that the individual members be considered and treated as persons and encouraged to take an active part in the ordering of their lives'. It follows that 'whether the enterprise is private or public ... every effort should be made that the enterprise should be a community of persons'. 'In such a way, a precious contribution to the formation of a world community can be made, a community in which all members are ... conscious of their own duties and rights, working on a basis of equality for the bringing about of the universal common good.'[37]

Yet in the course of the progress of industrial society this ideal of community has also lost its revolutionary power and been integrated into the industrial system. It has often been shown by sociologists

---

37 *Mater et Magistra*: ET as Appendix to E. Guerry, *The Social Teaching of the Church*, 1961, pp. 185, 190, 208.

and critics of culture that modern society is not by any means on the way to becoming a totalitarian ant-hill in which any and every activity is governed by rules and regulations, but that this age of conformity and indiscrimination, of vast organizations and economic combines, is at the same time also the age of small, specialist groups and of confidential relationships within narrow circles. The super-organizations and macro-structures in the economic world are answered by the micro-structures of informal groups, bodies, societies, clubs, etc. 'Here the isolation of man is checked, and these informal, unofficial institutions are manifestly acquiring increasing significance.'[38] Alexis de Tocqueville had already observed this in the American democracy of last century: 'The first thing that strikes the observation is an innumerable multitude of men, all equal and alike, incessantly endeavouring to procure the petty and paltry pleasures with which they glut their lives. Each of them, living apart, is a stranger to the fate of all the rest; his children and his private friends constitute to him the whole of mankind. As for the rest of his fellow citizens, he is close to them, but he does not see them; he touches them, but he does not feel them; he exists only in himself and for himself alone.'[39]

In the circle of his friends, his intimate colleagues, neighbours and children, at home, in the choral society and the local community, it is as if man's businesslike and inhuman outlook were suddenly blown away. Here he is 'man', and is permitted to be man. Perhaps, as A. Gehlen thinks, all these small ties provided by the intimate groups combine to form a sort of cement for the total structure of society: 'the vast utility organizations and the individuals pitchforked into them do not by any means constitute the whole of the truth.'

Amongst and between these small groups the church, too, as a congregation can have its place and carry out its function. Here it can become a refuge of the inner life, away from the supposedly 'soulless' world of affairs. Conditions in the vast industrial complexes transcend our intellectual range and can no longer be mastered morally. Responsibility for the 'modern world' as such can no longer be expected of anyone. The objectifications of our scientific technical civilization have reached such vast and independent

---

38 A. Gehlen, *op. cit.*, p. 74.
39 *Democracy in America* II, Book IV, ch. 6; ET by Henry Reeve, rev. ed., 1948, vol. II, p. 318 (World's Classics ed., 1946, p. 579).

proportions that they can no longer be re-subjectified. In return, they leave free a small-scale world, in which responsibilities can be assumed in limited communities. Here Christian congregations can offer human warmth and nearness, neighbourliness and homeliness, 'community' which is not utilitarian but nevertheless meaningful, and therefore also readily called 'genuine'. The 'authentic' living relationship between man and man is here not channelled and pre-scribed in patterns of behaviour appropriate to rational ends. Here life can still be carried on in freedom, it evades formal fashioning and cannot be subjected to constraint and control. Here, instead of complying with the technically necessary rules of conduct in society, it is possible in human spontaneity to produce ever new solutions in ever new combinations of circumstances. In this non-preformed, unorganized, unofficial realm which is left free by industrial society, clubs, sects and communities of every kind thrive. Here Christian communities and groups, too, can become a kind of Noah's ark for men in their social estrangement. They become islands of genuine co-humanity and of authentic life in the rough sea of circumstances which the ordinary man can after all do nothing to alter. Here the Christian churches can become rallying points for integration, and would thereby no doubt have fulfilled a social aim. For the subliminal existence of free communities of this kind is for modern society a most salutary thing, because in the domestic economy of the human soul it can provide a certain compensation for the economic and technical forces of destruction. This, however, does nothing to alter the stem reality of the loss of the human in 'society'. It provides only a dialectical compensation and a disburdening of the soul, so that in the alternating rhythm of the private and the public, of community and society, man can endure his official existence today.

It is entirely in harmony with the social significance of 'com-munity' in this sense when Christian theology of various persuasions sets over against the officially and legally constituted Church the 'true Church' as a 'genuine community', as a 'spiritual church' (R. Sohm), as a 'spiritual community of persons' (E. Brunner), as a 'community of faith' and a 'community in the transcendent' (R. Bultmann), and sees its existence as 'pure happening' and 'unex-pectable event' in spontaneous encounters and decisions. The Church is then an absolutely non-worldly phenomenon, which in contrast to the planned society of rational ends is described in the categories of 'community'. It is then still possible to speak of the Christian Church's responsibility for 'the world', but hardly any longer of Christian callings in the world. Yet it must surely be plainly recognized that such a church, as 'community' and as 'pure event', cannot disturb the official doings of this society and certainly cannot alter them – indeed, it is hardly any longer even a real partner for the social institutions. True, the man who feels estranged and longs for authentic life and genuine community, for the spontaneity of experience, of making his own decisions and of transforming himself, is here met halfway and has his longing fulfilled. But it is fulfilled only in the personal esoteric realm in which he is relieved of social demands. Nor does the emphasis on the genuineness and authenticity of life in this personal community prevent Christian neighbourliness being brought to a social standstill.

4. Religion as the Cult of the Institution

A third role in which modern society expects the Christian religion to be effectual is, surprisingly enough, once more to be found today in the institution with all it involves in the way of officialdom and official claims. Modern, post-Enlightenment culture is again more ready to play into the hands of religion than was the pre-industrial age of the eighteenth century.[40] After the hectic decades of the founding of industrialism, in which vast social dislocations made men uncertain in their behaviour and therefore also susceptible to ideologies, industrial society in the highly industrialized countries is today again consolidating itself in new institutions. These new institutions, however, in turn relieve man of the permanent pressure of decision to which he is subjected in times of uncertainty. Stereotyped patterns of conduct give them an enduring, stable and communal character. Thus there emerges a new store of unvarying customs and axioms in work, consumption and intercourse. A 'beneficial unquestioningness' (A. Gehlen) spreads over life. This kind of institutionalizing of official, social life certainly springs from the permanent need of security on the part of man, who experiences himself in history as a 'creature at risk' and therefore also endeavours to resolve the historic character of his history

---

40 A. Gehlen, *op. cit.*, p. 43.

into a cosmos of institutions. This institutionalizing, however, brings about at the same time by an inner logic the suspension of the question of meaning. 'The conduct which they have made habitual has the purely factual result of suspending the question of meaning. To raise the question of meaning is either to have taken a wrong turning, or else to express consciously or unconsciously a need for something other than the existing institutions.'[41] For the latter are of course relationships and modes of conduct which must be axiomatic and unquestioning. The institutionalizing of public life is today producing in the highly industrialized countries an everywhere perceptible disappearance of ideologies. Ideologies as a means of giving purpose and meaning to life are becoming increasingly superfluous. This makes them optional and private. To be sure, it can be said even in the midst of institutionalized life: 'In the world of machines and "cultural values", of great alleviations, life slips away like water between the fingers that would hold it because it is the highest of goods. From out of unfathomable depths it is called in question.'[42] Yet this questionableness is experienced only in the free realm of subjectivity, and no longer in terms of the uncertainty and the historic character of the outside world.

This tendency towards the institutionalization of public life, together with the fact that the arts and sciences have become so abstract that only caricatures of them can now find ideological application, has had the result that the Christian religion is left alone and unopposed on the field of ideologies and world views in the highly industrialized countries. Darwinism in its day was bitterly contested by the Christian confessions. Modern genetics, however, whose technical consequences are beyond our range of vision, does not disturb them, because this is a science of boundless complexity and cannot turn into a speculative opponent. Christian theology accordingly finds itself in a position of being able to assert a neodogmatism and say things which can neither be proved nor contested on the ground of real experience, and which can therefore acquire for modern man a binding character which he hardly even disputes any more. On the contrary, he is prepared to delegate to the Church as an institution the problems regarding his own believing decision, and to leave the detailed questions to

---

41 A. Gehlen, *Urmensch und Spätkultur*, 1956, p. 69.
42 *Ibid.*, p. 289.

theological specialists. If, however, the vital decisions are delegated to the Church as an institution, which is then regarded as an institute for relieving us of them, then the result is the religious attitude of an institutionalized non-committal outlook. 'Christianity' becomes a social axiom and is relegated to one's environment. Matters of theological dispute are regarded as 'confessional witch-hunting' and banished from public life. On the other hand, the ecclesiastical institution of religious modes of conduct acquires a new social significance. For indeed even the modern, institutionalized consciousness retains somewhere on the margin an inkling of the horrors of history. It does not find articulate expression in normal times. Yet this subliminal consciousness of crisis results in a general, if also non-committal, recognition of the religious institutions as the guarantors of life's security in general. The institution of the churches then has the effect of being an ultimate institution overshadowing the institutional security of life, and one from which security is expected against the ultimate fears of existence. In this respect, too, Christianity has a certain social significance for modern society. Yet it is the significance of an institutionalized non-committal outlook. This, too, is religious movement within the limits of a social standstill. It is Christianity as prescribed by the social *milieu*.[43]

This brief sketch of the new social roles of religion, of the Church and of the Christian faith has made it plain that these roles – 'religion as the cult of subjectivity', 'religion as the cult of co-humanity' and 'religion as the cult of the institution' – are not the result of the goodwill or illwill of individual men, nor can they be laid to the charge of theologies determined by the history of ideas, but arise from that which, difficult as it is to grasp, must be called the socially 'axiomatic'. The theological 'self-understanding' (*Selbstverstädnis*) of the Christian faith always stands in a relation to the socially 'axiomatic' (*Selbstverständliche*). Only where we become critically aware of this connection can the symbiosis be resolved and the peculiar character of the Christian faith come to expression in conflict with the things that are socially axiomatic. If Christianity, according to the will of him in whom it believes and in whom it hopes, is to be different and to serve a different purpose, then it

---

43 C. Amery, *Die Kapitulation oder der deutsche Katholizismus heute*, 1963, p. 117, demands an 'exodus from the environment': *'Sentire cum Ecclesia* is a thing which *can require us to break with existing Catholicism.'*

must address itself to no less a task than that of breaking out of these its socially fixed roles. It must then display a kind of conduct which is not in accordance with these. That is the conflict which is imposed on every Christian and every Christian minister. If the God who called them to life should expect of them something other than what modern industrial society expects and requires of them, then Christians must venture an exodus and regard their social roles as a new Babylonian exile. Only where they appear in society as a group which is not wholly adaptable and in the case of which the modern integration of everything with everything else fails to succeed, do they enter into a conflict-laden, but fruitful partnership with this society. Only where their resistance shows them to be a group that is incapable of being assimilated or of 'making the grade', can they communicate their own hope to this society. They will then be led in this society to a constant unrest which nothing can allay or bring to accommodation and rest. Here the task of Christianity today is not so much to oppose the ideological glorification of things, but rather to resist the institutional stabilizing of things, and by 'raising the question of meaning' to make things uncertain and keep them moving and elastic in the process of history. This aim – here formulated to begin with in very general terms – is not achieved simply by stirring up 'historicality', vitality and mobility in the realms which are socially unburdened but have been brought socially to general stagnation. It is achieved precisely by breaking through this social stagnation. Hope alone keeps life – including public, social life – flowing and free.

5. Christianity within the Horizon of the Expectation of the Kingdom of God

'Christianity' has its essence and its goal not in itself and not in its own existence, but lives from something and exists for something which reaches far beyond itself. If we would grasp the secret of its existence and its modes of behaviour, we must enquire into its *mission*. If we would fathom its essence, then we must enquire into that *future* on which it sets its *hopes* and expectations. If Christianity in the new social conditions has itself lost its bearings and become uncertain, then it must once again consider why it exists and what is its aim.

It is generally recognized today that the New Testament regards the Church as the 'community of eschatological salvation', and accordingly speaks of the gathering in and sending out of the community in terms of a horizon of eschatological expectation.[44] The risen Christ calls, sends, justifies and sanctifies men, and in so doing gathers, calls and sends them into his eschatological future for the world. The risen Lord is always the Lord expected by the Church – the Lord, moreover, expected by the Church for the world and not merely for itself. Hence the Christian community does not live from itself and for itself, but from the sovereignty of the risen Lord and for the coming sovereignty of him who has conquered death and is bringing life, righteousness and the kingdom of God.

This eschatological orientation is seen in everything from which and for which the Church lives. The Church lives by the word of God, the word that is proclaimed, that pronounces and sends. This word has no magical quality in itself. 'The proclaimed word is directed towards that which in every respect *lies ahead of it.* It is open for the "future" which comes to pass in it, yet which in its *coming to pass* is recognized to be still *outstanding.*'[45] The word which creates life and calls to faith is *pro*-clamation and *pro*-nouncement. It provides no final revelation, but calls us to a path whose goal it shows in terms of promise, and whose goal can be attained only by obediently following the promise. As the promise of an eschatological and universal future, the word points beyond itself, forwards to coming events and outwards into the breadth of the world to which the promised coming events are coming. This is why all proclamation stands in the eschatological tension of which we have spoken. It is valid to the extent that it is *made* valid. It is true to the extent that it announces the future of the truth. It communicates this truth in such a way that we can *have* it only by confidently *waiting* for it and wholeheartedly *seeking* it. Thus the word has an inner transcendence in regard to its future. The word of God is itself an eschatological gift. In it the hidden future of God for the world is already present. But it is present in the form of promise and of awakened hope. The word is not itself the eschatological salvation, but acquires its eschatological relevance from the coming salvation. What is true of the Spirit

---

44 On what follows cf. O. Weber, *Grundlagen der Dogmatik* II, 1962, pp. 564ff.

45 O. Weber, *op. cit.*, p. 570.

of God is true also of the word of God: it is an earnest of things to come, and binds us to itself in order to point and direct us to greater things.

The same is true of Baptism and the Lord's Supper. Baptism, too, is 'ahead of itself'. In baptizing men into the past death of Christ, it seals men for the future of the kingdom that is being brought by the risen Christ. It is only as an eschatological Church that the baptizing Church has the right to perform the act of baptism, i.e. its title to this judicial and creative act derives from its openness towards that which is as yet only on the way towards it. Likewise, the Lord's Supper is not to be regarded in terms of mystery and cult, but eschatologically. The congregation at the Table is not in possession of the sacral presence of the Absolute, but is a waiting, expectant congregation seeking communion with the coming Lord. Thus Christianity is to be understood as the community of those who on the ground of the resurrection of Christ wait for the kingdom of God and whose life is determined by this expectation.

If, however, the Christian Church is thus oriented towards the future of the Lord, and receives itself and its own nature always only in expectation and hope from the coming of the Lord who is ahead of it, then its life and suffering, its work and action in the world and upon the world, must also be determined by the open foreland of its hopes for the world.[46] Meaningful action is always possible only within a horizon of expectation, otherwise all decisions and actions would be desperate thrusts into a void and would hang unintelligibly and meaninglessly in the air. Only when a meaningful horizon of expectation can be given articulate expression does man acquire the possibility and the freedom to expend himself, to objectify himself and to expose himself to the pain of the negative, without bewailing the accompanying risk and surrender of his free subjectivity. Only when the realization of life is, so to speak, caught up and held by a horizon of expectation, is realization (*Verwirklichung*) no longer – as for romanticist subjectivity – the forfeiting (*Verwirkung*) of possibilities and surrender of freedom, but the gaining of life.

The Christian Church which follows Christ's mission to the world is engaged also in following Christ's service of the world. It has its nature as the body of the crucified and risen Christ only

---

46 Similarly also H. D. Wendland, 'Ontologie und Eschatologie in der christlichen Soziallehre', in *Botschaft an die soziale Welt*, 1959, pp. 141ff.

where in specific acts of service it is obedient to its mission to the world. Its existence is completely bound to the fulfilling of its service. For this reason it is nothing in itself, but all that it is, it is in existing for others. It is the Church of God where it is a Church for the world. Now this modern phrase 'Church for the world' is very vague. It could of course be understood to the effect that personal faith, or the fellowship of the congregation, or the Church as an institution loyally fulfils the social roles in which modern society expects it to be useful. 'Church for the world', however, does not mean a solidarity that is bereft of ideas and a co-humanity that is void of hopes, but service of the world and work in the world as and where God wishes it and expects it. The will and expectation of God are voiced in the mission of Christ and in the apostolate. The Church lays claim to the whole of humanity in mission. This mission is not carried out within the horizon of expectation provided by the social roles which society concedes to the Church, but it takes place within its own peculiar horizon of the eschatological expectation of the coming kingdom of God, of the coming righteousness and the coming peace, of the coming freedom and dignity of man. The Christian Church has not to serve mankind in order that this world may remain what it is, or may be preserved in the state in which it is, but in order that it may transform itself and become what it is promised to be. For this reason 'Church for the world' can mean nothing else but 'Church for the kingdom of God' and the renewing of the world.[47] This means in practice that Christianity takes up mankind – or to put it concretely, the Church takes up the society with which it lives – into its own horizon of expectation of the eschatological fulfilment of justice, life, humanity and sociability, and communicates in its own decisions in history its openness and readiness for this future and its elasticity towards it.

One of the first senses in which this happens is in the missionary proclamation of the gospel, that no corner of this world should remain without God's promise of new creation through the power of the resurrection. This has nothing whatever to do with an extension of the claim to sovereignty on the part of the Church and its officials, or with an attempt to regain the old privileges accruing

---

47 This is made specially clear in the Dutch Reformed Church's *Fundamenten en Perspektiven van Belijden* of 1949 in Art. 8 and Art. 13, as also in the corresponding *Kerkorde* Art. VIII, 'Van het apostolaat der Kerk'.

from the cult of the Absolute. 'Missions perform their service today only when they infect men with hope.'[48] This kindling of live hopes that are braced for action and prepared to suffer, hopes of the kingdom of God that is coming to earth in order to transform it, is the purpose of mission. It is the task of the whole body of Christians, not merely the task of particular officials. The whole body of Christians is engaged in the apostolate of hope for the world and finds therein its essence – namely that which makes it the Church of God. It is not in itself the salvation of the world, so that the 'churchifying' of the world would mean the latter's salvation, but it serves the coming salvation of the world and is like an arrow sent out into the world to point to the future.

What missionary proclamation of the promises of God means, becomes clear from the Old Testament background of the Christian mission. In the Christian mission of hope there begins to happen already what according to Old Testament prophecies, especially in Isaiah and Deutero-Isaiah, is to happen only after Israel has received salvation and Zion is established. With the resurrection of Christ the divine lordship that has drawn near enters into the process of realization, in that Jews and Gentiles, Greeks and barbarians, bond and free, come to the obedience of faith and thereby attain to eschatological freedom and human dignity. If we take seriously this eschatological background in the prophets, against which the proclamation of the gospel by Christianity takes place, then the goal of the Christian mission must also become plain. It aims at reconciliation with God (II Cor. 5.18ff.), at forgiveness of sins and abolition of godlessness. But salvation, σωτηρία, must also be understood as *shalōm* in the Old Testament sense. This does not mean merely salvation of the soul, individual rescue from the evil world, comfort for the troubled conscience, but also the realization of the eschatological *hope of justice*, the *humanizing* of man, the *socializing* of humanity, *peace* for all creation. This 'other side'[49] of reconciliation with God has always been given too little consideration in the history of Christianity, because Christians no longer understood themselves eschatologically and left earthly eschatological anticipations to the fanatics and the sects. Yet it is only in the light of this 'other side' of reconciliation

---

48 J. C. Hoekendijk, *Mission – heute*, 1954, p. 12.
49 W. Dirks, *Frankfurter Hefte*, 1963, p. 92. Cf. W. D. Marsch, 'Glauben und Handeln', *Monatsschrift für Pastoraltheologie* 52, 1963, pp. 281f.

that Christians can get beyond the religious relief functions which they are expected to perform for a society left to itself, and can gain new impulses for the shaping of man's public, social and political life. If the Christian mission which brings to all men righteousness by faith arises against the background of the Yahwist promise to Abraham (Gen. 12.3) and of the prophetic eschatology of Isaiah (Isa. 2.1–4; 25.6–8; 45.18–25; 60.1–22), by turning these expectations into present activity, then its horizon must embrace not only the establishment of the obedience of faith among the Gentiles (Rom. 15–18), but also that which the Old Testament hopes for in terms of blessing, peace, righteousness and fulness of life (cf. Rom. 15.8–13). This is anticipated in the power of that love which unites strong and weak, bond and free, Jews and Gentiles, Greeks and barbarians in a new community.

6. The Calling of Christians in Society

The coming lordship of the risen Christ cannot be merely hoped for and awaited. This hope and expectation also sets its stamp on life, action and suffering in the history of society. Hence mission means not merely propagation of faith and hope, but also historic transformation of life. The life of the body, including also social and public life, is expected as a sacrifice in day-to-day obedience (Rom. 12.1ff.). Not to be conformed to this world does not mean merely to be transformed in oneself, but to transform in opposition and creative expectation the face of the world in the midst of which one believes, hopes and loves. The hope of the gospel has a polemic and liberating relation not only to the religions and ideologies of men, but still more to the factual, practical life of men and to the relationships in which this life is lived. It is not enough to say that the kingdom of God has to do only with persons;[50] for one thing, the righteousness and peace of the promised kingdom are terms of relationship and accordingly have to do also with the relationships of men to each other and to things, and secondly, the idea of an a-social human personality is an abstraction. The reason why Christian hope raises the 'question of meaning' in an institutionalized life is, that in fact it cannot put up with these relationships

---

50 P. Althaus, *Evangelisches Kirchenlexikon* III, col. 1931.

and sees the 'beneficial unquestioningness of life' in them only as a new form of vanity and death. It is in fact in search of 'other institutions', because it must expect true, eternal life, the true and eternal dignity of man, true and just relationships, from the coming kingdom of God. It will therefore endeavour to lead our modern institutions away from their own immanent tendency towards stabilization, will make them uncertain, historify them and open them to that elasticity which is demanded by openness towards the future for which it hopes. In practical opposition to things as they are, and in creative reshaping of them, Christian hope calls them in question and thus serves the things that are to come. With its face towards the expected new situation, it leaves the existing situation behind and seeks for opportunities of bringing history into ever better correspondence to the promised future.

The Reformers' rediscovery of the 'universal priesthood of all believers' made it plain that the call of the gospel is issued to every man. Everyone who believes and hopes is *vocatus* and has to offer his life in the service of God, in the work of his kingdom and the freedom of faith. For the Reformers, this call in our earthly life took concrete shape in our 'callings'. The mission and call of the Christian Church fan out, so to speak, into the world in our earthly callings in services, commissions and charismata towards the earth and human society. In our worldly callings, the lordship of Christ and the freedom of faith penetrate into the world as '*politia Christi regnum suum ostendentis coram hoc mundo. In his enim sanctificat corda et reprimit diabolum, et ut retineat evangelium inter homines, foris opponit regno diaboli confessionem sanctorum et in nostra imbecillitate declarat potentiam suam*' ('the city of Christ in which he displays his kingdom in face of this world. For in these he sanctifies our hearts and restrains the devil, and in order to maintain the gospel among men he openly opposes the confession of the saints to the kingdom of the devil and declares his power in our weakness.')[51] Our earthly doings, as a result of the fact that since the Reformation they have been designated 'calling', i.e. *vocatio*, *klēsis*, have acquired a new theological significance. The *vita christiana*, the Christian life, no longer consists in fleeing the world and in spiritual resignation from it, but is engaged in an

---

51 Melanchthon, *Apologie* IV, 189. The significance and consequences of this statement have been emphasized by E. Wolf in many of his writings. Cf. H. Weber, 'Der sozialethische Ansatz bei Ernst Wolf', *EvTh* 22, 1962, pp. 58off.

attack upon the world and a calling in the world.[52] Only, as the Reformation progressed, it became obscure who actually appoints these earthly callings. The revolutionary social movements of the fanatics caused the Reformers more and more to neglect the call to discipleship in the freedom of faith and to concentrate on the concern for order and its preservation. The new idea of calling was transformed into a doctrine of the two kingdoms, in which it was more and more a matter of adjusting questions of competence as between the divine institutions of church, state, business and home.[53] Thus the Confession of Augsburg XVI declares that the gospel brings no new laws and ordinances into the world, and does not dissolve the political and economic orders, '*sed maxime postulat conservare tamquam ordinationes Dei et in talibus ordinationibus exercere charitatem*' ('but chiefly demands both the preservation of the ordinances of God and the exercise of charity in all such ordinances'). Our callings do remain the several places of love's orderly service to the world for God, only it remains an open question whence this 'severalness' derives. The vocational ethics of Protestantism has usually had recourse at this point to the postulate of a second source of revelation. The 'call' which leads to specific callings was derived by Karl Holl from the coinciding of two voices – the 'inner call' heard in the gospel, and the voice which comes to us from things themselves and their necessity. Like Bismarck, he would hear in each given historic situation itself 'the footsteps of the God who strides through history'.[54] Thus the call to our calling comes from both voices together – from the call of God in the gospel of Christ, and from the call of the God of history. At this point Emil Brunner put 'providence': 'The "place" of the action, the here and now ... is the place given by God.'[55] Others have sought amid the multiplicity of possibilities in society and history certain ever-existing, abiding basic orders such as marriage and family, church and state, on the basis of which the many possibilities are to be elucidated as variations. They have called

52 D. Bonhoeffer, *Ethik*, 1949, p. 198 (ET by N. Horton Smith: *Ethics*, 1955, p. 223).
53 E. Wolf, 'Schöpferische Nachfolge', in *Spannungsfelder der evangelisehen Soziallehre*, 1960, p. 36.
54 K. Holl, 'Die Geschichte des Wortes Beruf', *Gesammelte Aufsätze* III, 1928, p. 219.
55 E. Brunner, *Das Gebot und die Ordnungen*, 1932, p. 184 (ET by O. Wyon: *The Divine Imperative*, 1937, p. 200).

these basic orders God's 'created orders', his 'preserving orders', his 'mandates', his 'fundamental ordinances', or institutions given along with human nature. This means, however, that the place of call is always seen as something given or predetermined, so that the call and the obedience of faith can then bring about only inner modifications in the *exercitium caritatis* at this place and in the predetermined vocational role. Typical of this are the lines in Johann Heermann's hymn: 'Grant me with diligence to do thy will, thy statutes in my station to fulfil.' But the 'station' or the vocational role in society had then in terms of a theology of creation or of history to be accepted as fate and seen as God-given. The *'conservare'* of the Confession of Augsburg XVI has always set a highly conservative stamp on the vocational ethics of Protestantism. And since, once left to themselves, forces of a totally different kind took over the determination of the place and role of men's 'callings', the call and mission of the believer was able to work itself out only in the inward fulfilment of his calling. The determining of the concrete historic form of the above-mentioned 'orders' was left to what happened to be the prevailing powers.

In actual fact, however, the call to discipleship of Christ is not aimed at faithful and loving fulfilment of our calling under the prescribed conditions – whatever the God or the forces prescribing them. On the contrary, this call has its own goal. It is the call to join in working for the kingdom of God that is to come. The Reformers' identification of call and 'calling' was never intended to dissolve the call in the calling, but *vice versa* to integrate and transform the 'callings' in the call. The *call* according to the New Testament is once for all, irrevocable and immutable, and has its eschatological goal in the hope to which God calls us.[56]

Our *callings*, however, are historic, changing, changeable, temporally limited, and are therefore to be shaped in the process of being accepted in terms of call, of hope and of love. The call always appears only in the singular. The callings, roles, functions and relationships which make a social claim on man, always appear in an open multiplicity. Always man stands in a multi-layered network of social dependences and claims. Our modern society is conspicuously no longer a society of stations, but is rather to be described as

---

56 Rom. 8.29; 11.29; I Cor. 1.9, 26; Phil. 3.14; Eph. 4.11f.; Heb. 6–4ff. and frequently.

a society of mobile jobs. It lays open to man a multitude of chances and demands of him elasticity, adaptability and imaginativeness.

Amid this fulness and wealth of conditions and possibilities, the decisive question for Christian existence is not whether and how man in the fluctuating variety of his social commitments, or at the point of intersection of all these roles in which he is always only partially involved, can be 'himself' and can maintain his own identity and continuity with himself.[57] The point of reference of his expressions and renunciations, his activities and sufferings, is not a transcendental Ego upon which he could and must repeatedly reflect in the midst of all his distractions. But the point of reference is his call. It is to this, and not to himself, that he seeks to live. It is this that gives him identity and continuity – even, and indeed precisely, where he expends himself in non-identity. He does not require to preserve himself by himself, in constant unity with himself, but in surrendering himself to the work of mission he is preserved by the hope inherent in that mission. The callings, roles, conditions and claims which society lays upon him are therefore not to be examined in regard to whether and how they fully occupy his own self or estrange him from himself, but in regard to whether and how far they afford possibilities for the incarnation of faith, for the concretion of hope, and for earthly, historic correspondence with the hoped-for and promised kingdom of God and of freedom. The criterion for the choice of a calling, for changing our calling, for spare-time activities, as well as for the acceptance and shaping of the process of socialization, is constituted solely by the mission of Christian hope.

The horizon of expectation within which a Christian doctrine of conduct must be developed is the eschatological horizon of expectation of the kingdom of God, of his righteousness and his peace with a new creation, of his freedom and his humanity for all men. This horizon alone, with its formative effect on the present, leads a man in missionary hope to oppose and suffer under the inadequacies of the present, brings him into conflict with the present form of society and causes him to discover the 'cross of

---

57 This humanistic question is not one that theology can take over by identifying man's personal being with his being as God's creature, so that then not only his personal being, but also his creaturely being along with it, falls outside the framework of modern functionalized society and a theology of creation endeavours to rescue man's personality from being turned into a thing.

the present' (Hegel). The place and situation in which the call to the hope of the gospel reaches men is, to be sure, the concrete *terminus a quo* of their calling, but not its *terminus ad quem*. Only Christians who no longer understand their eschatological mission as a mission for the future of the world and of man can identify their call with the existing circumstances in the social roles of their callings and be content to fit in with these. But where the call is seen within the horizon of expectation proper to it, there our believing obedience, our discipleship and our love must be understood as 'creative discipleship'[58] and 'creative love'.[59]

'Creative discipleship' cannot consist in adaptation to, or preservation of, the existing social and judicial orders, still less can it supply religious backgrounds for a given or manufactured situation. It must consist in the theoretical and practical recognition of the structure of historic process and development inherent in the situation requiring to be ordered, and thus of the potentialities and the future of that situation. Luther, too, could claim this creative freedom for Christian faith: '*Habito enim Christo facile condemnus leges, et omnia recte judicabimus, imo novos Decalogos faciemus, sicut Paulus facit per omnes Epistolas, et Petrus, maxime Christus in Euangelio.*' ('For when we have Christ we shall easily issue laws, and judge all things aright, and even make new decalogues, as Paul does in all his epistles, and Peter, and above all Christ in the Gospel.'[60]) 'Creative discipleship' of this kind in a love which institutes community, sets things right and puts them in order, becomes eschatologically possible through the Christian hope's prospects of the future of God's kingdom and of man. It alone constitutes here in our open-ended history the appropriate counterpart to that which is promised and is to come. 'Presentative eschatology' means nothing else but simply 'creative expectation',[61] hope which sets about criticizing and transforming the present because it is open towards the universal future of the kingdom.

From this standpoint the nowadays increasingly difficult problem of 'man and society' or 'freedom and estrangement', or man and work, must find a different answer from that which is possible on

---

58 A phrase of Ernst Wolf's, *op. cit.*

59 Cf. W. Pannenberg's essay, 'Zur Theologie des Rechtes', *Zeitschrift für evangelische Ethik* 7, 1963, pp. 1ff., esp. 20ff.

60 *WA* 39, I, 47, quoted according to E. Wolf, *op. cit.*, p. 35.

61 E. Bloch, *Tübinger Einleitung in die Philosophie* II, 1964, p. 176.

the ground of a humanism of transcendental subjectivity. German Idealism and the European Romanticism which followed it were the first reactions to the new conditions created by the industrial revolution. From that age and that way of thinking comes the idea that man must become identical with himself because primarily and originally he was and is so. But in order to become identical with himself and live 'in constant unity with himself' (Fichte), he must again and again collect himself from his outgoings, recall himself from the lostness of surrender, turn from his distractions to reflect upon himself and his true, eternal Ego. All acts which man allows to issue from himself acquire an independent existence according to laws of their own, and thus rob him of his freedom. His products grow too much for him, so that the creator has to bow to the things he has created. His personal relationships change into factual relationships which develop a logic of their own and stand on their own feet. In so doing they estrange man from his true nature, and he can no longer rediscover himself in them. Consequently, the individual must be able to take these factualized, independent forces which have turned into complexes of constraint and subject them once more to himself, to appropriate them again and take them back into himself, to see through them and be conscious of them.[62] This return from estrangement is apparently possible in two ways – the way of *utopia*, and the way of *irony*. Karl Marx in his early days thought it possible on the ground of his social pathology of early industrial conditions to realize the classical German educational ideal of the 'profound and thoroughly versatile man' by means of the revolutionary abolition of capitalist exploitation, class society and division of labour in a future 'association of free individuals'. In Western social philosophy today, on the other hand, we repeatedly find attempts to retain the idea of estrangement and regain the human nature of man by means of transcendental reflection. 'I no longer coincide with my social "I", even if at every moment I am together with it. I can now in my social existence be conscious of the *role*, so to speak, which I take upon me or put up with. I see

---

62 On the significance of Fichte's idea of identity for Marx's theory of estrangement and Freud's theory of the complex, cf. A. Gehlen, *Über die Geburt der Freiheit aus der Entfremdung*, Archiv für Rechts- und Sozialphilosophie, 1952, p. 350. For this paragraph cf. also H. Plessner, *Das Problem der Öffentlichkeit und die Idee der Entfremdung*, 1960, and T. Litt, *Das Bildungsideal der deutschen Klassik und die moderne Arbeitswelt*, 1955.

myself and my roles falling apart.'⁶³ By means of such reflections, the self-consciousness of man withdraws itself from the compromising, confusing, social reality. In constant reflection, in irony and in criticism of the corruptness of conditions, it regains that detachment in which it thinks to find its infinite possibilities, its freedom and superiority. Yet this subjectivity reflecting upon itself, which does not expend itself in any social task, but soars above a reality that has been degraded into an 'interplay of roles' – this faith that feels itself bound to no reality, not even its own – turn man into a 'man without attributes' in a 'world of attributes without man' (R. Musil). They rescue the humanity of man in an inner emigration in which man now only 'accompanies' his outward life, and in so doing they abandon conditions to final corruption.

When, by means of reflection, subjectivity is withdrawn from its social reality, then it loses contact with the real conditions of society and robs these conditions of the very forces which it requires in order to give them human shape and vindicate them to the future.⁶⁴ 'Whoever attempts to get rid of the antinomy by proscribing the world of organized labour as being the result of a mistake, and by recommending a withdrawal into the inward life as being the only possible way of salvation from the consequences of this mistake, abandons that world to a disorder that will sooner or later also lay hold of his artificially defined spiritual world.'⁶⁵

A thing is alive only when it contains contradiction in itself and is indeed the power of holding the contradiction within itself and enduring it.⁶⁶ It is not reflection, recalling man's own subjectivity from its social realization, that brings him back his possibilities and therewith his freedom, but this is done only by the hope which leads him to expend himself and at the same time makes him grasp continually new possibilities from the expected future. Human life must be risked if it would be won. It must expend itself if it would gain firmness and future. If, however, we are thus to risk expending

---

63 K. Jaspers, *Philosophie* II, 1932, p. 30. Similar conclusions are reached also by R. Dahrendorf, *Homo Sociologicus. Ein Versuch zur Geschichte, Bedeutung und Kritik der Kategorie der sozialen Rolle*, 1960, and 'Soziologie: 1. Der Mensch als Rollenspieler', in *Wege zur pädagogischen Anthropologie*, 1963, where Dahrendorf endeavours to come to grips with the (to my mind justified) objections of Tenbruck, Plessner, H. P. Bahrdt, A. Gehlen and Janoska-Bendl.

64 H. Plessner, *op. cit.*, p. 20.

65 T. Litt, *op. cit.*, p. 123.

66 G. W. F. Hegel, *Werke* IV, p. 67.

ourselves, then we need a horizon of expectation which makes the expending meaningful – and moreover, a horizon of expectation which embraces the realms and areas in which and for which the work we do in our self-expending is to take place. The expectation of the promised future of the kingdom of God which is coming to man and the world to set them right and create life, makes us ready to expend ourselves unrestrainedly and unreservedly in love and in the work of the reconciliation of the world with God and his future. The social institutions, roles and functions are means on the way to this self-expending. They have therefore to be shaped creatively by love, in order that men may live together in them more justly, more humanely, more peacefully, and in mutual recognition of their human dignity and freedom. They have therefore not to be taken as 'reliefs' (A. Gehlen), and not as a lapse into estrangement or as a benumbing of life, but as ways and historic forms of self-expending, and hence also as events and processes which are open towards the future of God. Creative hope historifies these conditions, and thus opposes their immanent tendencies towards stabilization – and still more the 'beneficial unquestioningness' of life in them. Faith can expend itself in the pain of love, it can make itself 'into a thing' and assume the form of a servant, because it is upheld by the assurance of hope in the resurrection of the dead. For love, we always require hope and assurance of the future, for love looks to the as yet unrealized possibilities of the other, and thus grants him freedom and allows him a future in recognition of his possibilities. In the recognition and ascription of that human dignity of which man is deemed worthy in the resurrection of the dead, creative love finds the comprehensive future in view of which it loves.

As a result of this hope in God's future, this present world becomes free in believing eyes from all attempts at self-redemption or self-production through labour, and it becomes open for loving, ministering self-expenditure in the interests of a humanizing of conditions and in the interests of the realization of justice in the light of the coming justice of God. This means, however, that the hope of resurrection must bring about a new understanding of the world. This world is not the heaven of self-realization, as it was said to be in Idealism. This world is not the hell of self-estrangement, as it is said to be in romanticist and existentialist writing. The world is not yet finished, but is understood as engaged in a history. It is therefore the world of possibilities, the world in which we can serve the future, promised truth and righteousness and peace. This is an age of diaspora, of sowing in hope, of self-surrender and sacrifice, for it is an age which stands within the horizon of a new future. Thus self-expenditure in this world, day-to-day love in hope, becomes possible and becomes human within that horizon of expectation which transcends this world. The glory of self-realization and the misery of self-estrangement alike arise from hopelessness in a world of lost horizons. To disclose to it the horizon of the future of the crucified Christ is the task of the Christian Church.

Index of Names

Adorno, T. W., 275, 299
Alt, A., 114
Althaus, P., 26, 313
Amery, C., 307
Anselm of Canterbury, 18, 31, 40, 264
Anz, W., 47
Aristotle, 3, 30, 49, 77, 128, 281
Arndt, E. M., 220
Auberlen, C. A., 60
Auerbach, E., 245
Augustine, 9, 21, 48, 49, 50, 51, 75, 219, 259, 270

Bach, R., 113
Bachmann, T., 10
Bacon, F., 221, 277
Baeck, L., 111
Bahrdt, H. P., 301, 320
Balthasar, H. U. von, 32, 34
Barth, C., 196
Barth, H., 37
Barth, K., 25, 26, 30, 31, 37 39, 40, 41, 42, 43, 44, 45, 46, 47, 63, 66, 70, 74, 109, 131, 165, 213, 264, 265, 266
Baumgärtel, F., 98
Baur, F. C., 231, 234, 235, 236
Bengel, J. A., 58, 59
Benjamin, W., 253
Bernard of Clairvaux, 49
Bertram, G., 225
Biedermann, A. E., 62
Bismarck, O. von, 315

Bloch, E., 2, 66, 79, 194, 228, 229, 248, 249, 318
Blumhardt, C., 58, 62
Böhme, J., 60
Bollnow, O. F., 163, 239
Bonald, L. G. de, 221
Bonhoeffer, D., xxxvii, 70, 158, 315
Bornkamm, G., 130, 154
Braudel, F., 230
Brunner, E., 78, 304, 315, 316
Buber, M., 83, 89, 90, 104, 105, 111, 112, 113, 115, 202
Buchenau, A., 32
Bultmann, R., 26, 30, 31, 37, 38, 45, 46, 47, 48, 51, 52, 54, 67, 146, 151, 160, 165, 171, 172, 173, 176, 198, 199, 200, 204, 243, 259, 268, 298, 301, 304
Burckhardt, J., 218, 221, 231, 256

Calvin, J., 4, 5, 6, 49, 286
Campenhausen, H. von, 160, 161
Camus, A., xxxii, 9, 10
Cocceius, J., 57
Cohen, H., 111, 245
Comte, A., 81, 221, 222, 250
Constantine, 290
Conzelmann, H., 160, 172, 204
Crusius, C. A., 58

Dahrendorf, R., 320
Dante, 17
Descartes, R., 35, 50, 221, 224, 276

THEOLOGY OF HOPE

Diels, H., 13
Dietzfelbinger, C., 131, 136
Dilthey, W., 163, 222, 224, 238,
239, 240, 241, 242, 271
Dinkler, E., 283
Dirks, W., 312
Dostoievsky, F. M., 154
Droysen, J. G., 218, 236, 237, 238,
239

Ebeling, G., 50, 55, 68, 72, 199,
236, 257, 258, 259, 278
Ebner, F., 15
Eichholz, G., 264
Eichhorn, A., 222
Eliade, M., 85, 87, 280
Ellul, J., 108

Fascher, E., 170
Feuerbach, L., 6, 60, 156, 157, 158
Fichte, J. G., 57, 217, 220, 297,
319
Fiore, J. di, 249
Fohrer, G., 112
Fontane, T., 9
Freyer, H., 222, 295, 301
Friedrich, G., 126
Fuchs, E., 45
Fulling, E., 57

Gadamer, H. G., 93, 160, 177,
240, 277, 279
Galileo, G., 221
Gehlen, A., 293, 299, 303, 305,
306, 319, 320, 321
Geiselmann, R., 278
Gerlich, F., 58
Geyer, H. G., 66, 166
Gloege, G., 29, 43
Goethe, J. W., 10, 12, 61, 233,
234, 249
Gogarten, F., 52, 236, 297
Grass, H., 160, 172
Guerry, E., 302
Günther, G., 296

Hahn, F., 286
Hamann, J. G., 4
Hauck, W. A., 59
Heermann, J., 316
Hegel, G. W. F., 13, 34, 35, 36, 40,
43, 58, 60, 65, 71, 72, 79, 153,
155, 156, 157, 158, 197, 210,
216, 217, 220, 233, 234, 239,
247, 250, 252, 264, 291, 292,
293, 294, 297, 318, 320
Heidegger, M., 45, 157, 230, 241,
242, 243, 244, 296
Heimpel, H., 216, 252
Heine, H., 154
Heraclitus, 10
Herder, J., 34, 58, 216, 220, 247,
249
Herrmann, W., 38, 39, 40, 41, 42,
45, 46, 47, 49, 51, 222
Hesiod, 13
Heuss, A., 222, 251
Hinrichs, C., 163, 218, 232, 233
Hoekendijk, J. C., 312
Hölderlin, F., xxxi, 248
Holl, K., 315
Holmström, F., 24
Hölscher, G., 112
Homer, 13
Huizinga, J., 248
Humboldt, W. von, 80, 232
Husserl, E., 177

Iwand, H. J., 77

Jaeger, W., 85
Janoska-Bendl, J., 320
Jaspers, K., 35, 36, 48, 320
Jüngel, E., 131, 139
Justinian, 290

Kähler, M., 23
Kamlah, w., 290
Kant, I., xxxviii, 32, 33, 34, 35, 36,
37, 48, 63, 67, 114, 156, 217,
220, 238, 247, 249, 250, 259,
261, 264

324

For the Brave of Heart
& Free of Spirit

KATE HUMBLE
HOME MADE

recipes from the countryside

PHOTOGRAPHY BY ANDREW MONTGOMERY

CONTENTS

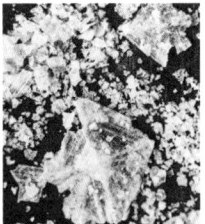

INTRODUCTION

In an age of the mass produced, of cheap imports and food grown or reared to cost as little as possible in order to meet political demand and consumer expectation, it was perhaps a foolish idea to think I could put together a book of recipes inspired by people who buck that trend. Would there still be folk out there who are producing the food we eat, and the tools we need to cook and serve it, in a sustainable way on a small scale? Would it make them a living, or would it have to be a hobby? Something they do alongside a 'proper job' that pays the mortgage?

I am delighted to tell you that there are. The twenty people whose stories I tell in this book represent many more artisans, whose dedication, hard work and belief keep their crafts and skills alive.

So, this is a book as much about people as it is about food, as one cannot exist without the other. But food there is! The recipes unashamedly suit my skill set. They are simple, easy – and often quick – to make, and don't require any specialist equipment. There are a few dishes that I suggest cooking over fire, but most of those can be cooked on a stove too. Some require the help of a food mixer, but many need little more than a few good ingredients and very little fuss.

The book is the result of a collaboration, as most of life's most enjoyable projects often are. Pooch Horsburgh, recipe guru and tester, photographer Andrew Montgomery and I all worked together for the first time on my last cookbook, *Home Cooked*. When my publisher asked for another book, the first calls I made were to those two and we sat together around Pooch's kitchen table to plot

and plan. This finished book is testimony to a joint effort and a very happy – if hard – few months.

I've dedicated this book to the brave of heart and free of spirit, and that sums up everyone involved in putting it together. It has been a joy and inspiration to write, and I hope it makes you feel similarly inspired and happy when reading it and cooking from it.

BASKET

⌣

Amanda Rayner • *Wyldwood Willow*

Amanda doesn't have a handbag. She has a basket. 'It holds all the detritus I can't fit in my pockets! My water bottle, my phone, purse, diary. There are always some tissues in there. Sometimes a half-eaten bar of chocolate.' Amanda made her basket from the willow she grows near her home, and it goes with her everywhere. But when she made her first basket, twenty-five years ago, she never imagined that it would become her way of life.

It was Amanda's great friend Phil who showed her how to make a basket one afternoon and then gave her a supply of willow. She didn't really get the appeal of basket-making that first time, she confesses. She'd just had a baby and had become used to doing everything in between looking after her in a rush. 'Basket-making is a journey, a process. But for me, that first time, it was just about getting it finished. I remember feeling a bit impatient with it. Wondering why it all was taking so long!'

Phil's willow sat, untouched, for several months, but when Amanda suffered a sudden and shocking bereavement, she was drawn back to the willow; found the weaving of it, the physical and mental process of it, started to help her heal. She now makes baskets of all shapes and sizes: for gathering and foraging, for logs and laundry. She makes beautiful, sculptural basket chairs, woven supports for flowers and vegetables, pergolas, hurdles and coffins. She's even made 'crazy baskets' for the Marvel films. 'My business has grown in a very slow, organic way, but I did realize very early on that I wanted to teach too. I wanted to share the magic of working with willow, because it is so good for body and soul.'

Amanda did a City & Guilds teaching certificate, which gave her the confidence to start offering willow-weaving workshops and, every summer, she packs up her van and does a tour of festivals. 'And that's what I love most, watching the transformation that happens to people who come to make a basket. It's quite a challenge – a small feat of engineering – because the way a basket comes together is quite complex. You have to be fully invested in the process, to concentrate completely on it. Whatever issues or problems you might be facing at home or at work, or even if you are just a bit worn down by the daily grind, all those things tend to get forgotten. People have said to me that when they are making a basket it feels like they are giving their brain a holiday; a rest from thinking or worrying about things for a while.'

Particularly rewarding is to see the people who return to her festival tent year after year to improve and develop their weaving skills. 'I love making baskets and at the end of the festival season I often can't wait to get back to my workshop and start weaving again. But passing on the skills I first learned all those years ago, seeing the ear-to-ear smiles of the people I've taught because they are so delighted with what they have made, gives me as much pleasure as taking a few lengths of willow and starting to weave.'

Cherry Compôte
& Some Lovely Things to Do With It

Amanda and cherries are synonymous in my mind, because she arrived at the farm one day with a basket brimming with the most beautiful cherries from her garden. They are my favourite summer fruit – I can eat my bodyweight in them in a single sitting – and they're all the more special because they are only available for a few weeks of the year. If I can stop myself eating them immediately, making this simple, versatile compôte makes them last a bit longer.

500g (1lb 2oz) cherries, fresh
    or frozen

2–3 tablespoons sugar, to taste
1 tablespoon lemon juice

Serves 4

Remove the pits from the cherries if using fresh fruit, then place into a saucepan along with 2 tablespoons of sugar and the lemon juice. Heat gently over a medium heat for about 10 minutes, until the cherries are starting to collapse and the juice has thickened a little. Taste (don't burn your tongue!) and add the extra sugar if needed. Leave to cool until warm, then pour into sterilized jars. Once cooled, the cherry compôte can be kept in the fridge for up to 2 weeks.

This goes really well as an accompaniment to a strong, salty goats' cheese. It's great on porridge, even greater with dark chocolate ice cream. Swirl into yogurt with a scattering of granola, or turn it into this pudding, which looks elaborate but couldn't be easier.

Cheat's Brûlée

8 tablespoons Cherry Compôte (see above)

450ml (16fl oz) Greek yogurt
4 tablespoons demerara sugar

Serves 4

Put 2 tablespoons of compôte into each of 4 flameproof ramekins. Divide the yogurt between the ramekins, giving it a gentle mix to lightly swirl the compôte into the yogurt.

Just before you are ready to serve, sprinkle 1 tablespoon of demerara sugar over the top of the yogurt in each ramekin and then, using a cook's blow torch or a grill preheated to high, melt the sugar until caramelized. Leave to cool and harden, then serve.

Leek & Pea Frittata with Leaves

I use the basket I bought from Amanda every afternoon when I go and collect the eggs from our hens and ducks. I've been keeping poultry for almost two decades, yet I still get excited by the small miracle of finding eggs tucked among the straw in the nest boxes, and by all the wonderful things you can cook with them. This frittata is a current favourite.

FOR THE FRITTATA

50g (1¾oz) butter

olive oil

200g (7oz) leeks, finely chopped

150g (5½oz) peas, defrosted if frozen

4 eggs

75g (2½oz) Caerphilly cheese, grated

a small handful of soft herbs (such
   as chives, chervil, lovage, dill,
   tarragon), chopped

sea salt and freshly ground
   black pepper

FOR THE LEAVES

3 tablespoons extra virgin olive oil

1 tablespoon lemon juice

2 handfuls of pea shoots

1 Baby Gem lettuce, leaves
   roughly chopped

any leftover herbs from the frittata

Serves 2–4

Heat a medium nonstick frying pan over a medium heat. Add the butter and a dash of oil then sauté the leeks with a good pinch of salt until softened, about 7 minutes. Add the peas, mix and heat through. Preheat the grill.

Lightly beat the eggs in a bowl. Mix in the cheese and herbs, season and then pour into the pan, over the leeks and peas, gently stirring to mix. Leave to cook over a medium-low heat for 5–7 minutes, until firmed up on the bottom and most of the sides. Then put under the preheated grill and cook for a further 3–4 minutes, or until just set.

To prepare the salad, whisk the extra virgin olive oil and lemon juice together in the bottom of a large bowl. Season. Add the pea shoots and lettuce, along with any herbs you have left over from making the frittata, then toss everything together to coat in the dressing.

Remove the frittata from the grill, loosen around the edges with a palette knife and slide out onto a plate. Serve hot, warm or at room temperature, in slices, with the leaves.

Frying Pan Pizza Bianca
with Porcini Mushrooms

✦

'I've just discovered there are porcini mushrooms growing in the lane I walk along almost every day,' Amanda told me. 'They are amazing on pizza!' She's right. They are.

FOR THE DOUGH

500g (1lb 2oz) plain flour or 00 flour,
    plus extra for dusting
7g (¼oz) packet of easy bake yeast
2 tablespoons olive oil, plus extra
    for oiling
300ml (½ pint) lukewarm water
sea salt and freshly ground
    black pepper

FOR THE TOPPINGS

250g (9oz) ricotta
2 garlic cloves, crushed
250g (9oz) fresh porcini (or other)
    mushrooms, thinly sliced
1 banana shallot, thinly sliced
150g (5½oz) cucina mozzarella,
    thinly sliced
leaves from 4 thyme sprigs

Serves 4

In a large bowl, mix the flour and yeast together until the yeast is evenly distributed. Make a well in the middle and pour in the olive oil, 1½ teaspoons of salt and the lukewarm water. Mix into a dough, adding a little more water if needed to bring everything together.

Tip the dough out onto a floured work surface and knead until soft, stretchy and smooth. This can take up to 10 minutes, so if you have a stand mixer you may prefer to do it in that.

Shape the kneaded dough into a ball and place into a large oiled bowl. Cover loosely with a piece of oiled clingfilm or a clean tea towel. Leave the bowl somewhere relatively warm (not in a very cold room or near a draught) to rise for an hour or two.

Tip the dough out onto a floured work surface and knock it back a little to get rid of any excess air. Divide into 4 balls and place these on an oiled plate to rest until you are ready to cook. The balls of dough will happily sit in the fridge overnight at this point, if necessary. Cover them with oiled clingfilm before popping into the fridge.

Once ready to cook, preheat the grill to its highest setting.

Prepare the toppings. Season the ricotta really well with salt and pepper, then stir in the crushed garlic, making sure it is evenly distributed.

Heat a large, heavy-based frying pan over a high heat. Shape one of the balls of dough into a pizza base the same size as your frying pan, either using your hands to stretch it or using a rolling pin.

Place the shaped dough into the hot frying pan and immediately spoon over one quarter of the ricotta. Spread it out with a spoon and top with one quarter of the mushrooms, seasoning them once added. Top with one quarter each of the sliced shallot and mozzarella. Be careful not to overload the pizza, otherwise it won't cook properly. Drizzle a little olive oil over the top and around the edge.

After about 3 minutes, lift the edge of the pizza with a palette knife or spatula and check the base. If it is golden and crisp, place under the grill, as close to the grill as possible, for a further 2–3 minutes until the top is golden and the cheese is bubbling and blistered.

Remove from the grill, slide the pizza out onto a board and sprinkle with thyme. Repeat the process with the remaining dough and toppings and eat immediately.

APRON

～

Toria & Simon Whitfield • *Field & Found*

Toria was taught to use a sewing machine by her mum when she was seven. By the time she was eleven, she was making her own costumes for the school play. 'I just loved it. I sewed all the time after that.'

After completing a degree in textiles, she set up an upcycling business with a friend. 'I taught myself basic pattern cutting, and I would cut up old tweed jackets, which we would remodel and embellish with lace and things, then travel around the festival circuit selling them. We did that for four or five years, until I met Simon, and we had our first baby.'

Simon is a polymath: a builder, a grower, a carpenter, an experimenter, but most of all, a foodie. He used to have his own business importing Mediterranean antipasti, oils and olives, selling them at farmers' markets and food festivals. He ran a deli-café, and now runs courses in sustainable building, does pop-up feasts and fire cooking as well as growing as much food as he can produce for his family.

After their second child was born, Toria found herself yearning to get back to designing and making things. A chance meeting with someone who had just taken over a building in their local town gave her the opportunity. 'They asked what I did, and I said, "I make clothes, but I'm not sure what direction I'm going in."'

She was offered a room in the building to use as a studio. 'Simon and I set to work, stripping back the walls to reveal the bricks, bringing in bits and pieces of timber and rope to create hanging spaces for the clothes I was going to make. I had an old pingpong table where I cut out the patterns, and a cot for my baby. It was an open studio. People could come and see me actually making the things they could buy.'

One of the very first things she made was an apron. 'I just had this idea to make one, based on the Japanese cross-back design. Still utilitarian, but something with a bit more shape and elegance.' She made it in some old linen that she had found and within twenty minutes of her finishing it and hanging it up, it was sold. 'So, I made another one. And then another one. And it just went from there. I even managed to incorporate my love of repurposing old objects. I had a collection of those old-fashioned men's braces, with the leather ends that attach them to trousers. I cut off those leather ends and used them on the straps of my aprons.' It's become her signature style.

The first person to buy one of Toria's aprons was a baker. And it continues to be craftspeople who make up the majority of her customers. 'I've made them for jewellers, printers, carvers, florists, gardeners, even a truffle hunter!' Simon has been the inspiration for many of her designs and road tests them all. 'Almost everything I do involves getting dirty, and different tasks require a different apron. When I'm gardening, I want a long apron that can double as a kneeler and have pockets and loops for my tools. I need another one for when I'm fire cooking and I'm greasy and hot. One for carpentry, one for metalwork. A smart one for hosting pop-ups… And everyone likes to feel good when they are working, so the design and look of them does matter, even though they are made with a purpose.'

It's been ten years since Toria made that first apron and they are still selling almost as fast as she can make them. She works now from a little studio she and Simon built in their garden from repurposed recycled finds. She has several designs that are regular favourites – all named after birds – but she relishes the challenge of making aprons that are bespoke. Adding a big leather patch to the side of an apron for a spoon carver was something she was asked to do most recently.

'I'm at my happiest when I'm making things. It's just a joy! Our life is a creative life. If there is any excuse for making something, we'll do it.'

All-in-One Campfire Hotdogs

Campfire bread – like potatoes or apples wrapped in foil and baked in the coals of a bonfire – is the food of childhood holidays. To take a simple, sticky mix of flour and milk, combine it into a paste, wrap it around a stick and cook it over a fire really did feel like performing a magic trick. But how even more magical would it be, I thought, to wrap your dough around a sausage and make yourself an all-in-one hotdog. I can't tell you how delighted I was when it worked!

You'll need four long, thin, freshly cut sticks for this. Sharpen one end of each stick to a point and scrape the bark off. You can use metal skewers, but they do get hot, so you might want to wrap the ends you are holding in a cloth. I've suggested using pre-cooked frankfurter sausages here, to avoid any worries that the sausages may not be cooked all the way through. This is definitely an apron-wearing recipe that pays homage to Simon's love of cooking over fire.

300g (10½oz) self-raising flour,
plus extra for dusting
1 teaspoon sea salt

175–200ml (6–7fl oz) whole milk,
or water if preferred
olive oil
4 large frankfurter sausages

Serves 4

Heat your barbecue or fire ready for direct grilling.

Put the flour into a mixing bowl and add the salt. Mix well, then slowly pour in 175ml (6fl oz) of milk or water along with a dash of olive oil, mixing as you go, until you reach a dough consistency. Add a little extra milk or water if needed. Knead the dough for a few minutes until smooth and elastic.

Thread the frankfurters onto the sticks or skewers so that the stick or skewer runs through from top to bottom.

Divide the dough into 4 and roll each piece into a long sausage shape. Mould one end of your dough to the stick above the frankfurter then twirl it around so there is a spiral of dough around the frankfurter, before securing it around the stick at the other end.

Once your fire is hot and the embers are glowing brightly, spread the embers out a little. Hold the hotdogs over the embers, but not touching them, turning the sticks often so that the dough cooks evenly. Cook until the outside of the dough is golden brown and has puffed up slightly. The inside should be cooked and the frankfurters warm. This could take up to 15 minutes.

Once cooked, slide the stick out of your magic hotdog and eat, wiping your fingers on your apron when you're done!

Herefordshire Antipasto

~∽~

Simon's challenge to himself is to make something they have grown part of every meal they eat. His early career, importing Italian vegetables preserved in oil, gave him the inspiration to do the same with the vegetables he grows at home. This dish is beautiful alongside cheese, cold meat, salads, or just straight out of the jar…

1 hard squash or pumpkin, about 750g (1lb 10oz) prepared weight
50g (1¾oz) sea salt, plus extra for sprinkling
50g (1¾oz) sugar
100ml (3½fl oz) vinegar

1 red onion, thinly sliced
4 garlic cloves, thinly sliced
2–4 long red chillies, halved lengthways, to taste
2 tablespoons fennel seeds
500ml (18fl oz) light olive oil

Makes 1 x 500ml (18fl oz) jar

Peel and deseed the squash or pumpkin, then slice into thin slices, about 2.5mm (⅛ inch), and small enough to fit into a large Kilner jar.

Put the salt and sugar into a large saucepan and fill the pan two-thirds of the way up with water. Bring to a simmer. Once the sugar and salt have dissolved, add the vinegar, onion, garlic, chillies to taste, fennel seeds and the squash or pumpkin. Bring back to a simmer then, keeping the squash or pumpkin submerged under the liquid, blanch for 2–3 minutes – just long enough to take the rawness off the vegetables.

Tip the contents of the saucepan into a colander over the sink. Shake dry, then tip out onto a large tray and spread out so that the vegetables can steam dry.

Once everything is dry, stuff it firmly into a sterilized Kilner jar, seasoning with a little salt as you add each layer. Pour over enough light olive oil to completely cover. Wait for any air bubbles to surface, top up with more olive oil if needed, then seal up.

Give the jars a good shake, then leave somewhere cool and not too bright for 1–2 weeks until tender and aromatic before tucking in. This will keep for up to 1 month.

The Whitfield Family Magic Potion

Elderberries may be tiny, and slightly annoying to remove from the stalks (a fork is a good secret weapon here – use the gaps between the tines to trap the berries and pull them off), but they contain every good thing you need to ward off winter sniffles. Simon inherited this recipe from his grandmother, who called it Red Rob, although it is more purple than red. They keep a big Kilner jar of it in the fridge and take a teaspoon of it neat at the first sign of a cold. But it can be used as a cordial in hot or cold water, or sparkling wine. If you can't get hold of elderberries, blackcurrants or blackberries are good substitutes.

300g (10½oz) elderberries,
  stalks removed
5cm (2 inch) piece of fresh root
  ginger, sliced
4 star anise
1 cinnamon stick
3 cloves
500ml (18fl oz) water
250g (9oz) honey

Makes about 500ml (18fl oz)

Put the elderberries, aromatics and water into a heavy-based saucepan and bring to a simmer. Simmer, squishing the berries a little (a potato masher works well here), until the liquid has reduced by half. This can take 20–30 minutes.

Strain the mixture through a fine sieve into a heatproof bowl or jug, then mix the honey into the liquid until completely combined. Pour into a sterilized jar or bottle. Once cool, store in the fridge until ready to use. Alternatively, to extend its life, store half in the fridge to use first and put the other half into the freezer for at a later date.

Whenever you feel a cold coming on, swallow 1 teaspoon of the syrup neat. It's also great turned into a hot drink by stirring into a mug of boiling water. Or use in place of a cordial in a refreshing cold drink with sparkling water, or Champagne.

KNIFE

～

Joel Black • *Joel Black Knives*

With his first pay cheque, Joel Black bought a knife. 'Were you one of those chefs who travel around with your own knives in a big canvas roll?' I asked him.

'Yes,' he laughs. 'I was a proper chef! Knives are the tools of your trade. Some professional kitchens will have knives to lend the more junior chefs, but as you rise through the ranks it is expected – and you want – to have your own. So each time I got paid, I would spend a few hundred quid on another knife. Then I always knew I had the right tool to do the job well; that it was sharp and had been looked after. I came to understand the value of a good knife.'

And Joel did rise through the ranks, becoming the head chef at an innovative, creative and sustainable restaurant in Bristol. And he loved cooking. Loved creating something from scratch. Taking the raw ingredients and transforming them. But the hours, he said, were punishing. 'All right when you're younger, but they get to you after a while.' And as a head chef, he spent more time managing than cooking. 'And I just loved making things. Considering all those different elements of a dish – taste, smell, look, nourishment. But ultimately I was creating something very transient. You make it, send it out of the kitchen, and it's gone. So I started to feel a bit disillusioned and to think about doing something else.'

He knew he wanted to continue making things, so he spent a day in the forge of an artisan blacksmith. The parallels to his own profession were immediately apparent. 'You take raw materials and through your understanding of how they behave and what they can do, using heat and the right technique, you can turn them into something beautiful.' He went on to do

an NVQ in blacksmithing and then a degree. And he specialized, perhaps unsurprisingly given his knowledge and affinity with them, in making knives for chefs. All the knives he made for his final degree show sold.

He had found his new vocation. But he was still unsure whether he could make a living from it. 'I remember when I first started knife-making, I wasn't sure how to make it a business. I said to my partner "I've never made anything and sold it. I've got no idea how this works!"' And she said, "That's what you've always done in your job! It's what you were doing when you were cooking. You make stuff and you sell stuff." But when it's food you're making, it's gone. The nice thing about making knives is they have some longevity. They go out there and remain. And I like the fact that I am making something a little more niche.'

Every knife Joel creates in his forge is unique and his approach to making each one is the same as the approach he adopted when creating a new dish in the restaurant. He thinks about the ingredients – their provenance, what will work well with what. He draws on his

knowledge and passion for the long, illustrious knife-making culture of countries such as Japan. He envisages how he wants the final product to look. How it will feel to hold it. How it will cut. His principal ingredients are steel and wood, but steel, like wood, can have different properties, and he likes to mix in other metals sometimes. Old wrought iron or, in the case of a knife he has on his workbench when I visit, a piece of meteorite that fell to earth in Argentina roughly five thousand years ago. 'And the handle of that knife is bog oak.' It is so dark, it is almost black. 'It was dug up from a place on the coast – it was from a forest that was submerged by rising sea levels, also about five thousand years ago. Now the sea has retreated again, this ancient wood has been discovered. I love that I have been able to bring these two ancient natural elements together and use them to create something, not just long-lasting, but also useful.'

He holds the knife in his hands. They are the hands of an artisan, nails rimmed with black, skin ingrained with a decade of working with metal. The knife is a work of art, the blade part polished to a high, gleaming sheen, part still raw and black. The back edge is thick, heavy, industrial, tapering to the finest, cleanest cutting edge I have ever seen. Looking closely, I can see the marks of Joel's hammer in places. It is his trademark. A knife that combines the raw and the refined. It looks far too beautiful and far too precious to be used. But Joel is emphatic. 'It is a tool and the fact that it is useful is the most important aspect of it. Making a useful object, a useful tool, is the goal. All the other things – the materials, the finishes – all of that is ancillary to it being a working knife which is there to cook with.'

French Onion Soup

This is a dish to test your knife skills! Joel told me he must have sliced, chopped and diced several tonnes of onions during his time as a chef and he never tired of it. He still loves making this deeply flavoursome soup. It takes lots of chopping and you need to allow plenty of time for the onions to achieve that rich depth of flavour, so this is one for a wet afternoon, when being in a warm, fragrant, steamy kitchen is a treat. A meal in its own right, it's well worth the wait.

75g (2½oz) butter
750g (1lb 10oz) onions (about 4 large
   or 6 small), thinly sliced
1 tablespoon plain flour
250ml (9fl oz) dry white wine or
   medium cider, or a mixture of
   the two
leaves from 2 thyme sprigs

750ml (1 pint 7fl oz) strong,
   best-quality beef stock
a dash of brandy (optional)
8 slices of baguette
150g (5½oz) Gruyère or Comté
   cheese, grated
sea salt and freshly ground
   black pepper

Serves 4 as a starter, 2 as a lunch

Heat a large, heavy-based pan over a medium heat and add the butter. Once melted, stir in the onions along with a big pinch of salt and pop a lid on the pan. Cook for 20 minutes, stirring now and again.

Remove the lid and continue to cook the onions over a medium-low heat for a further 20–30 minutes, stirring occasionally. You want them to be slightly caramelized and deeper than golden brown. If needed, cook for slightly longer, but keep a close eye on them as you definitely don't want them to burn.

Once the onions are ready, stir in the flour and cook for a couple of minutes. Deglaze the pan with a splash of wine or cider, scraping up anything stuck to the bottom. Then pour in the rest of the wine or cider, add the thyme and bring to a simmer. Simmer for

2 minutes, then add the stock. Simmer gently for 30 minutes, then taste the soup and adjust the seasoning.

Preheat the grill to high. Stir the brandy through the soup, if using, then divide the soup between heatproof bowls and place the bowls onto a baking tray. Place the baguette slices on top of the soup, sprinkle over the cheese and grill until golden. Serve immediately, being careful as the bowls will be very hot.

Halloumi & Tomato Salad
with Gremolata

My take on a caprese salad, using fried halloumi instead of mozzarella and a lovely, zingy mix of parsley, lemon and garlic in lieu of basil. A variety of tomatoes of different sizes, shapes and colours will look nicest.

500g (1lb 2oz) mixed tomatoes
2 handfuls of rocket, about
    40g (1½oz)
extra virgin olive oil
a small bunch of parsley, coarse
    stalks removed

1 garlic clove
1 unwaxed lemon
250g (9oz) halloumi, sliced
sea salt and freshly ground
    black pepper

Serves 2

Slice the larger tomatoes and halve any smaller ones. Place onto a serving platter with the rocket, season with salt and pepper, drizzle generously with extra virgin olive oil then toss to coat everything.

Finely chop the parsley, then using a fine grater, grate the garlic over the top of it. Using the same fine grater, zest the lemon on top too. Add a pinch of salt and chop everything again until really finely chopped and well mixed.

Heat a large frying pan over a medium heat and add a dash of oil. Fry the slices of

halloumi for 2–3 minutes on each side, until dark golden.

Meanwhile, squeeze a little of the lemon juice over the tomatoes and rocket and toss. Taste and adjust the seasoning or add more lemon juice if needed.

Once the halloumi is cooked, transfer to the serving platter on top of the tomatoes, drizzle with a little bit more oil, then sprinkle the gremolata over everything. Serve immediately.

Quick Pickled Fennel

The reward for a bit of careful slicing is a speedy, tasty, versatile accompaniment to cold meats or cheese, or smoked fish. It's great with smoked salmon, and I love it with roast pork.

2 large fennel bulbs, about 750g (1lb 10oz)

30g (1oz) sea salt

1.5 litres (2¾ pints) water

350ml (12fl oz) cider vinegar

30g (1oz) sugar

1 teaspoon coriander seeds

1 teaspoon fennel seeds

1 teaspoon mustard seeds

1 teaspoon celery seeds

Makes 1 x 750ml (1 pint 7fl oz) jar

Finely slice the fennel. Mix the salt and water in a medium-large saucepan and bring to the boil, making sure the salt has fully dissolved. Add the fennel to the pan and blanch for 2 minutes. Drain immediately and transfer to a large sterilized jar.

Meanwhile, make your pickling liquor. Heat the vinegar, sugar and spices in a small pan over a medium heat until the sugar is completely dissolved and the vinegar aromatic (about 5–10 minutes). Leave to cool for 5 minutes.

Pour the slightly cooled vinegar into the jar over the fennel, mixing everything together well so that the spices are evenly distributed. Push the fennel down under the level of the vinegar. Once cool, seal the jar and transfer to the fridge.

The pickled fennel is ready to use straight away, but can be stored for up to 8 weeks in the fridge and used as and when you like.

BOARD

~∾~

Jamie Gaunt • *Jamie Gaunt Designs*

In 2005, Jamie Gaunt set off with his cousin to travel the world by bicycle. Over three years, they managed to reach all seven continents without ever taking a plane, hitching lifts on container ships to get them across the oceans. Once they reached Australia, they wrote up the story of their adventures and sold it on the streets to passers-by. And that's how Jamie met the woman he was destined to marry.

They moved in together, and, because they didn't really have the money to buy furniture, Jamie decided to make it. 'I'd never made anything with wood before, but I just looked at how something went together and worked out how to do it. I made us a bed, a table. The first thing I made was a Welsh dresser! They were all very rough and ready, but people seemed to like them, and friends started asking me to make things for them too.'

The problem was it took months to make a table or a bed, so he'd have to charge way more than anyone could afford. That's when he decided to go into homewares. He started out by creating an oil burner from Tasmanian oak. 'I sold hundreds of them in the local market in Australia,' he says. He extended his range, adding wooden bowls and vases. But he became particularly well known for his chopping boards.

Now back in the UK with his wife and family, Jamie's self-taught wood-carving skills have become honed and refined. He uses mostly hand tools – Swedish carving axes and knives – and has discovered that, more often than not, it is the relationship between the tools and the piece of wood they are working that defines the final look of his pieces. He uses

almost exclusively oak, and his work celebrates the character of the wood – the grain and the knots, all the natural quirks and imperfections that make each piece unique. He continues to sell his work at markets and although some people buy his boards to put up on their walls, because they are as beautiful as a work of art, Jamie insists they are utilitarian and should be treated as such. 'I have boards for everything. A little board for chopping chillies, an onion and garlic board, one for fish, one for meat… And food – even the simplest of dishes – always looks so good, so inviting, when it's served on an oak board.'

Roasted Veg & Butter Bean Mash
with Feta, Herbs & Seeds

One of Jamie's favourite things to serve on one of his boards is a beautiful pile of roasted veg. The recipe below is something I put together one evening with what I had in the fridge and it's now become something of a favourite. And it does, indeed, look very pretty on a board.

FOR THE VEGETABLES

2 aubergines

olive oil

4 Romano peppers

8 unpeeled garlic cloves

3 courgettes

4 vines of cherry tomatoes, about
   350g (12oz)

a bunch of spring onions, trimmed

sea salt and freshly ground
   black pepper

FOR THE FETA SPRINKLE

2 tablespoons mixed seeds

50g (1¾oz) feta cheese

chilli flakes

zest of 1 unwaxed lemon

a handful of mixed herbs (such as
   mint, parsley, coriander, basil,
   oregano, dill), chopped

FOR THE BUTTER BEAN MASH

2 x 400g (14oz) jars or cans of butter
   beans, drained and rinsed

a knob of butter or slug of olive oil

extra virgin olive oil, to finish

Serves 4–6

Preheat the oven to 220°C (425°F), Gas Mark 7.

For the roasted vegetables, cut the aubergines into quarters lengthways and brush with oil. Leave the peppers whole and brush with oil. Put both onto a lined baking tray with the garlic and season well. Roast for 20 minutes, or until they start to soften and colour.

Halve the courgettes lengthways and chop into 3cm (1¼ inch) chunks. Brush them with oil. Place the courgettes, tomatoes and spring onions on a separate lined baking tray. Season well and cook in the oven with the aubergine and peppers for a further 20 minutes or until all the vegetables are soft and slightly charred. Remove and leave to cool slightly.

While the vegetables cook, prepare the feta sprinkle. Toast the seeds in a dry frying pan over a medium heat until golden. Crumble the feta into a bowl. Add some chilli flakes, lemon zest and chopped herbs and leave to stand.

Once the vegetables are out of the oven, make the butter bean mash. Heat the drained butter beans in a saucepan over a medium heat with the butter or olive oil. Squeeze the roasted garlic from the skins into the pan, season well and add any juices from the roasted vegetables too. Squash the garlic with the back of a spoon as you mix everything together in the pan. Once the mixture is hot but not boiling, tip into a food processor or use a stick blender and blitz to a smooth purée. Taste and adjust the seasoning if necessary.

Pile the butter bean mash up on a board, arrange the roasted vegetables on top and sprinkle over the feta mixture, finishing with the seeds and a drizzle of extra virgin olive oil.

Hoisin Pork Belly & Cucumber in Lettuce Cups

A lovely combination of flavours and textures, this is perfect outdoor food, to cook over a fire and pass around to eat with your hands, straight from the board you assemble it on.

1 tablespoon Chinese five spice powder
flavourless oil, such as sunflower

400–500g (14oz–1lb 2oz) pork belly slices, about 1cm (½ inch) thick
½ cucumber

4 spring onions, finely shredded
1 tablespoon rice vinegar
1 tablespoon toasted sesame oil
2 Little Gem lettuces, leaves
  separated

75g (2½oz) hoisin sauce
Chiu Chow chilli oil, to taste
  (optional)
sea salt

Serves 4

Fire up your barbecue or fire ready for direct cooking. Or if you want to cook the pork belly on the hob, see instructions opposite.

Rub the Chinese five spice powder and a dash of oil over the pork belly slices so that they are coated on all sides.

Cut the cucumber in half lengthways and scoop out the seeds with a teaspoon. Cut the cucumber into slices 2mm (¹⁄₁₆ inch) thick. Toss in a bowl with most of the spring onions, reserving a few for garnish. Drizzle over the vinegar and sesame oil and season with a little salt. Toss to coat.

Arrange the lettuce leaf cups on a board and divide the cucumber mixture evenly between them.

Once the barbecue or fire is hot (you shouldn't be able to hold your hand over it for longer than about 2 seconds), place the pork belly slices onto the grill and sprinkle with a little salt. Cook for a couple of minutes, then turn over.

Once turned, brush each slice with hoisin sauce and continue to cook for 1–2 minutes. Then turn them back over and brush the other sides. You are looking for caramelized crisp edges and bubbling fat. Keep turning, brushing with hoisin and moving between direct and indirect heat, until the pork is cooked through and crisping at the edges.

To cook on the hob, heat a griddle pan over a medium-high heat. Once hot, place the pork belly slices onto the griddle and sprinkle with a little salt. Cook for a couple of minutes until browned, then turn over. Once turned, brush each slice with hoisin sauce and continue to cook for 1–2 minutes, then turn them back over and brush the other side. Reduce the heat to low and keep turning and brushing with hoisin until the pork is just cooked through and crisping at the edges, which should take 10–12 minutes in total. Leave to rest for a few minutes.

Remove onto a chopping board and chop the pork into small bitesize pieces. Top each lettuce cup with some pork, drizzle over the chilli oil (if using), then scatter over the remaining spring onions and serve.

Two Seasonal Fruit Boards
with Meringues & Yogurt

When he was living in Australia, Jamie loved assembling a display of sliced, colourful fruits for breakfast or to finish off a meal. Inspired by that lovely simple dish, overleaf are two ideas – one for summer and one for autumn or winter – that are a little more elaborate, but don't require much effort. The recipes are on pages 54–5.

Summer

FOR THE MINI STRIPED
  MERINGUE BITES
2 egg whites, at room temperature
¼ teaspoon lemon juice
150g (5½oz) caster sugar, at
  room temperature
a few drops of pink gel or paste
  food colouring

FOR THE FRUIT BOARD
150g (5½oz) strawberries
150g (5½oz) raspberries
150g (5½oz) cherries (optional)
4 figs
½–1 teaspoon ground cardamon,
  to taste
150ml (¼ pint) Greek yogurt
honey or agave syrup
zest of 2 unwaxed limes
a small handful of mint leaves

Serves 4–6

Preheat the oven to 120°C (250°F), Gas Mark ½, and line 2 baking trays with baking paper.

In a large, very clean bowl, whisk the egg whites with a handheld electric whisk (or you can use a stand mixer) until frothy. Add the lemon juice and continue to whisk until doubled in size.

With the whisk still running, slowly add the sugar 1 spoonful at a time, whisking constantly until all the sugar has been added and you have reached a glossy stiff peak.

Using a fine paint brush, brush 3 stripes of food colouring on the inside of a piping bag fitted with a 1cm (½ inch) nozzle. Spoon the meringue mixture into the piping bag.

Secure the baking paper to the trays using a dot of meringue mix in each corner, then pipe meringue mix onto the trays at intervals, leaving a small gap between each. You are aiming for meringues that are about 2cm (¾ inch) wide at the base. To achieve a point at the top, pipe vertically down onto the tray, release the pressure and pull the piping bag upwards as you do so.

Bake for 1 hour in the oven. Then turn the oven off, leave the door ajar and leave the meringues inside the oven for a further 2 hours until completely cool. Once cool, they can be stored in an airtight container for up to 2 weeks.

When ready to serve, slice the fruit (remove any pits) and arrange in a lovely pattern on a board. Mix the ground cardamom to taste into the yogurt and add a little honey or agave syrup if you'd like it a little sweeter. Dot the yogurt over the fruit, if you like, or serve it in a small bowl for dipping. Top with the meringues, dotted around the board on top of the fruit, then finish with a sprinkling of the lime zest and a scattering of mint leaves.

Autumn/Winter

FOR THE BROWN SUGAR
  MERINGUES
2 egg whites, at room temperature
¼ teaspoon lemon juice
150g (5½oz) light muscovado sugar,
  at room temperature

FOR THE FRUIT BOARD
2 clementines, peeled and
  sliced horizontally

2 persimmons, sliced
a handful of blackberries
2 pears, quartered, cored and sliced
100g (3½oz) physalis in their husks
2 balls of stem ginger, plus
  1 tablespoon syrup
150ml (¼ pint) Greek yogurt
zest of 1 unwaxed orange or
  2 clementines
75g (2½oz) pomegranate seeds

Serves 4–6

Prepare the meringue mixture and cook the meringues following the recipe for the summer fruit board, leaving out the food colouring.

Once ready to serve, arrange all the fruit in a lovely pattern on a board, except for the pomegranate seeds which you'll use later. Finely chop or grate the stem ginger balls and mix into the yogurt along with enough syrup to sweeten it to your liking. Dot the ginger yogurt over the fruit, or serve it in a small bowl for dipping. Crumble the meringues over the top, then finish with a sprinkling of the orange zest and the pomegranate seeds.

PAN

‹⌇›

Alex Pole

'At eighteen, I was a big, ex-rugby-playing, profoundly dyslexic, punk drop-out who went travelling for a bit, was sent to study architecture, went travelling again, went to art school in Plymouth, walked into the jewellery department and thought, "This is what I'm going to do for the rest of my life."'

It was Alex's mother who sowed the seed of this epiphanal moment. A moment that still makes the hairs stand up on Alex's arms when he recalls it. She was an artist and jewellery-maker herself, and Alex spent hours as a child sitting beside his mother in her studio watching her work, or playing with the gemstones she kept in an old wooden chocolate box. She made, Alex says, beautiful silverware, and was particularly skilled at reticulation – the craft of creating a textured surface on metal. When, all those years later, he announced that he too wanted to become a jewellery-maker, she arrived one day with the entire contents of her jewellery workshop: 'All her tools, the gemstones – everything – which she'd given to a friend to keep in trust in case any of her children wanted to take up her craft.'

Next door to the jewellery department at his art school was the metalwork department. Alex found himself migrating over there too, learning hot steel work and how to make decorative gates and fences. For eighteen years, Alex was both jewellery-maker and blacksmith. The two skills appear to be at the opposite ends of the spectrum but, Alex insists, they are essentially the same trade and it is not unusual for a blacksmith to become a jewellery-maker and vice versa. 'The reason I found myself drawn to both crafts is that they are all about making something from nothing: taking raw materials and transforming them into something beautiful. It gave me a real sense of self-worth.'

But in 2007 he found himself in a rut. He and his partner, with their young family, had returned to the UK after living in Australia for a few years. Alex had set up a forge near where they lived. 'But there was a massive recession. I was literally repairing garden forks for

a fiver just to make any money at all, and I got to the point where I thought I might just have to give up. But my wonderful missus said, "Take some time. Go and find a way of being happy again."'

He went to do a course in Sweden. The proper, old-fashioned blacksmithing course he had never done, where you start by learning to make the tools you then work with, such as tongs, chisels and hammers. 'It is the equivalent of a chef learning how to grow his own vegetables.'

Alex failed the course. 'I was the only professional blacksmith there, and I failed! So, it was a lesson in humility, but it was pivotal in helping me find a new direction. I started making axes – something Swedish metalworkers are famous for – and knives. Knife-making introduced me to chefs. I started going to festivals with a local chef and doing demos. And that's when I discovered that I wanted to make kitchenware. Everyone thought I was mad.'

But he didn't think it was mad. Alex has always cooked. When he's not working, he cooks. 'It's my outlet. I love the theatre of it. If I wasn't a blacksmith, I might well have been a chef. And I thought, rather than work simply to make a living, I'd work doing something that would make me happy and not worry about the money. I love kitchenware because it is entirely functional; almost everything I started making were things we didn't have at home.

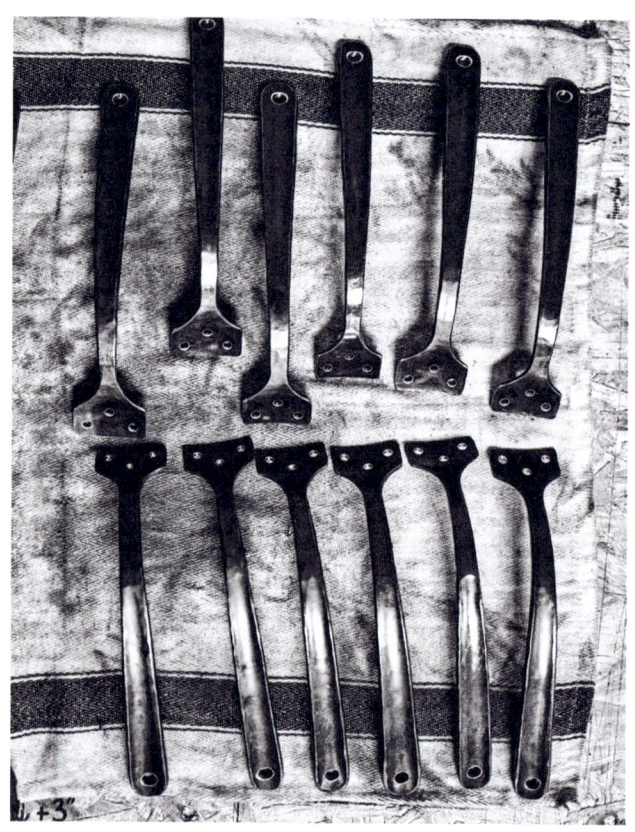

I took a huge drop in income – wiped out eighty per cent of my turnover overnight – but I had to hold my nerve and focus on doing what I really wanted to do.'

His forge is in a big old barn on a former dairy farm. Hanging on hooks and stacked on shelves are the kitchen tools, skillets, skewers and pans that have ended up in the hands of some of the leading chefs in the country. His frying pans are his most successful product. Made from carbon steel, each pan is spun by hand by traditional metal spinners in Bournemouth to Alex's meticulous design. 'We honed it and honed it. The first pan probably cost about £1,000 to make, but the guys down there are the best at what they do.' Once the pan is spun, it is sent up to Alex's forge where it is oiled and baked in a furnace to pre-season it. The handles for the pans are forged individually from stainless steel, so each handle is unique, and hand-riveted onto the pan with copper rivets.

'The carbon steel used for the pan is a good conductor of heat, so it's brilliant to cook with, and it's light and doesn't need any chemical coating. The stainless steel we use for the handles is a bad conductor of heat, so they don't get hot and burn your hands. Some people worry about using steel pans, but almost the worse you treat them, they better they become! Just don't put them straight onto a high heat. Let them warm up slowly. And don't scrub with a scouring pad when you're washing them up. When you're done, wipe them with a thin layer of oil and put them away somewhere dry. They'll last a lifetime and beyond. But just cook with them and keep on cooking with them!'

Chorizo, Prawn & Butter Bean Stew

⁓

This is a dish Alex cooks all the time. He has no fixed recipe and might replace the prawns with chopped boneless chicken thigh (cooked with the chorizo) or swap the butter beans for chickpeas. Chucking in a handful of spinach or two at the end works beautifully too.

olive oil

200g (7oz) cooking chorizo, cut into 5mm (¼ inch) slices

4 garlic cloves, thinly sliced

2 bay leaves

250g (9oz) cherry tomatoes, halved

100ml (3½fl oz) dry sherry

2 x 400g (14oz) cans of butter beans, drained and rinsed

200ml (7fl oz) chicken or vegetable stock

300g (10½oz) raw peeled king prawns

a small handful of chopped parsley

sea salt and freshly ground black pepper

hunks of bread, to serve

Serves 4

Heat a large frying pan or sauté pan over a medium heat. Add a dash of oil, then fry the chorizo until starting to brown on all sides. Add the garlic and bay leaves and stir for another minute or 2 until aromatic.

Stir in the tomatoes and leave to cook for 5 minutes, or until they are starting to soften, but are still holding their shape. Pour in the sherry and bring to a simmer.

Simmer for 2–3 minutes, then tip in the butter beans and the stock and bring the pan to the boil. Reduce to a simmer and stir well so that everything is coated in the sauce in the bottom of the pan. Simmer for 10 minutes, to warm the butter beans through. Taste and adjust the seasoning.

Once ready to serve, stir through the prawns and cook for 3 or so minutes, until just cooked through. Serve the stew in shallow bowls, scattered with the chopped parsley, with hunks of bread on the side to mop up the juices.

One-Pot Spring Chicken Casserole

ٮسٮ

Another simple, almost-no-washing-up-required dish that is perfect for cooking over a fire, although it can just as easily be done on the hob. Serve with some bread for mopping.

olive oil

4 chicken thighs, bone in,
   skin removed

a bunch of spring onions, trimmed

150ml (¼ pint) white wine

400ml (14fl oz) chicken stock

500g (1lb 2oz) small new potatoes

150g (5½oz) baby carrots

150g (5½oz) shelled broad beans
   (frozen are fine)

1 tablespoon Dijon mustard

100ml (3½fl oz) crème fraîche

leaves from a small bunch
   of tarragon

sea salt and freshly ground
   black pepper

Serves 2–4

Fire up your barbecue or fire, ready for direct and indirect cooking. Once hot, place a medium-large casserole dish over the direct heat and add a glug of olive oil. Fry the chicken thighs in the oil with a good pinch of salt until they are coloured on all sides. Transfer the casserole dish to indirect heat once the chicken is nicely coloured.

Chop the spring onions and reserve the green parts. Add the white parts to the pan and stir around with the chicken for a minute or 2 until they begin to soften. Pour in the wine and allow to bubble for a couple of minutes (you may need to move the casserole dish closer to the direct heat), then add the stock and bring to a gentle simmer over direct heat.

Add the potatoes and carrots and cover the casserole with a lid. Simmer gently over indirect heat for 20 minutes, or until the potatoes are tender.

Once the potatoes are ready, add the broad beans and continue to simmer for a further 2 minutes. Add the mustard and crème fraîche and stir through to mix well. Taste and adjust the seasoning if necessary. Finish by scattering over the tarragon leaves and the green parts of the spring onions, then serve.

Plum Tarte Tatin

I planted three plum trees when we first moved onto our smallholding. Nothing beats a just-picked plum eaten straight from the tree, but if you're going to cook them, this is a very fine way to do it. And using ready-made pastry means it is quick and easy too.

100g (3½oz) caster sugar

25g (1oz) butter, cubed

1 teaspoon ground cinnamon

6 ripe plums, halved and pitted

1 sheet of ready-rolled puff pastry

ice cream or double cream, to serve

Serves 6

Preheat the oven to 220°C (425°F), Gas Mark 7.

Heat an ovenproof frying pan, about 23–28cm (9–11 inches) in size, over a medium heat and sprinkle the sugar into the pan in an even layer. Swirl the pan over the heat for about 5 minutes, or until the sugar has melted and caramelized to a dark golden colour.

Remove the pan from the heat, dot the butter into the pan, sprinkle in the cinnamon and swirl again to mix it together to form a sauce, or use a wooden spoon or spatula to stir.

Place the plums, cut sides down, into the pan, arranging them in a nice pattern and packing them in as tightly as possible.

Cut the pastry into a disc about 2cm (¾ inch) wider than the top of the pan. Place the pastry over the top of the plums, tucking the edges down the sides of the pan to completely cover the plums. Prick the top of the pastry a few times with a fork.

Place into the oven and bake for 15 minutes, or until the pastry is golden and puffed up, then remove from the oven (be very careful as the pan handle will be really hot). Using a butter knife or palette knife, loosen the pastry from the edges of the pan. Carefully, place a large plate upended over the top of the pan, give the pan a little shake to make sure the tart is loosened and then flip the pan over, with the plate held tightly on the top of the pan, so that the tart drops out onto the plate with the plums facing upwards.

Serve with balls of vanilla ice cream, or whipped double cream, and enjoy while warm.

FIREPIT

⌣

Tim & Emma Ross • *Firepits UK*

'Tim's now become known as Dirty Boy on the trade show circuit,' laughs Emma, 'because he's always covered in black oil.' Tim went from being a corporate art dealer and designer and manufacturer of picture frames to making firepits. It happened, says his wife Emma, as a result of trying to stop a bunch of teenagers from ruining their home. 'Our fifteen-year-old son – he's now in his thirties! – was having a party and we didn't want him and all his friends smoking and drinking beer in our house. So, Tim came up with the idea of making a big metal box so they could sit around a safe, contained bonfire outside. They loved it! And it had the added bonus of not leaving a big burn mark on the lawn.'

Friends started asking if they could borrow Tim's ingenious invention for their own parties, and soon people were asking if he could make more. The timing couldn't have been more perfect. 'It was 2008,' Tim says. 'The time of the big financial crash. The family business that I started when I was twenty-two was struggling. It turned out to be to my advantage, as Emma and I were beginning to realize we had unwittingly hit on an idea that seemed to have potential.'

They started to refine their design, moving on from the utilitarian steel box, made by a local welding company, to a more aesthetically pleasing bowl. These were spun out of untreated steel in a factory in Yorkshire, then finished in their garage at home. Word of mouth got them an invitation to take a stand at a horse show in the neighbouring county. 'We set up our little stand with our firepits,' recalls Emma. 'And two hours later we had sold out. We were just very, very lucky to have had an idea to make something that at the time no one else was doing.' Their next big break came at the Chelsea Flower Show, where, once again, they were the only people selling firepits. They were approached by a man who owned a garden centre. 'He asked if he could buy our whole stand!' Emma laughs. 'We had never sold to trade, and didn't have a trade price, but he didn't care. He just bought the lot and took it away.'

The appeal of their firepits, Tim thinks, is that they are British made, very long-lasting and built to be practical. Even as more companies caught onto the idea and started making firepits, Tim and Emma's business has continued to grow. Tim's design background has allowed them to tinker with and adapt the original model. When customers asked if they could cook on the firepits, Tim came up first with a grill that could sit within the rim, then, thanks to cooking on their own firepit at home, as well as feedback from customers, he developed a grill on a swing arm that could be easily moved on and off, according to what sort of heat was required. 'So the firepit became multi-functional: something you could sit around enjoying the ambience of an open fire, then cook on, then enjoy the fire again once the cooking was done.'

It's been sixteen years since Tim built his first prototype firepit. They continue to be made just around the corner from their home, but now the whole manufacturing process is done in-house and they've expanded from one shed to several. But one thing hasn't changed. They still love going to shows, meeting their customers and selling direct. 'We're on the road a lot,' says Emma. 'We live in a converted horsebox and still really enjoy meeting our customers face to face.'

'The feedback we get is invaluable,' adds Tim. 'That's when I know I've got a design right, or if I need to go back and tweak it.'

But when they are not on the road, their perfect evening is spent around their own firepit with friends. Cooking, drinking wine and watching the sun go down behind the hills.

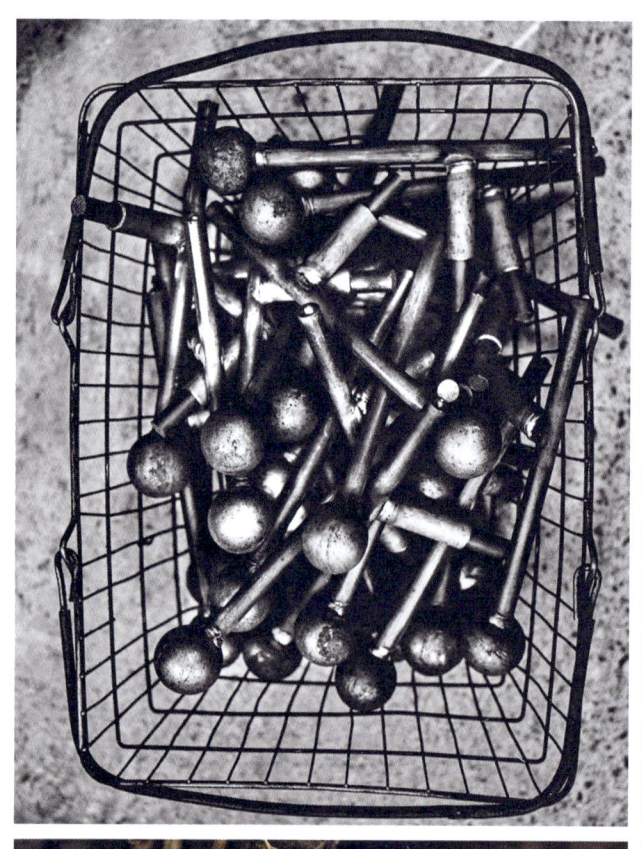

Lamb Skewers
with Quick Roast Chilli Sauce & Herbs
༜

Tim and Emma's favourite firepit dinner with friends is a butterflied leg of lamb, marinated in harissa. The recipe below incorporates all the elements of their favourite meal, but on a smaller scale, so you don't need to gather a crowd to have an excuse to cook it.

FOR THE SKEWERS

150ml (¼ pint) full-fat natural
    yogurt
2 tablespoons Dijon mustard
500g (1lb 2oz) boneless lamb leg
    meat, trimmed of any sinew or
    skin, cut into large cubes
olive oil
sea salt and freshly ground
    black pepper

FOR THE CHILLI SAUCE

2 long red chillies
1 garlic clove, peeled
1 tablespoon tomato purée
3 tablespoons natural yogurt, or
    more if you prefer less chilli heat

TO SERVE

4 flatbreads (see page 75 for
    homemade)
leaves from a small bunch of mint
small bunch of dill, torn

Serves 4

Mix together the yogurt and mustard, then toss the lamb in the mixture until all the pieces are covered. You can do this up to 24 hours in advance, then cover and chill.

Fire up your barbecue or fire, ready for direct grilling. When the barbecue or fire is almost ready to cook on, push a few of the burning embers to one side and place the chillies directly onto the embers. Turn them every minute or so, until charred and blackened all over with soft flesh. Remove and set aside to cool.

Once ready to cook, thread the pieces of lamb onto skewers, making sure not to pack them too tightly. Drizzle with a little olive oil and season well with salt.

Set a grill over the fire and place the lamb skewers over the direct heat. Cook for 2–3 minutes on each side, until caramelized and golden. This will give you lamb that is still a little pink on the inside. Cook a little longer if you prefer your lamb well done. Remove the lamb once cooked and leave to rest while you prepare the chilli sauce.

Peel the skin off the chillies and place the flesh (discarding the seeds) onto a chopping board. Grate the garlic over the top and then finely chop the chilli and garlic until it is almost paste like. Spoon the chilli mixture into a bowl, stir in the tomato purée and yogurt and mix well. Season well with salt and pepper.

Serve the lamb and chilli sauce with flatbreads and the herbs to scatter over everything.

Baba Ganoush with Flatbreads

I love a hummus. I will never say no to a guacamole. But the smoky silkiness of baba ganoush is hard to surpass. It is almost a waste to light a fire and not roast aubergines on it.

FOR THE BABA GANOUSH

3 large aubergines
1 garlic clove, crushed or grated
1 tablespoon tahini
2 tablespoons olive oil
juice of 1 lemon
½ small bunch of parsley, chopped
sea salt and freshly ground
  black pepper

FOR THE FLATBREADS

250g (9oz) plain flour, plus extra
  for dusting
1 teaspoon fine sea salt
1 tablespoon olive oil, plus extra
  for drizzling
150ml (¼ pint) water

Serves 4 as a dip or side

Fire up your barbecue or fire ready for direct cooking. Once the barbecue or fire is hot, pierce the aubergines in a few places with a fork, then place directly on the hot coals or wood, turning now and again for 20 minutes, or until they are charred all over and collapsed.

For the flatbreads, mix the flour, salt and oil in a bowl. Pour about two-thirds of the water into the flour, mixing all the time. Continue to add water until you have a dough that holds together and doesn't stick to the sides of the bowl. It shouldn't be sloppy or wet.

Sprinkle a board or your worktop with flour and tip out the dough. Roughly knead it for a couple of minutes until it becomes stretchy and elastic. Divide into 4 portions and roll out until 3mm (⅛ inch) thick. These flatbreads can be set to one side between sheets of baking paper until you are ready to cook them.

Meanwhile, for the baba ganoush, mix together the garlic, tahini, olive oil and half the lemon juice in a large bowl until completely combined.

Once the aubergines are ready, remove and leave until cool enough to handle. Slice them in half lengthways and gently scoop out the flesh into a sieve, discarding the skins. Press down on the flesh to remove as much liquid as possible. Then put the flesh into the bowl with the tahini mixture. Mix everything together really well to break up the aubergine flesh as much as possible. You want to retain a little texture, but still create a creamy, silky purée. Taste and adjust the seasoning and add more lemon juice if needed. Scatter with some of the parsley and roughly stir it through.

Cook the flatbreads for 2–3 minutes on each side over indirect or direct heat on the barbecue or fire, depending how hot it is. Cook until just starting to turn pale golden brown and bubbling up in places. Once cooked, drizzle with a little olive oil and scatter with sea salt flakes and a grind of pepper if you'd like.

Serve the warm flatbreads alongside the baba ganoush. Scatter the remaining parsley over everything just before serving.

Two Firepit Puddings

When it comes to firepit puddings, Tim and Emma are at loggerheads. Tim would go for simply baked bananas, Emma for peaches. Whatever you decide, both these puds are perfect for cooking at the end of a meal as the embers of your fire are starting to die down. You still need a bit of heat, but nothing like as hot as you'd need for direct cooking.

Tim's Fire-Baked Bananas with Ice Cream

2 ripe bananas   2 balls of your favourite ice cream

Serves 2

Either put the whole bananas in their skins directly on the embers if they're not really really hot, or put them on a grill above the hot embers. Leave for 5–7 minutes, turning now and again, until the skins are completely black and the bananas inside are soft and warm.

Once ready, place onto a plate or into a bowl and split open the banana skins. Serve with balls of your favourite ice cream on top.

Emma's Grilled Peaches with Clotted Cream & Amaretti Biscuits

1 teaspoon flavourless oil, such as   1 tablespoon sugar
  sunflower or vegetable   4 tablespoons clotted cream
2 ripe peaches, halved and pitted   amaretti biscuits, to serve

Serves 2

Brush a little oil on the cut sides of the peach halves, then place cut side down onto a clean grill rack over the hottest part of the embers. This can also be done in a griddle pan on the hob. Grill until the cut sides are caramelized and come away from the grill easily (3–4 minutes). Turn the peaches over so that the skin sides face down. Sprinkle the cut sides with a little sugar and continue to cook for 2–3 minutes, or until softened.

Transfer the grilled peaches to a plate, dot over the clotted cream and crumble some amaretti biscuits on top. Serve immediately.

BOWL

꘎

Michelle Mateo • *Michelle Mateo Crafts*

Watching Michelle Mateo work is mesmerizing. From what appears to be no more than a few simple wooden planks, a pole and some lengths of rope, she constructs a pole lathe, a beautifully simple, non-mechanized device that she operates with her foot. With it she can transform a hunk of wood into a bowl.

Like everyone who has devoted their life to their craft, she makes the process look effortless. 'It's not!' she laughs. 'It took me a long time to be able to make a bowl without swearing and getting frustrated. But it's good frustration: the sort of feeling that makes you more determined not to give up and instead keep trying to get better. The day will come when the penny drops. I remember when it happened to me. I could feel, from the way the wood was cutting, that I'd got the technique right.'

Her introduction to the craft came when she was volunteering at the Cherry Wood Project, just outside Bath. She was reading environmental management at university, with a view to going into woodland management, and volunteering was a way to gain experience. It was there she saw bowl turning for the first time and immediately thought, 'I want to learn how to do that!' But first she had to learn how to make the lathe and it wasn't until the final day of the course that she had a chance to put it to the test. 'Operating the lathe is not dissimilar to trying to pat your head and rub your tummy at the same time. It requires your foot to keep pumping the treadle to keep the lathe spinning while your hands guide the tools over the wood to shape the bowl. It was really difficult, but also sort of addictive.'

In the meantime, Michelle was discovering that jobs in woodland management were few and far between. She had finished her degree and taken an administration job in an office, just to earn some money. 'But I hated it.' Tim, the founder of the Cherry Wood Project, where she was still volunteering, came to her rescue, offering her both a job and somewhere to live. 'The job was cooking for the course and volunteer days. It is all off-grid there, so everything is cooked on fire and in cob ovens, which I'd never done before. I was thrown in at the deep end, but by the time I'd lived there for a few months, I was even baking cakes in cob ovens.' More importantly for Michelle, it gave her the time and space to keep practising and honing the craft that had, by now, become an abiding passion.

Her break finally came a year later when she got a job helping to manage a woodland in Bristol, but by then she had come to realize that she didn't want to be dependent on other people for work. 'I wanted to be able to be self-sufficient, but I didn't really think I had the skills to do anything that would earn me a living on my own.' It was her partner Charlie who pointed out that she did, indeed, have a skill. 'I never imagined bowl turning could be my profession. I just did it because I loved it. Loved the weight and feel of a piece of wood in my hands, of being able to shape and smooth it until it was no longer a hunk of wood, but something practical and useful.'

Emboldened by Charlie, she took out a small business loan and started putting the word out among the crafting community

that she wanted to teach. 'I'm lucky. The green woodworking community is very friendly and supportive. I had a great network from volunteering, and I was soon being asked to do demos and teach at various woodland skills centres all over the country.' In between teaching, she makes bowls on commission or to sell at craft fairs. The first bowl she sold was bought by a friend. 'I would have given it to her, but she insisted on paying for it. That gave me the confidence to believe that the bowls I was making had value and that people might actually want them!'

The woods she uses are native hardwoods such as beech and alder and, her favourite, cherry. 'As soon as you pick up a piece of wood, and you feel the density and the curves, it is already telling you what it's going to be. But I don't make ornaments. Using a bowl gives it life, makes it more beautiful. When someone has put so much effort into making something that is practical, use it every day and love it!'

Mushroom Spelt Risotto

Risotto made with spelt is an altogether earthier, more rustic affair, but every bit as delicious as one made with arborio rice. If you are after a comforting bowl of food that is both warming and full of flavour, look no further.

30g (1oz) dried mushrooms, such as
   porcini or mixed wild
750ml (1 pint 7fl oz) vegetable stock
250g (9oz) chestnut mushrooms,
   finely chopped
olive oil
50g (1¾oz) butter
1 onion, finely chopped
2 garlic cloves, finely chopped

200g (7oz) pearled spelt
175ml (6fl oz) dry white wine
25g (1oz) Parmesan cheese,
   finely grated
3 tablespoons chopped tarragon
   leaves
1 tablespoon balsamic vinegar
sea salt and freshly ground
   black pepper

Serves 4, or 2 very hungry people

Put the dried mushrooms and vegetable stock into a medium saucepan and bring to a simmer. Reduce the heat and leave on the lowest setting to keep warm.

Meanwhile, place the chestnut mushrooms, a glug of oil and a good pinch of salt in a sauté pan over a medium heat. Sauté the mushrooms for 7–10 minutes, until tender and starting to turn golden.

Add half the butter and the onion to the pan with the chestnut mushrooms and sauté over a medium-low heat for a further 10 minutes, until the onions are soft. Add the garlic and cook for a further 2–3 minutes, until cooked through.

With a slotted spoon, remove the rehydrated dried mushrooms from the stock. Chop roughly and leave to one side. Keep the stock over a low heat.

Stir the spelt into the onion so that it is coated in the buttery juices. Leave to cook for a couple of minutes, then pour in the wine. Bring to a simmer for 3–4 minutes, or until reduced and absorbed by the spelt.

Add the hot mushroom stock and the chopped rehydrated mushrooms to the pan and stir to mix. Put a lid on the pan and leave to cook over a medium-low heat, so that it's simmering but not boiling, stirring now and again, until almost all the stock has been absorbed and the spelt is tender, but with a slight bite. This will take about 20 minutes.

Remove the pan from the heat and stir through the remaining butter and the Parmesan. Season to taste. Mix well, then leave to rest for a couple of minutes. Add the tarragon and give it one last stir, then spoon into dishes and drizzle over the balsamic just before serving.

Thai-Spiced Fish Stew

This is heaven in a bowl and needs no more introduction than that!

300g (10½oz) firm white fish, cut
  into chunks

200g (7oz) raw peeled king prawns

flavourless oil, such as sunflower

2 lemon grass stalks, trimmed
  and bashed

3cm (1¼ inch) piece of fresh root ginger,
  peeled and finely chopped or grated

4 garlic cloves, sliced

3 spring onions, sliced

1 long red chilli, sliced

1 tablespoon tomato purée

150g (5½oz) cherry tomatoes, halved

160ml (5½fl oz) coconut cream

500ml (18fl oz) fish or vegetable stock

1 tablespoon fish sauce

1 teaspoon sugar

1 tablespoon tamarind paste

250g (9oz) sugar snap peas

leaves from a small bunch of Thai basil

sea salt and freshly ground
  black pepper

Serves 4

Put the fish and prawns into a bowl and sprinkle over 1 teaspoon of salt. Mix well and leave to one side for up to 1 hour.

Heat a large saucepan over a medium heat, add a dash of oil and stir the lemon grass, ginger, garlic, two-thirds of the spring onions and the chilli over the heat until the garlic turns light golden. Add the tomato purée and stir for a further minute.

Tip in the tomatoes, the coconut cream and the stock and mix to combine. Then stir in the fish sauce, sugar and tamarind and bring to a gentle simmer for 10 minutes. Taste and adjust the seasoning, bearing in mind the fish with its salt will be added shortly. More fish sauce will give a saltier flavour, extra tamarind will increase the sour.

Add the fish, prawns and sugar snap peas and mix through. Simmer gently for a further 3–4 minutes, or until the fish is only just cooked through. Remove the lemon grass stalks and discard. Serve in bowls, scattered with the basil and remaining spring onion.

Potato & Salsa Salad

Michelle likes to make dips and salsas. Her favourite is a mix of finely chopped tomatoes, spring onions, garlic, radishes, lime juice and lots of coriander. 'I love it because it goes with curries, Mediterranean dishes, barbecues... you get the gist!' she says. I've used it as a dressing for a potato salad, because Michelle loves potatoes and because it is infinitely nicer than those mayonnaise-based potato salads that taste, I think, as unappetizing as they look. This, on the other hand, is fresh, zingy and delicious.

500g (1lb 2oz) new potatoes, scrubbed and halved if large

juice of 1–3 limes, to taste

2 garlic cloves, finely chopped

300g (10½oz) tomatoes, finely chopped

3 spring onions, finely chopped

175g (6oz) radishes, halved and sliced

a bunch of coriander, stalks and leaves, chopped

extra virgin olive oil

sea salt and freshly ground black pepper

Serves 4

Boil the new potatoes in salted water until tender. Drain and run under cold water to cool. Leave to one side.

In a large bowl, mix together the juice of 1 lime, the garlic and a good pinch of salt. Leave while you get on with preparing the rest of the ingredients.

Add the tomatoes, spring onions, radishes and coriander to the bowl with the lime and garlic. Mix really well and season generously with salt.

Quarter the cooled potatoes, then stir them through the tomato mixture with a good drizzle of olive oil to bind everything. Taste and adjust the seasoning. You may need more lime juice and a bit more salt. The salad will sit happily for a few hours if needed, or can be eaten straight away.

PLATE

↜↝

Gill Thompson • *Sytch Farm Studios*

Gill Thompson made her first plate by mistake, but it was a formative moment. 'I was about six, at primary school in St Agnes in Cornwall where I grew up, and we were making pinch pots. You're given a lump of clay and you stick your thumb in it and pinch it round and round until you've got a pot. But mine collapsed and I smeared the clay about a bit and realized I'd made a plate. I was so proud of it! I asked Mrs King, my teacher, if I could eat off it and she explained it needed to be fired first. But still. I'd made something that was just one step away from being useful.'

She learned how to throw clay and use a kick wheel while doing A-level art, then, after a foundation course, went to Wolverhampton: 'The best place in the UK at the time to study ceramics.' It was here she honed her craft and developed her style making sculptural pieces, but she was still making pots as presents every Christmas. 'I was a poor student! And it became a bit of a family joke – what's this year's pot going to be like?!'

Gill went into teaching after she graduated. Pottery was something she did in her spare time for the sheer pleasure of it, and the school where she taught was happy for her to use the school kiln. She only thought to sell her work when a friend, who was running a Christmas fair, asked her to come along as she needed more stalls. Gill paid £8 for her table at the fair and came away with £180 in sales. That early success, she thinks, is because everything she made was practical. Made to be used. 'My philosophy then – and now – is if you're not going to use it, don't buy it.' It gave her the confidence to do more small county shows and

when she and her husband Jon moved from Shrewsbury to the Shropshire countryside, she was able to have a dedicated studio and space for a kiln.

I slept in Gill's old pottery, now the beautiful holiday let that Jon created in the space. He built Gill a new, bigger studio in their garden, converting an old pigsty into an oasis of light and calm, among the flowers and fruit trees, the pond, the allotment and the chickens.

Tom Kerridge spotted Gill's work at a festival, and that was the catalyst. Her collaboration with him – and subsequently with many other top chefs – enabled her to become a potter full time. She uses the beautiful stoneware clay from a clay pit in St Agnes where she grew up. Her potter's mark is an ammonite, which she presses into everything she makes to remind everyone who uses it of its provenance. She combines sober glazes with intense, vibrant bursts of colour. It's a style quintessentially hers. Eye-catching. But always practical. Always made to be used.

Courgette Gratin

Gill's allotment is a homage to her favourite vegetable. 'I just love courgettes. I love the beauty and exuberance of the plants. I grow every shape and colour I can find.' And her favourite way of cooking them is in a gratin. 'A French friend gave me her recipe; it's one of those dishes that is very forgiving and can be tinkered with happily without going wrong. But it does require time – you can clean the kitchen, do a crossword, while it quietly simmers away – and lots and lots of cheese.' This is my version of it and, like cauliflower cheese, it can be served either as a side dish or on its own as the ultimate comfort food.

50g (1¾oz) butter
olive oil
2 large onions, finely chopped
800g (1lb 12oz) courgettes
1 teaspoon caraway seeds
2 garlic cloves, crushed

1 tablespoon crème fraîche (optional)
50g (1¾oz) Parmesan cheese, grated
1 slice of dark rye bread, blitzed
   into breadcrumbs
sea salt and freshly ground
   black pepper

Serves 4 as a side, or 2 as a main

Heat a sauté pan or large saucepan over a medium heat. Add the butter and a dash of oil and, once melted, stir in the onions and a good pinch of salt. Sweat until the onions are completely softened, about 15 minutes.

Meanwhile, trim the ends off the courgettes, then partly peel them to leave strips of green. Chop them into 1cm (½ inch) cubes.

Stir the caraway seeds into the onions with the crushed garlic and cook for a minute or so until they become fragrant.

Stir in the courgettes, another glug of olive oil and another good pinch of salt and cook over a medium-low heat, covered with a lid, stirring every so often, for about 45 minutes. Until, Gill says, it looks a bit like porridge, although the courgettes still retain a bit of shape and texture.

Stir in the crème fraîche if using and cook for a further 5 minutes, uncovered, to allow any liquid to evaporate. Taste and adjust the seasoning; it may need a good grinding of pepper and another pinch of salt. This part can be done in advance, up to 2 days before serving if you'd like.

Once ready to cook, preheat the oven to 200°C (400°F), Gas Mark 6. Spoon the courgette mixture into a gratin or baking dish and sprinkle over the cheese. Scatter with the rye breadcrumbs and put into the oven for 15–30 minutes, depending on how cold the courgettes were when they went in. You want the dish to be bubbling and brown on top.

Leave to cool slightly before serving.

Courgette, Artichoke & Burrata Panzanella

~

This is another lovely way of using courgettes but, this time, involves no cooking at all. It is simply an assembly of ingredients that combine to make a fresh-tasting, beautiful-looking, satisfyingly delicious plate of food.

juice and zest of 1 unwaxed lemon

2 tablespoons capers

6 tablespoons extra virgin olive oil, plus extra for drizzling

200g (7oz) stale crusty bread, such as ciabatta

2 courgettes

200g (7oz) drained chargrilled artichokes in oil, roughly chopped

100g (3½oz) drained semi-dried or sunblush tomatoes in oil

a small handful of mint leaves

a handful of basil leaves

1 whole burrata, about 150g (5½oz)

sea salt and freshly ground black pepper

Serves 4

In a large serving bowl or deep platter, mix together the lemon juice and zest, capers, extra virgin olive oil and a good pinch of salt and pepper until completely combined. Tear the bread into chunks and toss in the dressing in the bowl.

With a vegetable peeler, shave the courgettes into ribbons (discarding the seeded part in the middle) and toss into the bowl with the bread, along with the artichokes and tomatoes.

Add most of the mint and basil leaves and toss again. Place the burrata on top and drizzle everything with a little more oil and season with salt and pepper. Scatter over the remaining herbs and serve.

Slow-Cooked Five Spice Hogget

⌇

Jon made this when I went to meet him and Gill at their studios. The hogget – meat from a sheep between one and two years old – had come from their neighbour, Sam. She rears Soays: small, native sheep, descended from a feral population on St Kilda. Cooking the meat with five spice was her suggestion, and it really works. Jon served it with roasted potatoes, gently crushed once cooked (an excellent way of soaking up the gravy), spring greens and balsamic-roasted red onions and beetroot that were soft and gloriously sticky. It was a feast.

FOR THE HOGGET

1 leg of hogget, about 2kg (4lb 8oz)
olive oil
2 tablespoons Chinese five
  spice powder
sea salt and freshly ground
  black pepper

FOR THE ONIONS & BEETROOT

6 beetroot, trimmed, scrubbed clean
  and cut into slim wedges
4 red onions, peeled and cut into
  thick wedges
leaves from 4 thyme sprigs
2 tablespoons balsamic vinegar
sea salt and freshly ground
  black pepper

Serves 6

A few hours before you want to cook, or up to a day in advance, marinate the meat. Prick the hogget all over with a sharp knife and rub with a little oil. Massage in the five spice powder and leave to marinate, either in the fridge or on the work surface if you're cooking it soon.

Preheat the oven to 150°C (300°F), Gas Mark 2, and get the meat to room temperature.

Place the hogget into a large roasting tray and pour 4cm (1½ inches) of water into the tray. Season the meat, then cover with foil, securing the edges to the tray.

Place in the oven and slow cook for up to 5 hours, basting the meat every now and then (ideally every 30–45 minutes). Top up the water in the tray if necessary, aiming to keep it at least 2cm (¾ inch) deep throughout.

Place the beetroot wedges onto a lined baking tray with the onions and thyme leaves. Drizzle over the balsamic, some olive oil, season really well and toss to coat all the pieces. Cover with foil, securing the edges to the tray. For the final hour of the hogget cooking time, place the tray of onions and beetroot in the oven.

Once the meat is really tender, remove from the oven. Leave the onions and beetroot in there, but remove their foil covering. Increase the oven temperature to 200°C (400°F), Gas Mark 6. Flake the meat off the bone into chunks and put back into the roasting tray, mixing with the juices. Return it to the oven and cook for a further 20 minutes to crisp up slightly.

Remove everything from the oven and leave the hogget to rest with the onions and beetroot. Pour any juices over everything before serving.

SPOON

༄

David White • *The Whittlings*

David White whittles spoons. He works in the studio he built in his garden, using green wood planks bought from a small woodland timber yard. Many of his tools are handmade too, the handles made from sturdy sticks cut to length, into which are embedded iron hooks of various shapes and sizes.

Green woodworking is an ancient craft, based, he says, on medieval-era technology using simple, blacksmith-made hand tools. But much of David's inspiration comes from the traditional Japanese understanding of the properties of wood. 'The beauty of working with green wood is that you end up with very fluid, loose shapes that warp and change as they dry. The secret to green woodworking isn't just the craftmanship. It's about fundamentally understanding how every type of wood behaves as it dries. Even different parts of the same tree will behave differently as they dry.'

The wood he uses is often windfall, sourced from the forests and woodlands around his North Wales home. 'The environmental aspect of green woodworking appeals to me too. I can use wood that is super-local and I'm making products that can last a lifetime and that grow in character the more they are used and the older they become.'

Although it was design and woodworking in which he excelled at school, 'in an era of flat-pack furniture, furniture-making didn't seem a viable career.' Instead, he became a graphic designer, using his artistic skills in a different but – ultimately for him – unfulfilling way. 'I found myself putting my heart and soul into designing something that ended up online and, because of the nature of the internet, was always going to be transient.' So when he and his family left the city and moved back to North Wales, he started taking green woodworking courses at the woodland skills centre near his home. 'I did nearly every course they offered and after a few years I started teaching green woodworking myself!'

Alongside design projects, he started doing food photography for restaurants and local producers. A top chef setting up in Wales wanted to work with local producers and makers, and saw some little cawl spoons David had made. Cawl is the soupy stew that is the mainstay of many a Welsh kitchen, and was traditionally eaten with a small oval-shaped ladle with a handle that tapered towards the end. Every village had a blacksmith who would make the hook tools to carve the spoons. The tools would be shared around the village and the shape of the spoons developed regional styles, somewhat dictated by the tools the local blacksmith created and the way they were made.

David's design is particular to him. 'I scaled my cawl spoon down to be dessertspoon sized, so it's more versatile, and went back to my love of the Japanese aesthetic. I wanted the simplest shape I could create that was still completely functional.' Cawl spoons, as well as dairy bowls and handwashing bowls, were often made from sycamore wood in Wales, an introduced species that wasn't valued for building but grows quickly and also has natural antibacterial properties. David also uses sycamore, finishing the spoons with a white oil which makes them look almost as if they were carved from bone. He uses walnut, too, for its beautiful, chocolate-brown colour. 'The chef asked if I could make him thirty cawl spoons! It was my first commission and I felt like an imposter. I was just a designer who happened to know how to make spoons, but I said yes. And then he asked for more tableware, and before long I had made him about two hundred different pieces.'

Other chefs followed suit. It became increasingly impossible to fit his design work around the woodwork commissions. 'So, I made the decision to give up being a graphic designer and become a spoon carver in the shed in my garden. Everyone around me was saying, "You're going to carve spoons for a living? Are you mad?!" But it was such a passion for me that I just couldn't turn down the chance.'

Root Vegetable Cawl

Cawl is usually made using meat – lamb, beef or ham hock – and vegetables, cooked in a deep, meaty stock. When his son turned vegetarian, David created a stock from roasted root vegetables to get the same depth of flavour. Pooch and I played around a bit, infused dried mushrooms in the liquid that would form the stock, and stirred in a good dollop of Marmite. Don't be put off if you're a Marmite hater: it gives the stock, which thanks to the roast veg is quite sweet, a more savoury note, but doesn't, I promise, taste of Marmite.

If you stick with tradition, cawl is eaten with bread and cheese. If it's wild garlic season, David recommends stirring in a handful of chopped garlic leaves. This cawl is also delicious topped with a little grated cured egg yolk or dried dulse seaweed, for an umami hit. For a heartier cawl, add a couple of handfuls of pearled barley along with the vegetables at the beginning of the cawl's cooking time. Cook until the barley is tender.

FOR THE VEGETABLE STOCK

2 large carrots, cut into chunks

2 onions, peeled and cut into wedges

1 leek, roughly sliced

400g (14oz) celeriac, peeled and cut into chunks

2 celery sticks, roughly cut

1 head of garlic, halved

olive oil

2 bay leaves

2 thyme sprigs

1 small rosemary sprig

2.5 litres (4½ pints) water

sea salt and freshly ground black pepper

FOR THE CAWL

2.25 litres (4 pints) vegetable stock

2 carrots, peeled and cut into small cubes

1 large potato, cut into small cubes

1 small swede, peeled and cut into small cubes

1 parsnip, peeled and cut into small cubes

2 leeks, trimmed and sliced into 1cm (½ inch) thick rounds

1 bay leaf

4 thyme sprigs

1 tablespoon Marmite

½ small bunch of parsley, chopped

Serves 4

Preheat the oven to 200°C (400°F), Gas Mark 6. Put the stock vegetables and garlic onto a large roasting tray (or divide between 2 trays if necessary, so they aren't too crowded). Drizzle with olive oil and season. Toss to coat, then roast in the oven for 30–40 minutes, stirring now and again, until golden and caramelized on the edges.

Tip the vegetables into a large saucepan, add the herbs and measured water, bring to the boil, then simmer rapidly for 45 minutes, squashing and mixing the vegetables (a potato masher is great for this) as much as possible so that they release all their flavour into the water.

Pour through a fine sieve into a large bowl, pushing as much of the solids through the sieve as possible. Discard the contents of the sieve. Your stock is now ready to use.

To make the cawl, heat the stock in a large saucepan. Add all the cawl ingredients, except for the parsley, and simmer with a pinch of salt until the vegetables are just cooked through. This will take about 20 minutes, or a little longer, depending on how large your chunks are.

Taste and adjust the seasoning, adding more salt if necessary. Remove the bay leaf and thyme. Stir through the parsley and serve in bowls.

Venison Kofte
with Wild Garlic & Fennel Butter
⌇

This is David's favourite way to eat the venison he buys direct from the man who helps control the deer population in the forests near his home. Venison is widely available now and this is a lovely way to cook it. If it's the wrong time of year for wild garlic, use parsley or another soft green herb of your choice. Or make the butter when wild garlic is in season and store in the freezer, where it will keep for up to a year. The Quick Pickled Fennel on page 42 goes really well with this too.

FOR THE WILD GARLIC &
FENNEL BUTTER
1 teaspoon fennel seeds

a handful of wild garlic leaves,
finely chopped
100g (3½oz) butter, softened

FOR THE KOFTE

1 small onion, grated

a handful of parsley leaves,
    finely chopped

a handful of mint leaves,
    finely chopped

2½ teaspoons ground cumin

1½ teaspoons ground coriander

½ teaspoon chilli flakes (optional)

2 teaspoons fine sea salt

500g (1lb 2oz) minced venison

olive oil

flatbreads, slaw and yogurt, or pitta
    breads and salad, to serve

Serves 4

Place all the kofte ingredients, except the oil, into a large bowl and mix together really well with your hands. You need to make sure all of the ingredients are evenly distributed before you start to shape your kofte.

Take small handfuls of the mixture and shape into torpedo shapes or patties. If you're planning to cook them over a fire or on a barbecue, then be mindful of the shape of your grill and which shape works best so that they don't slip through the grill bars. Place the kofte onto a plate and into the fridge to chill and firm up while you make the butter.

For the butter, toast the fennel seeds in a dry frying pan over a medium heat until fragrant, then finely chop them or crush roughly in a pestle and mortar. Mix with the wild garlic and butter until the flavourings are evenly distributed. Place a couple of sheets of clingfilm or baking paper on a work surface and spoon the butter on top. Using the sheets, roll the butter into a sausage shape and twist the ends of the sheets to secure. Place into the freezer or fridge to firm up.

Once ready to cook, heat a frying pan (or a barbecue) and drizzle a little olive oil over the kofte, making sure they are evenly coated. Cook the kofte until brown on all sides. You don't need to cook venison all the way through – the kofte are fine to serve pink – but cook them through if you'd prefer.

Transfer the kofte to a plate and dot with slices of the flavoured butter. Leave to rest for a few minutes to allow the butter to melt and coat the kofte. Serve while still warm. Delicious served with flatbreads, slaw and yogurt, or in warmed pitta breads with some salad.

Bircher Muesli

⌁

My Austrian friend Marina was the first person to introduce me to Bircher muesli and ever since it has become a breakfast regular, particularly when we have friends to stay. I'll make big bowls of it and, depending on what's in the garden, might serve it alongside stewed rhubarb, or baked plums. If it's blackberry season, they make a beautiful addition too.

125g (4½oz) oats
350ml (12fl oz) best-quality
  apple juice
250ml (9fl oz) milk of your choice
50g (1¾oz) sultanas

50g (1¾oz) almonds, roughly
  chopped
1 apple, grated, core discarded
4 tablespoons toasted mixed seeds

Serves 4

Place the oats, apple juice, milk, sultanas and almonds into a large bowl or Tupperware box and mix well. Leave overnight in the fridge to soften up and soak up the liquid.

Once ready to serve, give the Bircher muesli a really good stir, then mix in the grated apple. Stir again and divide into bowls. Top each bowl with a sprinkling of toasted seeds and serve immediately.

GLASS

 ‿

Emsie Sharp • *Sharp Glass*

In an old cow shed in the depths of the Dorset countryside, a woman is performing magic. I watch with wide-eyed delight as Emsie Sharp transforms the fiery blob of molten glass on the end of a long metal rod, deftly blowing, twisting and rolling it. It expands and begins to take shape, until it becomes, all of a sudden, a beautiful bottle in jewel-bright stripes.

Emsie did not do well at school. 'I failed everything! Even though I was good at art, I couldn't get into art school because I didn't get any O-levels.' She left school at 16 and did a Cordon Bleu cooking course. 'I loved the creative side of making beautiful desserts, but also the precision needed to do it right.' She started cooking professionally, but still she yearned to go to art school, so did evening classes in working with stained glass. She built up a portfolio of work and was accepted at Farnham Art School. The creativity and precision she had used to such great effect in her cooking transferred perfectly into the making of glass.

It was her first opportunity to work with molten glass. 'It was my first day and there I was in what was called the "hot shop" and it was like something just went click! There is something about glass that is unique and I knew this was the material I wanted to work with. It's exciting, it's fluid, it requires dexterity, it's fun. I loved the adrenalin rush that working with glass gave me. I loved the colour. And it was the first time anyone had ever said to me "Wow! You're good at this."'

But the techniques required to work glass successfully take a long time to learn and to hone. 'It's really hard and pretty much everything you make at first is terrible! I remember

my first attempt at making a wine glass. It had this really thick, chunky base and leaned to the left, but gradually you get better. It just takes practice.' And she got plenty of that when she took herself off to Murano, the glass-making centre of Venice, and asked for a job. She was turned down three times, but eventually she was offered a three-week, unpaid internship. She stayed for three years. 'I spoke no Italian, I was the only woman in the factory, and we were making a hundred wine glasses a day. I loved the intricacy of making wine glasses. The Venetians work really fast, they blow the glass really thin. The work is very focused and intense and sweaty. We worked ten hours a day. It was hardcore. But it didn't put me off. It made me even more passionate.'

In 2003 Emsie returned to the UK and got a grant to set up her own studio. When I step inside, the heat from the roaring furnace hits me. It burns at over 1,000°C and is full of molten glass. There's another, cooler oven where finished pieces are put to set – 'And where I cook baked potatoes!' – and there is also the so-called 'glory hole', a small furnace in which Emsie reheats the glass she is working on. On racks against the wall there are thick round bars of coloured glass – her equivalent of tubes of oil paint – and pots of pencil-like rods that she has stretched and cut, ready for the furnace. 'I work with lead crystal. Not many people work with it any more, but it's what I trained with, and I love it for its clarity, brightness and softness.'

And then there are the shelves containing her finished pieces. Most of her work is commissioned, although she does make some to sell online. It's the colours she uses that are so striking: rich and jewel-like. 'Brightening up your life with colour is really important. I always seek out colour. I've always loved it. And I've learned from mistakes. A lot of my designs, patterns and colours have come from mistakes.' She does some sculptural work, although most of what she makes is practical – bases for lamps, bowls, bottles for olive oil – but glasses are still the thing she makes most. 'It's what I love. It's alchemy. I still think it's amazing and I've been doing it every day now for thirty years!'

Two Prawn Cocktails

It was Pooch's idea to include a recipe for prawn cocktail, the dish synonymous with hotel starters in the seventies. It was her childhood favourite, one she always ate on holiday in Ireland, whereas I hate it. 'Wait until you taste mine,' said Pooch. And I had to concede that hers is very good indeed. However, just to be contrary, I came up with a version of my own.

Pooch's Prawn Cocktail

300g (10½oz) cooked shell-on
    prawns
½ Iceberg lettuce, outer leaves
    removed
2 lemon wedges
brown bread, sliced and cut into
    triangles
lots of Irish salted butter

FOR THE SAUCE
5 tablespoons mayonnaise
1 tablespoon tomato ketchup
¼ teaspoon brandy
a couple of shakes of Worcestershire
    sauce
pinch of cayenne pepper, plus extra
    for dusting
Tabasco sauce, to taste
a squeeze or 2 of lemon juice
salt and freshly ground black pepper

Serves 2 as a generous starter, or 4 as part of a lunch

Peel the prawns and leave to one side. Pooch says if you want to look swish, you could leave 2 unpeeled for garnish (although this definitely wasn't how they were served back in the late eighties or early nineties in Ireland!).

Shred the lettuce, favouring the whiter, crisper parts. If it is remotely limp, then place in iced water to crisp up. Drain and dry really well with kitchen paper or a clean tea towel before using.

Mix together the sauce ingredients, adding just a small squeeze of lemon juice and a shake or 2 of Tabasco. Taste, then go from there, adding a little more of each or either to taste. Season with a little salt and pepper – it won't need much of either, but benefits from a touch of both.

Place a dollop of the sauce into the bottoms of 2 glasses or serving dishes. Top with shredded lettuce, pushing it down into the glasses. Add the prawns on top, dividing them equally between the 2 glasses. Spoon the rest of the sauce over the prawns and dust the top with a little extra cayenne pepper. Add a lemon wedge to each glass.

Serve with triangles of brown bread with lots of butter on the side. Alternatively, take a leaf out of Pooch's book and add fries and a spicy bloody Mary for a brilliant lunch!

Kate's (Contrary) Prawn Cocktail

I used smoked sriracha made by Eaten Alive, which can be bought online. If you can't get hold of it, regular sriracha also works well.

5 tablespoons mayonnaise

1½ teaspoons smoked sriracha, or to taste

a squeeze or 2 of lime juice, plus 2 lime wedges to serve

1 Baby Gem lettuce, shredded

½ cucumber, deseeded and cut into matchsticks

300g (10½oz) cooked peeled king prawns

sea salt and freshly ground black pepper

Serves 2 as a generous starter, or 4 as part of a lunch

Mix together the mayonnaise, smoked sriracha and lime juice. Start with a small squeeze of lime juice, taste, then go from there, adding a little more if needed. Season with a little salt and pepper – it won't need much of either, but benefits from a touch of both.

Mix together the shredded lettuce and cucumber matchsticks.

Place a dollop of the sauce into the bottoms of 2 glasses. Top with the shredded lettuce and cucumber mixture, pushing it down into the glasses.

Mix the prawns into the remaining sauce and spoon over the lettuce in the glasses. Spoon any remaining sauce at the bottom of the bowl over the prawns and serve with a lime wedge attached to the side of each glass.

Tumbler Lemon Curd & Raspberry 'Cheesecake'

In contrast to Emsie's artwork of a pudding overleaf, this is very simple. It's a sort of deconstructed cheesecake that requires no cooking, can be made in an instant and is ridiculously good. Serve it, of course, in a glass tumbler. Or even a jar.

250g (9oz) raspberries

1–2 teaspoons caster sugar, to taste

juice of ½ lemon

500ml (18fl oz) Greek yogurt

2–3 tablespoons lemon curd, to taste

zest of 1 unwaxed lemon

80g (3oz) gingernut biscuits

mint leaves, to decorate

Serves 4

Divide the raspberries between 4 glass tumblers and sprinkle a little bit of sugar over them. Spritz with lemon juice and mix gently, then leave to one side.

Tip the Greek yogurt into a bowl. Add the lemon curd and taste to see if it is lemony enough, adjusting if necessary. Stir in the lemon zest.

Spoon the yogurt mixture into the tumblers on top of the raspberries, then crumble the gingernut biscuits over the top. Finish with a few mint leaves to decorate. Serve immediately.

Emsie's Hazelnut Meringue Roulade

٭

This is Emsie's favourite pudding of the moment. The day after I met her she was going to be making this for 150 wedding guests. Lucky them! As beautiful as her work in glass, this roulade takes some effort, but is so show-stoppingly gorgeous, it's worth it.

6 egg whites, at room temperature	sea salt
340g (11¾oz) caster sugar, at room temperature	350g (12oz) frozen raspberries
	lemon juice
100g (3½oz) roasted chopped hazelnuts	600ml (20fl oz) double cream
	200g (7oz) fresh raspberries

Serves 8

Preheat the oven to 180°C (350°F), Gas Mark 4, and line a large baking tray with baking paper. Emsie uses the one in her oven, about 36 x 34 cm (14½ x 13¼ inches).

In a large, very clean bowl, whisk the egg whites with a handheld electric whisk (or in a stand mixer) until doubled in size. With the whisk still running, slowly add the sugar 1 spoonful at a time, whisking constantly until all the sugar has been added and you have reached a glossy stiff peak. Gently fold in the hazelnuts, along with a pinch of salt.

Spread the meringue mixture out onto the lined baking tray then place on the middle shelf of the oven and bake for 20 minutes, or until the meringue is cracking a little, crispy on the top and a nice golden colour. It should still be chewy inside. Remove from the oven.

Place a clean tea towel on a work surface, or on top of a cooling rack. Flip the meringue out of the baking tray onto the clean tea towel and peel off the baking paper. Take the 2 corners of a long edge of the tea towel and gently roll the meringue and tea towel together into a log shape. Leave to cool.

Put the frozen raspberries into a medium saucepan over a medium heat and simmer with a squeeze of lemon juice until soft and bubbling. Simmer for 5 more minutes.

Pour the raspberries through a sieve suspended over a bowl, pushing any bits of flesh

through the sieve, but sieving out the seeds. If the resulting coulis in the bowl is too thin, place back over the heat and simmer until thickened to your liking. Leave to cool.

Whip the double cream to a soft peak consistency. Once the meringue is completely cool, unroll gently and spread the whipped cream over the meringue. Drizzle over three-quarters of the coulis, reserving the rest to finish the roulade at the end. Scatter over the fresh raspberries.

Using the tea towel for support, gently roll up the meringue again with the raspberries and cream enclosed inside. Carefully transfer to a serving dish. Drizzle with the remaining coulis and serve, or offer the coulis in a bowl on the side.

BREAD

꙳

Gerald Miles & Jacqueline 'Jam' Morgan
Caerhys Organic Community Agriculture

Gerald was born on the farm he took over from his father when he was sixteen years old. His father had run the 120 acres as a mixed farm, rearing livestock and growing wheat and a crop known as shipreys, a mixture of barley and black oats. Black oats – so called because the hulls of the seeds are black – ripen earlier than the more commonly grown white oats, so both barley and oats would be ready to harvest at the same time. It was, Gerald says, an excellent animal feed. 'In October, the cattle would be fed whole sheaves of shipreys, because the oats helped them put on condition before the winter and the spiky bits of the barley would worm them.'

When Gerald took on the farm, he moved away from cereal crops, concentrating more on growing potatoes and increasing the farm's dairy herd. 'It was a great buzzing farm back then. We used to employ thirty-four people here to plant and pick potatoes. It supported a lot of local families.' But in 1985 the price of potatoes dropped so dramatically – from £300 per ton to just £8 per ton in a week – that Gerald and other farmers like him were left in financial ruin. The bank agreed to a loan, but only if he would sign a banker's charge which, he recalls with pained disbelief, 'would have allowed them to sell the farm whenever they wanted without my permission and to own everything.'

He refused the bank's terms, contacted everyone he owed money to and told them it would be at least three years before he could pay them. His dairy herd kept him afloat until

the milk price dropped in the 1990s and that's when he stopped. 'We made a living from tourism – running a B&B. We kept a few horses for people and bought cows to rear for beef. And I became an activist!'

A demonstration outside the European parliament in Brussels against chemical giant Monsanto's grip on the seed market saw farmers exchanging seeds of the old crop varieties that were fast disappearing from the landscape. Gerald was given some emmer wheat. 'It's a variety that dates back to the time of the ancient Egyptians. I took ten kilos home on the Eurostar, through customs, and planted it here on the farm. It looked so good, it started me thinking about other old varieties that had been grown around here, and particularly the black oats my father used to have on the farm.'

It took a year to track down someone who had the seed, and then almost sixty years after he took on the farm, black oats were once again growing in the Pembrokeshire soil. And they flourished. 'They can grow anywhere. They don't need fertile soil. They can grow up a mountain or down in a valley.' Now aged seventy-six, Gerald is a key figure in the movement to promote and protect heritage varieties of cereal crops. 'These are the varieties that will feed us though climate change,' he says. And that was music to Jacqueline's ears.

Jacqueline grew up in a small fishing village on the Towey estuary, surrounded by a family for whom food was a way of life. 'I grew up growing vegetables with my grandfather, cooking with my grandmother and my mother, foraging with my great grandmother, and fishing with my father,' she says. 'It comes as second nature to me. Food is my first and foremost love.'

At fourteen, Jaqueline was earning pocket money cooking at her local community centre. At eighteen, she was cooking in a country pub, where she ended up running the kitchen. 'Lonwen, the lady who ran the pub, was the first person to realize my potential. She encouraged me to go and study professional cookery. And quite quickly I learned that I was quite good at it and that I really enjoyed it.' She was offered a two-week work placement as a pastry chef in a high-end restaurant. 'I had to make the bread every day, and classic French desserts like crème caramel. It was wonderful! I started dreaming about heading to London and Michelin stars!'

But as she continued to work in different kitchens in different establishments, she came to realize that many professional chefs had scant regard for provenance and sustainability; that the true value of food she had been made so aware of by her family was often overlooked. 'I saw a lot of misuse and lack of love for food within the industry and that disappointed me.'

For a while, she left her professional cooking career behind and went to university to do a degree in photojournalism. 'I wanted to make a difference to the attitudes people have towards food and felt maybe I could do it more effectively out of the kitchen, by writing.' But it was cooking that could provide an income, and as well as writing, she worked as a private chef doing supper clubs and dinners. It was at a dinner hosted by the Gaia Foundation that she met Gerald. 'And as soon as I did, I instantly felt I had come home. That I had found my kindred spirit.'

It was Jacqueline who baked the biscuits that gave Gerald his first taste of his own black oats. 'At that Gaia Foundation dinner, Jacqueline baked some really thin, crisp cheese biscuits and a few of us did a blind taste test. We had various crackers from different supermarkets but every one of us picked the biscuits Jacqueline had made as the best. It was the flavour of those oats, their sweetness, that set them apart.'

Jacqueline and Gerald have become collaborators, growing and cooking food that is responsibly and sustainably produced and benefits both farmers and the environment. 'My dream is to open a bakery,' Jacqueline says, 'and to make heritage, locally sourced grains attainable and desirable to everyone.'

A Heritage Loaf

٭

This is Jacqueline's recipe for a sourdough that uses fermented oats as a starter and Hen Gymro flour. Hen Gymro means 'old Welsh' and this ancient variety of wheat was commonly grown on the west coast of Wales and is having a bit of a resurgence, thanks to farmers. Look for it online. If you can't track down Hen Gymro flour, use the best-quality flour you can get your hands on (Hodmedods do a great range). The oats need soaking at least overnight, so this is a loaf to start one day and finish the next.

FOR THE FERMENTED OATS

70g (2½oz) porridge oats

½ teaspoon easy bake yeast, or
   5g (⅛oz) fresh yeast

15g (½oz) treacle

375ml (13fl oz) lukewarm water

FOR THE LOAF

160g (5¾oz) wholegrain Hen Gymro
   flour (see recipe introduction)

30g (1oz) wholegrain barley flour, or
   wholegrain wheat flour

310g (11oz) strong white bread flour,
   plus extra for dusting

75g (2½oz) whole oats

½ teaspoon easy bake yeast or
   5g (⅛oz) fresh yeast

10g (¼oz) fine sea salt

Makes 1 loaf

Combine the ingredients for the fermented oats in a bowl and mix well. Leave at room temperature for at least 12 hours or up to 24 hours to create fermented sour oats.

The following day, put all the ingredients for the loaf except for the fermented oats into a large mixing bowl, or the bowl of a stand mixer, reserving 25g (1oz) of the whole oats for the top of the bread. Briefly mix the dry ingredients together to incorporate and distribute them evenly.

Add the fermented oats and mix well using a dough hook if using a stand mixer, or by hand if not. Knead for 10 minutes on a low speed in the stand mixer, or by hand. The dough should come together into a soft ball. Turn the dough out onto the work surface and leave to rest for 30 minutes, covered with a damp clean tea towel.

Once rested, rub the top of the dough with flour, then turn it flour side down, folding the edges of your dough into the middle to create a ball shape. Pinch together the edges, then dust with flour and turn over once more.

Place the dough onto a piece of baking paper and put it in a large cast-iron casserole dish, or onto a baking tray if you don't have a suitable casserole. Rub the top of the dough with a little water and sprinkle over the reserved oats. Leave the dough to prove for 1 hour, ideally somewhere quite warm. The dough should double in size.

Preheat the oven to 220°C (425°F), Gas Mark 7. Once ready to cook, score the top of the loaf with a sharp knife and, as quickly as possible, put into the oven to bake. If you're using a cast iron casserole dish, cook with the lid on for 30 minutes, then remove the lid and cook for a further 15 minutes, until the loaf feels and sounds hollow if knocked on the bottom. If using a baking tray for the loaf, cook for 15 minutes, then reduce the oven temperature to 200°C (400°F), Gas Mark 6, and bake for a further 30 minutes. Remove from the oven and leave to cool completely before cutting.

And the Butter to Go With It

I helped to make butter once, in a place where it was still done entirely by hand. It involved stirring milk in a barrel for hour after muscle-aching hour. Now, you may think that making butter even with the considerable help of an electric mixer is a bit daft when it is so readily available to buy, but it gives me huge pleasure to watch cream become butter without the pain. And, like anything homemade, it does seem to taste better than the shop-bought stuff.

600ml (20fl oz) best-quality
double cream

fine sea salt

Makes about 150g (5½oz)
Pour the cream into a large bowl or the bowl of a stand mixer. Using a handheld electric whisk or the mixer, whip the cream at high speed until it looks like over-whipped cream and is starting to turn grainy. Scrape down the sides of the bowl now and again as you're whipping. Reduce the speed once the cream starts to firm up, and continue to whip until it separates into butter solids and buttermilk. This will take 7–10 minutes.

Place a sieve over a bowl and tip the butter solids into the sieve. Squeeze the butter solids to remove as much buttermilk as possible. Pour off and save the buttermilk that drains out to use in another recipe.

Put the butter solids (still in the sieve over the now-empty bowl) into the sink under the cold tap. Run the cold water over the butter solids and knead and squeeze out any buttermilk that remains. Do this until the water runs clear. Drain the butter and place into a bowl.

Add a big pinch of sea salt to the butter and knead it in. Add more salt to your taste.

Store the butter in a clean jar, or roll it into a sausage shape, wrap in baking paper and chill in the fridge until ready to use.

Legacy on Toast

When our dear friend David died, his wife and daughters celebrated his life in the garden he loved, surrounded by flowers, and colour, and the people he held most dear. One of them, who had known him for more than fifty years, described the supper he made for her when they first met, and I suspect it wasn't just me who went home that evening and recreated it. So, this is with love and thanks to David.

2 large handfuls of watercress, any thick stalks removed

2–4 slices (depending on size) of really good brown bread

1 small pear, quartered, cored and thinly sliced

125g (4½oz) blue cheese, crumbled

Serves 2

Preheat the grill to hot.

Place the watercress in a pan over a medium heat and stir until wilted a little. Remove from the heat.

Place the bread onto a baking tray and toast on one side under the grill. Remove the tray from the grill, turn the bread over and divide the watercress between the untoasted sides of the bread. Top with the slices of pear and then the blue cheese.

Place back under the grill and cook for a minute or 2, until the blue cheese has melted. Eat immediately.

Sarah's Nan's Bread Pudding

ᐧᐧᐧ

My friend, Farmer Tim, makes a mean bread pudding. When he first made it for us, I was expecting bread and butter pudding, but bread pudding is a different and, in my view, better joy altogether. It's eaten in hearty, comforting squares with a mug of tea, or as a pudding with, if you're Tim, a thick slick of custard. The recipe he uses is that of his wife Sarah's grandmother. This is heritage Welsh cooking. Treat it with reverence! And start making it the day before you want to eat it, because it requires overnight soaking.

There is no sugar in the pudding, just a little sprinkled on top, because I feel the dried fruit gives it all the sweetness it needs. If you like a sweeter pudding, however, add 125g (4½oz) with the breadcrumbs.

425ml (¾ pint) milk

150ml (¼ pint) cold, strong tea
  (made with 2 teabags)

110g (4oz) butter, melted, plus a little
  extra for the tin

1 tablespoon mixed spice

3 eggs, lightly beaten

350g (12oz) mixed dried fruit

450g (1lb) fresh breadcrumbs
  (brown or white, or a mixture
  of both)

2–3 tablespoons demerara sugar

Makes 12–16 pieces

In a large bowl, mix together the milk, tea, melted butter, mixed spice, eggs and dried fruit. Stir until well combined. Add the breadcrumbs and stir again until everything is really well mixed. Cover the bowl and leave to soak overnight.

Once you are ready to cook, preheat the oven to 180°C (350°F), Gas Mark 4. Butter and line a baking tin, about 28x20x4cm (11x8x1½ inches), then tip the mixture into the tin and spread it out evenly. Sprinkle with the demerara sugar.

Bake in the oven for 1¼ hours, until firm and golden. Leave to cool in the tin before removing the paper and cutting into squares.

SEASONINGS

David, Alison & Jess • *Halen Môn*

Forty years ago, David and Alison bought a derelict oyster hatchery on the island of Anglesey off the north coast of Wales. They grew mussels and oysters, kept lobsters and ran a fishmonger's shop. It was a precarious way to make a living, so they opened a public aquarium on the site too, but the seasonal nature of a tourism business meant that wasn't a sustainable idea either. 'There was a lot at stake,' David says. 'We had had to borrow a lot of money to set up the business and our house was secured on that loan, and we had lovely staff; we wanted to keep them on. So, we had to come up with an idea that could make money all year round.'

They drew up a list of forty ideas and neither Alison nor David can remember who added 'make salt'. 'We both think we came up with it!' they laugh. 'But as we were already paying for the licence to use sea water in the aquarium, it seemed like an idea that made sense.'

David's first attempt to extract the salt from the water around their Anglesey home was not promising. He put a pan of sea water on the Aga and 'boiled it to death'. The result was disappointing. 'I was left with salty sludge.' So he tried again, heating the water at a much lower temperature, watching the salt crystals gathering on the surface. 'It's alchemy,' says Alison. 'You heat the sea water, and these beautiful white flakes appear.'

'But only if you do it in a certain way,' adds David. 'In theory, it's simple. In practice, it's more difficult. And we had to find a reliable way to ensure we had a high-quality product every time we made it. That was the key.'

But would anyone pay significantly more for a product they could buy cheaply in every supermarket? 'We looked at real ale, artisan bread and single estate tea, everyday commodities that had value because they had a story; they had provenance. So, we pitched the idea of producing and selling Anglesey sea salt to a group of MBA students. They were very enthusiastic, with no preconceptions. They looked at things like how important the Welsh provenance was and said, yes, it'll work! But you have to charge a premium, you have to make the products look great and you have to tell their story. Their professor disagreed and thought it would never work.'

So, in 1995, David set about honing his salt-making technique. It was, he said, 'slightly wacky' and entirely down to trial and error, because only one other person, right on the

opposite side of Britain, was attempting to do the same. The test came when David and Alison went to their first trade food show in London with tubes of their salt, bearing navy blue labels David had run off on a photocopier. They had two buyers: one was a deli in Knightsbridge, 'who liked the packaging because it went with their décor,' and one was a butcher from Anglesey. 'About 10 miles from here. She still sells our salt now. The Knightsbridge deli went bust!' But it proved that they had a product people believed in and wanted to buy. 'The professor was wrong!' laughs Alison.

Their breakthrough moment came at a subsequent show where they met a Spanish distributor. David was sceptical that he would have any interest in their salt at all. 'But he tasted it, and he was absolutely blown away. One of his customers was El Bulli, at the time

the greatest restaurant in the world. When head chef Ferran Adrià said he loved our salt, we knew we'd picked the right idea from our original list of forty.'

The business that started as a sludgy mess in a saucepan in their kitchen has continued to grow and innovate because (Alison and David think) they are a very foodie family. 'My grandmothers were great cooks and my mother still is. We have three children, and they are all good cooks too. And we're all very greedy and all very competitive!'

Their daughter, Jess, has been instrumental in bringing some new seasonings to the range. They had already started producing spiced salts, but after tasting the popcorn made by her former boyfriend in his New York restaurant, she persuaded him to let them recreate the flavouring he used. 'It's a mixture of salt, nutritional yeast and a few other secret spices, and it is so moreish.' The idea for their Popeth seasoning (which means 'everything' in Welsh) came from an 'everything' bagel she ate in a New York deli – one with onion, garlic and sesame and poppy seeds. 'I added some salt and a hint of chilli too. When it's toasted, it smells and tastes wonderful,' Jess says.

'The thing about seasonings is you don't just add them to a dish for the sake of it. You add them because it will make a dish taste better,' says Alison. 'And when the best chef in the world tells you that if he was stranded on a desert island he would want only the best oil, the best bread and the salt we produce from Welsh sea water in Anglesey, you know the idea that everyone thought was mad was not so mad after all.'

Everything Nuts

࿔

Intrigued by Jess's take on the 'everything' bagel seasoning, I thought I would try it as a flavouring for nuts. I tested them out on some friends who were coming to supper that evening and they got a universal thumbs-up. If you make these, don't expect there to be any left for another day…

350g (12oz) mixed nuts of
  your choice
2 tablespoons of flavourless oil, such
  as sunflower or vegetable

4 tablespoons Halen Môn Popeth
  Everything Seasoning
sea salt

Serves 6–8 as a snack

Preheat the oven to 180°C (350°F), Gas Mark 4.

Put the nuts into a large bowl and drizzle over the oil. Toss to make sure they are completely coated in oil and then sprinkle over the seasoning and a good couple of pinches of salt. Toss again to completely coat. Transfer to a lined baking tray.

Bake in the oven for 15 minutes, stirring halfway through and keeping an eye on them – if the nuts are of very different sizes, some may cook faster than others.

Remove from the oven and leave to cool in the tray, stirring occasionally. Once cool, store in a large jar or airtight container.

Jess's Oak-Smoked Hummus

David and Alison had already tried smoking salt, which turned out to be a success: 'Scrambled eggs shouldn't be eaten without it,' according to David. But it didn't add the smoky potency Heston Blumenthal was after for a smoked risotto he was developing. So David came up with the idea of smoking water. It took a lot of experimenting until he cracked it, but the deep, savoury flavour it brings, not just to Michelin-starred risottos, but to mashed potato or guacamole – or this hummus, which is Jess's favourite way to use it – lifts a simple dish to new heights.

400g (14oz) can or jar of chickpeas
50g (1¾oz) light tahini
1 generous teaspoon sea salt
2 tablespoons extra virgin olive oil
50ml (2fl oz) Halen Môn oak-
    smoked water

juice of ½ lemon, plus extra to taste
1 garlic clove, crushed
crudités, to serve

Serves 4 as a snack or part of a main meal
Drain the chickpeas, reserving the liquid. Blend together all the ingredients, with 1 tablespoon of the chickpea liquid, using a stick blender or food processor to form a creamy, smooth dip.

Check the seasoning – you may need to adjust the hummus with a touch more lemon juice to brighten it up a little. If it is too thick, add a little more chickpea water until it is the consistency you like. Serve with crudités for dipping.

Margarita Granita

~❦~

This was Pooch's idea. I've never liked tequila, so I wasn't sure. And we were both sceptical, given the alcohol content, that the mix would freeze. But it did; just enough to give the perfect texture to the soft flakes of intensely flavoured ice. The taste is sophisticated, sharp and really refreshing. Served in a glass with a seasoned rim – Mexican tajin seasoning (find it online) is a winner – this is knockout, even if you don't like tequila. Thank you, Pooch.

175g (6oz) sugar
500ml (18fl oz) water
100ml (3½fl oz) tequila blanco
  or reposado
85ml (5½ tablespoons) lime juice
  (about 5 limes)

75ml (5 tablespoons) orange juice
  (about 2–3 oranges)
4 lime wedges
2 tablespoons sea salt
chilli flakes or tajin seasoning
  (optional)

Serves 4–6

Heat the sugar and water in a small pan over a medium heat, stirring as you go, until the sugar has completely dissolved. Remove from the heat and leave to cool slightly. Then add the tequila, lime juice and orange juice. Stir to mix and leave to cool.

Pour the mixture into a large Tupperware tub or baking dish and place in the freezer, resting it somewhere flat. Leave for 2–3 hours.

Give it a mix with a fork, dragging the fork through any icy areas that have formed, to break it up. Return it to the freezer. Repeat this process every hour or so, until there is no liquid left and it has all turned to a slushy ice. This will probably take a total of 6–8 hours, depending how deep the mixture is in the container. The granita can be made in advance and left in the freezer; just drag a fork back through it before serving.

Once ready to serve, rub a lime wedge around the rim of the serving glasses. Tip the salt (and chilli or tajin seasoning if using) into a saucer and up-end the glasses into the saucer, tilting them slightly to create a salted rim. Spoon the granita into the glasses and serve.

VEGETABLES

❧

Ben Ward • *Moor Park Garden*

In November 2018, Ben decided that he had had enough. No longer was he going to do a job he hated, sitting in an office day after day answering phone calls and emails. He handed in his notice, with no job to go to, but with the belief that if he didn't do something dramatic, nothing would change. He'd be the tech support man for a phone company for the rest of his life. The very next day a friend sent him a link to a job he'd seen advertised. 'It was my dream. And it was on my doorstep.' He met his prospective employers, they all liked each other, and in January 2019, Ben became a professional vegetable grower and custodian of an old walled garden in the Welsh hills.

Ben was born in the south east of England, but when he was three years old his parents bought a couple of derelict cottages with some land they had seen for sale in the *Exchange & Mart*. They moved their young family to the Welsh countryside and started a smallholding with goats, sheep, chickens and pigs, and a huge vegetable patch. 'Dad was a biology teacher and was obsessed with plants. One of my earliest memories is of picking peas and planting radish seeds in my own little patch.'

When Ben was in his teens, the family left the smallholding and moved to the local town. Ben went to university to study product design and, when he left, got a job in manufacturing. 'But I was made redundant in the early 2000s and I wasn't sure what to do next. I got an HGV licence, thinking that would stand me in good stead, and I drove trucks for a while. By then my dad had retired from teaching and had a picture-framing business in the town.

He had developed rheumatoid arthritis, so I went to work with him and helped him in the vegetable garden he had behind the house.'

Working in his father's vegetable garden brought back happy memories of his childhood and helped him reconnect with nature, becoming more attuned to the weather and the seasons. 'I enjoyed that feeling of immersion, of being re-engaged with growing plants again; getting excited when the first tomatoes ripened, when I could pick the first apples from the tree. And when you taste the success of the work you've done to produce something, it makes you want to grow more, try new things.'

Ben applied for an allotment and started growing vegetables for himself – 'Playing around and experimenting a bit.' He also volunteered at a local organic vegetable garden so he could learn from more experienced growers. He had no thoughts of it becoming a career. It was just something he loved doing. 'But then my mother bought me a place on a day course at Charles Dowding's garden in Somerset and that was an eye-opener. Vegetable beds are always hidden away at the bottom of gardens, but they shouldn't be. Charles's garden showed me that productive vegetable beds could also be beautiful. He was so inspiring and so helpful. By the end of the day, I was thinking the hobby that I loved might be my future. That I could do this!'

From then on, Ben spent as much time on his allotment as he could, trying to learn how to grow vegetables which had a taste and texture that set them apart. He experimented with different varieties, discovering which ones did best in his soil and climate and which had the best yields to make them worth growing. 'Aubergines were a challenge! They took a few attempts to find the right varieties that like growing here and still taste good. There is nothing like growing something that tastes better than you can get anywhere else. It was such a good feeling when I gave someone a tomato I had grown and saw their reaction to the taste, that almost disbelief that something could taste so wonderful and so different from anything they might have had from a supermarket. The first tomato of the year is always my greatest pleasure. I don't buy tomatoes now out of season, and I don't eat them unless I've picked them fresh or they have come from my freezer, so that makes me appreciate them even more.'

The job Ben was offered at the end of 2018 was in the old walled garden of a private house. For years, Moor Park Garden had been derelict, a choked tangle of nettles and brambles. The new owners had cleared it and created terraces of long, raised beds enclosed in sleepers, but nothing had been grown there for decades. It was Ben's job to bring it back to life, using the no-dig system he had learned from Charles Dowding. He started with compost, covering each bed in a layer several centimetres thick and planting straight into that layer. 'The compost feeds all the soil life you've left undisturbed by not digging, keeping the ecosystem that nurtures your plants intact and healthy. And it suppresses weeds and acts like a sort of sponge, keeping moisture in, so you don't need to use so much water.'

Ben's remit was to create a productive, commercially viable vegetable garden that could supply high-end restaurants. 'I had a massive case of imposter syndrome for about three years! It was hugely nerve-racking taking my vegetables to chefs to see if they liked them.'

One of his early customers – a chef – happened to have the same accountant as him, and he made an introduction. 'Josh had also had an allotment and had grown vegetables using the no-dig method, so we instantly had lots in common. He asked if I could supply him with some vegetables and he would see how it went. We've been working together ever since. Every winter we sit down and talk about what he wants for the year ahead. Sometimes he'll want very specific things for particular dishes he's designed: turnips a certain size, or nasturtium leaves no bigger than a 2p piece. He's really pushed my knowledge and growing skills. I can't imagine doing anything else now. I absolutely love it. I'm outdoors all day in a beautiful part of the world. I have my dog with me. And people love what I'm doing. I get huge satisfaction from that. There's very little that irks me. Apart from slugs.'

Ben's Packed Lunch

Simple, ingenious, healthy and tasty, you can use any mix of salad ingredients you like here. Play around! Swap hummus for the Baba Ganoush on page 75 or the Guacamole on page 230. Add feta, toasted seeds, or nuts. Try cider vinegar, sherry vinegar, red wine vinegar or balsamic vinegar in the dressing. This is an infinitely nicer, more satisfying lunch than a shop-bought sandwich.

FOR THE DRESSING

2 teaspoons white wine vinegar

2 tablespoons extra virgin olive oil

½ teaspoon Dijon mustard

½ teaspoon honey

sea salt and freshly ground
    black pepper

FOR THE SALAD

1 tomato, chopped

¼ cucumber, chopped

5 radishes, sliced

1 small carrot, peeled and grated

4 tablespoons Hummus (see page
    149 for homemade)

a handful of rocket or other
    salad leaves

Serves 1

Place the dressing ingredients in a large jar, roughly 500–700ml (18fl oz–1¼ pints) in size, along with some seasoning, and shake to combine. Taste and adjust the seasoning if necessary.

Spoon the salad ingredients into the jar in the order they appear in the ingredients list. Season as you go. Place a lid on the jar and you now have your own portable packed lunch salad.

Once ready to serve, open the jar and invert it into a bowl. Remove the jar, letting the salad fall out into the bowl and the dressing to coat it, then serve. Alternatively, if you're out and about, simply upend the jar for 2–3 minutes so that the dressing mingles with all the vegetables, then turn back up the right way and eat.

One-Pot Tomato, Spinach & Basil Pasta

﹌

When Pooch first showed me this way of cooking pasta, I didn't believe it could work. But not only does it work, the end result is absolutely delicious. It's simplicity itself to make and is the perfect quick, tasty supper. Try it!

350g (12oz) dried linguine

1 onion, thinly sliced

3 garlic cloves, finely chopped

300g (10½oz) cherry tomatoes, halved

100g (3½oz) baby leaf spinach

leaves from a small bunch of basil, roughly torn

1 tablespoon tomato purée

25g (1oz) butter

3 tablespoons extra virgin olive oil

900ml (1 pint 12fl oz) hot vegetable stock

1 teaspoon sea salt

Parmesan cheese, grated, to serve

Serves 4

Put all the ingredients except the Parmesan into a large, wide saucepan or sauté pan and bring to the boil. Boil gently over a medium heat for 8–10 minutes, stirring often, until the pasta is cooked to your liking and most of the liquid has evaporated.

Divide between serving plates and top with grated Parmesan cheese. Serve immediately.

Cauliflower Curry

✢

The one vegetable Ben struggles to grow is cauliflower. 'I've grown the occasional beauty, but to consistently produce good cauliflowers is fiendishly tricky.' Luckily there is nothing tricky about this curry, which makes the most of the cauliflower's ability to carry flavour.

1 tablespoon cumin seeds

1 tablespoon mustard seeds

4 curry leaf sprigs (optional)

1 red onion, thinly sliced

flavourless oil or ghee

4cm (1½ inch) piece of fresh root
   ginger, peeled and finely grated

4 garlic cloves, finely grated

2 tablespoons curry powder

450g (1lb) tomatoes, chopped, or
   a 400g (14oz) can of chopped
   tomatoes

1 cauliflower, cut into florets

250ml (9fl oz) vegetable stock

sea salt and freshly ground
   black pepper

a handful of fresh coriander,
   to garnish

Serves 4

Heat a large saucepan over a medium heat. Add the cumin and mustard seeds and the curry leaves, if using. Cook until the seeds start to pop, then immediately add the onion, a big pinch of salt and a glug of oil or 1 tablespoon of ghee and stir well. Cook over a medium-low heat for 10–15 minutes, until the onion is softened and turning golden.

Stir through the ginger and garlic and cook for a further minute. Then add the curry powder and stir through to mix. Tip in the tomatoes with a pinch of salt and mix well. Cook for a further 5 minutes over a medium heat, until the tomatoes are collapsed and soft.

Stir through the cauliflower and another good pinch or 2 of salt, mixing really well so that all the florets are coated in the spices. Add the stock, cover and bring to a simmer. Simmer for 15–20 minutes, stirring now and again, until the cauliflower is tender.

Taste and adjust the seasoning if necessary. Sprinkle the coriander on top and serve with steamed rice and mango chutney.

FISH

꘎

Hayden Scamp

Hayden Scamp grew up in the Cotswolds – 'About as far away from the sea as you can get!' he laughs. So, when his father took him fishing, it was in the ponds of the local trout farm and the freshwater streams near his home. He caught his first fish when he was three years old, with a small, old-fashioned rod and line, sitting on his father's knee. He, too, was hooked. Something that was instilled in him from the outset was to eat what you caught. 'I often caught my own tea,' he tells me – trout which he baked in the oven, or signal crayfish, an invasive but delicious species, which he would catch by the bucketful.

His love of fishing, and fascination for fish, grew as he got older. His career path was set, and he went to work at a trout farm – 'the one where I caught my second-ever fish!' for seven years, learning every aspect of aquaculture. But some aspects of his profession didn't sit well with his conscience. 'It felt wrong to be taking six kilos of wild fish out of the sea to make one kilo of fish meal, which in turn would produce one kilo of farmed trout. I felt that if I could catch fish straight from the sea, in a clean and sustainable way, that would be better.'

He did a new entrants' fishing course in Lyme Regis. He was terribly seasick, but the thrill he felt being out at sea was great enough to make him put up with it. At the end of his fifteen-day course, he was offered a job as crew on a small fishing boat. 'It is the most sustainable way to fish. The boat, like the one I have now, was under ten metres – a day boat that goes out for less than twenty-four hours at a time and fishes within the confines of where it can go in that time, which is not very far. So ultimately, we are fishing over the same piece

of ground and we have to look after it. My skipper really understood and cared about the marine environment. I couldn't have had a better teacher.'

On that first job he learned that gill nets – abhorred by many because of the indiscriminate way they catch marine life – can be a very sustainable way of fishing if used the right way: left out for just a short time, rather than for days, and placed in the right area with mesh sizes big enough to reduce bycatch. And that if he targeted high-value species, like lobster – 'We have a very good, carefully managed lobster fishery in Lyme Bay' – Dover sole, and rod-and-line caught sea bass, he could make a living.

Hayden has been a fisherman for four years. He leaves Axmouth Harbour in his little red boat every high tide when the weather forecast is good enough for the ten to twelve hours he'll be at sea. He sells his catch at Brixham Harbour and through Wylde Market, an online outlet for a range of hand-selected sustainable producers. He continued to be seasick for well over a year into the job. 'I tried everything – the wrist bands, the patches, every sort of medication – but the key, I discovered, was to have a really good breakfast. Bacon and egg roll. Bacon must be smoked and crispy. Fried egg with a runny yolk. Red sauce. That's the answer.'

Peanut-Stuffed Trout Cooked in Newspaper

꙳

Stuffing trout with dry-roasted peanuts and wrapping it in wet newspaper before it is cooked does, I grant you, sound very bizarre indeed. When Hayden told me this was his favourite way of cooking trout, I thought he was pulling my leg. I dare you to try it. It's a revelation!

newspaper, for wrapping
1 trout, 300–500g (10½oz–1lb 2oz),
   cleaned, gutted, gills removed
100g (3½oz) dry-roasted peanuts

25g (1oz) butter, cubed
sea salt and freshly ground
   black pepper

Serves 1

Preheat the oven to 220°C (425°F), Gas Mark 7.

Place 2 sheets of newspaper, one on top of the other, on a work surface, lay a sheet of baking paper on top and put the trout in the middle. Season the trout all over. Fill the cavity with the peanuts and butter. Roll the newspaper around the trout, enclosing it completely in a parcel.

Run the trout parcel under the cold tap until the newspaper is wet the whole way through. Then place the trout parcel onto a baking tray, making sure the newspaper can't unfurl.

Bake in the oven for 20–25 minutes, or until just cooked through.

Remove from the oven, unwrap the newspaper (the skin may come away with the paper – don't worry about this), transfer to a plate, pouring over the buttery juices and the peanuts, and enjoy. It's great served with steamed rice and some stir-fried greens. It's equally delicious eaten straight from the paper.

Scallops in Their Shells
with Samphire Garlic Butter

~

These scallops are cooked over fire in their shells with samphire (or you can use finely chopped parsley) butter, keeping them beautifully moist and soft. Please buy your scallops with care. Go for sustainable hand-dived scallops – they will be more expensive, but this dish is a real treat. One for high days and holidays!

50g (1¾oz) samphire, washed well

75g (2½oz) butter, softened

1 garlic clove, finely chopped

6 hand-dived scallops, cleaned and separated from their shells

2–3 tablespoons vermouth (or white wine if you prefer)

bread, for dipping

Serves 2 as a starter or as part of a bigger meal

Remove any woody stalks from the samphire, then chop the green parts. Place in a bowl with the butter and garlic. Mix well until completely combined. If making the butter in advance, spoon it onto a sheet of baking paper and roll into a sausage shape. Twist the ends to enclose the butter then chill or freeze until ready to use. Alternatively, just leave to one side while you fire up your barbecue or fire ready for direct cooking.

Once the barbecue or fire is hot, either spread the coals out into an even layer or place a grill rack over the hot coals or wood.

Place a scallop back into each shell and add a dash of vermouth on top. Then gently place the scallops in their shells either directly onto the hot coals or on the grill rack. They need to be relatively flat and stable.

Cook for 1 minute to heat up the shells, then add a slice of the samphire butter to each shell and cook for a further 3–4 minutes, until the butter has melted and the scallops are only just cooked through. If one side of the scallop is cooking quicker than the other, you can turn the scallop (not the shell!) over to cook more evenly.

Remove from the heat and serve on a platter or board with some bread for dipping.

Grilled Mackerel

with Mango Salsa & Watercress

⌇

Going out on a small boat in Lyme Bay, trailing a hooked line in the water and taking whatever we caught home for supper, is one of my happiest childhood memories. Mackerel is an oily fish that cooks beautifully over fire without drying out, but you can also roast it in the oven if you're cooking indoors. The salsa can be made with gooseberries, kiwi or segmented orange instead of mango, depending what is in season or more easily available.

2 very fresh mackerel, 300–350g (10½–12oz) each, cleaned, gills removed and gutted

olive oil

1 small-medium mango, peeled, pitted and finely chopped

2 spring onions, finely chopped

zest and juice of 1 unwaxed lime

chilli flakes

2 handfuls of watercress

sea salt and freshly ground black pepper

Serves 2

Fire up your barbecue or fire ready for direct grilling. Once your fire is hot and the embers are glowing brightly, set a grill over the top.

Cut 3 shallow slashes into both sides of each mackerel, then rub with a little olive oil. Season well both the inside and outside of the fish. Place directly onto the grill, or into a fish grill basket if you prefer. Cook for 3–4 minutes on each side, or until the flesh is cooked through. Alternatively, preheat the oven to 200°C (400°F), Gas Mark 6, and roast the mackerel on an oiled baking tray for 15–20 minutes, turning halfway through. You can finish it under the grill if you like, to create some charred skin and smoky flavours.

Meanwhile, make the salsa. Mix together the mango, spring onions, lime zest and juice, chilli flakes to taste, a good pinch of salt and pepper and a little drizzle of olive oil.

Once the mackerel is cooked through, transfer to a plate and serve with the watercress, drizzled with a little olive oil, and spoonfuls of the salsa on the side.

MEAT

Jake, Amie & Ed • *Wild by Nature*

It all started when Jake's parents saw a seventy-acre farm for sale, tucked in a valley, surrounded by verdant hills and woods, not far from where Jake had grown up. Too small to be commercially viable, it was, nonetheless, in a beautiful setting and they felt it had potential, they just weren't sure in what way. By then, Jake had left home and trained as a chef. He met Amie when working in New Zealand. She was a teacher, but later started working with Jake in hospitality, first in London and then running a ski chalet for a season. When they returned to London, they felt restless. 'We were both a bit sick of our jobs and were thinking about doing something different.' Jake's sister Fran and brother-in-law Ed, who were living in Cardiff, felt the same. The farm that Jake's parents had seen for sale offered the chance they were all looking for.

Ed and Fran moved onto the farm in 2015 to begin an entirely new way of life. The house and outbuildings were pretty much derelict and the whole place needed refencing. As work started on the buildings, Ed started to learn how to farm. 'I'd never driven a tractor before. I had no agronomy training, no animal husbandry training. I did a one-day lambing course. But there seemed to be two routes we could follow. We could farm the land intensively, chasing high yields, or we could farm it regeneratively, allow our livestock to grow slowly without any inputs. And that's what we decided to do. It made sense for us financially because it didn't require a huge outlay to get started, but we also believed – although we didn't know – that the meat we reared would taste better if it was produced more naturally.'

He started with six Belted Galloway cattle and Jacob sheep. 'The combination of wily native sheep and inexperienced farmers meant we spent an awful lot of time running around after them!'

The reality, though, was that making a living for them all by simply rearing the small number of livestock they could produce on a seventy-acre farm was never going to work. They had always planned to use what they produced themselves: add value to it by selling it direct to consumers in meat boxes, or by starting a hospitality business to run alongside the farm. Jake loved the idea of a farm-to-fork model. 'I remember working in kitchens in London and seeing all this amazing produce coming through the door. As a chef, the idea of being able to see and be part of that process from start to finish, to understand different breeds of animal, the influence of the seasons – that was the dream. I just didn't quite know what form that was going to take. This place was the catalyst for all those ideas coming together.'

They started by offering catered camping weekends and Jake and Amie produced charcuterie from the meat they reared. They had discovered, as soon as their first animals came back from the slaughterhouse, that the way they were raising them really did make a difference to the fat quality and taste of the meat. Then someone asked if they could hold their wedding at the farm, because they loved the setting. 'And it snowballed from there,' says Ed. 'The following year we hosted six weddings, the year after that, twelve. Now we do two a week and all the catering is done here using the meat and vegetables we produce in the fields around the wedding barn. And people really like that.'

In 2020 they took on the village pub, which had been closed for almost seven years. By now they had added to their livestock, rearing Angus and Shorthorn cattle as well as Galloways, and Herdwick and Llyn sheep. The meat they produce supplies the pub's restaurant as well as the weddings. It is an entirely different way to run a kitchen, Jake says. One that is based on collaboration and communication between farmer, butcher and chef. 'It's made us all more appreciative of the cuts of meat that have fallen out of favour, and the taste of meat that has come from an animal that has grown slowly and naturally. An old man who was doing some work here tasted some and gave us the ultimate compliment. He said it tasted like the beef he ate as a boy. My challenge as a chef is making sure nothing goes to waste, and finding ways of using every part of an animal. But that's a wonderful challenge to have.'

Open Steak Sandwiches

Ed suggests using bavette steak here – an underrated cut that I love too. This sandwich is something Ed cooks all the time for his family and it's now become a regular on their pub menu as well. The anchovies don't make the dish taste fishy at all, but just add a rich saltiness that complements the beef perfectly.

2 bavette steaks, 150–200g (5½–7oz) each, at room temperature
olive oil
60g (2¼oz) butter
3 anchovy fillets in olive oil, drained

2 tablespoons capers, drained
2 thick slices of sourdough
sea salt and freshly ground black pepper
parsley leaves, to serve

Serves 2

Heat a large, heavy-based frying pan over a medium-high heat. Rub the steaks all over with a little oil then season well on each side with salt.

Once the pan is really hot, fry the steaks for 1–3 minutes on each side, depending on thickness. You're after as much colour and crust as possible on the outside, but still rare or medium-rare on the inside. Bavette does not respond well to being overcooked. Remove the steaks from the pan and leave to rest on a warm plate.

Place the pan back on the heat and reduce it to a medium-low. Add the butter, anchovies and capers to the pan and stir until the anchovies have dissolved into the butter. Pour over the resting steaks.

Toast the sourdough and divide between 2 plates. Slice the steaks against the grain and place them on top of the toast. Pour over the anchovy and caper butter, along with any resting juices. Scatter with parsley leaves and tuck in immediately.

Seasonal Collar of Pork Steaks in Brioche Buns

Collar of pork is the meat that comes from the shoulder. Jake can't understand why more people don't eat it as steaks because, as you will discover, it is a succulent and tasty cut of meat that goes beautifully with seasonal herbs: parsley and lovage in spring and summer, or rosemary and thyme in autumn and winter. Get the pork from your local butcher and ask them to prepare the steaks for you; they are also sometimes called pork rib eyes.

a small handful of seasonal herbs
   (such as parsley and lovage, or
   rosemary and thyme)
olive oil
2 pork collar steaks, 175–200g
   (6–7oz) each

2 brioche buns, halved
mustard
a handful of rocket
sea salt

Serves 2

Pick the leaves from the herbs and finely chop them. Mix in a large bowl or deep plate with a couple of glugs of olive oil. Remove 1 tablespoon of the herby oil and leave to one side in a small bowl.

Add the pork steaks to the large bowl and massage the herby oil all over them. You can leave this to marinate overnight in the fridge if you'd like. Leave to one side while you prepare a barbecue for direct cooking, or heat a large, heavy-based frying pan or griddle pan over a medium-high heat.

Once ready to cook, season the pork steaks really well on each side with salt. Place on the barbecue or in the pan and cook for 2–3 minutes on each side until well coloured with areas of char. Then move to a cooler part of the barbecue or reduce the heat under the pan and cook for a further 3–4 minutes on each side, depending on the thickness. Ideally you're after pork steaks that are still a little pink inside, around 60–62°C (140–144°F) on a temperature probe. And yes, it's fine to eat pork pink, provided you are confident of its provenance.

Remove from the heat and leave to rest for at least 5 minutes, ideally 10, covered in foil and keeping warm.

Open out the brioche buns and spread a little mustard on the inside. Top with some rocket. Slice the rested pork steaks and place on top of the rocket. Drizzle over a little of the reserved herby oil and any resting juices. Close up the brioche buns and enjoy immediately.

Oxtail Ragù

Oxtail was one of those old-fashioned cuts of meat that went out of fashion. But happily, because it tastes so good, it is back on menus and in recipe books and much easier to get hold of. Don't be put off by the bones (which get removed before the end of cooking) or the length of cooking time. This is a dish to make on a rainy Saturday, in between solving crossword clues, and the end result can be used in multiple ways. Serve with pasta, bake in a pie or simply serve as a rich and satisfying stew. It will store really well in the freezer if you'd like to get ahead or make a big batch.

olive oil

1.5kg (3lb 5oz) oxtail on the bone,
cut into 5cm (2 inch) pieces

1 onion, finely chopped

2 celery sticks, finely chopped

1 large carrot, peeled and
finely chopped

2 bay leaves

200ml (7fl oz) great-quality red wine

400g (14oz) can of best-quality
chopped tomatoes

500ml (18fl oz) beef stock

sea salt and freshly ground
black pepper

pasta, to serve (optional)

Serves 4–6

Heat a large, heavy-based casserole dish over a medium-high heat. Add a dash of oil, season the oxtail all over and brown it in batches until really nicely coloured on all sides. Remove and leave to one side.

Reduce the heat to medium, add another dash of oil if needed and add all the vegetables, a big pinch of salt and the bay leaves. Start to sauté the vegetables, then place a lid on the pan, reduce the heat a little and leave, stirring occasionally, for 20–25 minutes, or until the vegetables are really soft.

Increase the heat and pour in the wine. Bring to a simmer and leave to bubble for 3–4 minutes. Scrape up any bits stuck to the bottom of the pan and mix into the vegetables. Then add the tomatoes and stir to mix.

Tip the meat back into the pan and mix well, then stir in the beef stock. Bring it to a gentle simmer, taste and adjust the seasoning if needed. Place a lid on the pan and cook over a low heat for 4 hours. Alternatively, you can do this in a low oven at 140°C (275°F), Gas Mark 1. Check the liquid levels every now and again: if the pan is looking at all dry, add a little water.

Once the meat is meltingly soft, remove from the heat and leave until cool enough to handle. Alternatively, leave to cool and pop in the fridge, ready to finish off tomorrow.

Once cool enough to handle, strip the meat off the bones. Place the meat back into the pan with the sauce and mix well, breaking up any large chunks. Your ragù is now ready to use. Simply reheat gently before serving with pasta, if you like.

CHEESE

～

Roman & Hamish • *Aberdyfi Cheese Company*

It was Tom, who owns our local deli, who introduced me to a new Manchego-style cheese he'd just discovered. 'But it's not made in Spain,' he said. 'It's made in Aberdyfi.'

Aberdyfi is a small seaside town which sits at the mouth of the Dyfi estuary on the west coast of Wales. Inland from its sandy beaches are green rolling hills, trees and marshes, where cuckoos call in spring and ospreys nest in summer. When Roman first came here he was seventeen years old and on a school trip from his native Bavaria. It proved to be a pivotal experience, one that made him choose to go to university in the UK and, once he had qualified as a lawyer, to settle in London. 'But I visited Aberdyfi whenever I possibly could.'

In London he met Hamish, who was born in Australia but had spent much of his career travelling the world, working in fashion. Soon after they got together, Roman brought Hamish to see his favourite place, and he fell in love with it too. But it is a long journey from London – too far to do in a weekend – and an idea started to creep into their heads. Could they make Aberdyfi their home? 'We had both spent so much of our working lives travelling,' says Roman, 'that the idea of committing to one place felt really appealing. And we didn't want to wait until we retired. We wanted to have the time and energy to devote to an entirely new way of life.'

They found a converted stable with six acres of land, perched on a hillside overlooking the mouth of the Dyfi estuary. It was perfect. They bought it in December 2019 and in the summer of 2020 they moved in. For the first year they continued their old jobs, working from

home. But all the time they were considering new and different ways of making a living. 'We thought about having alpacas, but realized very quickly that we would earn almost nothing from the sale of their wool. Our neighbours both farm sheep, which they sell for meat, but

we knew with just six acres we couldn't keep enough to make that work. And that's when we considered the possibility of making cheese. Our favourite cheeses are Manchego and pecorino – both made from sheeps' milk – so it was an idea that seemed to make perfect sense.'

Except that neither Hamish nor Roman had ever made cheese, or even seen it being made. Undaunted, they attended a cheese-making course at Coleg Menai in Anglesey and spent some time with celebrated cheese-maker Carrie Rimes in North Wales. Carrie also makes cheese from sheeps' milk – one of just a handful of people in Wales who do – and her course and ongoing support inspired Roman and Hamish to buy a dozen French Lacaune sheep and go into business.

'Our neighbours were – and are still – amazing. They have helped us with everything. One of them even came with us to the Midlands to help us buy the sheep. We knew absolutely nothing about how to look after them. One ewe died in the first week and we thought, at this rate, we won't have any sheep left by Christmas,' says Roman.

'It was tough, but it was an important part of the learning curve,' says Hamish. 'Thankfully all the other ewes have gone on to do well.'

And the learning curve just kept getting steeper. 'We were kept on our toes for the whole of our first year. We had to build and equip our cheese-making workshop, at the same time as we were lambing. Then there was mastering the cheese-making itself.'

They got their sheep in October of 2021 and had their first lambs the following February. In March 2022 they were ready to start making cheese. But first they had to milk the sheep,

and that's when they discovered that walking into a milking parlour and obligingly standing still while the milking clusters are attached to their udders is not something the ewes do naturally. 'Once they are in the habit of it, it's easy, but we had to teach them the habit, and we weren't really sure how to.' Bribery and patience finally paid off.

Some of the early cheeses they made were not a success. 'The cheese curds just wouldn't knit together to form a solid cheese and looked more like bits of cottage cheese loosely stuck together.' They phoned Carrie, who told them that it could be a number of things that had gone wrong and gave suggestions. 'We just had to keep trying. Without the support of Carrie, the teacher from Coleg Menai and fellow sheep-milking farmers, we would not be where we are now.'

Six months later they had cheeses maturing on the shelves of their dairy. Roman's mother came to visit and they made the nerve-racking decision to try one. 'We had no idea whether it would have the right texture and taste good or whether we would have to throw the whole lot away.' It was good. Good enough to give Roman and Hamish the confidence to do a tasting in the local town. 'And one of the first people to buy our cheese was a friend of some friends who lived near Abergavenny in the east of Wales. She liked it so much she took some to her local deli.' That deli was Tom's. They had made their first sale.

A year on and a new batch of cheese is on the shelves waiting to go to their growing list of restaurants, shops and delis. They've started making ricotta too, and a chef buys the whey they produce to make ice cream. They're even making a profit – not big enough for them both to live on yet but that, they believe, will come. 'This is our life now. We'll never look back.'

Grilled Asparagus
with Edible Flowers, Herbs & Sheeps' Cheese

Cooking asparagus over a fire is a lovely way to do it, but this dish can just as easily be made by steaming your asparagus on the hob until the stalks are al dente. It's such a pretty, colourful dish, one that celebrates spring and the asparagus season.

14 asparagus spears, woody
   ends removed
olive oil
50g (1¾oz) sheeps' cheese, such
   as pecorino
leaves from 4 lemon thyme sprigs

6 dill fronds, torn
6 primrose flowers, or other
   edible flowers
sea salt and freshly ground
   black pepper

Serves 2 as a starter or side

Fire up your barbecue or fire ready for direct cooking. Once it's hot (you shouldn't be able to hold your hand over it for longer than about 2 seconds), toss the asparagus in a drizzle of olive oil until completely coated and season with salt.

Place the asparagus onto a grill over the barbecue or fire and leave to cook for 3–4 minutes, turning now and again. You are after tender spears with a little bite, with some blistered and charred areas.

Once the asparagus is cooked, remove to a serving plate or platter. Use a vegetable peeler to add shavings of the sheeps' cheese, then scatter with the thyme leaves, torn dill fronds and some pepper. Finally, finish with the primrose flowers, arranging them on top.

Roasted Tomatoes
with Ricotta & Garlic Butter

꩜

This looks impressive, takes very little effort to make and is dangerously moreish! I love this as a weekend lunch with a big green salad alongside, but in that case, might only share it with one other person, rather than three.

350g (12oz) cherry tomatoes on the vine	2 garlic cloves, finely sliced
olive oil	sea salt and freshly ground black pepper
250g (9oz) ricotta	focaccia, cut into cubes, or focaccia crispbreads, to serve
50g (1¾oz) butter	

Serves 4 as a snack or starter, or as part of a main meal

Preheat the oven to 220°C (425°F), Gas Mark 7.

Put the tomatoes on a baking tray, drizzle with oil and season well. Roast in the oven for 10–15 minutes, until lightly charred in places.

Meanwhile, season the ricotta really well with salt and pepper. You can do this in the tub, just mix it all together. Taste and add a little more seasoning if needed.

Heat the butter and garlic in a small pan over a medium heat. Let the butter start to bubble and the garlic turn golden, but remove from the heat before the garlic starts to burn or the butter turns too dark.

Once ready to serve, spoon the ricotta on to a plate and then spread out with the back of the spoon, creating waves and undulations. Place the roasted tomatoes and any roasting juices on top and pour over the warm garlic butter, allowing it to pool in the ricotta. Serve with cubes of focaccia or focaccia crispbreads and eat (with lots of napkins) while the tomatoes and butter are still warm.

Apple, Cheese & Honey Tart

＋〜＋

When I suggested we try to make a tart that shamelessly incorporates some of my favourite things into one dish, Pooch was understandably doubtful. But, without wanting to sound too smug, it worked! And because it is neither completely sweet nor completely savoury, it can be eaten in any way you like, at the beginning of a meal as a starter, at the end as a sort of pudding and cheese combined, or as a meal on its own with a salad.

1 sheet of ready-rolled puff pastry
100g (3½oz) hard cheese, such as
   Cheddar, grated
2 small eating apples, quartered,
   cored and finely sliced

1 tablespoon honey
50g (1¾oz) walnuts, crumbled
leaves from 4 thyme sprigs
sea salt and freshly ground
   black pepper

Serves 4

Preheat the oven to 200°C (400°F), Gas Mark 6.

Unroll the puff pastry sheet and place onto a baking tray. Sprinkle the cheese over the pastry, leaving a 1cm (½ inch) margin all the way round the pastry. Top with the apples, arranging them in a nice pattern on top of the cheese.

Put the honey into a small bowl, add a tiny bit of hot water and mix into the honey to loosen it to a brushable consistency. Brush the apples with the honey. Sprinkle over the walnuts and season with a little salt and pepper.

Place in the oven and bake for 20 minutes, or until golden all over. Remove from the oven and scatter over the thyme leaves. Leave until cool enough to handle, then cut into slices and serve either hot, warm or at room temperature.

PRESERVES

Nick & Annette Tonkin • *Coedcanlas*

'I had this idea that I was going to restore an old wooden boat, sail it to the Russian Arctic and spend the winter in Yakutsk. I'd been travelling for about ten years, working on farms and fishing boats, and when I came back to the UK, I found an old boat in Pembrokeshire, moved into a disused oyster farm and that became my boat yard. At weekends my dad would help me and in return I said I'd rear him some queen bees. And then I met Annette and, well, I never went to Yakutsk.'

Nick grew up on a honey farm in Devon. It was a family business but it seemed to Nick, as a teenager, 'an awful lot of work for very little return,' so as soon as he left school at eighteen, he left the bees and Devon behind. But when he wasn't working on boats, honey farms in New Zealand were all too keen to employ him. It was there that he first learned about raising queen bees. And soon he was selling queen bees commercially, rearing them among the flower-rich fields and woods near his boat yard. 'The spin-off of rearing bees is that you end up producing lots of honey. So almost unintentionally we had created a business that could provide us with a living in a place we both loved being.'

The Arctic dreams started to fade, thanks, Nick says with a laugh, to the 'siren' who was running the village post office. When he met Annette, he realized that there was something else that was becoming more important to him than going away again. And that was to stay.

Their honey, carefully extracted without using excessive heat to preserve the aromatic flavours of the flowers the bees have fed on, has now been joined by a few other products,

which are produced by people they have met and who have the same gentle respect for nature and for food as Nick and Annette. They buy maple syrup from a Mennonite community in Ontario. Their olive oil comes from a friend in Trapani. The organic oranges and lemons used for the marmalade that they make every year in two copper pans come from the friend of a Sicilian beekeeper they know. They buy their blackcurrants and raspberries from the same farms on the Welsh borders every year and turn them into true 'preserves' using a Russian recipe that uses a far greater quantity of fruit to sugar than traditional jams.

'The business just grew organically,' says Nick. 'It came together with the contacts we made through life, the people we know, the things we've learned. We think of it as eclectically cohesive! It is just a part of us: what we love and what we believe in.'

Maple & Miso Baked Fish
with Noodle Salad
୰

This is a lovely combination of flavours and textures, and although the ingredients list looks a little daunting, it is more assembling than cooking, so takes a lot less time than you'd expect and is absolutely delicious. Choose any fish you like, such as salmon, coley, hake, halibut, cod or haddock.

FOR THE NOODLES

75g (2½oz) vermicelli rice noodles or soba noodles

1 carrot, peeled and cut into matchsticks or julienned with a julienne peeler

100g (3½oz) radishes, sliced

100g (3½oz) shelled cooked edamame beans, or sliced sugar snap peas

2 spring onions or ½ bunch of chives, finely sliced

1½ tablespoons white miso paste

1½ tablespoons rice vinegar

1 teaspoon soy sauce

2½ tablespoons sesame oil

1½ tablespoons maple syrup

2 tablespoons black or white sesame seeds

chilli flakes (optional)

FOR THE FISH

2 garlic cloves, thinly sliced

2 thick fillets of fish, 150–175g
(5½–6oz) each (see recipe
introduction)

1–1½ tablespoons white miso paste

2 tablespoons maple syrup

knob of fresh root ginger, peeled and
finely grated

1–2 tablespoons rice vinegar,
or to taste

1 tablespoon flavourless oil, such as
sunflower or vegetable

1 long red chilli, sliced

2 spring onions, finely sliced

sea salt and freshly ground
black pepper

Serves 2

Cook the noodles according to their packet instructions, then drain and rinse under cold running water. Place into a large bowl.

Add the carrot, radishes, edamame beans and spring onions and mix well. Mix together the miso, vinegar, soy, sesame oil and maple syrup to form a dressing. Toss into the noodle salad. Season with salt if needed and leave to one side while you prepare the fish. This salad can be made in advance and stored in the fridge for up to 24 hours if you need.

Preheat the oven to 220°C (425°F), Gas Mark 7, and place 2 large pieces of baking paper on a baking tray. Divide the garlic between the pieces of paper, then season the fish fillets and place on top, skin side down if they have skin.

Mix the miso, maple syrup, ginger, vinegar and oil together in a small bowl until well combined. Taste and adjust the flavour if necessary. You may find you need a little extra miso or vinegar to achieve a balanced flavour. Spoon over the fish, dividing it equally, then scatter over the sliced chilli. Fold the paper up around the fish to make 2 enclosed parcels, leaving space for it to steam. Secure the edges by folding or rolling them over.

Bake in the oven for 10–15 minutes, depending on how thick your fillets are, or until just cooked through. Carefully open the parcels at the table and scatter over the spring onions. Sprinkle the sesame seeds and chilli flakes (if using) over the noodle salad and serve alongside the fish.

Marmalade on Toast Semifreddo

Semifreddo is ice cream without the need for an ice-cream maker. This one is a combination of Pooch's love of brown bread ice cream and my love of marmalade on toast. It will be absolutely fine for three months in the freezer once made.

FOR THE BREADCRUMBS
2 slices of brown bread, 75–100g (2¾–3½oz) in total, crusts removed
50g (1¾oz) butter
60g (2¼oz) caster sugar
sea salt

FOR THE SEMIFREDDO
4 eggs, separated

100g (3½oz) caster sugar
300ml (½ pint) double cream
150g (5½oz) marmalade of your choice

FOR THE MARMALADE SAUCE
3 tablespoons whisky
2 tablespoons water
4 tablespoons marmalade

Serves 6–8

Preheat the oven to 180°C (350°F), Gas Mark 4, and line a 900g (2lb) loaf tin with baking paper or clingfilm.

For the breadcrumbs, either use your hands or a food processor to turn the bread into chunky breadcrumbs. Heat a small saucepan over a medium heat and add the butter. Once melted, keep cooking until it starts to turn a nutty brown. Remove from the heat and stir the breadcrumbs into the melted butter. Sprinkle in the sugar and a pinch of salt and mix well so that the sugar is evenly distributed.

Pour the breadcrumb mixture onto a lined baking tray and bake in the oven, stirring often, for 15–20 minutes, or until the bread is dark and toasted, but not burned. Leave to cool. Once cool, break up any chunky bits that have stuck together during cooking.

For the semifreddo, put the egg whites into a large bowl, the egg yolks and sugar into a separate bowl and the double cream in a third bowl. With a handheld electric whisk, whisk

the egg whites until stiff. Then whisk the yolks and sugar until thickened and lightened in colour. Then whip the cream until thick enough to be scooped up with a spoon and hold its shape. There is no need to clean the whisk between each stage if you whisk in this order.

Fold the cooled breadcrumbs into the cream. Then fold the egg yolk mixture into the cream. Fold half of the egg whites into the cream mixture and then gently fold in the marmalade. Finish by folding the remaining egg whites into the mixture until everything is completely combined.

Gently spoon the mixture into the prepared loaf tin. Smooth out the top, then cover with clingfilm. Transfer to the freezer and freeze overnight.

Once ready to serve, prepare the marmalade sauce. Warm the whisky in a small saucepan over a medium-low heat until almost simmering. Remove from the heat, add the measured water and marmalade and mix until you have a lovely glossy sauce. Up-end the semifreddo onto a serving plate or platter and remove all the wrappings. Serve in slices and eat immediately with the sauce drizzled over, before it melts too much!

Honey, Almond & Olive Oil Cake

Nick and Annette's favourite cake is an almond and honey cake. I've used honey instead of sugar in the cake mix and incorporated some of the other wonderful ingredients they source from their friends in Italy – olive oil and lemons – then finished the cake, as they do, with honey poured over the top when it's fresh from the oven. The result is moist, dense and delicious. A cake that can happily be eaten on its own or as a pudding, perhaps alongside poached figs or apricots, with yogurt or cream.

300g (10½oz) ground almonds
1 teaspoon baking powder
1 teaspoon freshly ground cardamom
zest of 2 unwaxed lemons
3 large eggs

120ml (4fl oz) olive oil, plus extra for
   the tin
120ml (4fl oz) best-quality
   flavoursome runny honey
salt

TO FINISH THE CAKE

2 tablespoons flaked almonds

1–2 tablespoons best-quality
   flavoursome runny honey

Serves 8

Preheat the oven to 160°C (325°F), Gas Mark 3, and oil and line a 20cm (8 inch) springform tin.

In a large bowl, mix together the ground almonds, baking powder, a pinch of salt, the cardamom and lemon zest, making sure they are all well combined and any lumps have been broken up.

In a second bowl, whisk the eggs, then add the olive oil and the honey. Whisk together and then pour onto the dry ingredients. Mix well (I use a silicon spatula for this) and when you have a glorious, golden batter, scoop it into your lined tin and put in the oven. Bake for 35–40 minutes.

While the cake is baking, toast the flaked almonds in a dry frying pan until they are golden, then leave to cool.

When the cake has had its cooking time and is fragrant and golden brown, test with a skewer to make sure it's cooked through. If the skewer comes out clean, poke a few more holes into the surface of the cake, then spoon over the rest of the honey, spreading it as you do so to glaze the top of the cake. Sprinkle with the toasted almonds, let it cool for a few more minutes, then take it out of the tin and cool on a rack.

FRUIT

†⁓†

Jo & Beth Marsden • *Spring Mills Community Garden*

Jo and Beth bought a piece of land. It had once been a colliery and beneath a wild tangle of brambles and gorse, the earth was a mixture of shale, rock and subsoil. They cleared a small strip, made soil by mixing aggregate from a local foundry with manure from a nearby farm, and planted potatoes. They brought in pigs to clear another area for an orchard. 'I grew up in Cambridgeshire,' says Jo, 'and spent much of my childhood mucking about in orchards and going scrumping.' They went to a local apple-tasting day to choose the varieties they wanted, ones that would be good for eating, cooking and making cider. They planted pears too, as well as cherries, plums and greengages – another fruit that had been in the orchards around Jo's childhood home.

It was the beginnings of the Spring Mills Community Garden, although neither Beth nor Jo had originally planned it to be anything other than somewhere to grow food for their family. 'But a footpath and cycle track ran alongside it,' says Beth. 'And every day, Howard, a retired potato farmer who lives in the village, would walk past with his dog. I'd be there, toiling over the potatoes, and he would stop and have a chat, and usually comment about something or other I was doing wrong. Then one day, perhaps because he saw I was struggling a bit, he said, "Why don't you leave your hoe in one of the gullies and every time I come past with the dog, I'll tickle your potatoes." Before I knew it, all the potatoes were tickled, and I could get on with growing other things. A week or so later he asked if he could plant runner beans on the site, because his garden wasn't sheltered enough from the wind.

Then our neighbours asked if they could also keep some pigs on our land, so we could share the work and the costs and clear more ground for growing. And some other people in the village asked if they could join in. Entirely by accident we became a group of about twenty – families, couples and individuals of all ages. We've cleared over an acre of land now and have gone from mixing our soil in wheelbarrows to using a JCB!'

The garden has been running for fifteen years. There are no individual plots. Everyone helps with everything and when it comes to harvesting, all the produce is divvied out between all the members of the group. There are no rules, Jo says. 'We just get together for a big cook up once a year and decide what we are going to grow the following year, based on what everyone likes or wants to try.'

Alongside the vegetables are two fruit cages full of gooseberries, black-, red- and whitecurrants, strawberries, raspberries and blackberries. 'And all the kids love physalis, those beautiful little orange-coloured fruits that grow in paper lanterns.' They planted a new orchard this year too, with figs, mulberries, plums and damsons. 'We prune all our trees and fruit bushes in the winter, and I love it because you get to have a conversation with each of them about the year ahead and review what impact your meddling had last year. Trees respond to your suggestions either by taking you seriously and adopting the shape you've given them, or telling you you're wrong and putting out shoots where they see an opportunity. It might be for light or water, or just

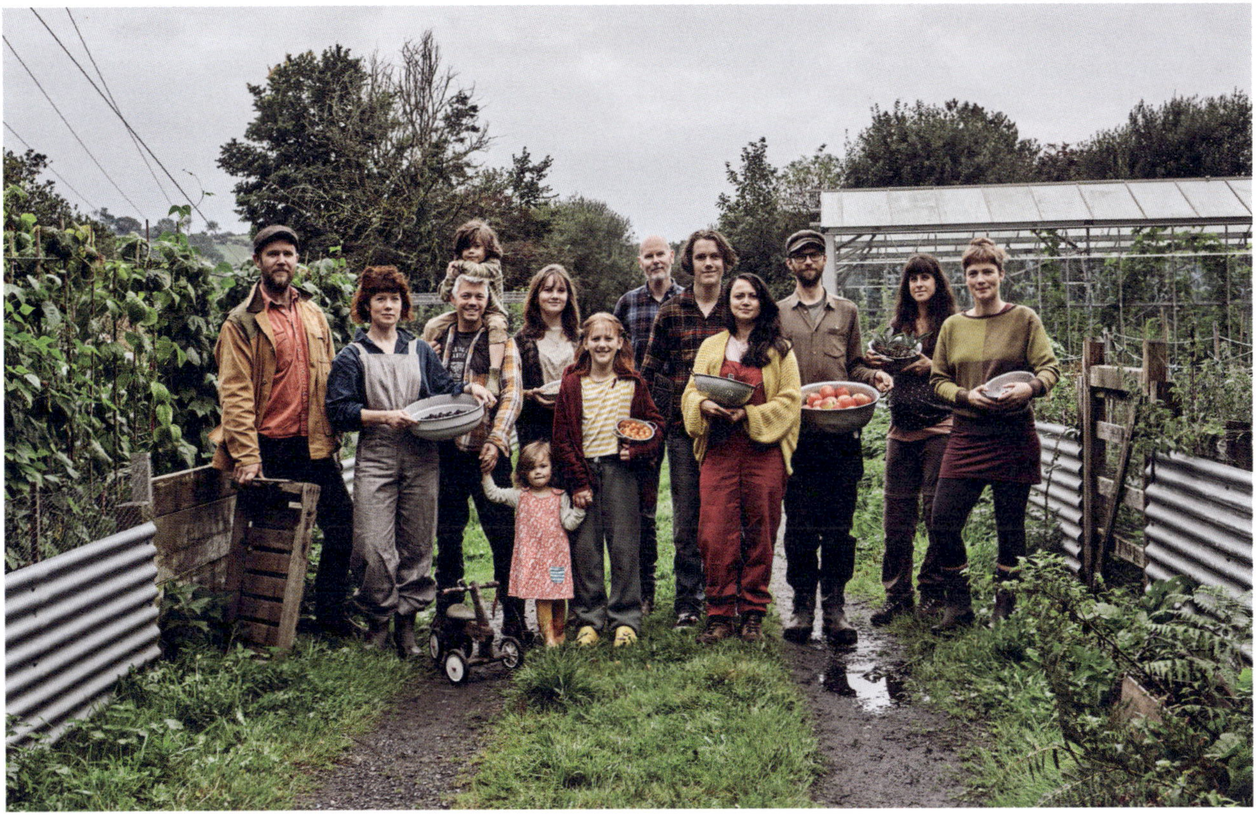

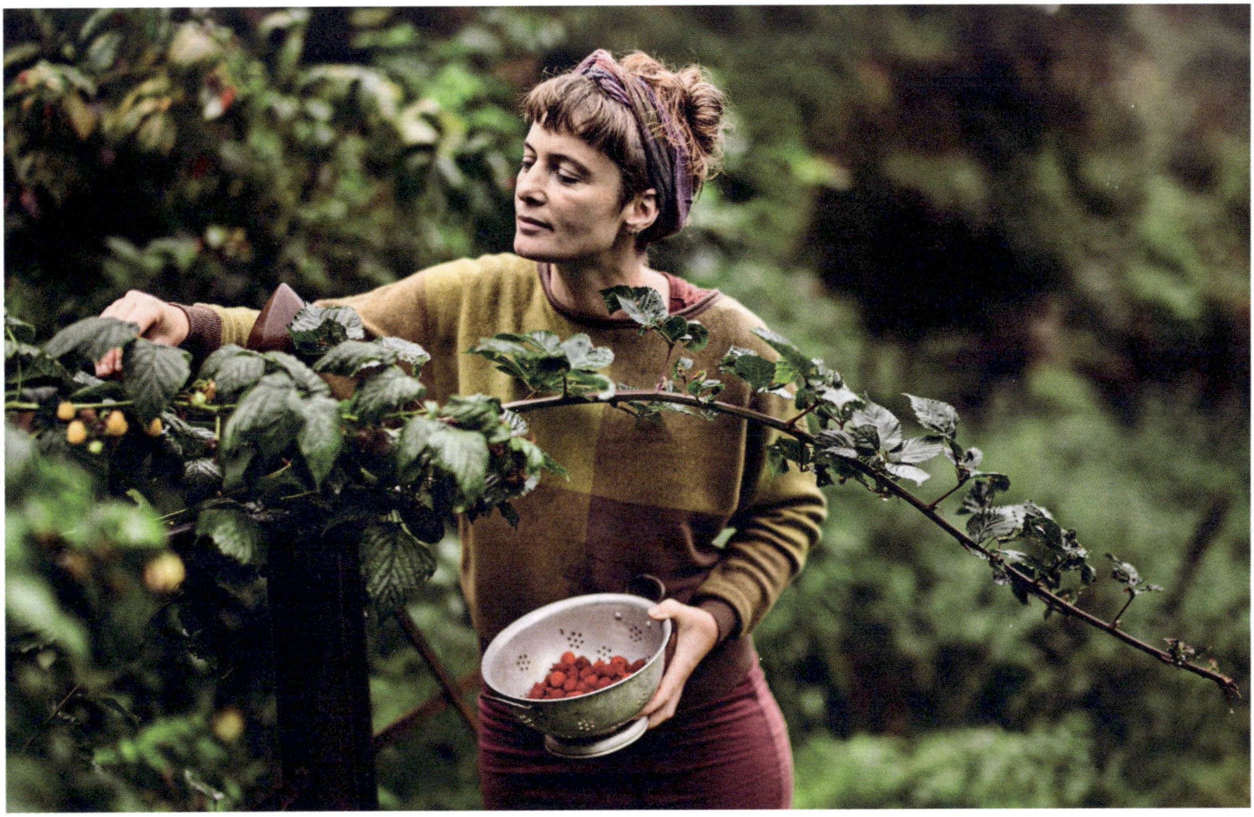

because they're naughty! Different varieties of apple tree all have different personalities. I love thinking about them like that and it helps me understand how, why and where to prune. It is gently and surprisingly rewarding.'

This year, the garden got a greenhouse. 'It had been used by a commercial grower for tomatoes and he wanted to get rid of it,' says Beth. 'It's absolutely enormous. We've only used a part of it and even that took Jo two months to erect.' As well as growing tomatoes, peppers, aubergines and chillies, they are experimenting with grapes and kiwi fruit. 'We've planted their roots outside the greenhouse so they can take advantage of the rain, but we're training the vines inside, which not only helps provide shade but will hopefully mean we might have our own grapes and kiwis in the years to come.'

There are annual rituals that involve everyone: blackberry picking, making elderflower 'Champagne', pressing apple juice and making cider. They share ideas and recipes for their produce, and Jo has started Pickle Club – 'Because whenever you are making jam or chutneys, there are always too many jars for one family, so our policy is that we give away our excess preserves and receive spares from other members of the group in return,' she says.

'We always hope that Hannah will make too much of her crabapple and chilli jam,' laughs Beth. 'It's incredible. Creating this garden has given us all the opportunity to share. To share time, to share skills and to share knowledge. It's absolutely lovely.'

Pear, Beetroot, Feta & Mint Salad

This is a delicious mix of flavours and textures and colours. It was invented by Pooch's great friend, milliner Cozmo Jenks. The perfect lunch for a late summer or early autumn day.

FOR THE DRESSING

1 tablespoon poppy seeds

1 teaspoon mustard powder

½ teaspoon onion powder or
  granules (optional, but delicious)

1 teaspoon caster sugar

2 tablespoons balsamic vinegar

6 tablespoons olive oil

sea salt and freshly ground
  black pepper

FOR THE SALAD

2 firm but ripe pears

juice of ½ lemon

4 raw beetroot, peeled

150g (5½oz) sugar snap peas

100g (3½oz) pine nuts, toasted

200g (7oz) feta cheese, crumbled

leaves from a small bunch of mint,
  roughly chopped

Serves 4–6

Put all the ingredients for the dressing into a clean jam jar along with a good pinch of salt and shake vigorously to mix. Taste and adjust the seasoning if necessary.

For the salad, quarter and core the pears (if the skin is tough, peel them too). Slice each quarter into 2 or 3 wedges, then chop these into chunks. Toss the chunks in the lemon juice in a large bowl.

Coarsely grate the beetroot and add to the bowl. Slice the sugar snap peas diagonally into 4 or 6 and add to the bowl. Mix everything together until evenly distributed and season well.

Dress the salad with the dressing, taste and season again if needed.

Transfer the salad to a serving platter, then scatter over the toasted pine nuts, feta and mint. Give it one last gentle toss and serve. Any leftovers will still be delicious the next day if stored in the fridge overnight.

Grilled Pineapple
with Rum, Chilli & Lime

It's worth lighting your barbecue just to make this dish. It is ludicrously delicious and pretty. Eat this and it feels sunny, even on a cloudy day. But it can also be cooked indoors in a griddle pan. Heat the pan over a medium-high heat and, once hot, follow the barbecue instructions. When you get to the rum stage, remove the pineapple from the griddle pan and place on a serving platter, then drizzle over a little rum, along with the lime juice, zest and chilli.

1 large ripe pineapple, skin removed

100g (3½oz) golden caster, demerara
   or soft brown sugar

2 tablespoons dark rum

zest and juice of 1 unwaxed lime

1 long red chilli, finely chopped

Serves 4–6

Fire up your barbecue or fire ready for direct cooking (or see recipe introduction).

Cut the pineapple lengthways into 6–8 wedges, leaving the core in. Sprinkle the sugar on a plate and dip the wedges in the sugar, trying to get all sides covered.

Once your barbecue or fire is hot, place a grill rack over it and, when hot, place the pineapple on the grill. Cook for 3–4 minutes until caramelized on one side, then turn and repeat with the other side until the pineapple is caramelized all over. Drizzle a little rum over each piece and cook for a further 1–2 minutes.

Place on a serving platter or board and squeeze over the lime juice, then scatter over the lime zest and chilli. Serve straight away, or it is also delicious at room temperature.

Blackcurrant Vinegar

Beth and Jo make this every year from their blackcurrant crop. It has become their go-to condiment, used neat on salads and over roast vegetables. A drizzle of it over a poached pear is heaven! Use fresh or frozen blackcurrants, or even a mixture of blackcurrants and redcurrants, if you like.

500g (1lb 2oz) blackcurrants, stalks removed

300ml (½ pint) red wine vinegar
golden caster sugar

Makes 450–500ml (16–18fl oz)

Wash the blackcurrants under plenty of cold running water and pick out any bits, such as leaves or leftover stalks. Place into a large glass bowl or a large Kilner jar and pour over the vinegar. Squish the fruit a little with a wooden spoon or potato masher and leave, covered, for 4 days to macerate. Every now and again, give the fruit another squish.

Weigh a large saucepan and make a note of the weight. Line a sieve with some clean muslin and place over the saucepan. Pour the blackcurrant vinegar mixture into the sieve and leave to drip through. Don't force it through, or you will get cloudy vinegar. Once all the liquid is in the pan, remove the sieve and weigh the pan again. Calculate the difference. This is the amount of liquid you have in the pan.

For every 250g (9oz) of liquid, add 85g (3oz) of sugar to the pan. Place the pan over a medium heat and stir until the sugar has dissolved. Then increase the heat and boil the mixture for 5 minutes.

Leave the blackcurrant vinegar to cool slightly in the pan, then pour into sterilized bottles or jars. Once cool, put lids on and they are ready to store. The vinegar should last up to a year if kept somewhere cool and out of direct sunlight.

CHOCOLATE

❧

Iris & Bob • *Solkiki*

Iris's first attempt at chocolate-making was not a success. 'I grew up in Holland. My mother wouldn't allow me in the kitchen but I loved experimenting and making things. I tried making chocolate by mixing cocoa powder with water into a paste. It was disgusting, so I put it in the freezer to harden, hoping it might taste more like chocolate. It didn't!' Bob didn't have to make his own chocolate. His parents ran a convenience store and as soon as he could crawl, Bob would make his way to the chocolate counter. 'Then when I was tall enough to reach the hob, I started cooking. I loved experimenting too. Exploding toffee was my speciality.'

But their sweet-making childhoods were left behind for more conventional careers. They met in Amsterdam, moved back to the UK, and Iris gave birth to their first child in 2007. 'Kiki was born very prematurely. For the first months of her life she had a lot of catching up to do and she slept a lot. I wanted something that was comforting and therapeutic to do while she slept. At that time I had a craving for white chocolate. But I'm vegan; I couldn't find any that didn't contain milk powder, so I thought I'd try to make some.'

She went to the supermarket to look at the ingredients listed on a bar of white chocolate, substituted milk powder for soy milk powder, bought some cocoa butter, added sugar and vanilla and it worked. She made more, then felt a little bit guilty and self-indulgent. 'I thought I should try selling some of it, just to pay for the ingredients. If I was looking for vegan white chocolate, perhaps other people were too.' And it turned out her hunch was right, so she continued to make small batches of chocolate in her kitchen and sell it on Etsy.

The chocolate Bob brought back from a business trip in San Francisco in 2008 introduced them both to what Bob describes as a 'chocolate revolution'. It was the beginning of the bean-to-bar movement, which saw small-scale chocolate-makers going right back to the raw product – the cacao beans – rather than buying bricks of ready-made chocolate, which they would then melt, mould and process. 'I was blown away by the flavours of this chocolate. Honeysuckle, heather, smoke. And they weren't added – they were the natural flavours that came from the beans themselves. Before that moment, I'd had no idea there was more than one type of cocoa bean. I now know there's about six thousand!'

They couldn't buy bean-to-bar chocolate in the UK, because nobody was making it, so, true to form, Iris decided to try making it herself. She was still doing things on a micro-scale at home, not least because Bob's job involved them moving almost constantly. He was asked to go to Quebec, where the family had to live in a hotel for a while before moving into an apartment. He was at the top of his game, with offers coming in from all over the world. 'But by now our son Sol had been born and we felt the children needed more stability. So in the end we decided to come back to England and make chocolate!'

In 2014 they bought a pair of derelict cottages in Dorset, not far from Bob's childhood home. One was to live in and the other was to become their chocolate factory. 'I never thought chocolate-making would become our business,' Iris laughs. 'It was always something I did as a sideline . I imagined when the kids were grown up I might go back into psychology, but…'

They discovered that although it had been possible for them to buy cacao beans while living in Canada, it was impossible to find them in the UK. They had to start their own chocolate revolution and became the first people in the country to make and sell chocolate using named, traceable cacao. 'It was slow progress,' says Bob. 'We are naturally risk averse. We don't like getting into debt. And we're fiercely independent, so we declined approaches from investors and remain entirely self-funded.'

Over the years they have built up relationships with cacao growers and cooperatives from all over the cacao-growing world. The beans are fermented, sundried, put into jute sacks and sent straight from the farms to Bob and Iris's workshop in Dorset. The first thing they do is try the beans in their raw state, and that first taste will start them thinking about

how to use them, how to roast them, what ingredients they might add. Not everything works. 'We've made several thousand test batches over the years. The sixty that we sell now are the only ones we are completely happy with.'

'I tried making a black garlic chocolate once,' Iris says with a grimace. 'It wasn't good.'

'We love to push the boundaries with chocolate,' smiles Bob. 'It's an all-consuming passion. The core ingredient is the key. We just treat it very nicely.'

Venison Chilli
with Grilled Tortilla Chips & Guacamole

This is very much a campfire version of chilli, where everything is cooked in the easiest way possible. If you're making it in your kitchen, it's nice to brown the minced venison well in oil first, then remove it before continuing with the recipe as written. Chipotle pastes can vary quite a lot, so taste before adding so you get the level of heat you like. The chocolate used here doesn't make the dish sweet, but adds a layer of deep, satisfying flavour. This is a no-bean chilli and is, in my opinion, all the better for it.

olive oil

2 red onions, peeled and finely chopped

2 peppers (mixed colours if possible), deseeded and chopped

4 garlic cloves, chopped

up to 3–4 tablespoons chipotle paste or chipotle in adobo (see recipe introduction)

1 tablespoon ground cumin

1 teaspoon ground coriander

1 teaspoon ground cinnamon

600g (1lb 5oz) minced venison

400g (14oz) can of chopped tomatoes

250ml (9fl oz) beef stock

50g (1¾oz) dark chocolate

sea salt and freshly ground black pepper

FOR THE TORTILLA CHIPS

4 large soft tortilla wraps

2 teaspoons smoked paprika

FOR THE GUACAMOLE
1 large ripe avocado
1 spring onion, finely chopped

½ small bunch of coriander,
    finely chopped
juice of 1 lime

Serves 4

Fire up your barbecue or fire ready for direct and indirect cooking.

Once hot, place a casserole dish over the direct heat and add a glug of olive oil. Sauté the onions and peppers with a good pinch of salt until softened. Add the garlic and cook for a further minute or 2, then stir in the chipotle paste and cook for another minute.

Add the spices and cook for a minute or 2 until fragrant, then stir in the minced venison and another good pinch of salt. Continue to stir until everything is mix together well and the mince has broken down. Add the tomatoes and half the stock, stir them in and bring to a simmer. Put a lid on the casserole dish and move to indirect heat to allow it to gently simmer away while you get on with everything else. It will happily simmer away for hours if needed, or will be ready to eat within about 40 minutes if easier. If you're cooking for a long time, you may need to add the rest of the stock.

Meanwhile, prepare your tortilla chips. Drizzle each wrap with a little olive oil and sprinkle over some smoked paprika and salt. Put the wraps on top of each other and cut the pile into 8 wedges, in the same way you would a pizza. Grill the wedges in small batches on a grill over direct heat, for 30–60 seconds on each side, or until crisped up and golden. Place in a bowl once cooked and repeat with the remaining pieces.

For the guacamole, put the flesh of the avocado into a bowl and season with salt and pepper. Mash with a fork until crushed, but not completely smooth. Stir in the spring onion, coriander and lime juice until mixed well. Taste and adjust the seasoning if needed.

Once the venison chilli is cooked, add the chocolate and stir through until melted and mixed in. Taste and adjust the seasoning. If it needs thickening a little, then move onto the direct heat and bubble away until thickened.

Serve the chilli in bowls with tortilla chips for dipping and the guacamole on top or in a small bowl on the side.

Chocolate Chip Cookies

Based on a recipe developed by Head Chef at Byron Burgers, Fred Smith, and inspired by Iris's idea of using chopped chocolate rather than chips, these cookies are about as indulgent as you can get. You can use any chocolate you like, but I tried them using Solkiki's miso chocolate and they were out of this world. If you can't get hold of miso dark chocolate, then use plain dark chocolate and add 2 teaspoons of white miso paste, loosened with 2 teaspoons of warm water, with the eggs, making sure it is well mixed in before adding the flour.

150g (5½oz) butter, softened

300g (10½oz) light soft brown sugar

1 egg, plus 1 egg yolk

300g (10½oz) plain flour, sifted

½ teaspoon baking powder

pinch of sea salt

250g (9oz) miso dark chocolate (or
    see recipe introduction), chopped

Makes about 20

Preheat the oven to 180°C (350°F), Gas Mark 4, and line 2 baking trays with baking paper.

Cream the butter and sugar together in a large mixing bowl with a handheld electric whisk. Once combined, mix in the whole egg and the egg yolk. Add the flour, baking powder, salt and chocolate, then mix in. Roll the cookie dough into balls the size of golf balls and place on the baking trays, spacing them apart to allow for spreading.

Bake in the oven for 12–15 minutes, or until golden but not too browned. Remove from the oven once cooked (the cookies will firm up more once they begin cooling, but will still have a soft middle) and leave on the trays for a couple of minutes to firm up before transferring to a wire rack for cooling.

Eat while warm, or leave to cool and store for up to 3 days in an airtight container.

Iris's Speculaas Hot Chocolate

Iris's way of making hot chocolate is rich, indulgent and flavoured according to your every whim. She suggests adding cayenne to the speculaas mix for a hint of heat. Instead of the speculaas mix, Iris and Bob also recommend trying hot chocolate with ground ginger, freshly ground black pepper, nutmeg, cloves or sea salt. Iris also loves using finely grated fresh ginger and orange zest, vanilla and anise powder. She even makes a summer version: melt the chocolate as described below, but add cold milk instead of hot, and some ice cubes.

FOR THE SPECULAAS SPICE MIX

4 teaspoons ground cinnamon

1 teaspoon freshly grated or ground nutmeg or mace

1 teaspoon ground ginger

½ teaspoon freshly ground black pepper or ground white pepper

1 star anise

4 cardamom pods

1 teaspoon cloves

FOR THE HOT CHOCOLATE

25g (1oz) chocolate of your choice, broken into chunks

½ teaspoon Speculaas Spice Mix (see left)

2 tablespoons recently boiled water (allow to cool to about 80°C/176°F)

200ml (7fl oz) milk of your choice, dairy or non-dairy, warmed

Serves 1

To make the spice mix, mix the ground spices together. Grind the star anise, the seeds from the cardamom pods and the cloves together in a spice grinder or a pestle and mortar until powdered. Add to the other spices and mix together. Transfer to a jam jar or airtight container. The spice mix will keep for 6 months and can be used for lots of different dishes.

To make the hot chocolate, place the chocolate pieces in a mug with ½ teaspoon of the spice mix and the hot water. Stir together until the chocolate has melted (I promise this works). Now fill the mug with warm (not boiling) milk. Mix together until completely combined. Sit on the sofa in your favourite woolly socks and purrrr…

DRINK

Alistair Frost • *Pentire*

Alistair 'Frosty' Frost is, first and foremost, a surfer. 'It's our office policy. When the waves are good, anyone who wants to can go for a surf.' Yet he didn't grow up by the sea. Home was inland, amid the green fields of rural England. It was seaside holidays as a child that introduced him to surfing. At seventeen he went on a surf trip to Cornwall and didn't go home. 'I paid my way by working in bars, and then I qualified as a surf instructor. I loved it,' he says. 'Loved the rapport I built with people of all ages and backgrounds who came to learn to surf. And I loved being outdoors all day, even when the weather was wild.' But the moment came when he had to decide whether he was going to continue teaching surfing or do something else. 'Most of my friends were heading up to London to start different careers, so I thought I would go up there for three months over the winter and see how I got on.'

He got a job as a glass washer in a Champagne bar and restaurant, which gave him a taste of the hospitality business. 'I loved the vibe, the atmosphere, the fun. So I stayed and worked my way up from glass washer to eventually becoming the general manager.' And as general manager he had a big say over which drinks the bar would stock. He got to know the people from the various brands, many of them start-ups, that over the years he saw become household names. And it got him thinking. Would it be possible to develop something that had a connection with a job he really enjoyed and turn it into a business?

It was a bold idea, not least because the market for drinks is crowded and competitive. He needed to come up with something that was different but would also have wide appeal.

And he knew the inspiration for that would come from the place he loved best. The coast. 'Attitudes were beginning to change. It was becoming cool to be healthy and demand was growing for non-alcoholic drinks,' Frosty says. 'I started thinking about creating a drink that had all the elements of something you might order in a cocktail bar, but wouldn't stop you going for a surf!'

It was a walk on Pentire Head, above his favourite surfing beach, that helped formulate his plan. He was in the company of Ian, a botanist, who introduced him to the huge array of edible plants that grow on that part of the Cornish coast. 'He told me that this area has one of the biggest varieties of botanicals anywhere in the UK. I had walked this path so many times and had no idea. I had never imagined that the plants growing around my feet were going to be pivotal to my future.'

He started experimenting in his kitchen. 'I'd never tried distilling before, but I borrowed some equipment, bought some other bits off the internet and with the help of YouTube and quite of lot of experimenting, I managed to learn a lot. And we've got some wonderful distillers and brewers in this part of Cornwall who helped me too. I just needed to come up with a recipe that tasted good and captured all the things I love about being by the sea.'

It was his old boss from the Champagne bar, Claude, who helped him turn the sea purslane, ice lettuce and rock samphire that grows on Pentire Head into a non-alcoholic spirit that captured Frosty's favourite place in the world in a bottle.

Frosty knew from his time as the manager of the Champagne bar that creating a drink he thought was good was only the first step. Now he needed to persuade people to try it. And buy it. 'It was pure hustle from day one and there were quite a few knockbacks.' The breakthrough came when some of the top local chefs, who loved the provenance of the drink and the taste those fresh, green coastal plants gave it, started to stock it. 'That's when other restaurants and bars started to list it too. I still get a real kick when I'm out somewhere and I see someone order it. And I'm really excited to see how the idea might develop, where it will end up next. But most important of all is still having time to surf!'

Mussels with Parsley & Thyme

Frosty's friend Jack Adair Bevan gave him this delicious and simple recipe for mussels with parsley and thyme. Warm and comforting, this is perfect winter's day food without the stodge.

1kg (2lb 4oz) mussels
olive oil
3 shallots, finely chopped
2 bay leaves
leaves from a handful of thyme
1 garlic clove, crushed
150ml (¼ pint) white wine or
   dry vermouth

60g (2¼oz) butter, cubed
a handful of flat leaf parsley,
   chopped
sea salt and freshly ground
   black pepper
flatbreads, to serve (optional)

Serves 2

Rinse the mussels under cold running water, giving them a good scrub to remove any barnacles and bits of dirt. Some may have 'beards'; these should be removed with a sharp tug. Mussels with broken shells should be discarded. To check if any open mussels are alive, give them a tap. Discard them if they don't close after around a minute. Then pop them in cold water in the fridge until it's time to cook them.

Heat a splash of olive oil in a large, heavy-based pan. Add the shallots, bay leaves, thyme and garlic and cook for a few minutes before adding the wine or vermouth. Simmer over a medium heat for 10 minutes, until the shallots are softened.

Drain the mussels and add these to the pan. Cover with a lid and cook until they open – this should take 2–3 minutes.

Finally, add the butter and parsley and give the mussels a good stir, allowing the butter to melt. Season to taste. Discard any mussels that haven't opened, and serve immediately. These are great with flatbreads to dip into the wonderfully aromatic sauce.

Dress Up Your Drinks

～

A garnish can make all the difference to the taste – and of course to the look – of a drink. Here are some of Frosty's top tips. There are, he says, no rules as such. 'Explore the flavours that suit you best: experimentation can often lead to wonderful surprises!'

Leaves

Rosemary offers a lovely scent with each sip, plus it's a great stirring device. It works well with sweet, acidic flavours such as citrus (lemon, lime, orange), cranberry and tomato.

Bay is a great way to invigorate a drink with a delicate flavour. It's a lovely pairing with lemon, and adds a rich dark green accent of colour too.

Rock Samphire has an aromatic warm taste and adds a salty crunch when eaten. Great with spiced flavours, or a lovely contrast to citrus.

Scots Pine is a wonderfully fragrant and decorative garnish, an excellent choice in the winter months.

Sage has an aromatic taste and scent. It pairs well with lime and both sweet and bitter flavours.

Mint offers that reassuring freshness and scent. It's a brilliant pairing with citrus and other fruit flavours in drinks.

Fennel has a refreshing, liquorice flavour and looks beautiful in a drink. It complements sweet, savoury and bitter flavours.

Tarragon has a subtle, anise-like note and works well with citrus and fruit flavours.

Citrus

Lemon Zest cannot be overlooked as a sturdy garnish for many drinks. Beautifully bright, it adds aromatic essential oils as well as citrus and bitterness.

Grapefruit offers the same quality, with added bitterness. Brilliant with lime, berry fruit flavours or simply on its own with tonic.

Flowers

Nigella is an exquisite edible flower with a delicate fragrance and a mild, fresh taste.

Food

Olives are a great option if fresh ingredients are low, and the perfect foil for herbal, woody flavours. Most iconically used in a martini.

Spice

Turmeric offers delicate spice with its vibrant orange-yellow hue. Excellent paired with other spice notes, it is also bursting with anti-inflammatory antioxidant properties.

Ginger helps cleanse the palate and adds another brilliant spiced dimension to a drink.

Pentire Collins

※

Frosty's non-alcoholic take on the classic Tom Collins cocktail. Citrusy and fresh, with the added bonus that you can drink as many as you like and still safely go surfing!

ice cubes
75ml (5 tablespoons) Pentire
25ml (5 teaspoons) fresh lemon juice

1 teaspoon sugar or a squeeze
  of honey
150ml (¼ pint) soda water
lemon slice or zest, to serve

Makes 1

Begin with a glass full of ice. Pour in the Pentire, lemon juice, sugar or honey and top with the soda water. Give it a quick stir and serve with a lemon slice or lemon zest.

ARTISANS & PRODUCERS

BASKET	APRON	KNIFE	BOARD	PAN
Wyldwood Willow	Field & Found	Joel Black Knives	Jamie Gaunt Designs	Alex Pole
www.wyldwoodwillow.co.uk	*www.fieldandfound.com*	*www.joelblackknives.com*	*www.jamiegauntdesigns.com*	*www.alexpoleironwork.com*
@wyldwoodwillow	*@fieldandfound*	*@joelblacksmith*	*@jamie_gaunt_designs*	*@alexpoleironwork*

FIREPIT	BOWL	PLATE	SPOON	GLASS
Firepits UK	Michelle Mateo Crafts	Sytch Farm Studios	The Whittlings	Sharp Glass
www.firepitsuk.co.uk	*www.michellemateocrafts.com*	*www.sytchfarmstudios.co.uk*	*www.thewhittlings.co.uk*	*www.sharpglass.co.uk*
@firepitsuk	*@chelle.mateo*	*@sytchfarmstudio*	*@thewhittlings*	*@emsiesharpglass*

BREAD

Caerhys Organic
Community Agriculture
www.coca-csa.org
@caerhysorganic

SEASONINGS

Halen Môn
www.halenmon.com
@halenmon

VEGETABLES

Moor Park Garden
@moorparkgarden

FISH

Hayden Scamp
www.wylde.market
@wylde_market

MEAT

Wild by Nature
www.wildbynaturellp.com
@wildbynaturellp

CHEESE

Aberdyfi Cheese Company
www.aberdyficheeseco.com
@aberdyficheeseco

PRESERVES

Coedcanlas
www.coedcanlas.cymru
@coedcanlas

FRUIT

Spring Mills
Community Garden
This is a community garden,
so doesn't sell to the public.

CHOCOLATE

Solkiki
www.solkiki.co.uk
@solkiki_chocolatemaker

DRINKS

Pentire
www.pentiredrinks.com
@pentiredrinks

INDEX

ACKNOWLEDGEMENTS

First thanks must go to Pooch Horsburgh and Andrew Montgomery, for their enthusiasm, ideas, tireless creativity and patience. And to Pooch's husband, Jason, and her son Alfie, for letting us take over their house for the recipe testing and photo shoot.

Andrew's beautiful photographs owe much to Pooch and to Lizzie Evans, who between them cooked and styled more dishes in one day than I thought humanly possible.

Thank you to Alex Stetter for your ever-careful editing and Jonathan Christie for putting words and pictures together to create another beautifully designed book.

To Stephanie Jackson and the team – five books in, and I still love working with you! Thank you for you continued support and belief.

Rosemary Scoular at United Agents – thank you for your guidance, encouragement, advice and friendship over so many years, and to Natalia Lucas for keeping me in the right place at the right time and making me laugh.

And it is with unfailing gratitude and admiration that I thank all the people in this book who invited me to their homes, their studios, farms or workshops to share their inspirational stories and their love of food.

Kate x

First published in Great Britain in 2024 by Gaia,
an imprint of
Octopus Publishing Group Ltd
Carmelite House, 50 Victoria Embankment, London EC4Y 0DZ
www.octopusbooks.co.uk

An Hachette UK Company
www.hachette.co.uk

ISBN 978-1-85675-505-4

A CIP catalogue record for this book is available from the British Library.
Printed and bound in China by 1010 Printing International Ltd
1 3 5 7 9 10 8 6 4 2

Publisher: Stephanie Jackson
Creative Director: Jonathan Christie
Senior Editor: Alex Stetter
Photography: Andrew Montgomery
Home Economist: Anna Horsburgh
Assistant Home Economist: Lizzie Evans
Senior Production Manager: Peter Hunt

Kate Humble is a writer and broadcaster. She started her television career
as a researcher, later presenting programmes such as 'Animal Park',
'Springwatch' and 'Autumnwatch', 'Lambing Live', 'Living with Nomads',
'Extreme Wives', 'Back to the Land' and 'Escape to the Farm'. Her book
Thinking on My Feet was shortlisted for both the Wainwright Prize and the
Edward Stanford Travel Memoir of the Year.

www.katehumble.com | 𝕏 @katehumble | ⬜ kmhumble

Also available:

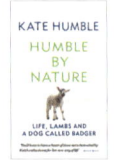 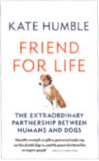 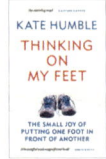 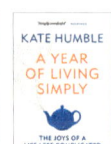 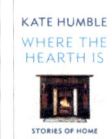